A MANUAL OF COSTUME AS ILLUSTRATED BY MONUMENTAL BRASSES

" And Dekker, in his "Gull's Horn Book," published in 1609, contrasting the fashions
" of his day with the simplicity of the old times (though where he found simplicity in
" any later than the Deluge I am not aware), says :—' There was then neither the
" Spanish slop nor the skipper's galligaskins ; the Danish sleeving, sagging down
"like a Welsh wallet ; the Italian's close strosser, nor the French standing collar ;
" your treble, quadruple Dædalion ruffs ; nor your stiff-necked rabatos, that have
"more arches for pride to row under than can stand under five London bridges,
" durst not then set themselves out in print, for the patent for starch could by no
" means be signed. Fashion then was counted a disease, and horses died of it.'
" The disease is a very old one, and Dekker would have been puzzled, I fancy, to
" point out an age in which it was not deplored as epidemic."—J. R. PLANCHÉ,
A General History of Costume in Europe, 1879, p. 230.

Sir John D'Aubernoun 1277. Sir John D'Aubernoun 1327.
Stoke D'Abernon, Surrey.

A MANUAL OF COSTUME
AS ILLUSTRATED BY
MONUMENTAL BRASSES
BY HERBERT DRUITT

WITH 110 ILLUSTRATIONS

GENEALOGICAL PUBLISHING CO., INC.
Baltimore   1970

Originally Published
London, 1906

American Publishers
GENEALOGICAL PUBLISHING COMPANY
Baltimore, Maryland
Published in Conjunction with
TABARD PRESS
Wiltshire, England

Library of Congress Catalog Card Number 74-126136
International Standard Book Number 0-8063-0428-6

Printed in Great Britain
Bound in the United States of America

PREFACE

The aim of this book is to give, as far as possible, a straight-forward account of the costume to be found represented on that large class of sepulchral memorials known as Monumental Brasses. The student of Costume, to whom this volume is addressed, has before him the task of clothing one of an earlier age than his own "in his habit as he lived." If his period be the first quarter of the nineteenth century he collects and compares the fascinating copper-plate engravings of that time; if the seventeenth century claims his study, he consults the portraits of Van Dyck, Kneller, and Lely; but if his attention be turned to the costume of the fourteenth or fifteenth century, he finds his examples less easy of access, and mainly to be sought in illuminated manuscripts and in sepulchral effigies. Of the latter, in England, a large number consists of memorials in brass. Of these he must collect examples, either by means of heel-ball rubbings or of photography. By these methods he will be able to show the various styles of armour, the vestments of the clergy, the dress of the merchant, the fashions of the ladies, so that his collection will form a valuable companion to the study of English History.

In dealing with such a subject as Costume, the enormous scope of the study renders necessary a strict adherence to stated limits, and a plain statement of those limits. The present volume treats of Costume,[1] so far as it appears on English Monumental Brasses, including an introductory chapter dealing generally with this class of memorial. The author has not commented upon the beauty or

---

[1] Two classes of costume, if such they may be considered, have been omitted:—the swaddling clothes of infants with the class known as "Chrysom Brasses," and the class represented by "Shroud Brasses."

ugliness of English fashion, holding that, at the most, such
treatment conveys but the expression of individual taste,
and that it is futile to criticize adversely a fifteenth-century
head-dress, merely because it may not be supported by the
sanction of a nineteenth-century mode. Dresses which
appear to us to be graceful, or the reverse, occur in every
age. The light which they throw on the manners of their
period constitutes their importance, and justifies an intelligent study of their origin, use, and development.

The adequate acknowledgment of an author's indebtedness to authorities, in a work of this kind, presents many
difficulties. It was intended that a Bibliography should
have been printed at the end of this book,[1] which would
have shown the range of these obligations; but it was
found to be impossible to include this, as it would have
increased unduly the size of the book. This bibliography
will be issued, with some additions, in a separate form at
a later date, when it is hoped that it will prove of service
to the student. But it must be stated here that the
author's chief indebtedness is to the Rev. Herbert Haines'
Manual of Monumental Brasses, now, unfortunately, out of
print, and comparatively costly, but which for more than
forty years has been and still remains the standard work
on the subject.

Many of the illustrations are from photographs, taken
directly, of the brasses themselves. The author's grateful
acknowledgments are due to Mr. E. M. Beloe, junr., for
his photographs of the Elsing brass; to Mr. W. H. H.
Rogers, F.S.A., for his kindness in allowing the use of
some thirty blocks, made from his own carefully prepared
rubbings; and to Mr. H. K. St. J. Sanderson for the use
of his block of the brass at Cople.

The author thankfully records his indebtedness to many

---

[1] This will explain the reference on p. 145, and the absence of the list
of books there mentioned. In the Index of Persons the names of authors
cited will be found printed in italics. The author has endeavoured by
means of footnotes to show the sources of statements in the text.

of the clergy and to others, who have given him information and assistance, more especially to the Rev. Canon
C. H. Mayo, Professor E. C. Clark, LL.D., F.S.A.,
and to Messrs. Mill Stephenson, F.S.A., and Albert
Hartshorne, F.S.A.

That errors and many imperfections must exist in his
work the author is well aware. He will be grateful to any
one who, detecting such, will bring them to his notice.

CONTENTS

INTRODUCTION.—OF MONUMENTAL BRASSES

Rise of this branch of archæology—its literature—its importance—Haines' classification of monumental effigies—Incised slabs—Limoges enamels—inlaying slabs with colour and metals—inlaying of brasses—advantage of use of brass for sepulchral monuments—material used—how made and engraved—brass inlaid in marble slab—cost of brasses—artists and engravers—devices and signatures—thirteenth century brasses—development of brasses following that of architecture—arrangement in periods with their characteristics—fourteenth century—fifteenth century—sixteenth and seventeenth centuries—rarity of brasses in eighteenth century—modern brasses—distribution of brasses—their size—some account of the treatment to which they have been subjected from the sixteenth to the nineteenth centuries—modern recoveries, practices, restorations—palimpsest brasses—three classes described, with examples—palimpsest at Burwell described—Flemish brasses—list of those in England of fourteenth century—some fine Continental examples—Flemish palimpsests—brass of Abbot Delamere described—effigy of abbot, British Museum—the Lynn brasses—those at North Mimms, Wensley, and Elsing—characteristics of fourteenth century Flemish brasses—fifteenth and sixteenth century Flemish brasses—foreign brasses in London museums—brasses showing French influence—English brass of Bishop Hallum at Constance

CHAPTER I.—OF ECCLESIASTICAL COSTUME ON BRASSES

Origin of vestments—early examples on brasses—brasses of cardinals—division into mass and processional vestments—Mass Vestments: 1. Amice; 2. Alb; 3. Stole; 4. Maniple; 5. Chasuble—examples of priests in mass vestments, and of

b

CHAPTER II.—OF ACADEMICAL COSTUME ON BRASSES

Difficulty of subject—some authorities—ecclesiastical origin of universities and of their costume—its regulation—Articles of dress: 1. The Under or Body Garment; 2. Cassock; 3. Gown: *a. cappa clausa; b.* gown with two slits, or sleeveless *taberdum talare; c.* sleeved tabard; *d.* sleeveless *taberdum ad medias tibias;* 4. Tippet; 5. Hood; 6. Pileus: *a.* skull-cap; *b.* Pointed—Order of precedence of faculties

Examples in academicals and other costume—Sacræ Theologiæ Professor, Doctor of Divinity—Decretorum or Juris Canonici Doctor—Legum, or Juris Civilis Doctor—Utriusque Juris Doctor—Medicinæ Doctor—Licentiati (in decretis)—Sacræ Theologiæ Baccalaureus—Artium Magister (Haines'

CONTENTS

M.A. I. and M.A. II.)—Sacræ Theologiæ Scholaris—Juris
Canonici or In Decretis Baccalaureus—Juris Civilis or Legum
Baccalaureus—Utriusque Juris Baccalaureus—Physicæ Bacca-
laureus—Artium Baccalaureus—Student of Civil Law—
Undergraduate—Schoolboys—Note : Doctor of Music   -   119

CHAPTER III.—OF MILITARY COSTUME ON BRASSES

Surcoat Period—examples—mail—hawberk—coif de mailles
—chausses—genouillières or poleyns—prick spurs—hauketon
—surcoat—ailettes—shield—sword—brasses of Sir John
D'Aubernoun—Sir Robert de Trumpington (with tilting
helm)—Sir Robert de Bures—Sir Robert de Setvans—two
half-effigies—matrices of the Surcoat Period

Transitional Period—brasses at Pebmarsh and Gorleston—
brassarts (rerebraces and vambraces)—coutes or coudières—
roundels—jambs or jambarts—sollerets

Mixed Mail and Plate Period, called Cyclas Period—
examples—cyclas—camail—brasses of Sir John de Creke, Sir
John D'Aubernoun II., Sir John de Northwode

Transitional Period—brasses of Sir Hugh Hastings, Sir John
de Wantyng, and Sir John Giffard described

Camail Period—hawberk—chausses—camail—bascinet—
rerebraces—vambraces—coutes—epaulières—cuisses — genouillières—jambs—sollerets—rowell spurs—gauntlets—jupon—
bawdric—sword—basilard or misericorde—tilting helm—
examples

Transitional Period—breastplate or cuirass—skirt of taces
—examples

Complete Plate Period (Lancastrian)—bascinet—gorget or
standard—breastplate—backplate—skirt of taces—epaulières
—brassarts—coutes—roundels — palettes — gauntlets—cuisses
—jambs— genouillières — sollerets — rowell spurs — sword—
misericorde—tuilles—heraldic tabards (brasses of heralds)—
examples

Yorkist Period—demi-placcates—pauldrons—gardes de bras
—hausse-col or collar of mail—tuilles—tuillettes—examples
showing lance-rest—gussets of mail—shell-backed gauntlets—
salade—mentonière—examples of the Yorkshire school showing it—examples of heraldic tabards—early examples of period
—examples of the London school—later examples—examples
with short mail-skirt showing signs of transition—examples of
the Norwich school

Early Tudor or Mail Skirt Period—its characteristics—pike
guards—cuirass—its tapul—lamboys or bases—tuilles—skirt
or petticoat of mail—sabbatons—other characteristics—examples—examples showing heraldic tabards

CONTENTS

[1] The term *Civilian* is here used in a broad sense, not in its academical significance.

ILLUSTRATIONS

Those marked * lent by W. H. H. Rogers, Esq., F.S.A.

The author is indebted for much information concerning this brass to
Mr. Albert Hartshorne, F.S.A., whose account of this monument will
appear in the *Archæologia*. The treatment of the Elsing figure resembles
in some respects that of Sir John de Wantyng's brass at Wimbish, and
it is not improbable that they are of French rather than of Flemish
workmanship. With regard to the figures in the side shafts, coloured
pigments seem to have been employed in the backgrounds and on the
heraldic jupons. The shields of the Lords Grey de Ruthin, Stafford, and
St. Amand probably contained their respective arms in enamel, which
has long since disappeared.

The following illustrations, with the exception of that of the figure of
Thomas Beauchamp, Earl of Warwick, are *from photographs taken by
Mr. E. M. Beloe, junr.*

The diapered background of this figure is similar to that of the
opposite figure of the Earl of Lancaster.

The opposite figure, lost, was that of Edward le Despenser.
P. 155, the arms have disappeared from the shield.

The diapered background of this figure is similar to that of the
opposite figure of Lord Grey de Ruthin.
P. 155, the arms have disappeared from the shield.

In the *Connoisseur*, July, 1905 (Vol. XII., p. 182), is an illustration showing a piece of fifteenth-century tapestry "exhibited by Count of Valence de Don Juan at the Madrid Exhibition, 1892-93." The costume of the lady therein represented bears much resemblance to that of Jane Keriell, and reveals the nature of the latter's head-dress :—the horse-shoe ornament being formed of some costly material surmounting the horned cauls of the head-dress and falling behind.

ILLUSTRATIONS

INTRODUCTION

INTRODUCTION.

OF MONUMENTAL BRASSES

Rise of this branch of Archæology

THE study of Monumental Brasses, as a branch of Archæology, may be said to have arisen in the nineteenth century. A collection of impressions, now in the British Museum, was made towards the close of the previous century by Craven Ord, Sir John Cullum, and the Rev. Thomas Cole, at which time also Richard Gough published his great work on Sepulchral Monuments in Great Britain. In the year 1819 appeared Cotman's work on the brasses of Norfolk. About the middle of last century Boutell and Haines gave system and classification to the subject; in 1853 Hudson's work on the brasses of Northamptonshire appeared; whilst the Messrs. Waller produced a splendid series of engravings. Some years later the Rev. W. F. Creeny published the results of his labours on the Continent. Besides these a large literature exists, in books devoted to the treatment of separate counties, and in scattered articles, the work, for the most part, of Archæological societies in the Universities and different English counties: work, doubtless of varying merit, but all to a greater or less degree adding to our knowledge of the subject. These papers, moreover, are in many instances accompanied by illustrations, which gain in absolute accuracy what they lack in artistic merit by the substitution of photographic processes for the more costly, though less trustworthy, line-engraving.

Importance of the study

The importance of the subject is sufficiently proved by the fact that this class of monument affords matter of interest to the students of different branches of art and antiquities. The architect finds the contemporary style mirrored in the canopies, surviving on many brasses; the herald may trace the history and development of armorial bearings through a fine series of shields, though he may complain that time has deprived them of their original tinctures; the genealogist finds in the frequent dating of brass inscriptions evidence often denied him by other monuments ; the student of costume, to whom the present volume is more particularly addressed, has before him a set of durable and trustworthy fashion-plates of military. and civil dress throughout four centuries; the ecclesiologist observes the use of vestments, the form of the chalice and many other details of importance; the student of palæography has valuable data of the use of different styles of lettering; the philologist of the changes in language. Besides which there are many subjects upon which brasses give information, such as the manufacture in Europe of alloys of copper.　Wherefore we do not feel guilty of exaggeration in saying that it would be difficult to overestimate the importance, from an historical point of view, of an intelligent study of the contemporary evidence afforded by the sepulchral monuments of our churches, of which so goodly a proportion is furnished by engravings on brass.

Haines' Classification of Monumental Effigies

Haines[1] divides Monumental Effigies into three classes :

1. Sculptured figures in complete or low relief, executed in stone, wood, or copper.

2. Figures incised on stone or engraved on brass plates fastened to stone.

3. Representations of the deceased painted on wood or glass.

It is with the second of these groups that we have to deal; though it should be noted that sometimes a monument may be found to combine the characteristics of two classes.[2]

---

[1] Introduction, p. i.

[2] As for instance at Hereford Cathedral, where Bishop Richard Mayo (*d.* 1516) is commemorated by a brass (*see* p. 81) as well as by a sculptured effigy.　Haines (Introduction, p. i.) writes :—"The incised memorials "forming the second class may indeed be considered merely imitations of "the sculptured effigies on a flat surface, and the progressive history of the "art shews that such was their origin."

INCISED CROSS SLAB,
New Romney, Kent.

INTRODUCTION

Incised slabs can be traced to a much greater antiquity Incised Slabs
than brasses. Of this kind of monument two sub-classes
may be said to exist :—those which are incised in the strict
sense of the word, and those which are formed by cutting
away the surface of the stone, thereby leaving the pattern
or figure in low relief with a raised border, as in the case
of so-called Keltic crosses.[1] Many examples of each sub-
class exist, usually in the form of crosses on slabs. The
slab proper probably derives its origin from the lid of the
stone coffin, which, gradually becoming more ornate,
reached its highest development in the stately altar-tomb.
About the twelfth century the representation of the
deceased in bas-relief on the stone coffin seems to have
come into use, being superseded later by the incised slab
proper. The best examples of this latter form are to be
found on the Continent, due, no doubt, to the greater
prevalence of a harder stone than that employed in
England. Creeny mentions as early examples those of
St. Piatus at Seclin, near Lille, c. 1142, and of Bishop
Barthelemy de Vir at Laon, 1158, each in pontificals; and
that of Antone de Loncin, c. 1160, at the Palais de Justice,
Liége, in armour, said to be the earliest incised slab in
Belgium.[2]

An early fragment representing an ecclesiastic with
pastoral staff, possibly of the twelfth century, exists at
Carisbrooke, Isle of Wight.[3] At Salisbury Cathedral are
two slabs commemorating respectively Bishop Roger, 1139,

---

[1] This classification may possibly invite the criticism that this latter
sub-class really belongs to Haines' first class. But the two sub-classes
(called by Rev. E. L. Cutts in speaking of crosses, respectively Incised and
Raised Cross Slabs, see p. 1, *A Manual for the Study of the Sepulchral Slabs
and Crosses of the Middle Ages*, 1849) are so closely connected that it would
merely encourage confusion to separate them.

[2] See Plates 1, 2, and 3, "Illustrations of Incised Slabs on the Continent
of Europe from Rubbings and Tracings," by W. F. Creeny, M.A., F.S.A.,
Norwich, 1891.

[3] In the Church. The lower part, very much worn, is in the porch of
the priory farm-house.

and Bishop Jocelin, 1184,[1] which combine the two sub-classes, lines being incised on the figure in relief. A cross-slab at Bosbury in Herefordshire shows the head of the cross in low relief, whilst the stem, two other crosses and a sword are incised. A small incised slab exists at Steeple Langford, Wilts., representing a man with a hunting horn, c. 1200. Another interesting specimen is at Bitton, Gloucestershire, Sir Walter de Bitton, 1227, wherein the upper part of the body is in bas-relief, whilst the lower part is incised.

Besides these may be mentioned a cross-legged knight, c. 1260, at Avenbury, Herefordshire; the slab of Bishop St. William de Byttone, 1274, at Wells; that of Johan de Botiler, c. 1285, at St. Bride's, Glamorgan; and that of William de Freney, Archbishop of Rages, c. 1290, at Rhuddlan, N. Wales. It is of interest to note that these five slabs belong to the thirteenth century, and are, there-fore, contemporary with the earliest brasses, of which we have any knowledge, in this country. Of later date may be mentioned James Samson, Rector, 1349, Middleton, Essex, in mass vestments; Gerard Sothill, Esq., 1401, Redbourne, Lincs.; John Cherowin, Esq., 1441, Brading, Isle of Wight, probably of Flemish work; and John Stone, Vicar, 1501, Aldbourne, Wilts., in mass vestments and holding a chalice.[2]

An engraving, taken from a drawing in a manuscript in the British Museum,[3] is given in the first volume of the

---

[1] But see Rev. Canon W. H. Jones ("The Bishops of Old Sarum," A.D. 1075-1225—Vol. XVII., 1878, *Wiltshire Archæological Magazine*) who considers the older slab to belong to Bishop Jocelin, and the other, therefore, not to be that of his predecessor, Roger (1107-1139).

[2] The first is illustrated in *Trans. of Essex Archæological Society*, New Series, Vol. VIII., 1903, p. i. :— "Two Essex Incised Slabs by Miller Christy and E. Bertram Smith." The second in *The Reliquary*, Vol. XV., 1874-5, p. 154. The third in *Walks round Ryde*, by Henry Richard Holloway, 2nd edition, London, 1848, p. 107 (the length of the spurs is remarkable). The fourth in *Wiltshire Notes and Queries*, Vol. II., June, 1898, p. 447.

[3] Add MS., No. 10,292, fol. 55 v°. Also illustrated in Boutell, p. 162 (*Monumental Brasses and Slabs*, 1847).

Archæological Journal (1845, p. 301) representing the process of incising two stone slabs in the fourteenth century.[1] For a long time after the introduction of sepulchral brasses, incised slabs seem to have run in a parallel line, keeping the characteristics due to their different material, but exhibiting an identical scheme of design and arrangement. This is best seen on the Continent, where the Flemish brass may be said partly to have derived its quadrangular shape from that of the incised slab.

Haines (Introduction, pp. viii.-xiii.) produces much evidence to show the origin of the monumental brass from the Limoges enamel. This art of enamelling on copper, named after the town where it flourished, was used in the decoration of Church vessels soon after the tenth century. Later, we find it used for monumental purposes, as on the plate of copper in the Museum at Le Mans, which shows an enamelled effigy with canopy and diapered background of the twelfth century.[2] Another exists at St. Denis, 1247.[3]

Limoges Enamels

---

[1] Another example is afforded by MS. Royal 14, E iii., British Museum: " Here Flegentyne bids them build three Tombs near Tarabel," reproduced in " Early Fourteenth Century Costume," by Oswald Barron, F.S.A., *The Ancestor*, No. VIII., January, 1904, p. 152.

[2] This enamel, formerly in the Church of St. Julien, has been supposed to represent Geoffrey Plantagenet, Count of Anjou (*d.* 1150), father of Henry II. It has, also, been assigned to William D'Evereux or Fitz-Patrick, Earl of Salisbury, *c.* 1196. *See* " Remarks on an Enamelled Tablet, preserved in the Museum at Mans and supposed to represent the effigy of Geoffrey Plantagenet," by J. R. Planché.—*Journal of Brit. Arch. Assoc.*, Vol. I., 1845, pp. 29-39. M. Darcel considers the work to show German influence,—see *Musée du Moyen Age et de la Renaissance*, Série D. Notice des Émaux et de l'Orfévrerie par Alfred Darcel, Paris, 1867, pp. 10, 11. This is an early instance of a shield bearing arms, see *Some Feudal Coats of Arms*, by Joseph Foster, 1902, in which the plate is reproduced, p. xxxviii. It may be found also in Stothard's *Monumental Effigies*, and in Planché's *Cyclopœdia of Costume. Dictionary*, 1876, p. 455, *sub.* shield, where it is assigned to a " Norman Nobleman."

[3] Reproduced in Willemin's *Monuments*, " Tombeau en bronze doré et émaillé de Jean fils de St. Louis, 1247, conservé à l'Eglise royale de St. Denis." Mr. J. Starkie Gardner writes " There are two in St. Denis, of " the children of St. Louis, 1243 and 1248 ; one of Blanche of Cham- " pagne, only slightly enamelled, in the Louvre, 1283 ; and two or three

This species of enamelling is known as *champ-levé*, consisting of a field of copper indented to receive and separate the different coloured enamels. Here, then, we see a very obvious connection between this treatment and the filling up of the engraved lines of the brass with some black or coloured substance. Instances of the use of enamel on monuments may be seen on the tomb of William de Valence, Earl of Pembroke, 1296, in Westminster Abbey,[1] and on that of Edward the Black Prince, 1376, in Canterbury Cathedral. The tomb of Walter de Merton, Bishop of Rochester, 1277, in his Cathedral, which was destroyed in the seventeenth century, was decorated with Limoges enamels by artists from that place. There can be no doubt that the antiquity of the Limoges enamel is superior to that of the monumental brass; and from this fact and from the great similarity of design seen in the Continental brasses and in these enamels Haines was of opinion (Introduction, p. viii.) "that the use of Limoges works led the way to the employment of brass plates on the ground."

Inlaying slabs with colour and metals The principle of inlaying with different substances and colours is common alike to incised slabs and brasses, and may reasonably be derived from the Limoges enamels. Many instances are known of incised slabs having been inlaid with different material in order to gain additional effect. An instance of a dark slab being inlaid with a white composition is that of Jehan Rose, *d.* 1328, and his

---

"others in Spain."—*See* "Enamels in connection with Ecclesiastical Art," by J. Starkie Gardner, F.L.S., F.G.S.—*Trans. of St. Paul's Eccles. Society*, Vol. III., 1895. Stothard and Haines mention an enamelled tablet, formerly in the Church of St. Maurice, Angers, but destroyed at the Revolution, representing Ulger, Bishop of Angers, 1149. *See* Plate in Planché's *Cyclopædia of Costume. Dictionary*, 1876, *Sub. Chasuble*, p. 94. These enamels are of the kind called *champlevé*. The Chinese *cloisonné* enamel is formed by separating the colours by means of wires attached to the metal groundwork.

[1] In connection with this monument see *Proceedings of the Society of Antiquaries*, Vol. XVIII., pp. 411-12 (June 20th, 1901). Sir J. Charles Robinson, F.S.A., exhibited a shield of Limoges enamel on copper with the arms of England and De Valence quarterly.

wife, *d.* 1367, in the Cathedral of Meaux, an illustration
of which is given in the *Archæological Journal,* Vol. IX.,
1852, p. 384.   A black substance fills the incised lines of
a slab upon an altar-tomb at North Mimms, Herts.
(Margaret Beresford?, 1584).   Creeny gives (Plate 9) a
black marble slab, commemorating Asscheric van der
Couderborch, *c.* 1250, which was found with some fifty
others serving as the bottom for the sluice of a bridge at
Cuypgat near Ghent, by Mons. van Duyse, secretary of
the Ghent Municipal Museum.   The lines of the design,
which somewhat resembles that of the Wyvill brass at
Salisbury, were filled with coloured material.   The slab of
Thiebauz Rupez, *c.* 1260, at St. Memmie, near Chalons-
sur-Marne (Creeny, Plate 10) has its lines filled with lead.[1]
Haines mentions (Introduction, p. x.) a slab from Villers
in Brabant, of which " the figure most artistically drawn
" has the lines usually incised on a brass, in relief, the inter-
" vening spaces, having been hollowed out and inlaid with
" thin plates of copper enamelled."   Instances of incised
slabs which have had portions of their effigies, heads, hands,
etc., inlaid in brass may be seen in Lincolnshire at Ashby
Puerorum (Priest in Mass Vestments), and at Boston,
worked in a foreign blue marble.[2]   The Gough Collection
of Drawings in the Bodleian Library contains examples of
slabs inlaid with coloured material.[3]   Indeed, it is reasonable to infer that the habit of inlaying stone slabs with
coloured substances, copper, or brass gradually led to the
increase in importance of the latter; work in brass usurping
that hitherto seen in the surface of the stone itself, till, in
the case of English brasses, the slab is used merely as the

[1] Cutts (p. 4) mentions a similar treatment of an incised slab at Atten-
borough, Notts.

[2] *See* pp. 3, 14, *A List of the Existing Sepulchral Brasses in Lincolnshire,* by
the Rev. G. E. Jeans, 1895.

[3] This Collection, acquired by the Bodleian Library in 1810 on the
death of Richard Gough, consists of sixteen folio volumes, being part of
the Collection of Drawings of Monuments in France formed about 1700
by M. de Gaignières, the remainder of which is in the Bibliothéque
Nationale, Paris.

background for the brass effigy and ornaments; the matrix, into which the brass is fitted in the shape of the figure, being the only survival of the sculpture on the stone itself.

Inlaying of brasses
The use of enamel on copper plates let into brass is proved by the shields on the brass of Sir John D'Aubernoun (1277), a well-known example; and traces of colour may be found on the Hastings brass (1347) at Elsing, on that of Sir John Say (1473) at Broxbourne, and in other instances. But this can hardly have become the general practice owing to the costliness of the process. Moreover, the choice of enamel for a permanent memorial, however suitable, as was gilding, when applied to a brass raised on an altar-tomb, would be prevented by its frailty when exposed to wear and tear on the pavement of a church. An examination of extant brasses leads to the conclusion that, as a rule, it was part of the design to fill the incised lines with different substances of varied colours, thereby relieving the monotony of the metal, and producing a rich effect. In some cases a white metal was used for a similar purpose, as, for instance, in portraying the almuce. That the softer material no longer remains is not to be marvelled; but we see the lines cut for its reception and to secure its adherence. It is due to the disappearance of these compositions, which probably filled the grooves, that the student is enabled to obtain an accurate reproduction of a brass by means of that which the Rev. C. H. Hartshorne termed "this little piece of heel-ball, uniting even fragrance with its economy and portableness."[1]

Advantage of brass for sepulchral monuments
The necessity for not overcrowding a church with monuments so cumbersome as the altar-tomb,[2] gives

---

[1] P. 56, *An Endeavour to Classify the Sepulchral Remains in Northamptonshire*, etc., by the Rev. Charles Henry Hartshorne, M.A., F.S.A., 1840.

[2] William Fitz-William (*d.* 1474) by his will directed that he should be buried in the Choir at Sprotborough, Yorkshire: "ita quod impedimentum in aliquo non fiat eundo et redeundo ministrantibus circa Divina officia in choro prædicto" (*Test. Ebor.*, Vol. III., p. 211). For account of his brass see "Ancient Memorial Brasses remaining in the old Deanery of Doncaster," by F. R. Fairbank, M.D., F.S.A.—Vol. XI. *Yorkshire Archæological and Topographical Journal.*

sufficient reason for the adoption of a style of memorial which, by becoming a part of the pavement of the church, performed a function as useful as it was ornamental. The incised slab or effigy in very low relief soon became worn by the feet of the faithful. Limoges enamels would soon be broken by a like cause. Brasses engraved in deep lines filled with coloured cements were found best suited to resist the detrimental influences, practically unavoidable in the conduct of the services of the Church. Hence the very general adoption of this kind of monument in England from the thirteenth to the seventeenth century.

The material employed for monumental brasses was an alloy of copper,[1] which appears to have been generally known as latten or laton (*Belg.* lattoen). The chief place for its manufacture was Cologne, from which we find it called " Cullen plate." [2] The industry was confined for a long time probably to North Germany and Flanders, where are such splendid examples of the sepulchral brass. The plates were imported into England[3] from the beginning of the thirteenth century. It is not till the latter half of the sixteenth century that we find records of the manufacture in this country at Isleworth and elsewhere.[4]

The following quotations from Waller (*A Series of*

Material used

---

[1] The analysis of the Cortewille Flemish brass, 1504, in the South Kensington Museum is :—copper 64·0, zinc 29·5, lead 3·5, tin 3·0 in the hundred parts.

[2] *See* Appendix for Dugdale's account of the construction of the Beauchamp tomb, 1439, at Warwick.

[3] Doubtless in connection with the exportation of wool to Flanders. This accounts for the use of monumental brasses by the Wool-merchants of Gloucestershire, and for the prevalence of these memorials in the counties on the East coast.

[4] " At the close of the 16th century the manufacture of brass was in-" troduced into England. Patents were granted in 1565 to several " persons, and mills were established in various places about London and " elsewhere. Norden in his account of Middlesex mentions the ' copper " ' and brasse myll' near 'Thistleworth or Istleworth' where 'the workmen " ' make plates, both of copper and brasse, of all syces, little and great, " ' thick and thyn, for all purposes.' This metal was of improved manu-" facture ; the copper was beaten out with heavy hammers worked by

Monumental Brasses, p. ii.) give some account of the process of making and engraving the plates :—

"The sheets of metal were cast to near the size required
"in a mould formed of two cakes of loam; there was no
"hammering, except by wooden mallets, an operation now
"known as planishing, the object of which is to get rid of
"any twist or bend. The average size of the sheets is
"generally from 2 ft. 6 in. to 2 ft. 8 in.; but there is one at
"Higham Ferrers, Northamptonshire, somewhat over 3 ft.,
"and the Flemish brass just alluded to ("Cortewille") has
"plates measuring 3 ft. 2 in. by 1 ft. $10\frac{1}{2}$ in. The thickness
"or gauge is about $\frac{1}{8}$ of an inch, but being always unequal,
"varies much in the same plate. The mode of manu-
"facture was not calculated to produce a substance of
"homogeneous structure; thus it is often found full of
"air-bubbles and flaws; and a brass, much worn, will show
"a number of small holes upon its surface. The Lynn
"brasses exhibit these defects in a remarkable manner. . . .
"In English work the burin or lozenge-shaped graver is
"more constantly used. Broad lines are produced by
"repeated parallel strokes, running into each other, and
"the channel thus made is in some cases roughened by
"cross hatching as in a fine example of John de Campeden,
"1382, at St. Cross, near Winchester. But, in the Flemish,
"a broad chisel-shaped tool has been chiefly used; the
"channels are not so deep, and are always smooth at the
"bottom. Simple as it seems to be, this difference of
"practice has materially affected the character of the
"designs. This is especially noticeable in the treatment
"of draperies in which the Flemish brasses fall short of
"the grace and elegance to be found in English examples;
"and the reason appears to be that the broad-cutting tool
"admitted of less freedom in execution."

"water power; and the plates thus produced were saturated with oxide
"of zinc. But they were thin, and when used for brasses, upon the pave-
"ment, are always found much bent and defaced."—*A Series of Monumental Brasses from the Thirteenth to the Sixteenth Century,* drawn and
engraved by J. G. and L. A. B. Waller, p. ii.

A slab of stone, or of marble of the Purbeck or Sussex Inlaid in marble slab
kind, was prepared to receive the brass[1] when finished,
being hollowed out so as to form a casement, matrix, or
indent in which the brass was laid, imbedded in pitch and
fastened to the slab by means of rivets.

Some evidences of the cost of these monuments have Cost of brasses
come down to us. Sir Iohn de St. Quintin, 1397, left
xx marks for a marble stone with three images of laton
to be placed over himself and two wives at Brandsburton,
Yorkshire. Katherine, widow of John Fastolff (d. 1445),
by her will dated 20th November, 1478, orders a stone to
be provided to the value of 7 or 8 marks, inlaid with the
arms of John Sampson and John Fastolf, her late husbands,
of Roger Welysham, her father, and with those of Beding-
feld. There is no mention of the two effigies in the will;
but they are reproduced in Suckling's *Suffolk*, 1848, Vol. II.,
p. 40, in the account of the Church of St. Michael at
Oulton.[2] The contract for the tomb of Richard, Earl of
Warwick, gives much information on this subject. (*See*
Appendix.)[3]

The following extract (for which we are indebted to
Canon Mayo) from the will of "Thomas Denny, son and
"heir of Edmunde Denny late one of the Barons of the
"Eschequier, 10 May, 1527; 19 Hen. VIII." gives
instructions for making a memorial brass. Unfortunately,
no such brass remains in Cheshunt Church, Herts. Possibly
the executor did not fulfil the testator's wishes :—"To be

---

[1] An instance of a brass originally fixed on wood is at Bettws-Cedewain,
near Newtown, in Montgomeryshire, John ap Meredyth de Powys, 1531,
in mass vestments.

[2] They were stolen, together with that of Adam de Bacon, *c.* 1310,
in February, 1857. The brass of Katherine Fastolff afforded a good
example of the butterfly headdress.

[3] *See* also "Some Notes on the Montacutes, Earls of Salisbury," by
Edward Kite, *Wiltshire Notes and Queries*, Vol. IV. (No. 47, September,
1904), p. 490, for codicil to will of Thomas de Montacute, 4th Earl of
Salisbury (d. 1428), directing a tomb to be made at Bisham, Berks, for
himself and wives, the Ladies Alianore and Alice, "which tomb I desire
"to be made of marble, with portraitures of each in brass, and epitaphs."

" buried in parish Church of Chesthunt, where I doe dwell
" at the altar's end on the south side next before the pewe
" where I was wonte to sitte, and there I will a stone to be
" layd on me by my execut', and a picture of dethe to be
" made in the saied stone w^t roules having this writing
" about hym to be written in the sayed roules, *As I am so*
" *shall ye be, nowe praye for me of yor charitie w^t a p$\bar{r}$ n$\bar{r}$ and*
" *an ave mary, for the rest of the soule of Thomas Denny*
" *whiche dyed the xth day of May in the yere of or Lorde god*
" *m^{l}v^{c}xxvii*, and at the hed of the saied picture in two
" roules having this sculpture *D$\bar{n}$e secund$\bar{u}$ actum meum noli*
" *me judicare* unto the one syde, and on the other syde
" *Delicta juventutis mee et ignorantias meas ne memineres*
" *domine*.   Also I will it to be made by myne execut' a
" litle stone of halfe a yerde brode and thre quarters long
" and to be set in the wall over where I doe lye and therein
" a picture of me to be made kneling and holding up
" my hands, ingraven and gilted w^t my armes another side
" and a picture of or Lorde suffering his passon in the
" upper corner and a roule gilted with this ingraven
" comyng frome my hands and upwards *M$\bar{\imath}$as tuas dne in*
" *etern$\bar{u}$ cantabo* and underneth in the foote of the saied
" stone one other plate graven and gilted with this therein
" written *Every man that here goeth by pray for him that here*
" *doth lye wt a p$\bar{r}$ n$\bar{r}$ & an ave mary, for the reste of the soule*
" *of Thomas Denny which died the xth day of May in the yere*
" *of or Lorde God m^{l}v^{c}xxvii*" (28 Jankyn P.C.C.).

Artists and engravers   Very little is known as to the artists who designed or the men who engraved the brasses.   But from differences in locality and style it may be inferred that, like other craftsmen, they formed themselves into guilds with centres at large towns, such as London, York, or Norwich. There is little to go by but a similarity of design, from which, however, it is obviously unsafe to infer that because any two brasses have similarities, they were, therefore, either designed or worked by the same hand.   The most important school of engravers was that settled in London, which supplied the greater number of brasses.   Provincial

engravers, as a rule, show inferior workmanship, though
there is good local work to be found in Yorkshire and
Lincolnshire, probably executed by engravers making York
their headquarters. The special characteristics marking
the Norwich school are to be met with throughout Norfolk
and Suffolk. Some peculiarities seen in Cambridgeshire
and Essex (as for instance on the brasses of ladies, mentioned on p. 283) may prove the existence of several
engravers at Cambridge in the sixteenth century; and
proofs of a school supplying the Midlands may be seen in
the local work, such as the ecclesiastical brasses at Coleshill (William Abell, 1500) and at Whitnash (Richard
Bennett, M.A., 1531), Warwickshire. Sometimes an
extraordinary and grotesque effect is produced, owing to
lack of craftsmanship. Such may be seen at Preston,
Lancashire, where the effigy of Seath Bushell, woollen
draper, 1623, has more the appearance of a modern
caricature by "Max" than of a sepulchral memorial.[1]

A device, which may be an artist's signature,[2] or possibly
the mark of the brass manufacturer, occurs on the brass of
Lady Creke, c. 1325, at Westley Waterless, Cambs.,
representing the letter N reversed over which is a mallet,
and on the dexter side a crescent and on the sinister
a star of six points. The N reversed is also found on the
Camoys brass, 1424, at Trotton, Sussex. Waller, in
his description of the Creke brass, mentions a seal of
Walter the Mason, attached to a deed, on which a
mallet with a crescent and a star of five points appears.
This device of a star and crescent is mentioned in the
Archæological Journal (Vol. III., 1846, p. 345), as used by

---

[1] *See* illustration in *The Monumental Brasses of Lancashire and Cheshire*, by
James L. Thornely, 1893. *See* also *Records of the Parish Church of Preston
in Amounderness*, by Tom. C. Smith, F.R.Hist.Soc., Preston, 1892, pp.
258-9 and 287-8.

[2] Boutell gives an illustration (*Monumental Brasses and Slabs*, p. 149) of
a palimpsest fragment now in the British Museum, of a Flemish inscription, formerly in Trunch Church, Norfolk, on which is a shield charged
with a crescent and star and the letter W.

Hawisia de Wygornia for a seal to a document, dated 1254.[1]

Signatures are, occasionally, found in later years, particularly on inscriptions of the seventeeth century. The Flemish brass of Margaret Svanders, 1529, at Fulham, has the initials G. O.[2] The initials A. H. and R. H. found respectively on the brasses of Bishop Henry Robinson and Provost Airay, both 1616, at Queen's College, Oxford, have been supposed by Haines to refer to Abraham and Remigius Hogenbergh; but it is possible that the latter may refer to Dr. Richard Haydock, fellow of New College, whose work is to be seen in the brass of Erasmus Williams, 1608, at Tingewick, Bucks, and who composed the inscription to Thomas Hopper, 1623, at New College.[3] An engraver's monogram occurs on the brass of William Waller (1636), St. Paul's, Bedford.[4] The Filmer brass (1638) at East Sutton, Kent, is signed: " Ed. Marſhall sculpſit." At Tamworth, in Warwickshire, the inscription to Anne, wife of John Chambers, 1650, is signed, " J.C. composuit, E.C. sculpsit, W.C. dedit."[5] In the

---

[1] " The name of an artist was recorded on the brass of Bishop Philip, " 1241, formerly at Evreux, 'Guillaume de Plalli me fecit,' and another " was on an incised slab, formerly in the church of St. Yved de Braine, " in France, representing Robert, Count de Dreux, who died 1223. It " was inscribed upon the fillet at the feet of the figure thus : ' Letarous me " fecit.' Drawings of these are preserved in Gough's Collection in the " Bodleian Library, Oxford. These instances are of particular interest, " and suggest to us the question, whether we have here the name of the " designer, or of him who executed the work. It is scarcely possible that " the workman and the designer were one."—Waller, *A Series of Monumental Brasses*, Introduction, p. iv.

[2] Possibly those of her husband, Gerard Hornebolt, the painter.

[3] See *A Catalogue of the Brasses in Queen's College, Oxford*, by P. Manning, M.A., F.S.A., pp. 67-79 ; *Journal of the Oxford University Brass Rubbing Society*, Vol. I., No. 2, June, 1897, p. 78.

[4] See *Transactions of the Monumental Brass Society*, Vol. II., p. 90.

[5] Her children's names were William, Edmund, John, and Elizabeth. *See* " A Few Notes on Monumental Brasses with a Catalogue of those existing in Warwickshire," by Charles Williams, *Transactions of the Birmingham and Midland Institute (Archæological Section)*, 1884-5, Birmingham, 1887, p. 47. A brass in Chichester Cathedral, William Bradbridge and wife Alice, is signed " Fynished in July, 1592, A. L. B."

Gwydir Chapel, Llanrwst, Denbighshire, the brass of
Mary, wife of Sir Roger Mostyn, 1653, is the work of
"Silvanus Crue"; that of Sarah, wife of Sir Richard
Wynne, 1671, of "Guil. Vaughan." In Yorkshire there are
several signed brasses.[1] The name of "Gabr. Hornbie"
occurs on an inscription at Nunkeeling (George Acklam,
1629); that of "Fr: Grigs" on the brass of John and
Grace Morewood, 1647, at Bradfield, near Sheffield. It
is also found, 1640, at Upton Cressett, Shropshire (Richard
Cressett and Wife), and at St. Osyth's, Essex (John Darcy,
Serjeant-at-Law). "Tho. Mann Eboraci sculp." occurs
on brasses at Lowthorp (John Pierson, 1665); Normanton
(Richard Mallet, 1668); Ingleby Arncliffe (Elizabeth
Mauleverer, 1674); Rudstone (Katherine, wife of John
Constable, 1677). "J. Mann Ebor. sculp^t" occurs on the
brass of John Wilson, 1681, at Bedale. "P. Brigges,
Ebor." signs the brass of Roger Talbot, 1680, at Thornton-
le-Street, and "Ric. Crosse" that of Peter Samwaies,
rector, 1693, at Bedale. "George Harris Fecit" occurs
on an inscription at Deddington, Oxon. (Thomas Higgins,
1660).

A few brasses, by the fineness of their engraving, are
evidently the work of goldsmiths, as in the case of the
palimpsest reverse, c. 1500, at Berkhampstead, Herts, to
Thomas Humfre, goldsmith, of London (see p. 64, note 2).
A later example is at St. Andrew's, Auckland, Durham,
to Fridesmonda, wife of Richard Barnes, Bishop of
Durham.[2]

The use of engraved plates of brass for sepulchral
monuments seems to have arisen early in the thirteenth

Thirteenth Century Brasses

---

[1] See Mr. Mill Stephenson in Vols. XII., XV., and XVII. of the *Yorkshire Archæological Journal*.

[2] Mr. J. G. Waller writes (*Archæologia Aeliana*, Vol. XV., p. 81):—
"In Raine's *Auckland Castle*, p. 72, is an excerpt from the bishop's
accounts, 1583, which tells of a payment 'to the gouldsmythe at Yorke
for a plate to sett over Mrs. Barnes, 32s.'"

century ;[1] but very few remains of that period have come down to us. Leland records an inscription on brass, once existing in St. Paul's Church, Bedford, to Simon de Beauchamp, Earl of Bedford, c. 1208.[2] An engraving (Planche 18), in the second volume of Montfaucon's *Monumens de la Monarchie Françoise*, 1730, gives an early design of a brass, commemorating Philippe and Jean, the sons of Louis VIII. (1223-1226). On a quadrangular plate the two boys are portrayed beneath a double canopy, above which four angels, holding incense boats, swing censers ; the background is composed of *fleurs-de-lis*.[3] The oldest extant brass is that at Verden, representing in pontificals Ysowilpe Graf von Welpe in Lower Saxony, who became the thirty-first Bishop of Verden in 1205, and died on the nones of August, 1231. It consists of one

---

[1] Boutell aptly writes (*Monumental Brasses and Slabs*, p. 7) : "Nor is it less "worthy of remark that these incised monumental plates were produced "in abundance, and in high perfection, more than two centuries previous "to the discovery of the art of engraving plates of metal for the purpose "of impression. To Mazo Finiquerra, a goldsmith of Florence who "flourished about the year 1460, is assigned the distinguished honour "of having made the discovery of copper-plate engraving, properly so- "called : and thus, during no less a period than 250 years, with an "abundance of engraven plates in existence, all of which were expressly "calculated to produce fac-simile copies by means of impression, the art "of taking impressions remained altogether unknown."

[2] *See* "The Brasses of Bedfordshire," by H. K. St. J. Sanderson, *Transactions of Cambridge University Association of Brass Collectors* (now the Monumental Brass Society), Vol. II., p. 41-2.

[3] "La planche suivante nous montre Philippe et Jean de France, fils de "Louis VIII. et de Blanche de Castille, comme marque l'inscription tout "au tour, en quatre très-mauvais vers Latins. Ils moururent tous deux "fort jeunes. Leurs corps gisent sous la même tombe de cuivre au milieu "du chœur de Notre Dame de Poissi. Ils ont chacun une espece de "petite couronne, et un sceptre qu'ils portent de la main droite, et qui se "termine en haut par une fleur de lis. Celui qui est à la droite, tient de la "main gauche un gand. C'est le gand de la main qui soutenoit l'oiseau "que les grands Seigneurs, les Princes et les Rois mêmes se faisoient un "honneur de porter. C'est Philippe qui le tient, et qui comme aîné de "Jean, paroît avoir cette prérogative sur lui."—Montfaucon, Vol. II., p. 120.

sheet of brass, over six feet in length, surrounded by a fillet on which is an inscription in Lombardic capitals, spaces for the nails being allowed for in the arrangement of the lettering. The style of the design and engraving much resembles that of the incised slabs of the period, from which, no doubt, this was a departure. An illustration of this brass may be seen in Creeny's book of *Facsimiles of Brasses on the Continent*, where a similar thirteenth century one, that of Bishop Otto de Brunswick, 1279, in the Cathedral of Hildesheim, is given.

We have evidence of the former existence in England of various brasses during this century; such as that of Bishop Bingham of Salisbury;[1] of Richard de Berkyng, Abbot of Westminster, 1246, etc.; but the earliest effigies that survive to this day are those of Sir John Daubernoun, *c.* 1277, at Stoke d'Abernon, Surrey, and of Sir Roger de Trumpington, 1289, at Trumpington, near Cambridge. At Wimborne Minster, Dorset, is a brass commemorating St. Ethelred, King of the West Saxons, 872; but the half-effigy and shield belong to the fifteenth, and the inscription on copper in Roman capitals to about the end of the sixteenth century.[2] At Ashbourn in Derbyshire, a Lombardic inscription recording the dedication of the church, 1241, is probably a copy of an older plate.[3] In Westminster Abbey an important slab survives, showing a portion of the stem of a brass cross, with a marginal inscription in Lombardic lettering, enclosed in narrow brass fillets, of which eight letters (LAME :.........RLEA) still remain, the space between the stem and the inscribed border being filled in with glass mosaic in red, white, and gold. This

---

[1] The matrix, showing a demi-effigy with mitre and crozier in the centre of a cross flory, is illustrated in Kite's *Monumental Brasses of Wiltshire*, p. 6.

[2] *See* some remarks in *A History of Wimborne Minster*, by Charles Mayo, London, 1860, pp. 7 and 135. Haines gives the date of the effigy, *c.* 1440.

[3] Illustrated *Transactions of Monumental Brass Society*, Vol. III., p. 209, April, 1899.

may be the memorial of John de Valence or de Varleance, son of William de Valence, Earl of Pembroke, *c.* 1270.[1] At Hereford Cathedral is a small figure of St. Ethelbert, part of the brass, formerly existing, of Bishop Thomas Cantilupe, 1282.

Development similar to that of architecture The history of the development of design in English brasses is, practically, identical with that of English architecture.   As in the buildings, so in the brasses, we note an insular individuality of style.   Indeed, in many respects our brasses may be distinguished from those on the Continent; perhaps the most noticeable departure being the difference in shape.   For, whereas the foreign brasses, as a rule, consist of quadrangular sheets of metal, this form, putting aside the later mural brass, is the exception in England; and when it does occur in the earlier periods may, usually, be attributed directly to Flemish influence.[2]

It is no part of this essay to trace the development of Gothic architecture in England; but an acquaintance with its main features is necessary, if an intelligent study of brasses be desired.   This may be cultivated in Rickman, and Parker, and in other works, and, above all, in the buildings themselves.   Unfortunately, but few of the Decorated Canopies of the fourteenth century remain to us, though their beauty of form may be traced in surviving indents; but of the Perpendicular work of the next century many fine examples exist.   Indeed, so accurately do they reflect the architecture of their time, that were no other proof available, the date of a brass could often be fixed by comparing its canopy with well-known dated

---

[1] An excellent reproduction of this slab, made from a water-colour fac-simile done by Miss E. M. Vincent, will be found in *A Series of Photolithographs of Monumental Brasses in Westminster Abbey*, mostly from rubbings taken by E. M. Beloe, junr. 1898.

[2] It is possible that the costliness of the brass, due to the fact that it was not manufactured in England, may account for the shape of English brasses.   There was not the same need of economy in Flanders, the material being more easily procured.

examples in stone. Like Gothic architecture, the monumental brass, which can hardly be considered other than an accessory of the style, reached its perfection in the fourteenth century, and shared the stately decline of the Perpendicular period. The succeeding Renaissance, owing either to inferiority of craft and material, or to some subtle lack of sympathy in the classical spirit with a medium, so successful during the Gothic age, did not reach in brasses that perfection which it attained in other arts. Possibly there may be something essentially Gothic in this art, a quality born of tradition, since, theoretically, there is no reason why the classical treatment should not be equally successful. But it is curious to note that this view has been supported by the practice of the Gothic revivalists of the nineteenth century. The Renaissance artists, moreover, with their love for work in relief, may have found the necessary limitations of the flat surface of the brass irksome to them.

The arrangement of brasses in periods presents the same difficulties which we encounter in architecture owing to the overlapping of styles, and to the fact that the gradual growth of ideas with their concrete embodiment, though, doubtless, witnessing to the flight of time, does not, necessarily, take account of artificial divisions into reigns or centuries. The Rev. H. W. Macklin in his excellent handbook [1] divides brasses into seven periods, the final one beginning with the reign of Charles I. Haines groups them, in a somewhat broader survey, into three periods:—(1) The fourteenth; (2) the fifteenth; (3) the sixteenth and seventeenth centuries. In following this latter arrangement we have to consider some of the main characteristics, leaving the changes in costume for separate treatment. *Arrangement in periods*

The first period covers the fourteenth century, extending from the beginning of the reign of Edward I., 1272, to the end of that of Richard II., 1399, and in many respects is *The XIV. Century*

---

[1] *Monumental Brasses*, 4th edition, 1898, pp. 15-17.

the most important of the three. In it we include the
brasses at Stoke D'Abernon and Trumpington, already
mentioned as the only brass effigies of the thirteenth century
left to us in England. Its finest work was that seen in
the Flemish brasses of the middle of the century, of which
we treat below. The engraving was executed on thick and
hard plates, in bold and graceful lines without shading,
and deeply cut. It is indicative of the excellence of the
work and material used in this century that these earlier
brasses, where they have escaped deliberate vandalism, are,
usually, to be found in far better preservation than those
of a later period. The general treatment is revealed in
the use of the recumbent position and in the absence of
any apparent effort at portraiture. Ecclesiastics have the
grave countenances befitting their profession. To the
earlier part of this period belong the few cross-legged,
mail-clad knights that survive. The figures are usually
about life-size, though we find them somewhat diminished
after the introduction of canopies under Edward II. Half-
length figures and busts seem to have been in fashion.
The Floriated cross was a favourite form of brass, its head
frequently enclosing a figure of the deceased, and it is de-
plorable that so few remain of what was once a numerous
class. Its use led to the development from it of the so-
called Bracket-brass, of which some beautiful examples
survive. The representation of children on brasses is rare,
and when it occurs the figures are usually not much inferior
in size to that of the parents. The canopies of this period
have suffered much from spoliation ;[1] they appear to have
grown in elaboration similarly to the stonework, which
they imitated. The earliest inscriptions are in Lombardic
characters, each letter being fixed into its own matrix on
the slab, and in some cases enclosed in narrow fillets of

---

[1] That of Lady Joan de Cobham, c. 1320, at Cobham, Kent (see Chap. VI.),
is the only specimen left of the pedimental canopy of the earlier part of
the century.

brass.[1] This rather insecure method gave place to engraving the words on fillets of brass placed as a border to
the slab.[2] At the beginning of Edward III.'s reign black
letter[3] was introduced with Lombardic capitals,[4] and we
find inscriptions placed beneath the figures. Generally
speaking, the inscriptions are of a simple nature. Latin
is used, as a rule, for priests, and Norman-French frequently occurs for knights and their ladies. Dates are
the exception rather than the rule. An early instance
occurs on the palimpsest inscription in Denchworth Church,
Berks (1333, St. Margaret's Day, the date of the surrender
of Berwick), recording the laying of the foundation-stone
of Bisham Priory by Edward III. At Cholsey, in the

---

[1] In Kite's *Monumental Brasses of Wiltshire*, p. 10, is an illustration of
a stone slab, not earlier than 1322, showing indents of a cross fleury surmounted by the half-effigy of a priest, and of a Lombardic marginal
inscription, once of brass, as witness the inscription in Norman-French :—
"+ SOUTZ · CESTE · PERE · LETTERE · OV · LATON · GIST · WILL'M · LA · SEINT ·
IOHN · DE · RAMM · ESBVRY · PERSONE · ET · FER · POR · SA · ALME · PRIER ·
ORASON · QARANT · IOVRS · ASSVRON · DE · P'DON."
The matrix of the brass of Boneface de Hart, Canon of Aosta, *c.* 1320,
at Hornchurch, Essex (a cross fleury with two half-effigies of ecclesiastics
and Lombardic marginal inscription), retains a small piece of the outer
fillet, the letters N and F in "BONEFACE," and the upper dot of the
colon after "SIRE." *See* "Some Interesting Essex Brasses," by Miller
Christy and W. W. Porteous, in *The Reliquary and Illustrated Archæologist*,
N.S., Vol. VII., 1901. At Peterborough are preserved a letter V and a
circular stop from the inscription of Abbot Godfrey de Croyland, 1329,
and at Watlington, Norfolk, five diamond-shaped stops remain on the slab
of Sir Robert de Montalt, 1329. *See* "Notes on some early matrices in
the Eastern Counties," by E. M. Beloe, junr., *Journal of the Oxford University Brass Rubbing Society*, Vol. II., No. I., Feb., 1900, pp. 35-39. In
the British Museum are preserved the Lombardic letters A D M N and
T, *c.* 1330. That these letters appear to have been imbedded in pitch
without rivets is sufficient reason for their scarcity at the present day.

[2] In the *Essex Review*, Vol. X., 1901, "Some Interesting Essex
Brasses," by Miller Christy and W. W. Porteous, p. 87, three fragments
are cited, as existing, of the fillet inscribed with Lombardic lettering to
Sir — Fitzralph, *c.* 1320, at Pebmarsh, Essex.

[3] An early example is at North Ockenden, Essex, Iohan bauchoñ, *c.* 1330.

[4] As at Stanstead Montfitchet, Essex, Robert de Bokkyngg, vicar, 1361.

same county, the French inscription to John Barfoot bears
the date 8th October, 1361.

The second period begins with the reign of Henry IV.
in 1399, and ends with the death of Henry VII. in 1509,
following the fortunes of the Houses of Lancaster and
York to their union in the latter monarch.   Great delicacy
distinguishes the early work of this century ; cross-shading
is introduced and the lines are finer than in the former
period.   Gradually, as the century advances, convention-
ality of treatment becomes more marked, and shading is
more frequently introduced, often to the disadvantage of
the composition.   The greater extension of the use by all
classes [1] of this form of monument leads to a greater diversity in artistic merit.   The figures become smaller, and
the presence of flowers and of grass beneath the feet begins
to denote an erect attitude.   The greater extravagance in
dress, especially in the development of the ladies' head-
dress, is noticeable, and led to the frequent use of the
figure in profile instead of the former full-face attitude,
still retained by the clergy.   The demi-figure, except for
priests, is not so frequent a feature as in the last century.
The portrayal of children on the brasses of their parents
becomes of common occurrence, sometimes placed beneath
the parents, sometimes standing beside them as diminutive
figures.   Brasses of children, alone, are to be found, as at
Blickling, Norfolk, 1479.   The mural brass with kneeling
figures, a form that became very common in the next
century, is introduced.   Floriated crosses of very fine
work are to be found in the earlier part of the century, as
at Stone, Kent (John Lumbarde, Rector, 1408), but are
superseded by the simpler cross fleury.   Fine examples of
bracket-brasses exist, as at Upper Hardres, Kent, 1405,
and Merton College, Oxford, 1420, in the former of which

---

[1] This fact adds greatly to the value of these memorials, ranging as they
do from the Duchess of Gloucester, wife of Thomas of Woodstock, 1399,
in Westminster Abbey, to the blacksmith at Beauchampton, Bucks
(William Bawdyn, 1600).

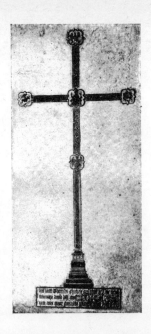

CROSS BRASS. THOMAS CHICHELE AND WIFE AGNES, 1400,
HIGHAM FERRERS, NORTHANTS.

C.B.]

BRACKET BRASS. JOHN STRETE, 1405,
UPPER HARDRES, KENT.

we see a good instance of the introduction of figures of
Apostles, as of other sacred personages and scenes at this
time. The canopies, of which there are many very fine
specimens, follow the progress of the Perpendicular style,
the gradual deterioration of which towards the close of the
century is very noticeable in the treatment of the crockets
and finials. The ogee is the favourite shape for the arch.
A curious feature of this period is seen to advantage in
Yorkshire, and later in Norfolk in the adoption of devices
with inscriptions, such as the chalice for a priest. Inscriptions are frequently formed of raised lettering,[1] and
in some instances the spaces between the words are filled
with grotesque figures of animals and flowers. At the end
of the century the letters are often crowded together and
consequently difficult to read. The Norman-French
language and Lombardic capitals go out of use, and are
succeeded by Latin with the occasional use of English,[2]
and Gothic black-letter or church-text. Arabic numerals
exist, but are uncommon. An example, late in the century,
is afforded by the brass of Thomas Greville, Chrysom,
1892, at Stanford Rivers, Essex. The disagreeable practice, introduced from the Continent, of presenting emaciated figures or skeletons in shrouds is a characteristic of
this century, and is sometimes carried to an unsavoury
excess. Examples are found in the eastern counties, where
they show an English individuality of treatment. It is
difficult to understand what satisfaction such a monument
can have given either to the person commemorated, if
worked in his lifetime, or to his relatives after his decease.
It betrays an attitude of mind, which, though found in so
eminent a person as Dr. Donne, we may hope has long
since disappeared.

The third period, in which the similarity of design XVI. & XVI
Centuries

---

[1] A good example, of the next century, is the inscription at Flam-
borough, Yorkshire, to Sir Marmaduke Constable, Knt., *c.* 1520.

[2] An early example is at Holm-by-the-Sea, Norfolk (Herry Notingham
and wife, *c.* 1405).

admits of the treatment of the two centuries in one division, spreads over the reigns of the Tudor and Stuart Dynasties. This is the age of the deterioration of brasses and of their final extinction in the seventeenth century; but in many respects this decadence is important. As already mentioned, the medium does not appear to have gained the sympathy of the best Renaissance workmen, from which fact, in England at all events, brasses may be defined as essentially Gothic in spirit. The workmanship, with few exceptions, is much coarser and weaker than in the former periods, and the practice of shading becomes an abuse. The quality of the metal, moreover, especially after the reign of Elizabeth, when it was first manufactured in this country, is much inferior to the earlier material, being much thinner and more easily worn. The erect attitude has become the favourite; the figures standing on a marble pavement or low, rounded pedestal. Haines observes (Introduction, p. ccxv.) that this attitude is adopted in brasses long before it came into use for the sculptured effigy. The mural brass becomes common, frequently set in a stone or marble framework of classical design. In it the deceased are often represented kneeling at faldstools, husband and wife facing each other with their sons and daughters grouped on either side behind them.[1] It should be noted that these mural brasses, which are of a moderate size, usually consist of a rectangular plate, the background being filled in with classical architectural details, armorial bearings, etc. A certain lack of dignity is often to be seen, as in the portrayal of domestic events, *e.g.*, at Heston, Middlesex (Constance, wife of Mordecai Bownell, 1581), or of occupations, as at Walton-on-Thames, Surrey (John Selwyn, 1587). Brasses of children become common, and we find the variety known as the

---

[1] The demi-effigy is uncommon. *See* mural brasses in York Minster, representing (1) Elizabeth Eynns, daughter of Sir Edward Nevell, one of the gentlewomen of the privy chamber to Queen Elizabeth, 1582; and (2) James Cotrel, Esq., 1595. Also at Little Warley, Essex (Anne Tyrrell, 1592).

CHRYSOM BRASS.
ELYN, DAUGHTER OF SIR EDMOND BRAY, 1516,
STOKE D'ABERNON, SURREY.

"chrysom," denoting the early death of the infant in a regenerate state. The influence of the Reformation is quite as visible as that of the Renaissance. Of the triumph of the latter, one of the best examples is the brass of Don Parafan de Ribera, Duke of Alcala, at Seville, 1571.[1] The influence of the former gives us many mournful or allegorical symbols, which replace those of an earlier age. Skulls and crossbones, hour-glasses, and other funeral ornaments succeed the evangelistic symbols, and the emblems of the Trinity or of the Passion. The Prayer for the dead is omitted from the inscriptions, which are much more ornate than in the former periods, epitaphs displaying, at times, elaborate eulogies, which are as foreign as possible to the good taste and reticent simplicity of a former age. There is, too, a more pompous display of heraldry, the shield commonly being surmounted by an elaborate helmet and mantling. English becomes the usual language of inscriptions, often badly spelt, though Latin is frequently retained by the clergy. In the sixteenth century Roman capitals came into use. The later Gothic canopies become very much debased; the best instances of the Renaissance style of building occur on Continental brasses. The class of effigies, described above as shroud or skeleton brasses, is common. A disgusting instance of this unpleasantness may be seen at Oddington, Oxon., c. 1510 (Ralph Hamsterley, rector, Fellow of Merton College, Oxford, died 1518).

In the eighteenth century there are very few instances of the use of brass effigies for sepulchral monuments. XVIII. and XIX. Centuries

[1] The inscription in Roman capitals runs :—
" Hoc jacet in tumulo, quem virtus vexit ad astra :
Quem canet ad summum debita fama diem.
Tempore diverso duo regna amplissima rexit :
Barchinoem juvenis Parthenopenque senex.
Dum fuit Eöis fulsit quasi sidus Eöum :
Dum fuit Hesperiis, Hesperus alter erat.
Flere nefas illum, qui fœlix vivit ubique,
Ante homines vivus, mortuus ante deos.
See Creeny's Book of Facsimiles of Brasses on the Continent.

Two occur at St. Mary Cray, Kent, namely those of Philadelphia Greenwood, 1747, and Benjamin Greenwood, 1775. Although of some interest as fashion-plates, they possess no artistic value. The revival of Gothic architecture in the nineteeth century, aided by the religious movement at Oxford, has resuscitated an art long dormant. Instances of good work are not uncommon. A favourite form was a cross engraved on a rectangular plate; but the cross proper has some representatives of merit in the nave of Westminster Abbey. Instances of effigies are increasing. A good example of a large brass is that of the Rev. Richard Temple West (*d.* 1893) in mass vestments in the church of St. Mary Magdalene, Paddington:[1] of a small one that of Martin White Benson (1878), son of Archbishop Benson, in the cloisters of Winchester College. A fine brass, designed in the Flemish manner by E. R. Singer, is in Bristol Cathedral (Rev. Jordan Roquette Palmer-Palmer, 1885). Both Haines and Creeny are appropriately commemorated by brasses; the former in Gloucester Cathedral, the latter in St. Michael-at-Thorn, Norwich.

Distribution of brasses

The next point for consideration is the distribution of brasses. Many thousands must have existed in former times on the continent of Europe, as well as in England, of a large proportion of which not even matrices remain. Creeny gave two hundred as the probable limit to the number of brasses left on the Continent.[2] In England more than five thousand survive, owing to the preservation of which the study of brasses may be said to have

---

[1] See *In Memory of the Rev. R. T. West, M.A., First Vicar of Saint Mary Magdalene, Paddington. A Description of the Memorial Brass,* with illustration [by J. G. Wood].

[2] " One small one at Amiens and some few unimportant ones at Douay are all that now remain in that land [France]. In Germany about seventy-five, and in Belgium about sixty or seventy, almost complete the catalogue," p. iv., Creeny's book of *Facsimiles of Monumental Brasses on the Continent.* A few exist in Denmark, and at least three are known in Spain.

become, pre-eminently, an English pursuit. Moreover,
an accurate exploration of a county, such as that conducted
by the Rev. Edmund Farrer in Norfolk, or that made by
Messrs. Miller Christy, and W. W. Porteous in Essex,
may be found to increase very considerably the number
above that given by Haines in 1861.[1] Both in Scotland
and in Ireland matrices occur, but brasses are very rare.
In the former kingdom there is a mural brass, 1613, at
Aberdeen; another exists at Glasgow, 1605; a third commemorates the Regent Murray, 1569-70, in St. Giles's,
Edinburgh. In St. Patrick's Cathedral, Dublin, are four
mural brasses; in Christchurch Cathedral one. The Prin-
cipality of Wales has preserved about a score. At Peel,
in the Isle of Man, is the brass inscription of Bishop
Rutter (1662). In the Channel Islands matrices may be
seen. The presence and survival of so many brasses in
this country may be attributed to a superior stability of
government, and the consequent greater prosperity of the
nation. They are scattered, very unequally, over the
different counties; those on the east coast (Kent, Essex,
Norfolk, and Suffolk) containing the greater number;
after which come the home counties. As a general rule,
the farther north and west we travel, the sparser do the
brasses become, until we find Northumberland represented by three brasses, one being the Flemish brass at
Newcastle-on-Tyne; and Westmorland by but two brasses
bearing effigies.[2] The chief cause of this unequal distribution must be the greater intercourse of the eastern
counties, and of those surrounding London with the
Continent, and especially with Flanders.

Brasses are of all sizes. The largest known is that at   Their size
Schwerin, representing Bishops Godfrey (1314) and
Frederic de Bulowe (1375), which measures 12 ft. 7 in.

---

[1] In Norfolk, counting inscriptions, over one thousand brasses are
known to exist; in Essex nearly five hundred.

[2] A third effigy exists on the reverse of the Palimpsest inscription at
Morland.

by 6 ft. 4 in.   Among the largest in England is the Walsokne brass at King's Lynn, 10 ft. by 5 ft. 7 in.   The slab
at Durham, in which is the matrix of Bishop Beaumont's
brass (died 1333), measures 15 ft. 10 in. by 9 ft. 7 in.
One of the smallest in existence must be the mural
inscription at Long Burton, Dorset, commemorating
Nathaniel Faireclough, intruding Rector of Stalbridge,
1656, which is 5½ inches square.   A very diminutive
effigy may be seen at Cheam, Surrey (John Yerd, c. 1480).

Some account
of the treat-
ment to which
they have been
subjected

A large book might be filled with records of the
spoliation and misusage to which brasses have been subjected; we must be content with a short survey of their
treatment.   And we must be grateful that Fate has dealt
more kindly with England than with other countries in
this respect.   If we review the history of Scotland or that
of France, it is easy to find sufficient cause for the disappearance of sepulchral monuments.   In the latter
country, indeed, in a great many cases what religious
fanaticism spared in the sixteenth, the Revolution of the
end of the eighteenth century destroyed.[1]

In Pre-Reformation times, moreover, it is not improbable that the tomb of a benefactor or illustrious personage
may have usurped the burial-place of some humbler individual; since interments in their churches became a source
of emolument to the monastic orders.[2]   But the extent of
such transactions must have been trifling when compared
with the havoc wrought in the sixteenth century.   The

---

[1] Many of the monuments no longer in existence are described and
engraved in Montfaucon.   We have already referred (p. 7, *note* 3) to the
Collection of Drawings, made under the supervision of M. de Gaignières,
c. 1700, and now preserved in the Bodleian Library.

> "And in beldyng of toumbes
> Thei traveileth grete,
> To chargen her cherche flore
> And chaungen it ofte."   (Referring to the Friars.)

lines 997-1000, The Creed of Piers Ploughman.   See *The Vision and
Creed of Piers Ploughman*, edited by Thomas Wright, M.A., F.S.A.
London, 1856.   Vol. II. (2nd edition), p. 480.

suppression by Henry VIII., in 1536, of the lesser
monasteries, followed, in 1539, by that of their more
wealthy brethren, whatever political justification may support it, can only be regarded by the antiquary as an almost
incalculable calamity. With the destruction of the religious houses their monuments disappeared, except in
those cases in which the preservation of a portion of the
fabric was due to the grant of its use as a parish church.
For, the laton being a marketable metal, all orders of the
realm were not slow to follow the example of greed and
rapine, set by the king and his commissioners. The class
of brasses known as "*Palimpsest,*" of which we treat below,
was largely added to at this time, an old brass being
bought and then adapted or re-engraved to suit the taste
or purpose of the purchaser. Sometimes, not only the
brass, but the slab in which it was laid, was taken.
Gough,[1] quoting Blomfield, records that Robert, Earl of
Sussex, paved his hall, kitchen, and larder with the slabs
containing brasses taken from the chancel of Attleborough
Church, Norfolk, granted him by the king at the dissolution of the college. Gough also[2] cites a document, then
in the Augmentation Office, giving particulars of the sale
of monastic property, 1538-9 :—

"County of Warwick, Mirival, six gravestones with
brasses on them, 5s.

"County of Stafford, Darley, the tombs and gravestones with the metal on them, and roof of the church,
isles, etc., sold for £20."

In Nichols' *Leicestershire,*[3] is an extract from the
Churchwardens' Accounts of St. Martin's, Leicester, 1547,
quoted by Haines,[4] as follows :—" By the commandment
" of Mr. Mayor and his brethren, according to the King's

---

[1] *Sepulchral Monuments,* Vol. I., Part I., p. cxxii.

[2] The same, p. cxx.

[3] Vol. I., pp. 570-71.

[4] pp. cxlii.-iii., Introduction.

"Injunctions, in the year of our Lord 1546, and the first
"year of the reign of Edward the Sixth, . . . Four
"hundred and a quarter of brass was sold for 19s. per cwt.
"to one man; and three hundred weight and three
"quarters was sold to another at the same price, and one
"hundred to William Taylor."[1]

Throughout the short reign of Edward VI. many monuments must have fallen a prey to reforming zeal. At
Wigtoft, in Lincolnshire, in 1550, 8s. 4d. was given for
"xxiii stone of leten," and Gough relates[2] that when the
materials of St. Andrew's Church, Lincoln, were sold in
1551, the plate in the chapel with the plate of other stones
in the church was valued at 40s. The destruction of
monuments must have received some check from the
short counter-reformation of the next reign; but when
Elizabeth ascended the throne it seems to have been in
baneful progress, as we find from the account given by
Weever in his *Ancient Funeral Monuments*, 1631 ; so much
so that the queen issued a proclamation in 1560, to put an
end to this wanton practice;[3] but in spite of her efforts
we find, in 1579, Dean Whittingham of Durham appro-
priating to his use many of the slabs in that cathedral.
Indeed, so constantly must the war against valuable monuments have been waged that we find at Horshill, Surrey,
in 1603, inscriptions to John Fayth and Thomas Sutton,
ending, "Gentle reader, deface not this stone";[4] and
Haines cites[5] the will of Archbishop Harsnett, February
13th, 1630-1, which gave suitable directions for the proper
fastening of his brass in Chigwell Church, Essex.

In the period of the Civil War and Commonwealth
brasses fared badly. "The Journal of William Dowsing,

---

[1] The Churchwardens' Accounts of St. Thomas the Martyr, Salisbury,
reveal a similar transaction at the rate of 18s. the hundred.

[2] *Sepulchral Monuments*, Vol. I., Part I., p. cxxi.

[3] *See* Appendix.

[4] *See* "Horsell Church," by Thomas Milbourn, Architect, *Surrey
Archæological Collections*, Vol. VII., 1880, p. 152.

[5] Introduction, p. ccliii.

"of Stratford, Parliamentary Visitor appointed under a
"warrant from the Earl of Manchester for demolishing
"the superstitious Pictures and Ornaments of Churches,
"etc., within the County of Suffolk in the Years 1643 and
"1644," shows us what damage that pestilent fanatic
wrought in one county. His attention seems to have been
specially directed against inscriptions of the "ora pro nobis"
type, and the comely elevation of the altar above the level
of the body of the church seems to have been a great offence
in his eyes:—

"Alhallows, Sudbury, Jan. the 9th [1643]. We brake
"about twenty superstitious pictures and took up thirty
"brazen superstitious inscriptions, 'ora pro nobis' and
"'Pray for the soul,' etc.

At Orford, January 25th: "Eleven popish inscriptions
in brass."

At Wetherden, February 5th: "there was taken up
nineteen superstitious inscriptions that weighed sixty-five
pounds."

In all nearly two hundred brass inscriptions must have
been subjected to the rigour of his intolerance.[1]

Other instances could be multiplied. The Churchwardens of St. Margaret's, Westminster, in 1644, received
£1 13s. 6d. "for 29 pound of fine brass at 4d. a pound
and 96 pound of coarse brasse at 3d. a pound taken off
from sundrie tombe-stones in the Church." At Christchurch, in Hampshire, March 30th, 1657, the Churchwardens were ordered to "deliver unto Mrs. Hildesley
or her Assignes one Marble Stone, now lying in the East
end of the church being loose."

The cathedral churches suffered much during the

[1] *See* "A true copy of a Manuscript found in the library of Mr.
Samuel Dowsing of Stratford, being written by his Father, William
Dowsing's own hand, carefully and almost literally transcribed, Sept.
5th, 1704." Reprinted and published by Parker, Oxford, 1840, bound
in the same volume with "The Rich Man's Duty to contribute liberally
to the building, rebuilding, repairing, beautifying, and adorning of
churches. By Edward Wells, D.D." 1715.

seventeenth century. At Lincoln, where but one small brass, engraved with a coat of arms, remains, in 1718 we find Browne Willis counting 207 " gravestones that had been stript of their brasses; " though, fortunately, Gough adds,[1] " the better half of them preserved in Bishop Sanderson's MS. account of the monuments there, and printed in Peck's *Desiderata Curiosa.*" Durham has been thrice despoiled. First, under the authority of Dean Whittingham, 1563-79, who " defaced all such stones as had any picture of brass or other imagery work." Secondly, by the Scots in 1640. Thirdly, by the destruction of the Chapter House in 1799.[2]

In the eighteenth century, not infrequently, the clergy, when non-resident, left the care of the church fabric in the hands of ignorant local agents and churchwardens, whose contempt for anything inexplicable by them, must have greatly aided the disappearance of brasses by more or less dishonourable means. Gough writes[3]:—" In the " body of York Cathedral, of an hundred and thirteen " epitaphs, not twenty were left at the time of new paving, " 1734, and half of these were cut in stone, which plainly " proves that the poor lucre of the brass was the great " motive to the defacing these venerable remains of an- " tiquity. Of fifty-two epitaphs in the church, which " Mr. Drake gives, near thirty were entire and legible " before the above paving, being preserved by the doors " being kept shut." A like fate befel the brasses at Hereford at the hands of workmen engaged in repairing the west front. The following quotation[4] shows what happened at King's Lynn :—

---

[1] *Sepulchral Monuments*, Vol. I., Part I., p. cxx.

[2] See p. 339, *Transactions of the Monumental Brass Society*, Vol. II. ; pp. 338-42, *Durham Cathedral: An Account of the Lost Brasses*, by R. A. S. Macalister and H. Eardley Field.

[3] *Sepulchral Monuments*, Vol. I., Part I., p. cxx.

[4] See *Transactions of the Monumental Brass Society*, Vol. II., p. 57. "A list of Brasses existing in the Churches of St. Margaret and St. Nicholas, King's Lynn, in the year 1724," by E. M. Beloe, junr.

" 17th Iune, 1742 : resolved that eighteenpence be paid
to the contractors for every grave stone they have
taken up."

" 16th May, 1746, " it was ordered that the old Brass
and old Iron be immediately sold by the Churchwardens."

From the same place the fine Flemish brass of Robert
Attelath and Iohanna his wife (see p. 49) was taken,
some time before 1813, and sold to a brassfounder for five
shillings.

In the collection of impressions made by Craven Ord,
and now in the British Museum, is one of a knight (Sir
Miles Stapleton, c. 1400) from Ingham Church, Norfolk.[1]
Cotman says[2] :—" In 1800 the chancel at Ingham was
" completely swept of all its beautiful memorials of the
" Stapleton family. They were sold as old metal, and it
" was commonly reported by whom they were sold and
" bought ; but nobody sought to recover them : neither
" minister nor churchwarden cared for any of those things."
A similar fate overtook the brasses at Sheepy Magna,
Leicestershire, in 1778. It is not uncommon to find despoiled slabs used again, without compunction, as tomb-
stones, as at Christchurch, Hants. Probably, in course of
time many slabs will be discovered to have been turned
over, in some cases, even, retaining their brasses. Among
the uses to which brasses have been put may be mentioned
the following :—At Meopham, Kent,[3] they were added to
the metal of the bells when these were recast. At Luton,
Beds, they were melted down, to make a chandelier. At
Royston, Herts, an inscription was found employed as a
door-scraper.

The revival of interest in brasses, which has taken place

---

[1] Reproduced in *Transactions of Cambridge University Association of Brass
Collectors*, No. IX., March, 1891, illustrating " Note on a brass formerly
in Ingham Church, Norfolk," by E. M. Beloe, junr.

[2] *Engravings of the most remarkable of the sepulchral brasses in Norfolk*,
1819, p. v. (2nd edition, p. x.).

[3] *See* Gough's *Sepulchral Monuments*, Vol. I., Part I., p. cxx.

during the nineteenth century, has led in many parts of the country to the exercise of an intelligent care for the well-being of these monuments.   But, in spite of good work done, there are only too many instances to record of irreparable damage wrought by deliberate dishonesty, by ignorant carelessness, or by an injudicious and misdirected zeal.   Losses by theft have been far too frequent.[1]   In 1857 the important brasses at Oulton, Suffolk, were stolen.   In August, 1889, two of the Washington brasses were stolen from Sulgrave Church, Northants.[2]   At Wicken, Cambs., the effigy of John Peyton, *c.* 1520, was taken, the thief fortunately leaving the inscription.

The mania for restoration, consequent on the revival of Gothic architecture in the middle of the century, and the demolition of churches have contributed their share to the causes of the mutilation and disappearance of brasses. The Giffard brass suffered severely when the church of Bowers Giffard, Essex, was rebuilt in 1830.   The brasses in St. Mary Magdalene, Canterbury, were lost when that church was pulled down in 1871; those at Chipping Norton, Oxon, have been much disturbed and shamefully treated.[3]   At St. John's College, Cambridge, a brass from the old chapel is now fixed to the wall in the new building; the slab from which it was taken lying exposed to the weather in the court.   In several churches alterations have been made detrimental to the objects of

---

[1] When such occur the incumbent should make every effort in his power to recover the Church property, as becomes "a good steward." This, we fear, in some cases, has not been done.   We have seen it stated that brasses are sold for large sums in America, a fact that reflects nothing but dishonour on the parties to such sordid and questionable proceedings. This should set the clergy and their officials on their guard; the loss of a brass should be made an occasion for the exercise of archidiaconal functions.

[2] *See* the correspondence in the *Standard* newspaper, beginning in August and continuing throughout September, 1889.

[3] *See* the Rev. H. W. Macklin's List, in the *Transactions of the Cambridge University Association of Brass Collectors*, No. VII., February, 1900, p. 14.

our care, such as the removal of portions of monuments,
the concealing of brasses under organs, pews, or stoves,
and the unscholarly, and truly feminine desire for uniformity of pavement and for general, so-called, tidiness,
including frequently much ecclesiastical upholstery. We
may hope that these exhibitions of bad taste are not on
the increase. It would be unreasonable to demand the
same high level of intelligence from all the clergy; but
where such lapses occur, *quis custodiet custodes?*

We have, however, much cause to be thankful that
several discoveries have been made, leading to the restoration of brasses to their churches, or to the removal of the
obstructions that have concealed them. A notable example
is that of the brass of Bishop Bell, of Worcester (*d.* 1556),
in St. James's, Clerkenwell. On the destruction of the
old church in 1788, the brass was sold, coming into the
possession of Richard Gough, the antiquary, and later of
Mr. J. B. Nichols, till, in 1884, it was placed on the wall
of the present church at the expense of the late Mr. Stephen
Tucker, Somerset Herald. The discovery at Roding, in
Essex, of the Borrell brass, long lost from Broxbourne,
Herts, led to its return. At Aldermaston, Berks, three
brasses were found beneath the floor of the Forster chapel.
A fine military effigy, 1408, was discovered in 1894,
beneath pews in Otterden Church, Kent.

We must not leave unnoticed the practice that has
grown of late years, usually during the " restoration " of
a church, of taking a brass from its slab on the floor and
placing it against the wall. This seems to us justifiable
only in extreme cases, in which it is the sole means of
preserving brasses, and in that of "palimpsests" (*see* p. 41).
The slab and brass together form one monument, and
should not be separated. Together, and in their original
position and state,[1] they often form valuable historical

---

[1] As in the case of all specimens of architecture or of archæological
remains in general, " Let well alone " has not been a maxim of much
weight with the majority of restorers.

evidence. The Purbeck marble, frequently, is very beautiful, forming a fine setting and background for the metal plate; indeed, the position of the brass on the slab is the result of design. It is, therefore, well-nigh as unreasonable to remove a brass from its original slab, as it would be considered to cut out the background of a portrait, leaving only the figure intact. Moreover, the fixing of a brass on the wall often leads to the disappearance of the slab, and to the impossibility of finding the original site of the brass. But if removal to the wall has become indispensable, the whole monument should, with the utmost care to prevent damage, be taken up and fixed in the wall; for a brass, if fastened to the plaster, may be injured by corrosion from the lime. At Cheriton, Kent, a small slab has been placed in the floor to indicate the original site of a brass, removed to the wall.

But it seems to us that there are few churches in which the space, occupied by the brasses in their position on the floor, cannot, with a little consideration, be spared to them; to say nothing of a sentiment of reverence, producing a disinclination to disturb a tomb. Besides which we know that mural brasses were not in general use before the sixteenth century, and should be careful not to be guilty of a kind of anachronism in dealing with those of an earlier date. The preservation of the brass with its slab can easily be secured, and at much less expense than by its removal to the wall—by placing a rope-rail round it, or even by covering it with a piece of matting or carpet; though, in the case of the adoption of the latter expedient, the dust that accumulates beneath the covering should be frequently and regularly removed.

If placed on the wall, a brass should be fixed at no great distance from the ground. When fastened at a height like that of the Beauchamp brass at Warwick, or, in a less degree, like the brass at Aldborough, near Boroughbridge, Yorkshire, great difficulty is experienced in examining it at all thoroughly, and, as a memorial, its value is obviously decreased.

Before passing to the consideration of "Palimpsests," we may mention that several restorations have been carried out with much care and ability during the nineteenth century by the Messrs. Waller and others. A good example is furnished by Winchester College Chapel, where the brasses, the originals of which disappeared in 1877, faithfully reproduced from rubbings, were laid down in 1882, at the expense and under the supervision of Dr. Freshfield.

The term "*Palimpsest*,"[1] first employed for this purpose by the late Mr. Albert Way, has become so generally used of a brass appropriated for other than the person originally commemorated, that it might appear pedantic to discard it. At the same time, strictly speaking, its use is only justifiable in the case of very few and exceptional monuments. Terms such as "*retroscript*," "*rescript*," "*reversed*," "*adapted*," seem better suited accurately to describe the condition of the brass; but for our present purpose we will retain the word "Palimpsest," contenting ourselves with pointing out where the term is applied more or less loosely.

PALIMPSEST BRASSES

Three classes of Palimpsest may be said to exist :—[2]

Three classes of palimpsest

1. In which the brass plate, turned over, is re-engraved and again laid down.

---

[1] "παλίμψηστος (ψάω) scratched or scraped again; usually of parchment from which one writing has been erased to make room for another." —LIDDELL AND SCOTT.

[2] The best authority on this subject is, "A List of Palimpsest Brasses, compiled by Mill Stephenson, F.S.A.," in Vol. IV. of the *Transactions of the Monumental Brass Society*. Mr. Stephenson divides palimpsests "into "two main classes. A. Appropriated and converted brasses. B. Brasses "which bear on their reverse side engravings of figures, inscriptions, etc., "either of English or foreign workmanship. This class may be sub-"divided into three heads : (1) Wasters from the workshop. (2) Spoil "from the destruction of the monastic houses and chantries in our own "country. (3) Imported plate and spoil from the destruction of the "religious houses in the Low Countries." P. 326, Vol. IV., *Transactions of Monumental Brass Society* (Part 8, October, 1903).

2. In which the original engraving is altered, without reversing the plate.

3. In which the original effigy is appropriated either entirely or in part, a new inscription replacing the true one.

Cases are known in which two or even three of these classes are represented in one monument.

(1) Of the first class many examples are known, and probably many more will be discovered as from time to time brasses become unfixed from their slabs. Sometimes we find the whole original memorial reversed, as in the case of that of Amphillis Peckham, 1545, at Denham, Bucks, in which a fifteenth-century effigy, representing John Pyke, probably a schoolmaster, an inscription to his memory, and a shield have, all three, been reversed to form a memorial for that lady.[1] In other cases part only of the original is used, or the whole of the original forms a part of a later memorial, as at Denchworth, Berks, where the reverse of the inscription below the effigies of William Hyde, 1557, and wife, records the laying of the foundation-stone of Bisham Priory by Edward III. (*see* p. 21); or the figure is mutilated to suit the outline of the usurping effigy, as at Fryerning, Essex, *c.* 1560; or the later brass is made up of pieces of others, frequently of Flemish design,[2] in which case it is often difficult to decide whether the fragments are parts of memorials, once in proper position, or merely the waste from the engraver's workshop. A good example of a brass composed from pieces of others, probably brought from Bury St. Edmund's Abbey, is that of Margaret Bulstrode, 1540, at Hedgerley, Bucks. Another is to be seen at St. Lawrence's, Reading, composed of portions of that of Sir John Popham, 1463.

(2) Examples of the second class are rare, in spite of the fact that it is the only one which can be said to afford

---

[1] Illustrated in the *Proceedings of the Society of Antiquaries,* 2nd Series, Vol. XV.

[2] For Flemish palimpsest fragments, *see* below, p. 44.

a sufficient analogy to the palimpsest manuscript, to make
the use of the term a scholarly one.   The best instance is
that at Waterpery, Oxon (Walter Curzon, Esq., and wife,
1527), in which the details of the armour have been altered
to suit the fashion of a period nearly a hundred years later
than that of the original brass.[1]   Another interesting
specimen, now practically destroyed, was that at Okeover,
Staffs, to Humphrey Oker, Esq. (1538), his wife and
children; curious, moreover, as belonging to all three
classes.   The brass appears to have been that of William,
Lord Zouch, and his two wives (c. 1447), beneath a triple
canopy.   The central figure was altered by the addition of
a tabard over the plate armour; the figure of one Lady
Zouch left untouched (class 3) to represent Oker's wife;
that of the other reversed and engraved with figures of
the children and arms of the appropriator; whilst other
shields were inserted in the canopy.[2]   At Chalfont St.
Peter, Bucks, is the effigy of a priest, c. 1440.   This has
been altered by shading and by rounding the pointed toes,
and furnished with a fresh inscription attributing the
memorial to Robert Hanson, vicar of that place and of
Little Missenden, who died 1545.

(3) The third class, in which the original brass is adapted
with as little expense as credit to the requirements of a
later monument, by merely adding a new inscription in

---

[1] *See* Haines' Introduction, p. xlviii.   "In the male figure a new head
"and shoulders have been substituted for the original; a skirt of plate
"armour has been altered into mail, the plates in front of the armpits have
"been partially erased, additional defences placed over the breastplate,
"gussets of mail added at the insteps, the pointed toes rounded, and the
"various edges of the armour invecked and shaded: in the lady's figure
"the upper half is a fresh plate, or the old one reversed; the lower half
"shows the engraving of the original brass, altered by the addition of
"shading and an ornament suspended by a chain."

[2] *See* illustrations in the *Portfolio of the Oxford University Brass-Rubbing
Society*, Part I., February, 1898, and in the *Portfolio of the Monumental Brass
Society*, Vol. I.

place of the old, is represented by several examples. At
Bromham, Beds, the brass, attributed to Thomas Widville,
1435, and his two wives, was, by the substitution of a
different inscription, used to commemorate Sir John Dyve,
1535, with his mother and wife. Among other instances
we may mention the Dalison brass at Laughton, Lincs
(*c.* 1400 and 1549), and the Wybarne brass at Ticehurst,
Sussex (*c.* 1370 and 1510). A curious case of adaptation
occurs at Hampsthwaite, near Ripley, W. Yorks, where
the small brass of a civilian of the fourteeth century has
been converted to the use of another some two hundred
years later, by the simple expedient of cutting an inscrip-
tion across the figure, " Prayse god for ye | soule of Ad
dyxon | Uncle to | vycar | dyxon | Aug 18 | 1570."

The chief cause of the existence of these so-called
Palimpsest brasses was, undoubtedly, the spoliation consequent on the suppression of the monasteries. This is
sufficiently proved by the fact that the greater part of the
obverse figures or inscriptions belong to the sixteenth
century, and that they disclose when reversed older engravings, which may be taken for genuine memorials torn
from their original positions. " Palimpsests " previous in
date to the Dissolution are uncommon, and, when they
occur, must be attributed either to dishonesty or to errors
in workmanship, the latter explanation probably being
correct, when the two engravings are of about the same
date. An example may be seen at St. Albans, where part
of the figure of an abbot, attributed to John de la Moote,
c. 1400, shows, when reversed, the lower half of a female
figure with a dog at the feet. At the Temple Church,
Bristol, is the figure of a priest vested in cassock, surplice,
and cope, *c.* 1460, the reverse of which reveals the figure
of a widow of similar date. In St. Margaret's, Rochester,
the half-length figure of Thomas Cod, Vicar, 1465, vested
in cassock, surplice, *amice*, and cope, when reversed shows
a figure similarly vested, with the exception that an *almuce*
takes the place of the *amice*. This alteration probably was

effected soon after his death, if not before that event.
But the most remarkable example of alteration is that at
Burwell, Cambridgeshire, in the brass, commemorating in
all probability, John Laurence de Wardeboys, last Abbot of
Ramsey, Hunts (1508–1539, died 1542),   He was originally represented, probably during his lifetime and under
his own supervision, in full vestments befitting his rank,
the lower part of the figure revealing these when reversed.
But owing, very possibly, to prudential reasons, either by
his directions or those of his executors, the figure was
altered to that of a canon in cassock, surplice, and almuce,
the upper part of the figure being engraved on a new
plate, since the old piece must have been unsuitable for
turning owing to the mitre and other differences of
costume affecting the outline.   A fine triple canopy
originally completed the design, but of this only the
central pediment remains, on the reverse of which portions of an early engraving (c. 1320?) are found, apparently representing a deacon, vested in amice, dalmatic
and maniple.

Occasionally a brass may be suspected of being palimpsest, if it is a thick piece of metal, whilst its date is later
than the first quarter of the sixteenth century, since the
later sheets of brass used were thin and very inferior in
quality to those of a former period.   When found to be
palimpsest a brass should not be fixed either on its slab
or on the wall, so as to prevent the reverse from being
seen, but should be fastened by means of screws, or placed
in a hinged frame, in order to make it accessible for in-
spection.   This may appear a violation of what we have
already laid down as to the undesirability of unfastening
brasses from their slabs; but in the case of palimpsests
it seems but a tardy act of justice to the person originally
commemorated.   Indeed, could we be sure that they
would receive skilful and harmless treatment in the
process, we should hail a systematic examination of
the reverse of every brass and slab in the kingdom.   For
thereby much valuable information would be gained, and

any doubts as to the palimpsest nature of a brass finally set at rest.[1]

FLEMISH
BRASSES

To estimate with any degree of accuracy all the influences which continental art may have exercised over English brass engraving would be no easy task. But we are fortunate in possessing in England some specimens of a style which is as superior to as it is different from the ordinary work of the English school. This style, from the position of similar work in Europe, is known as that of the Flemish school—and, as from its marked characteristics it is easily recognized, we are able to attribute to it, with certainty, a few brasses now existing in this country. Belonging to the fourteenth century, and, in England, speaking broadly, attributable to the reign of Edward III., they illustrate in a signal way, and form a most appropriate accompaniment to the most beautiful, as, indeed, the most ornate, period of Gothic architecture, constituting a series of designs of remarkable richness, ere the fifteenth century ushered in the Perpendicular style.   In enumerating these Flemish brasses it is more than ever necessary to bear in mind that the date given on the brass, though doubtless a trustworthy genealogical statement, is at the same time but an approximate date to which the engraving of the work may be attributed.   The style of treatment is the surest guide.   For the practice, instances of which occur in all ages, of the person commemorated personally superintending the execution of his memorial, is sufficient indication that in many cases the date on the brass itself cannot be identified with that of its engraving.

List of
those in
England,
XIV.
Century

The examples of this school in this country are as follows [2] :—

---

[1] Mr. Mill Stephenson's *List of Palimpsest Brasses*, already referred to, gives a detailed account of all brasses of this nature known to exist in England, up to the date of publication.

[2] The brass of Robert Attelath, and wife, 1376, stolen from King's Lynn at the beginning of the nineteenth century, was a good example of this class.   It is possible that the fine brass at Higham Ferrers, Northants (Laurence de St. Maur, 1337), is of foreign work.   Bishop Beaumont's brass at Durham, of which the matrix survives, was similar in style.

SIMON DE WENSLAGH,
c. 1360,
WENSLEY, YORKSHIRE.

Fourteenth century :—

Sir Hugh Hastings, Elsing, Norfolk -	1347
Adam de Walsokne, and wife, St. Margaret's, King's Lynn - - - - -	1349
Robert Braunche, and two wives, in the same church - - - - -	1364
Alan Fleming, Newark, Notts - - -	1361
Abbot Thomas Delamere, St. Albans' Abbey, dated 1396, but probably engraved - - - - - -	c. 1360
Priest in mass vestments, called Sir Simon de Wenslagh, Wensley, Yorkshire -	c. 1360
Priest in mass vestments, Thomas de Horton, North Mimms, Herts - -	c. 1360
Ralph de Knevynton, Aveley, Essex -	1370
Thomas de Topcliff, and wife, Topcliffe, near Thirsk, Yorkshire - - -	1391
A fragment of a large brass, representing an abbot, formerly in the possession of the late Mr. Pugin, but now in the British Museum ; which Boutell supposed might be that of Michael de Mentmore, Abbot of St. Albans,[1] who died 1342 - - - - -	c. 1350

Here it will not be out of place to mention some brasses of the same school on the Continent, to which reference will be made below [2] :— Some fine Continental examples

---

[1] But *see* "The Brasses and Indents in St. Albans' Abbey," by William Page, F.S.A., p. 12 (reprinted from the *Home Counties Magazine*, Vol. I., 1899). "But Mr. Mill Stephenson has ascertained that Mr. Pugin "obtained his brass from abroad, it is therefore improbable that it could "have come from St Albans' Abbey."

[2] Reproductions of these brasses are in Creeny's book of *Facsimiles of Monumental Brasses on the Continent of Europe*, 1884, folio. The brass of St. Henry of Finland (Bishop of Upsala, *d. c.* 1158), representing him in pontificals, at Nousis in South Finland, is a fine example of Flemish work of the next (fifteenth century). It will be found illustrated in *Proceedings of the Cambridge Antiquarian Society*, Vol. X., p. 215 (No. iii., 1903),

King Eric Menved and Queen Ingeborg
of Denmark, at Ringstead, in Zea-
land - - - - - -   1319
Bishops Ludolph and Henry de Bulowe,
at Schwerin, in Mecklinburg   - 1339, 1347
Bishops Godfrey and Frederic de Bulowe,
at Schwerin - - - - 1314, 1375
Burchard de Serken and Iohn de Mul, at
Lübeck - - - - - 1317, 1350
Albert Hövener, in the Church of St.
Nicholas, Stralsund - - -   1357
Johan von Zoest and wife, at Thorn, in
Prussian Poland- - - -   1361
John de Heere, and Gerard de Heere, at
Brussels - - - - - 1332, 1398

Flemish
palimpsests

These seven brasses may well be considered the finest
in existence, and form the best examples of the Flemish
school. It is to be noticed that they all belong to the
fourteenth century, the period which gave us the finest
Gothic architecture and for its appropriate concomitant
the finest brass-engraving.

Several palimpsest brasses are known, the reverse sides
of which show portions of Flemish work. Waller finds
a cause for this in " those events in Flanders, following
" the establishment of the league of the Gueux in 1566,
" when so large a number of churches in Brabant and
" Hainault were completely ravaged." [1] For it is remarkable that the greater part of these remains occurs on the
reverse of brasses of the latter part of the sixteenth century. It is probable, moreover, that in addition to pieces
sacrilegiously torn from tombs, many spoiled plates were
imported into this country from the Continent. Such

"The Sepulchral Brass of St. Henry of Finland," by Dr. M. R. James,
and also in the Portfolio of the *Monumental Brass Society*, Vol. II., plates
35-8. Dr. James' paper is reprinted in the *Transactions* of the latter
society, Vol. IV., p. 336.

[1] *A Series of Monumental Brasses*, Introduction, p. ix.

may be the case at Topcliffe, where the reverse of the
Flemish brass (1391), when removed from its slab, was
found to be engraved. An early example of a Flemish
palimpsest occurs at Great Bowden, Leicestershire. On
the reverse of an inscription to William Wolstonton, 1403,
rector, is an engraving of a civilian, c. 1350. Waller
mentions [1] that a fragment found in Leicestershire proved
to be a piece of a fine brass at Stralsund. Of fourteenth
century Flemish work palimpsests exist at, amongst other
places [2]:—Ewelme, Oxon. (1494); Tolleshunt Darcy,
Essex, c. 1375, where the obverse and reverse are portions
of ornate Flemish borders, similar in treatment to the
palimpsest at Margate (1582); Sall, Norfolk (c. 1480);
Winestead, E. Yorks (c. 1540); Pottesgrove, Beds (1563);
Cookham, Berks (1577); Wardour Castle, Wilts, on the
reverse of memorials of the Arundell family (1573 to
1586), removed from Mawgan, in Cornwall; Constantine,
Cornwall (1574); Isleworth (1544); Harrow (1574); and
Pinner (1580), Middlesex. Of the fifteenth century at
Hadleigh, Suffolk (1555); Yealmpton, Devon (1580);
Aveley (1584); Stondon Massey (1573), Essex; Camber-
well, Surrey (1582); Walkern, Herts (1583). Of the
sixteenth century at Aylesford, Kent (1545); St. Peter
Mancroft, Norwich (1568); St. Peter-in-the-East, Oxford
(1574); Paston, Norfolk (1596).

The presence on some of these brasses of fragments of
inscriptions; as at Harrow and Margate, " Int + Jaer +
ons + heren " (in the year of our Lord); at Constantine
" bidt . voer . die . ciel " (pray for the soul); [3] and at
Pinner " Hier + Licht " proves that they were never in-

---

[1] The same, p. xii.

[2] These fragments present similar characteristics to the brasses described
below. They are dealt with in Mr. Mill Stephenson's List, referred to
above. The dates, given in the text, are those of the obverse sides
of the brasses.

[3] For similar inscription existing at Topcliffe, *see* Waller's *Series of
Monumental Brasses*, p. ix.

tended for English memorials, nor laid down as such in this country, but merely imported to be re-engraved.

Delamere brass described Among the illustrations will be found one of the brass of Abbot Delamere in St. Albans' Abbey, considered by many the finest brass in England. The following description will furnish most of the characteristics which distinguish this class from the ordinary brass memorials in this country. Originally on a large marble slab in the choir, easily distinguished by its quadrilateral matrix, this brass now lies on a wooden frame, placed on the slab in the chantrey of Abbot John of Wheathamstead on the south side of the altar, in which chapel are other brasses taken from different parts of the church. Engraved during his lifetime (he died 1396), and probably under his personal supervision, we have no adequate reason for doubting that this is a thoroughly satisfactory representation of the abbot, clad in his pontificals, about the year 1360. It is well to mention the peculiarities common to this and other works of the same school. The monument is composed of several square pieces of brass, not shaped to the figure or making use of the slab for background in the ordinary English way, but joined together to make one large rectangular plate, in this instance 9 ft. 3 in. by 4 ft. 4 in. in size. Over this plate is spread diaper work which acts as a background to the whole, and from which the figure and architectural details stand out, as though in relief. This diaper work, which is practically the same as that in the Fleming brass at Newark, is very similar to that on the Continental brasses, enumerated above, and to the apparel of the alb and other embroidery on the Wensley brass. In the centre of the plate is the figure of the abbot, clad in amice, alb, stole, maniple, tunicle, dalmatic, and chasuble.[1] On his head is the *mitra pretiosa*; on his hands, which lie crossed downwards, the right hand over the left, are jewelled gloves; on his feet, resting on two fighting winged dragons, embroidered sandals. On his left arm

---

[1] For descriptions of these vestments, *see* pp. 65 *et seq.*

ABBOT THOMAS DELAMERE, *c.* 1360,
St. Alban's Abbey, Herts.

rests his pastoral staff in the crook of which is a representation of *Agnus dei*. The embroideries on the vestments are very fine. Dragons occur on the apparels of amice and alb; leopards' heads alternate with quatrefoils on the maniple; on the orphreys of the chasuble, and on the mitre, as on the vestments of Bishop Burchard de Serken at Lübeck, occur medallions of heads. The method of treating the mouth should be noticed, as it seems similarly treated in the other brasses of this style. The effigy is enclosed in a rich canopy of tabernacle work, in the compartments of which are figures and geometrical tracery, as in an elaborate shrine, outside which on three sides we see the diapered background continued between the architectural ornament and the marginal inscription. In the centre over the abbot's head sits Christ enthroned, two angels standing on each side, two of whom swing censers. In the top compartments of the side shafts sit St. Peter (dexter) and St. Paul (sinister). Beneath St. Peter is a larger figure of St. Alban with cross and sword; facing whom, under St. Paul, occurs St. Oswyn, King of Northumbria, with crown and spear. Beneath these on each side are three double compartments, in which the background behind the canopies in the upper part, is made to appear " masoned." The inner ones contain, apparently, six apostles with bare feet, nimbus, and implement of martyrdom; the outer ones six prophets or Old Testament saints, shod, wearing caps, and with labels. This difference of attire Creeny notes as prevalent in Western art since the schism between the Eastern and Western Churches. Between what we may well call the shrine and the inscription the diapered background is visible. The inscription, which was never completed, runs as follows, in Lombardic capitals :—

HIC + JACET + DOMINVS + THOMAS + QVONDAM + ABBAS
+ HVIVS + MONESTERII,

and is preceded by a saltire, evidently referring to the arms of the Abbey, azure, a saltire, or. At the corners were the evangelistic symbols within quatrefoils, one of which has disappeared. In the centre of each of two sides, within a quatrefoil, is a shield bearing on a bend three eagles displayed. Outside the inscription runs a marginal border of quatrefoil flowers.

Effigy of
Abbot,
British
Museum

Very similar in treatment, and indeed more ornate, is the fragment of an abbot's brass, now preserved in the British Museum. Boutell's conjecture that it might be the effigy of Michael de Mentmore, Abbot of St. Albans [1] (died 1342), is probably disproved by the fact that Pugin obtained it from the Continent. Here the curious treatment of the soul, a characteristic of the Flemish school, is noteworthy. Held in a sheet by the Deity, it appears as a diminutive nude figure, in this case wearing a mitre.[2] A similar convention is to be seen in the Topcliffe brass; whilst in the Walsokne one at King's Lynn the soul is upheld in a sheet by two angels.

The Lynn
Brasses

The Lynn brasses are, perhaps, our best examples of the Flemish school, bearing, as they do, so striking a resemblance in treatment to the Continental examples mentioned above. Each consists of a large rectangular sheet, composed of smaller pieces, on which is the diapered background, and beautiful architectural work, in the manner described above in the account of the Delamere brass. In the Walsokne brass we have a husband and wife; in the Braunche a husband between two wives. The costumes of Adam de Walsokne, Robert Braunche, and Alan

---

[1] *See* Gough's *Sepulchral Monuments*, Vol. I., p. 96, quoting inscription, extant in Weever's time.

[2] *See* Viollet le Duc's *Dictionnaire Raisonné de l'Architecture Française*, Paris, 1868, Vol. IX., p. 53, for illustration (*sub nom.* Tombeau) of a similar mitred soul painted at the head of the tomb of Archbishop Pierre de la Jugée, in Narbonne Cathedral. In the Exhibition of Pictures of the School of Siena, held at the Burlington Fine Arts Club, 1904, was shown a panel, belong to the Earl of Crawford and Balcarres, representing Scenes from the lives of the Hermits of the Thebaid and the Founders of the Religious Orders, "possibly by some Pisan follower of Pietro Lorenzetti," in which is depicted, *inter alia*, "a bishop's soul held by two devils in a boat." The little nude figure wears a mitre.

THOMAS DE HORTON, *c.* 1360,
NORTH MIMMS, HERTS.

Fleming are very similar; the Newark figure, however, has slits for pockets in the *cote-hardie*.[1]

It is fortunate that in the Douce collection at the British Museum, an impression is preserved of the brass of Robert Attelath. This fine brass was stolen early in the nineteenth century, owing to local unscrupulousness or ignorance.[2] It must have much resembled the other Lynn brasses and that at Newark. The costume is almost identical with that of Johannes von Zoest at Thorn. A long tunic, or *cote-hardie*, is fastened with many buttons in pairs. Attached by four buttons on the right shoulder (in the Zoest brass there are six) hangs a loose mantle or cloak with a small hood. The under-tunic is visible at the wrists, whence the sleeves are continued over the hand, and are fastened by a row of small buttons. They are finely embroidered as at Thorn. The dress is completed by a narrow waistbelt and long pointed shoes, with buckles. The inscription, given by Gough, runs as follows:—" Hic " jacet Robertus Attelath, q'dam burgensis Lenne, qui obiit " A° Dni MCCCLXXVI, xii die mensis Novembris. " Orate pro eo. Hic jacet Johanna, q'dam uxor Roberti " Attelatte, que obiit A° Dni MCCC...... Anime eorum " per misericordiam Dei requiescant in pace. Amen."

The brasses, one at North Mimms, and one at Wensley, as also that of Sir Hugh Hastings at Elsing, differ from those mentioned above in that they are not rectangular, and that the diapered background is omitted; but their style is unmistakeably Flemish. *Those at North Mimms, Wensley, and Elsing*

In the North Mimms brass, Thomas de Horton, vicar, is represented clad in mass vestments, with a chalice and paten lying on his body below his clasped hands.[3] The feet rest on a stag, below which a kind of bracket is

---

[1] The costume on these brasses will be found described in Chap. IV.

[2] *See* above, p. 33. It is figured in Gough's *Sepulchral Monuments*, Vol. I., Plate xxxvi., and described Vol. I., p. 138. It was engraved by J. S. Cotman in his *Norfolk Brasses*, 1819.

[3] At Wensley the chalice lies above the hands, which are crossed as in the St. Alban's brass.

supported by two lions addorsed, between which is a shield, a saltire between four crosses-crosslet fitché. On this bracket rest the bases of the shafts of the beautiful canopy of tabernacle work, with saints in niches, and the Deity holding the soul whilst two angels swing their thuribles. The mutilated Elsing brass possessed a less ornate canopy, though of great interest from the historical personages represented in the niches; but it probably gained in enamelling what it lacked in architectural detail. The Wensley brass is composed of at least three pieces, forming the figure of a priest, similar to that at North Mimms; but the embroidered work is finer. The head reclines on a cushion upheld by graceful angels, treated very similarly to the Albert Hövener brass at Stralsund. The slab is used as background for the brass, and originally there was a marginal inscription with evangelistic symbols in quatrefoils at the corners.

Characteristics of Flemish brasses

Before leaving the fourteenth century, it were well to mention some of the characteristics which distinguish this Flemish school of brass-engraving. We have already noticed the rectangular shape of the plates, as in the seven Continental instances given, and in the St. Albans', Lynn, Newark, Aveley, and Topcliffe examples, and the exceptions to this shape at Wensley, North Mimms, and Elsing. The diapered groundwork, too, has been noted, of varied pattern, a favourite one being dragons and foliage in trefoils. In the Walsokne diaper, butterflies and other curious figures are introduced. The place of diaper in the Wensley and North Mimms brasses is supplied by the stone slabs which act as background. The architectural details are strikingly similar in the various examples of the Flemish school, taking the form of ornately tabernacled canopies of geometrical Gothic with side and centre shafts, the niches filled with figures of apostles and prophets as at St. Albans, of civilians as in the Braunche and Fleming brasses, of members of noble families as in the Hastings brass, of angels playing musical instruments as at Topcliffe, or of mournful figures called "weepers." The canopies are single or double according to the number

of effigies to be represented.   In the Braunche brass we
have an instance of a triple-arched canopy.   An attempt
to give in perspective the vaulting of these arches is
sometimes observed, as in the Braunche brass, and in the
foreign brasses of Zoest and Heere.   Sometimes the centre
shaft of the canopy is made to pierce the marginal inscription, as on the Thornton brass, at Newcastle-on-Tyne (to
be mentioned below).   The central compartment of the
canopy above the effigy is usually treated in a manner that
we may call peculiar to Flemish brasses.   A venerable
figure, seated on a throne, evidently intended for the
Deity, holds in a sheet a little nude male or female figure,
representing the soul of the deceased.   In the fragment in
the British Museum the little figure wears a mitre.   On
either side we find angels with thuribles, as at St. Albans,
Topcliffe, and King's Lynn, or bearing candles as in the
palimpsest fragment at Wardour Castle.   In the Hastings
brass at Elsing a somewhat different treatment was adopted,
the soul being held in a sheet by two angels beneath the
canopy, immediately above the knight's head, whilst above
it on brackets are figures of the Deity and the Virgin, an
angel above censing them.

   In the faces of the principal figures the conventional
treatment of the mouth is noticeable.   Another feature,
frequently observed, is the cushion of elaborate embroidery
placed under the head of the deceased.   Those in the
Hövener, Zoest, and Heere brasses bear a striking resemblance to those at Wensley, Newark, and King's Lynn.
These cushions are usually supported on each side, as in
the above instances, by angels, sometimes of most graceful
design, as at Wensley and Stralsund.   At Topcliffe one
angel holds the cushion from above.   The brass of
Archdeacon William de Rothewelle, 1361, in Rothwell
Church, Northants, shows many signs of Flemish influence,
including this one of a cushion upheld by angels.[1]

---

[1] In the brass at Hever, Kent, the head of Margaret, wife of William
Cheyne, rests on two embroidered cushions, upheld by two angels, clad in
amice and alb.   This convention is frequently found in sculptured effigies.

Beneath the feet a favourite design seems to have been that of two animals addorsed, as at Wensley, North Mimms, and in the lost Attelath brass. Another form displays monsters fighting; winged dragons, as at St. Albans; a lion or eagle attacking a savage man, as at King's Lynn, Newark, and Thorn in Prussian Poland.

Between the feet of the figure and the marginal inscription an historical or legendary scene is sometimes shown. The famous instance of the former is what is known as the "Peacock Feast" on the Braunche brass at King's Lynn, representing a banquet, at which peacocks are being served, supposed to depict the entertainment of King Edward III.[1] The same place in the Walsokne brass is occupied by rustic scenes and fables, in which a windmill figures. In the foreign brasses mentioned above we find wild men or "wodehouses" feasting, in the Zoest, and Godfrey and Frederic de Bulowe brasses; scenes from the life of St. Nicholas below the effigy of Bishop Burchard de Serken, and from that of St. Eligius below that of Johan de Mul at Lübeck; a stag-hunt in the Hövener brass, and a woodland scene beneath the lady's feet in the Zoest brass.

The inscription, which is sometimes in Lombardic characters, as at St. Albans, sometimes in black letter, as at Topcliffe, acts as a border to the whole work, supplemented on the outside by a row of conventional flowers, as in the Walsokne, Braunche, and Topcliff brasses, or by a border of foliage, as at Newark. The corners of these inscription-borders usually bear the Evangelistic symbols

---

[1] An excellent description of this part of the brass is in the *Surrey Archæological Collections*, Vol. IV., 1869, pp. 285-6, in "Remarks on Timber Houses," by Charles Baily, Architect.

In *The Arts in the Middle Ages and the Renaissance*, by Paul Lacroix (English edition, revised by W. Armstrong. London, Virtue, 1886), this representation is reproduced (p. 11, fig. 8), where it is described as "A "State Banquet in the Fifteenth Century, with the service of dishes "brought in and handed round to the sound of musical instruments "(Miniature from a MS. in the Bibliothèque Nationale in Paris)."

in quatrefoils. Frequently we find the centre of each of the two sides ornamented with a quatrefoil containing, as in the Delamere, Braunche, and Topcliff brasses, a coat of arms, or as at Newark, a merchant's mark.

In the Introduction to Cotman's work,[1] the presence of Flemish brass work at King's Lynn is, doubtless correctly, attributed to the intercourse with Flanders occasioned by the wool trade. The fact of the whole plate being composed of separate pieces is explained as due to the greater facility of transport thereby obtained, and the great prevalence of brasses in the county of Norfolk as owing, in great measure, to these Flemish examples.

It may, perhaps, be doubted whether the North Mimms and Wensley brasses were originally intended for the places which they occupy, since they seem somewhat too ornate for memorials of parish priests, but we know so little of Thomas de Horton or of Simon de Wenslagh that we are not justified in belittling their importance during their lives. We should rather be grateful for the fine quality of their monuments.

Of the general characteristics of this school of brass engraving, Haines wrote [2]: "The foreign brasses are dis-"tinguished from the English by a peculiarity of engraving. "The principal lines are broader and more boldly drawn, "though less deeply cut, and wrought with a flat chisel-"shaped tool, instead of the ordinary engraving burin. "'Stippling' or dotted shading is found on early examples [3] "in the folds of the drapery, bases of canopies, etc." Except in the case of the Hastings brass we can only conjecture to what extent these brasses were enamelled or coloured in any way. But colour adds so greatly to the richness of these memorials that it is reasonable to suppose that the lines of the figure, coats of arms, etc., in several

---

[1] Engravings of the most remarkable of *The Sepulchral Brasses in Norfolk.* 1819, p. v.

[2] Introduction, pp. xx-i.

[3] At Wensley, for instance.

instances, were filled in with enamel or some substitute for it, and the surface burnished and polished, to produce a splendid effect.

XV. and XVI.
Century
Flemish
brasses

The following are some brasses, later in date, of Flemish workmanship, but inferior to those mentioned above [1] :—

Roger Thornton and Agnes his wife, 1429, at Newcastle, excepting palimpsests, the only example of Flemish work of the fifteenth century in this country. Two figures in civilian costume, their heads on cushions supported by angels, are placed beneath fine canopies, containing in niches figures of saints. Fourteen children are represented below the parents under small canopies. There is a marginal black-letter inscription, bearing at the corners evangelistic symbols and in the centre of each side a coat of arms.[2]

Thomas Pownder and wife, 1525, St. Mary Quay, Ipswich,

---

[1] The following contract for brasses of Flemish workmanship, to commemorate Sir William Sandys, Knt., and Margaret, his wife, and William Lord Sandys, formerly in the Chapel of the Holy Trinity, annexed to Holy Ghost Chapel, Basingstoke, Hants, is taken from *A History of the Ancient Town and Manor of Basingstoke*, etc., by Francis Joseph Baigent and James Elwin Millard, 1889, pp. 158-9. "A contract for "two tombs between Thomas Leigh, merchant, and Cornelius Herman-"zone, acting on behalf of Lord William Sandes, with Arnold Hermanzone, "native of Amsterdam, established at Aire in Artoise, was proved before "a notary at Antwerp on Monday the 1st March, 1536. One tomb "was to be of Antoing stone, eight Flemish feet long, by four and a half "broad, and four feet and a quarter high; the slab to be inlaid with a "copper or brass cross, of similar length, and the name of William Sans "and Margare Sans, and dates also in brass three inches wide. On each "side of the tomb were to be three coats of arms. The other tomb was "to measure seven feet by four, but only the slab and sides were to be of "Antoing stone, as the ends would join a wall; the cross to be four feet "long and four inches broad, and the inscription three inches. The tombs "to be delivered at Antwerp, in all respects conformable to the design "given, within seven months, and thence to be shipped to England; the "said Arnold to go over and set them up and finish them off properly. "He was to receive £30, Flemish currency, and also the expenses of his "maintenance during his journey and stay at Basingstoke."

[2] *See* illustration in *Archæologia Aeliana*, New Series, Vol. XV.

ANDREW EVYNGAR AND WIFE ELLYN, 1535,
ALL HALLOWS' BARKING, LONDON.

having merchants' marks and the arms of Ipswich and of the Merchant Adventurers. The inscription is in black-letter.

Margaret Svanders, 1529, Fulham, Middlesex, wife of Gerard Hornebolt, showing half-effigy in shroud, two angels holding the inscription. On a lozenge-shaped plate fixed to the wall.

Andrew Evyngar, and Ellyn, his wife, 1536, All Hallows, Barking, London. The Ipswich brass is very similar. A merchant's mark appears at the base. At the top on the dexter side are the arms of the Merchant Adventurers, on the sinister those of the Salters' Company. The classical treatment of this brass well exemplifies the change in style forming a great contrast to the splendid geometrical Gothic of the fourteenth century brasses.

Boutell [1] classes the brass at East Sutton, Kent, 1638, of Sir Edward Filmer, his wife and eighteen children as Flemish, being on one large plate of metal, but without diaper work. But this alone is no proof of Flemish origin. Waller attributes it to foreign manufacture, as also that of Archbishop Harsnett, 1631, Chigwell, Essex, to which he compares it. [2]

Three foreign brasses are in London Museums :—

---

[1] *Monumental Brasses and Slabs*, 1847, p. 23.

[2] See *A Series of Monumental Brasses*, drawn and engraved by J. G. and L. A. B. Waller, but the instructions in the Archbishop's will, dated Feb. 13, 1630-1. "My body I will to be buried within the Parrishe "churche of Chigwell, withoute pompe or solempnitye at the foote of "Thomazine late my beloved wief havinge only a Marble stone layde "uppon my grave wth a Plate of Brasse moulten into the stone an ynche "thicke haveinge the effigies of a Bysshoppe stamped uppon it wth his "Myter and Crosiers staffe but the Brasse to be soe rivited and fastened "cleare throughe the Stone as sacrilegious handes maye not rend off the "one w[thoute] breakinge the other" (PCC. 78. St. John), would seem to point to the employment of local workmen. Moreover, the Filmer brass is signed "Ed. Marſhall sculpſit."

1. Ludowic Cortewille and wife, 1504, from Cortville, near Liége, formerly in the Museum of Practical Geology, Jermyn Street, but now at South Kensington.
2. Henry Oskens, priest, 1535, originally at Nippes, near Cologne, now at South Kensington.
3. Nicolas le Brun (Bailly de Jeumont), *d.* 1547, and wife, Françoise du Fosset, *d.* 1531, in the British Museum.

Two curious Flemish palimpsest inscriptions exist. (1) At Norton Disney, Lincolnshire, recording, on the reverse of a memorial to William Disney, 1540, his wife, and son (1578), the foundation in 1518 of a mass by Adrian Adrianson and the lady Paesschine van den Steyne at the altar of St. Cornelius. (2) At West Lavington, Wilts, recording on the reverse of a brass to John Dauntesay, 1559, a gift to the masters of the Holy Ghost at Westmonstre, a church at Middleburgh in Walcheren, destroyed in 1575; and apparently referring to the same matter and persons as the Norton Disney inscription.[1]

Brasses showing a French influence are rare in England. The best instance is that at Minster, Kent, in which the costume of Sir John de Northwode and his wife, Joan de Badlesmere, *c.* 1330, has many features in common with that of French monuments, preserved to us in the pages of Montfaucon's *Monumens de la Monarchie Françoise.* The lady's dress, in particular, resembles that worn at the French Court during the fourteenth century.[2] Another

Brasses showing French influence

---

[1] *See* Mr. Mill Stephenson in the *Transactions of the Monumental Brass Society*, Vol. IV., Part v. The Norton Disney inscription was offered by the Rev. Dr. Disney to Gough the Antiquary, whose refusal did him much credit. *See* Gough's *Sepulchral Monuments*, Vol. I., p. cxxii. (Part i). Other examples of palimpsest Flemish inscriptions are at Oxford, St. Mary Magdalene (Jane Fitzherbert, 1574), St. Peter-in-the-East (Richard Atkinson, 1574).

[2] Varieties of the same peculiarity in her dress, a kind of fur-lined tippet, may be observed in the effigies of Jeanne de S. Veraen, *d.* 1297; of Jeane Reine de Navarre, wife of Philippe le Bel, *d.* 1304; of Marguerite de Beaujeu, wife of Charles de Montmorency, *d.* 1336; of Marie de France,

instance of French influence may be the brass of Margaret de Camoys, 1310, at Trotton, Sussex, whose dress was ornamented with nine small enamelled shields, now lost. A similar treatment may be seen on the surcoat of William de Valence, Earl of Pembroke, 1296, in Westminster Abbey. The slab of Sir John de Brewys, 1426, in Wiston Church, Sussex, is *semée* with scrolls, alternately bearing the words "Jesus" and "mercy." Several examples similarly designed are known; and it is not unreasonable to suppose that this very decorative treatment originated in France. Some authorities consider the brass at Horsmonden, Kent, to John de Grovehurst, priest, *c.* 1340, to be French work.

Having now dealt with foreign brasses in England, it will not be out of place to mention an instance of an English brass on the Continent. Such is that of Robert Hallum, Bishop of Salisbury, envoy of Henry V. to the Council of Constance, who, dying there in 1416, was buried in the Cathedral. It represents the bishop in full pontificals, beneath a canopy, with a marginal inscription on fillet with Evangelistic symbols. It is noteworthy that after the manner of English brasses, the metal is cut to the shape of the figure, and is laid in a marble slab, prepared to receive it. Of this method there are other examples on the Continent, the earliest being the brass of Bishop Bernard de Lippe, 1340, at Paderborn. At Florence, in San Lorenzo, is the gravestone of John Caterick, Bishop of Exeter, 1419, with a brass marginal inscription.[1]

English brass of Bishop Hallum at Constance

---

daughter of Charles IV., *d.* 1341; of Jeanne, wife of Philippe, Comte d'Evreux, *d.* 1349; and of Jeanne, wife of Jean d'Aragon, Duc de Gironde, *d.* 1373; all given by Montfaucon. *See* below, Chap. VI.

[1] See *Transactions of the Monumental Brass Society*, Vol. III., p. 114, but see *Transactions of Devon Association*, Vol. XVIII., 1886, p. 229. "The Bishopric of Exeter, 1419-20: a Contribution to the History of the See," by T. N. Brushfield, M.D., wherein the slab is illustrated; is stated to be in the Church of Santa Croce, and the inscription and shields said to be of black marble inlaid.

NOTE.—The following account of costume is divided into large and distinct groups :—

A. Ecclesiastical, with a sub-branch—Academical.

B. Military.

C. Civilian, contiguous to which we have placed brasses of Lawyers.

D. Female.

In England there is one brass of a king,[1] a half-effigy representing Ethelred, King of the West Saxons, 872 (engraved c. 1440) at Wimborne Minster, Dorset (see p. 17). The costume consists of a close-sleeved under-garment, a mantle, and a cape or tippet of ermine. His right hand is placed on his breast; his left holds a sceptre; on his head is a crown. At Ringstead, in Zealand, is the fine brass of King Eric Menved, of Denmark, and his Queen, Ingeborg, 1319. The king holds in his right hand a sword, in his left a sceptre. His long *cote*, over which is a mantle, bears the arms of Denmark (or semée of hearts gules three lions passant guardant in pale az. crowned or). This brass is reproduced by Creeny, who also gives the fine series of brasses ranging from 1464 to

---

[1] In Lincoln Minster a brass once existed, representing Queen Eleanor, which was placed there c. 1310. See p. 33. "The Architectural History of Lincoln Minster," by the Rev. G. A. Poole in *Transactions of the Lincoln Diocesan Architectural Society* (*Associated Architectural Societies Reports and Papers*, Vol. IV., 1857-8). A small brass inscription in Peterborough Cathedral commemorates Queen Katherine of Aragon (1536). At Tewkesbury Abbey a brass plate marks the supposed site of the grave of Prince Edward of Wales, killed 1471. At Sherborne, a modern brass marks the place of burial of the Saxon kings, Ethelbald and Ethelbert. At Malmesbury, Wilts, an inscription shows the probable site of the interment of King Athelstan (914). In St. Martin's, Canterbury, is a brass with inscription, composed by Bishop Claughton to commemorate Bertha, Queen of Ethelbert, King of Kent, who is supposed to have been baptized through her influence in 597.

ST. ETHELRED,
KING OF THE WEST SAXONS.
ENGRAVED c. 1440.
WIMBORNE MINSTER, DORSET.

1539, of the Ducal House of Saxony at Meissen.[1] At
Basle is the brass of Isabella, Duchess of Burgundy, 1450;
at Nymwegen that of Katharine de Bourbon, wife of
Adolphus, Duke of Gueldres, 1469; at Cleves, 1483,
that of John and Elizabeth, Duke and Duchess of Cleves.

---

[1] They are—1464 Frederick the Good, Duke of Saxony.
          1486 Ernst, Duke of Saxony.
          1500 Albert, Duke of Saxony.
          1502 Ameleie, Duchess of Bavaria.
          1510 Sidonia, Duchess of Albert, Duke of Saxony.
          1510 Frederic, Duke of Saxony.
          1534 Barbara, Duchess of Saxony.
          1537 John, Duke of Saxony.
          1539 Frederic, Duke of Saxony.
The brass of John Ernst, Duke of Saxony, 1553, is at Coburg.

CHAPTER I.

Of Ecclesiastical Costume on Brasses

RICHARD DE HAKEBOURNE, c. 1311,
MERTON COLLEGE, OXFORD.

CHAPTER I.

OF ECCLESIASTICAL COSTUME ON BRASSES

In dealing with ecclesiastical vestments it is no part of our scheme with St. Jerome '*spiritualis intelligentiæ vela*' *pandere*, by discussing the various symbolical meanings which have grown up round them in course of centuries. Such meanings may be of importance from a devotional aspect, but do not come within the scope of this book.[1] Vestments cannot reasonably be considered to be either the outcome of divine revelation, or a legacy from the Levitical priesthood, but they represent the adaptation of Roman civil costume to the special needs of a class, the conservative tendencies of which have preserved for us through many centuries, with comparatively slight alterations, a dress of great antiquity. We do not propose to enter into a minute discussion of the origin of these vestments or of the constitutions of the Church regulating their assumption. They concern us only so far as they are represented on brasses. We are, therefore, brought directly to the thirteenth century, in which we find the earliest ecclesiastical brass known to exist, that of Bishop Yso Wilpe, 1231, at Verden. Another thirteenth-century instance is that of Bishop Otto de Brunswick, 1279, in the Cathedral of Hildesheim. We have shown above (Introduction, p. 17) that some ecclesiastical brasses were laid down in England during this century, but none survive.[2] There are but few examples left of the early part of the fourteenth century, towards the latter part of which they become numerous. Among these may be mentioned the demi-figure of Richard de Hakebourne,

---

[1] Some sensible remarks on the many meanings given to vestments may be read in *Eccclesiastical Vestments; their Development and History*, by R. A. S. Macalister. London, Elliot Stock, 1896.

[2] A fragment, representing St. Ethelbert, from the brass of Bishop Cantilupe, 1282, is preserved at Hereford Cathedral.

c. 1311,[1] Merton College, Oxford, in the head of a floriated cross (lost); Archbishop Grenefeld, 1315, York Minster; Nichol de Gore, *c.* 1320, Woodchurch, Kent (figure in cross); and a Priest (head), *c.* 1320, Chinnor, Oxon. (in floriated cross). With the Minor Orders, which include *ostiarius, lector,* and *acolytus,* we are not concerned, as they do not occur on brasses. The Major Orders (an elaboration of the three orders, Bishop, Priest, and Deacon), in which are ranked sub-deacon, deacon, priest, bishop, and archbishop,[2] are represented chiefly by effigies of priests, and by a small number of bishops and archbishops.

---

[1] The brass of Adam de Bacon (?), priest, *c.* 1310, was stolen from Oulton, Suffolk, in February, 1857. It is engraved in Cotman, Boutell, and Haines.

[2] We have no brasses in England of cardinals. The crypt of Canterbury contains the slab which held the brass of Cardinal John Morton (1500), in which is the indent of his Hat. At Cues is the brass of Cardinal Cusanos, 1464; at Cracow that of Cardinal Cazmiri, Archbishop of Gnesen, 1493 (*see* Creeny). At Great Berkhampstead, Herts, is a palimpsest brass, the reverse of which commemorates Thomas Humfre, goldsmith of London, and Joan, his wife, *c.* 1500. The initial letter O of the inscription contains the seated figure of St. Jerome attired as a cardinal, holding a cross-staff in the right hand. William Whappelode (1446), on his brass at Chalfont St. Peter, Bucks, is described as *Seneschallus domus* to Henry, Cardinal of England and Bishop of Winchester. At Carshalton, Surrey, was the brass of Thomas Ellenbridge, Esq., 1497, *hostiarius* to Cardinal Morton, Archbishop of Canterbury. His will is printed in *The Reliquary,* Vol. XXI., 1880-1, p. 196: "The Will of Thomas Elyngbrigge, of Carshalton, co. Surrey, Esq., A.D. 1497. P.C.C. 15 Horne," by Robert Garraway Rice. On the palimpsest inscription lost from the brass of John Marsham, 1525, and wife, St. John Maddermarket, Norwich, was a request for the prayers of the faithful, ending "xii "Cardinals have granted you xii[c] dayes of Pardon." On the pardon brass of Roger Legh (1506) and Elizabeth his wife (1499), Macclesfield, Cheshire, St. Gregory is represented kneeling before an altar, on which stands a chalice with a missal, and wearing a triple crown, and a chasuble with cruciform orphreys on front and back. This subject is well shown in the little triptych "*La messe de St. Gregoire,*" by Hans Memling (1435-1495), formerly in the Huybrechts Collection (illustrated in *The Connoisseur,* Vol. IV., p. 20, September, 1902). See also a piece of sculpture at Stoke Charity, Hants (illustrated in *Journal of the British Archæological Association,* Vol. V., 1850, p. 258, "On certain Church Brasses in Cheshire and Lancashire," by J. G. Waller).

Brasses of the monastic orders, monk and nun, prior and prioress, abbot and abbess, form a small but important class, after which we have to consider some other forms of clerical habit, and academical costume as it is represented in brasses, principally in the college chapels of Oxford and Cambridge, a subject closely connected with that of the costume of the clergy.

Ecclesiastical Vestments may be divided into two main groups :—

1. MASS (sometimes called eucharistic) to which the term *vestment* pre-eminently belongs.

2. PROCESSIONAL (a rather loose title).

The Mass Vestments, as their title implies, were worn at mass time. They were put on in the following order, a short prayer being said with each :—

1. AMICE (*amictus, anabolagium, epomis, humerale, super-humerale*), of mediæval origin, intended primarily for a hood, was a rectangular piece of linen (about 36 in. by 25 in.) with an *apparel*,[1] sewn along one edge, and a cross embroidered in the centre. Being placed for a moment on the head, it was then lowered to the neck, to which the apparel, resting on the shoulders, afforded a kind of loose collar, to the ends of which strings were attached, which, carried under the arms, crossed on the back, and tied in front, kept the vestment in position. The amice appears constantly on brasses, and must not be confused with the almuce, amys, or amess, a kind of fur cape (described below,

---

[1] APPAREL (*parura, etc., barare*) is the name given to the strips of embroidery, often of great elaboration and enriched with jewels, adorning the amice and alb. The term is used, apparently, only of the decoration of these vestments. They were sewn or attached, one to the amice, and six to the alb. On brasses they present much variety of ornament, and are seen at the wrists and in front at the foot of the alb.

ORPHREY (*aurifrigia, phrygio*, an embroiderer in gold, for which art the Phrygians were famous) : term applied to the narrow strips of embroidery on other vestments, such as the chasuble and cope.

p. 86); a mistake rendered easy by the similar sounding of the words.

2. ALB (*alba, tunica alba, στοιχάριον*).   The ancestor of the alb and of its apparels would seem to have been the *tunica talaris* of the Romans with its *lati clavi* for senators, and *angusti clavi* for equites.   This garment was long and loose; being originally sleeveless, it was called *colobium*, but afterwards becoming sleeved, was known as *tunica manicata* or *dalmatica*, which latter variety seems to have been established for ecclesiastics instead of the former in the fourth century.   The alb being inconveniently loose for baptisms, a close-fitting variety came into use, which is the mediæval alb known to us on brasses.   The ecclesiastical dalmatic and tunicle, to be described below (pp. 72-3), are probably derived from the loose variety.   The alb, as we know it, is a long, close-fitting vestment reaching to the feet, usually of white linen, though occasionally coloured or of more costly material.   Passed over the head, it is fastened round the waist by a *girdle* or *cord* (*baltheus, zona, cingulum*).   But, as the alb is drawn through the girdle, so as to obscure it, the latter is not seen on brasses, though its presence is evident, where the crossing of the stole is visible, as at Horsham, Sussex, 1411, and Upwell, Norfolk, 1435.   The alb is decorated with six pieces of embroidery, which are possibly the remains of the *clavi* (purple bands), and *segmenta* or *calliculæ* on the *tunica talaris*.   These apparels are placed one on the back, one on the breast, one on each wrist, and on the lower skirt of the garment in front and behind. They were either sewn on the alb, or attached to it by strings, thereby causing less injury to the embroidery when removed for the necessary washing of the vestment.

3. STOLE (*orarium,* ἐπιτραχήλιον, ὠράριον) originally a napkin or scarf for wiping the face (*os*), which was worn *outside*

the outer cloak (*pallium*), thereby rendering the derivation of the shape from the *clavi* of the *tunica* improbable. The *orarium* seems to have become a mark of distinction or favour, the use of which as such by the Roman people was first granted by Aurelian; indeed, the archiepiscopal *pall* may be be derived from a like distinction. Since the seventh century the stole has been worn in the Western Church by priests round the neck, crossed on the breast and passed beneath the girdle;[1] by deacons over the left shoulder. It consists of a long strip of silk, embroidered throughout, nine or ten feet long, and two or three inches wide. Originally of equal width throughout, this has varied from time to time. The ends are fringed. Nowadays, in the middle and at each extremity a cross is embroidered; though, from the evidence afforded by brasses, the terminal cross does not appear to have been by any means obligatory.[2] Being worn beneath the chasuble, usually only the fringed ends are visible, which fact may have

---

[1] Bishops are said to wear it not crossed (an accessible example is shown in the painting by Jacopo da Empoli (1554-1640) of San Zenobio restoring to life a dead child, in the National Gallery. The stole passes beneath the girdle of the alb, and is worn with a cope and mitre); but instances of bishops with crossed stoles are known: a small figure of St. Peter on the brass of Ralph, Lord Cromwell (1455), Tattershall, Lincs, is vested in cope and crossed stole. A wood-carving of late fifteenth or early sixteenth century work at Barneck, Northants, affords an example, showing a bishop in alb, crossed stole, cope, and mitre (engraved in Vol I., *Carter's Specimens of Ancient Painting and Sculpture*). In the Church of the Annunziata, Florence, Angelo Marzi, Bishop of Assisi (1546), is represented in marble by Francesco di S. Gallo, wearing girded alb, crossed stole, and mitre. (*See* Plate 186, *Brindley and Weatherley. Ancient Sepulchral Monuments*, 1887.)

[2] Indeed, we know of no instance of the presence of crosses on stoles in brasses, unless the so-called Fylfot-cross be so considered. We have no means of detecting (on a brass) whether a cross were embroidered in the centre. The regular use of these crosses is probably of late rather than of mediæval origin; unless it may be said to constitute a return to an earlier usage.

led to the concentration of ornament at the extremities.   But the brasses with copes at Horsham (where
the stole is embroidered throughout) and Upwell,
mentioned above, show its arrangement; as does that
at Sudborough, Northants (*c.* 1430), which gives a
figure without chasuble or cope.

4. MANIPLE or FANON (*mappula*, ἐγχείριον, ὀθόνη, *fanon*,
sudarium, *manipulus*), originally a napkin.   Pope
Sylvester in the third century ordered deacons to
wear a *pallium linostimum* on their hands.   Gregory
the Great mentions a *mappula*.   It would appear that
the use of this vestment was first confined to Rome;
then granted to Ravenna, and so spread.   The
maniple, originally of linen, was worn over the fingers
of the left hand, as seen in the figure of Archbishop
Stigand in the Bayeux tapestry; but on brasses it
has lost its original use, having become like the stole,
a piece of silk, some three feet in length, with ornamental embroidery and fringed ends, forming in
shape a kind of miniature stole, hung over the left
fore-arm, beneath which it is secured by a button or
hook.   On the maniple, possibly of the tenth century,
found in 1827 with the remains of St. Cuthbert at
Durham, is worked a figure of Pope St. Sextus (third
century) wearing this vestment.[1]   An instance of the
maniple being represented on the right arm may be
seen at Newnton, Wilts (John Erton, 1503), probably
an engraver's error; but in the case of the brass at
Naudhausen, of Jacob Capillan, 1395 (a kneeling
priest, holding up a chalice), it may be that this
change is intentional.   In the MS. known as the
Bible of Charles le Chauve (840) is a representation
of that monarch receiving a Bible, in which ecclesi-

---

[1] Figured p. 33, and described p. 206, of "Saint Cuthbert, with an
account of the state in which his remains were found upon the opening
of his tomb in Durham Cathedral in the year MDCCCXXVII.," by the
Rev. James Raine, M.A., Durham, 1828.

astics appear wearing maniples over their right hands
(reproduced in Planché's *Cyclopædia of Costume*, Vol. II.,
1876, p. 31).

5. CHASUBLE (φαινόλιον, *casula*, *planeta*. Old English,
chesible, *vestment*).[1]   The Roman toga seems to have
become a very inconvenient garment, and was superseded by successive modifications, the *pænula*, *casula*,
and *planeta*.   From one of these forms, probably the
planeta, the ecclesiastical chasuble is derived.   Its
use, except when worn folded at certain seasons
(*planeta plicata*), was confined to the celebrant at
Mass.   Its earlier form was circular with a large
aperture in the centre through which the head passed.
Later it seems to have become a pointed oval (*vesica
piscis*), a shape known *now* as the Gothic chasuble;
which form would give more freedom in the use of
the hands.[2]   As the vestment became heavier with
embroidery it was found necessary to split up the
sides, as in the modern Roman chasuble.   At the
period when it appears frequently on brasses, it was
a vestment of great costliness, made of silk, cloth of
gold, etc., often elaborately decorated.   The material
used in earlier brasses, such as Bishop Yso Wilpe's,
is much more pliable than the stiff fabrics of a later
day.   The orphrey work sometimes took the form

[1] The word *vestimentum* is occasionally found applied to a set of mass
vestments.   In the provincial constitutions of Walter Gray, Archbishop
of York, 1250, the parishioners are to provide "Vestimentum ipsius
"ecclesiæ principale, viz., casula, alba munda, amictus, stola, manipulus,
"zona."   Wilkins' *Concilia Magnæ Britanniæ*, Vol. I., 1737, p. 698.

[2] This is a disputed point.   The pointed or Gothic chasuble of modern
times may be without authority.   Father Lockhart contends (*The Chasuble;
its Genuine Form and Size*, 1891) that the pointed form seen on sepulchral
monuments is caused by the position of the arms affecting the rounded
chasuble.   *See* the ample rounded chasuble worn by St. Cuthbert in
initial H of the fourteenth century M.S. of the Postils or Commentaries
on the Bible of Nicholas de Lyra, at Durham (reproduced, p. 131, in
Raine's *St Cuthbert*, 1828).   But the chasuble of St. Thomas à Becket
at Sens seems to support the contrary view.

of a border alone, round the edge of the garment. At others a perpendicular strip appears, as in the brass of Bishop Yong at New College, or a *Gamma* (γ) or *Psi* (ψ) shaped orphrey is seen. Occasionally the chasuble is quite plain.[1]

The following are good examples of priests in mass vestments[2] :—

1337.   Laurence de St. Maur, Higham Ferrers, North-ants.

c. 1340.   John de Grovehurst, Horsemonden, Kent.

c. 1360.   Esmound de Burnedissh, Brundish, Suffolk.

c. 1360.   Thomas de Horton, North Mimms, Herts (Flemish).

c. 1360.   Simon de Wenslagh, Wensley, Yorkshire (Flemish).

c. 1370.   A priest (with a franklin), Shottesbrook, Berks.

c. 1370.   A priest (? Nicholas de Caerwent), Crondall, Hants.

c. 1370.   A priest, Stoke-in-Teignhead, Devon.

c. 1375.   Peter de Lacy, Northfleet, Kent.

c. 1380.   A priest, Beachamwell, Norfolk (? Thomas Chervyll).

c. 1390.   A priest, Fulbourn, Cambs.

1395.   John de Swynstede, Ashridge House, Bucks.

c. 1400.   A priest, Stanford-on-Soar, Notts.

c. 1430.   A priest, Saffron Walden, Essex.

1432.   William Byschopton, Great Bromley, Essex.

1477.   Geoffrey Byschop, Fulbourn, Cambs.

c. 1500.   Philip Eyre, Ashover, Derbyshire.

1519.   Hen. Dodschone, Stanton Harcourt, Oxon.

---

[1] *e.g.*, *c.* 1380.   Thomas Chervyll (?), Beachamwell, Norfolk.

c. 1400.   A priest, Stanford-on-Soar, Notts.

c. 1425.   Robert Fyn, Little Easton, Essex.

c. 1460.   John Spicer (?), Monkton, Kent.

1522.   Edmund Assheton, Middleton, Lancs.

The chasuble of Richard Thaseburgh, 1389, Hellesdon, Norfolk, has a very simple hem-like border.

[2] Other examples are mentioned, p. 101.

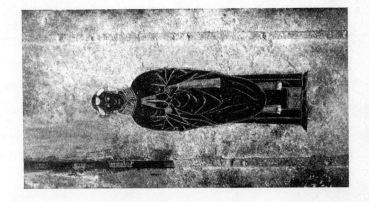

PRIEST, *c.* 1480,
CHILDREY, BERKS.

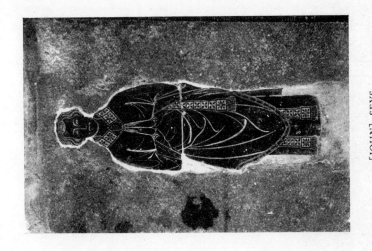

[JOHN] SEYS,
PRIEST *c.* 1370,
WEST HANNEY, BERKS.

There are numerous examples of demi-figures in similar vestments :—

c. 1311. Richard de Hakebourne, Merton College, Oxford.

c. 1320. Thomas de Hop, Kemsing, Kent.

c. 1320. A priest, Wantage, Berks.

c. 1340. Richard de Beltoun, Corringham, Essex.

c. 1340. A priest, Great Brington, Northants.

c. 1360. Walter Frilende, Ockham, Surrey.

c. 1364. William Darell, Brandsburton, Yorkshire.

c. 1365. Radulphus Perchehay, Stifford, Essex.

c. 1370. John Verieu, Saltwood, Kent.

c. 1380. John Alderburne, Lewknor, Oxon.

1398. Roger Campedene, Stanford-in-the-Vale, Berks.

c. 1430. A priest, Upton Lovel, Wilts.

c. 1450. Esperaunce Blondell, Arundel, Sussex.

1474. Robert Warde, Arundel, Sussex.

1494. John Taknell, Winchester College.

1498. William Branwhait, Ewelme, Oxon.

1514. John Tylbert, Winchester College.

1514. John Crewaker, Winchester College.

Some variant brasses must be mentioned, which, with the exception of the first example given below, appear to show a combination of mass and processional vestments:—

c. 1430. John West, Sudborough, Northants, in amice, alb, and crossed stole.

c. 1411. Henry Clark, Vicar, Horsham, Sussex; 1432, John Wyllynghale (half eff.), Fellow, Winchester College; 1435, Henry Martin, Rector of Yaxham, Upwell, Norfolk, vested in amice, alb, crossed stole, and cope, thereby allowing the arrangement of the stole to be seen. The orphreys of the cope in the first instance bear the initials H.C.

1472. Thomas Tonge, LL.B., Beeford, Yorks; (a similar effigy to which was formerly at Romaldkirk, N. Yorks), and two half effigies of

Fellows at Winchester College (1445, Richard
North, and 1473, Edward Tacham) vested in
amice, alb, and cope.

1465.   Thomas Cod, Vicar, St. Margaret's, Rochester
(half eff.), in cassock, amice, *surplice*, and cope
(*see* p. 40).

In addition to the vestments, above mentioned, bishops
wore the following:—

1. DALMATIC (*tunica dalmatica*). The origin of this vestment has been touched on whilst considering the alb.
Its name is derived from that of the country whence
it came. Its use as a separate vestment was given,
as a privilege, to the Roman deacons; and it is still
worn by the Deacon at Mass. Originally a close
white linen robe reaching below the knees, with
sleeves and purple or black *clavi*, it soon became a
subject for ornament, being decorated, before the
twelfth century, with vertical or horizontal bands of
embroidery. Later it became embroidered throughout, as on Bishop Goodryke's brass, 1554, at Ely,
and was made of similar material and colour to the
chasuble. The bishop wore this vestment immediately beneath the chasuble. The episcopal dalmatic
was fringed on both sleeves and on both sides; the
deacon's properly on the left sleeve and side only.
Examples of deacons on brasses are exceedingly rare.
The reverse of the canopy of the brass at Burwell,
Cambs, shows an ecclesiastic, *c.* 1320, so vested (*see*
p. 41).[1] The brass of Eghardus de Hanensee,

[1] The figure of St. Lawrence, vested in the dalmatic, occurs on the
following brasses:—
1401. William Ermyn, Rector, Castle Ashby, Northants, in which the
saint wears the episcopal dalmatic and a stole (priest-fashion).
1429. Roger Thornton and wife (Flemish), Newcastle-on-Tyne.
1468. John Byrkhed, Harrow, Middlesex.
A saint in deacon's vestments appears on the brass of Laurence de
St. Maur, 1337, Higham Ferrers, Northants, and on that of Bishop
Rudolphus, 1482, at Breslau; a figure of St. Quentin on that of Abbot
Leonardus Betten, 1607, at Ghent.

Provost, 1460, at Hildesheim (figured by Creeny) shows the dalmatic fully exposed.

2. TUNICLE (*tunica pontificalis*, *tunicella*), a plainer variety of the dalmatic, with narrower sleeves and frequently a fringed border. It was the vestment peculiar to the Sub-Deacon at Mass. The bishop wore it immediately below the dalmatic, but not until about the twelfth century. Originally of white linen, it underwent similar enrichment to the dalmatic. In the brass of Bishop Trilleck (1360) at Hereford, this vestment does not appear, probably because it is hidden beneath the dalmatic. This difficulty was solved by representing the dalmatic as shorter than the tunicle, the fringed hem of which, thereby, appears.[1]

3. BUSKINS or STOCKINGS (*caligæ*, *sotulares*, *tibialia*, Old English *sabatyns*), fastened at the knee, were first made of linen, then of silk embroidered. Originally reserved for the Pope, their use was gradually extended.

4. SANDALS (*sandalia*, *campagæ*). These, from an intermediate state of open work or fenestration, passed to shoes with strings (in the fourteenth century), on which three orphreys, somewhat of a *Psi* (Ψ) shape, frequently occur.

5. GLOVES (*chirothecæ*, *manicæ*) had come to be of white netted silk or other delicate material, though originally, probably of leather and intended for warmth. Jewels were set in the gloves, or a plate enamelled or jewelled, called a *monial*, was placed in the centre of

---

[1] In the directions for revesting the Abbot of Westminster at Evensong, instructions are given to lay ready the dalmatic with longest sleeves above the other. This implies that the tunicle had longer sleeves than the dalmatic: the term "dalmatic" is applied to both vestments, the fourteenth-century Inventory of Westminster speaking of pairs of dalmatics. *See* "On an Inventory of the Vestry in Westminster Abbey, taken in 1388." By J. Wickham Legg, F.S.A., in the *Archæologia*, Vol. LII., 1890, p. 195.

the back of the glove.[1]   In the brasses of Bishops
Stanley (1515), Yong (1526), Goodryke (1554), Bell
(1556), and Pursglove (1579), the gauntlets are wide,
ending in tassels.

6. RING (*annulus*) was worn, not near the knuckle, but
above the lower finger-joint on the middle finger of
the right hand, and was kept in place by a guard ring.
Either it was passed over the glove, or the finger of
the glove was cut away so as to show it.   The stone
was frequently a sapphire, unengraved, set in gold.[2]
Sometimes rings appear on several fingers, as on the
brass of Bishop Yong, 1526, at New College.   These
rings were called "*pontificals*."   That there should be
but one episcopal ring seems fitting, but in the Revesting of the Abbot of Westminster (quoted footnote, p. 73) "hys glovys and pontyfycales" are
mentioned, implying more than one ring.[3]   Bishop
Stanley (1515) wears a large ring on his right thumb.

7. MITRE [4] (*mitra, cidaris*, borrowed from similar Greek),

---

[1] "Item, a paire of gloves with broches sowedde upon eche of them
with perles and stones."   At St. Paul's, in 1552.   See *Hierurgia Anglicana*, revised and considerably enlarged by Vernon Staley.   London,
Moring, Part I., 1902, p. 60.

[2] "Item, a pontificale of golde with a great saphyer in it of playne
worke."   St. Paul's, 1552.   *See* the same, p. 60.

[3] *See* "On an Inventory of the Vestry at Westminster," by J. Wickham
Legg, F.S.A., *Archæologia*, Vol. LII., 1890, p. 214, note *b*.   "Item fouer
ringes of silver called pontificalles" in Henry VIII.'s Jewel Book.   It
has been held that the ring symbolizes a mystical marriage.   This idea
would be supported by the fact that the see impales with its arms those
of the bishop.   On the brass of Bishop Bernhard de Lippe, 1340, at
Paderborn, the coat of Lippe (azure, a five-petalled rose gules) is borne
on an escutcheon of pretence in the centre of the arms of the see, gules
a cross or.   An article, "On Episcopal Rings," by Edmund Waterton,
F.S.A., will be found in the *Archæological Journal*, Vol. XX., 1863, p. 224.

[4] *See* Papers "Ecclesiastical Head Dress," by Charles Browne, M.A.,
F.S.A., *Transactions of St. Paul's Ecclesiological Society*, Vol. III., 1895,
p. 155, and "The Evolution of the Mitre," by Henry Philibert Feasey,
O.S.B., *The Reliquary and Illustrated Archæologist*, Vol. x., 1904, p. 73.

the head-dress of a bishop, probably developed from a plain skull-cap. An illumination (reproduced in Marriott[1]) in a MS. in the British Museum (Cotton, Claud A3) shows St. Gregory the Great wearing a low cap with two lappets (*infulæ*, *vittæ*) which, originally, in all probability, being tied under the chin, kept the cap in place.[2] Possibly it was not before the eleventh century that the mitre began to show signs of the shape with two peaks, with which it is usually associated. The earlier forms are comparatively low and triangular, as in that of Archbishop Grenefeld, 1315, at York,[3] but later they become higher and are crocketed in accordance with Gothic taste (1395, John de Waltham, Bishop of Salisbury, Westminster Abbey; 1554, Bishop Goodryke at Ely); finally they become curved and bulged (1631, Archbishop Harsnett, Chigwell, Essex). They were made first of linen, then of silk or other costly material, and were of three kinds, worn on occasions of varying dignity :—

1. *Mitra simplex*, of white linen or silk, without much ornament.

2. *Mitra aurifrigiata*, with gold-embroidered orphreys.

3. *Mitra pretiosa*, overlaid with gold plates, set with jewels frequently of great value.

8. PASTORAL STAFF or CROZIER[4] (*virga* or *baculus pastoralis*,

---

[1] Plate XLIV, *Vestiarium Christianum*, 1868.

[2] In the brass of Lambert von Brun at Bamberg, 1399, the *infulæ* appear as though tied behind. In the Westminster Inventory, quoted above, the strings (*labellæ*) of a mitre are mentioned adorned with precious stones and eight silver-gilt bells. *Archæologia*, Vol. LII., p. 220.

[3] Bishop Pursglove (1579) wears a mitre, similarly depressed, but that of Bishop Stanley (1515) was of a considerable height.

[4] The term "Crozier" is frequently applied to the cross-staff borne before an archbishop. See the *Archæologia*, Vol. LI. (2nd Series, Vol. I.), 1888, p. 351, "Episcopal Staves," by the Rev. Frederick George Lee, D.D., F.S.A., and Vol. LII. (2nd Series, Vol. II.), 1890, p. 709, "On

cambuca, ferula, pedum). The usual form is obviously adopted from the shepherd's crook, denoting the bishop's pastoral authority. The staff was frequently of some precious wood, such as cedar, and often overlaid by plates of metal. The shape of the head varied greatly. Early instances occur of knobs or Y-shaped tops. Some Irish staves have a crook shaped like an inverted U. The usual form, however, is that of a volute, richly carved, frequently having in the centre a sacred symbol, such as the *Agnus Dei*. Below the crook a knob is seen, possibly used as a reliquary. Figures of saints in tabernacle work are not uncommon. To the knob a scarf or veil (*infula, vexillum*) is seen fastened, often having a tasselled end. This by some has been derived from the banner of Constantine; but a more likely, though humbler, explanation is that it served as a napkin to prevent the plated staff from getting tarnished: a view that is adequately supported by the manner of holding the staff seen on brasses. Much misconception exists as to the representation of the pastoral staff on sepulchral monuments, a popular idea being that the crook of a *bishop's* staff is turned outwards to show his diocesan authority; that of an *abbot* turned towards his body to show a jurisdiction restricted to his convent. But monuments give us no such clue; the heads of staves being turned, indifferently, either way.

It is held usually in the left hand, or rests between the left arm and the body; but in instances such as the palimpsest at Burwell, Cambridgeshire, it is on the right side; the reason for it being held in the left hand probably being that the right hand is raised

---

the use of the terms Crosier, Pastoral Staff, and Cross," by the Rev. J. T. Fowler, M.A., F.S.A. In the Westminster Inventory ("Revestyng of the Abbot") we read: "Hys myter and *crose* beyng Redy" (*Archæologia*, Vol. LII., 1890, p. 214). Archbishop Harsnett's will (1630) mentions a crozier-staff, which on the brass is identical with a pastoral staff.

to give a benediction. The pastoral staff has a pointed end, with which a bishop took off the vestments of an ecclesiastic on deprivation. Mr. R. A. S. Macalister[1] gives the following inscriptions, as supposed to have been engraved :—round the crook, " Cum iratus fueris, misericordiæ recordaberis "; on the ball of the crook, " Homo "; on the spike at the bottom, " Parce." On the brasses of Bishop Henry Robinson, 1616, at Carlisle, and at Queen's College, Oxford,[2] the pastoral staff bears :—on the shaft, " Ps. 23. Corrigendo SVSTENTANDO "; on the crook, encircling an eye, "Vigilando, Dirigendo"; on a short veil, " Velando."

Besides these vestments, archbishops have two additional ornaments :—

1. CROSS STAFF, which, as its name denotes, has for its head a cross or crucifix. That this ornament does not, in the case of an archbishop, necessarily supply the place of the episcopal crozier or pastoral staff is sufficiently demonstrated by the presence of both cross-staff and crozier on some archiepiscopal monuments ; notably the brass of Bishop Lambert von Brun, 1399, in Bamberg Cathedral,[3] who holds the cross-staff in his right hand and the pastoral staff in his left ; the brass of Archbishop Jacobus de Senno, 1480, at Gnezen, with pastoral staff in right hand and cross-staff in left ; and the monument of Archbishop Albrecht von Brandenburg, 1545, at Mayence. For, although the cross-staff was usually borne in front of the archbishop, rather than held by him ; yet, as in

---

[1] *Ecclesiastical Vestments*, p. 132.

[2] Illustrated in *Portfolio of Oxford University Brass Rubbing Society*, Part I., February, 1898.

[3] The Bishops of Autun, Bamberg, Le Puy, Lucca, Ostia, Pavia, and Verona are entitled to the archiepiscopal pall. Hence, probably, the presence of the cross-staff in this instance may be similarly explained. The Bishops of Dol were entitled to an archiepiscopal cross-staff.

the case of Archbishop Cranley's brass at New College,
1417, it is shown on his left side, partly, probably,
for pictorial effect, and also to accentuate the evidence
afforded by the pallium, of his metropolitan rank.

2. PALL (*pallium*, ὠμοφόριον), like the stole, probably derived from the *orarium*.   Dr. Rock, however, considers it to be descended from the Roman toga.[1]   The
ecclesiastical vestment is very dissimilar from the
Roman pallium, or cloak.   It was early set apart as
the symbol of authority delegated by the Pope to the
Metropolitans, and was sent by him to each of them
when consecrated.   Made of white wool, of three
fingers' breadth, in the sixth century mosaics at
Ravenna, it appears in a different form to that of later
times.[2]   But, finally, the vestment assumed a T or Y
shape in front and behind, as we see it represented in
the few brasses on which it occurs, and in the arms
of the See of Canterbury.   In earlier examples it is
represented as of great length, as in Bishop Yso
Wilpe's brass, where it has a Tau-like end.[3]   Later
it becomes somewhat shorter, as in Archbishop
Cranley's effigy.   The pall was at first fastened by
gold pins to the chasuble, to keep it in place.   These
may, possibly, be represented by the purple crosses
(*paté fitché* in the Cranley brass) shown on the pall,
which vary in number.   Later a plummet of lead,

---

[1] *The Church of our Fathers*, Vol. II., 1849, p. 129.   For an account of
this vestment see "The Blessing of the Episcopal Ornament called the
Pall," by J. Wickham Legg, F.S.A., *Yorkshire Archæological Journal*,
Vol. XV., 1900, p. 121.

[2] Being passed from the front, over the left shoulder, then from behind,
over the right, looped round in front, and passed again over the left
shoulder, thereby appearing double on that shoulder and single on the
right, the two ends hanging loose, one in front and one behind; but
afterwards, by being knotted, the tails (*lineæ*) were brought to hang
symmetrically before and behind.

[3] It is difficult to understand why this bishop wears a pall, unless it
were conferred as a mark of favour, as in some modern instances.

THOMAS CRANLEY, ARCHBISHOP OF DUBLIN, 1417,
NEW COLLEGE, OXFORD.

sewn inside at the end, was found to have this effect without injuring the orphrey of the chasuble. The pall was worn, correctly, only within the archbishop's province, and at his death was buried with him. The effigy of Albrecht von Brandenburg, 1545, at Mayence, shows two short palls, probably denoting thereby that he was Archbishop of Magdeburg as well as of Mayence. Care must be taken not to confuse the pall with the Y-shaped orphrey, frequently seen on the chasuble.

A list of brasses of Archbishops and Bishops in Pontificals :—

ARCHBISHOPS.

1315. William Grenefeld, Archbishop of York, York Minster.

1397. Robert de Waldeby, Archbishop of York, Westminster Abbey.

1417. Thomas Cranley, Archbishop of Dublin, New College, Oxford.

At Edenham, Lincolnshire, is a small sixteenth-century brass, representing an archbishop, 18 in. high, fastened some forty feet from the ground on the outside of the west wall of the tower.[1] But it may be questioned whether it be a *sepulchral* brass. One theory suggests that it is a representation of St. Thomas of Canterbury, who is depicted on the canopy of Thomas Nelond, Prior of Lewes, 1433, at Cowfold, Sussex, and also, possibly, as the archbishop on the orphrey of the cope of Simon Bache, 1414, at Knebworth, Herts. At All Saints', Maidstone, was formerly a brass for Archbishop William Courtenay, who died there in 1396, but was buried at Canterbury. In the latter cathedral, in the Transept of the Martyrdom, lie the

---

[1] In some districts, in which the local stone is unsuitable for carved inscriptions, brass plates may be found in the churchyards. This is the case in some Gloucestershire parishes. In the close at Chichester there is a brass to Thomas Farrington and wife, 1664.

matrices of the brasses of Archbishop John Stafford,[1] 1452, and Archbishop Henry Dene,[2] 1502-3.   At Sandal Parva, W. Yorks, was formerly the kneeling effigy of William Rokeby, Archbishop of Dublin, 1521.   The inscription alone remains.

BISHOPS.

1360.   John Trilleck, Bishop of Hereford, Hereford Cathedral.

1375.   Robert Wyvill, Bishop of Salisbury, Salisbury Cathedral.

1395.   John de Waltham, Bishop of Salisbury, Westminster Abbey.

1478.   John Bowthe, Bishop of Exeter, East Horsley, Surrey; a kneeling figure, in profile, showing the vertical orphrey on the back of the chasuble and its jewelled border.[3]

1496.   Richard Bell, Bishop of Carlisle, Carlisle Cathedral.

1515.   James Stanley, Bishop of Ely, Manchester Cathedral.

1526.   John Yong, titular Bishop of Callipolis, New College, Oxford, of which society he was Warden.

1554.   Thomas Goodryke, Bishop of Ely and Lord Chancellor, Ely Cathedral; holding book and great seal.

1556.   John Bell, Bishop of Worcester, St. James', Clerkenwell, Middlesex.

---

[1] See illustration of matrix.   *Wiltshire Notes and Queries*, No. 29, March, 1900 (Vol. III., p. 193).

[2] This brass had disappeared before 1778.   His will is printed in the *Archæological Journal*, Vol. XVIII., 1861, p. 256.   "The will of Henry Dene, Archbishop of Canterbury, A.D. 1502-3, communicated by the Rev. John Bathurst Deane, M.A., F.S.A."

[3] An example of a priest kneeling in mass vestments is at Blockley, Worcs. (William Neele, 1510).   For some account of the Bowthe family, *see* "The Booths or Bothes, Archbishops and Bishops, and the Derbyshire Family to which they belonged," by Llewellynn Jewitt, *The Reliquary*, Vol. XXV., 1884-5, p. 33.   With the Boothe brass may be compared the matrix of that of Thomas Cornish, 1513, Bishop of Tenos, in Wells Cathedral.

JOHN YONG,
BISHOP OF CALLIPOLIS, 1526,
NEW COLLEGE, OXFORD.

1579. Robert Pursglove, suffragan Bishop of Hull, Tideswell, Derbyshire.

At Adderley, Shropshire, is a full-length figure in episcopal vestments, c. 1390, without tunicle, stole, or gloves, holding a crozier in the right hand and a book in the left.[1] At Hereford Cathedral is preserved a figure of St. Ethelbert, which is all that remains of the brass of Bishop Thomas Cantilupe, 1282. In the same cathedral is a plate bearing twelve Latin hexameters, part of the memorial of Bishop John Stanberry, 1474. At St. Andrew's, Norwich, a scroll and shield survive from the cross-brass of Bishop John Underwood, 1541, titular Bishop of Chalcedon, and suffragan to the Bishop of Norwich.

At St. John Maddermarket, Norwich, is a palimpsest brass, commemorating Robert Rugge, 1558, the reverse of which shows portions of a figure in episcopal vestments, of early date, c. 1320, holding a pastoral staff in the right hand and a book on the breast in the left.[2] At Upminster, Essex, a small brass of a civilian, c. 1540, has on its reverse side a lower part of a figure in pontificals, probably of early fifteenth century date. Other instances occur at Tolleshunt Darcy, in the same county, and at Hedgerley, Bucks.

Several matrices of episcopal brasses exist. Perhaps the most notable is that of Bishop Beaumont (1333) at Durham.[3] At Hereford Cathedral was a small brass to the east of the tomb of Bishop Richard Mayo (1516), representing him kneeling in pontificals before a figure of the Virgin, supporting the dead Christ, and with a shield bearing Argent

---

[1] The head with mitre and crozier-head are lost. *See* illustration, *Archæological Journal*, Vol. LII., 1895, "Monumental Brasses in Shropshire," by Mill Stephenson, F.S.A. Bishop Richard Bell, 1496, Carlisle Cathedral, holds an open book in his right hand, on which is inscribed, "Haec spes mea in sinu meo."

[2] Illustrated in the same author's "List of Palimpsest Brasses" (*Transactions of the Monumental Brass Society*, Vol. IV.)

[3] Reproduced Vol. XIII. (Series II.) *Proc. Soc. Ant.*, and Vol. I., *Portfolio of Monumental Brass Society*.

on a fess sable between three roses gules a lily of the first. This was well restored in 1857 by Magdalen College, Oxford, of which the Bishop was President. A small brass is preserved in the cathedral library at Lincoln, consisting of a crocketed mitre (*pretiosa*) surmounting a shield bearing a chevron between three crosses-croslet fitché, with a curious inscription, through which it has been ascribed to Bishop John Russell (1494). The reverse of the shield on the brass of Thomas Fromond, Esq., 1542, at Cheam, Surrey, shows the arms of the see of Lincoln, *c.* 1420.

A few general remarks will now be in place as to the representation of the foregoing vestments on brasses. The earlier examples of the fourteenth century have the hair long and flowing, the ears large, and the shaven part of the face represented by dots. The vestments are less rigid than in later monuments; the chasuble, especially, showing by its many folds, that it was of pliant material. In the earlier examples, the ends of the stole and maniple are frequently broadened, and the apparels of the alb are continued round the wrists (as at Corringham, Essex, Richard de Beltoun, half eff., *c.* 1340), being represented later by a square piece only, on the upper side of the sleeve. In some instances the mitten sleeves of the undergarment appear over the hands beyond the alb. In the fifteenth century a greater stiffness in the vestments becomes visible; the hair is shown straight, and not in the graceful manner noticed at first. The Reformation brings this class of brass to an end. Instances of omission are well known, due, in all probability, to the mistakes of the engraver. For example, the stole is omitted at Blisland, Cornwall (John Balsam, 1410); Chelsfield, Kent (William Robroke, 1420); and at Newton Bromshold, Northants (William Hewett, 1426); the maniple in Bishop Yong's effigy at New College, 1526; both stole and maniple at Coleshill, Warwickshire (William Abell, 1500); at Sawston, Cambs. (Edmund Richardson, 1522); and at Middleton, Lancs. (Edmund Assheton, 1522). The

THOMAS DE HOP, c. 1320,
KEMSING, KENT.

JOHN VERIEU, c. 1370,
SALTWOOD, KENT.

tunicle is not visible on the brass of Bishop Trilleck,
1360, at Hereford.   The stole worn by Bishop Goodryke,
1554, at Ely, is placed between the tunicle and the
dalmatic.

The ornamentation of the mass vestments is usually of
a geometrical kind, the lozenge being a favourite device,
squares and circles also being found.   These are frequently filled in with the quatrefoil, or simple forms of a
floral origin.   The cross is exceedingly rare.   It occurs on
the brass of John de Waltham, Bishop of Salisbury, in
Westminster Abbey.[1]   The device known as the "fylfot"
cross may be seen on several brasses (e.g. Richard de
Hakebourne, c. 1311, Merton College, Oxford; Walter
Frilende, c. 1360, Ockham, Surrey, half-eff., etc.).   Personal devices seldom occur on the chasuble, probably
because of its superior sanctity, but the initials I. B.
(arranged $\frac{I}{B}$) occur on the vertical orphrey of that vestment at Arundel, Sussex (John Baker, fellow 1445).   On
the chasuble worn over his armour by Sir Peter Legh
(1527), Winwick, Lancs. (which shows an embroidered
collar, usually concealed in the priestly effigy by the
apparel of the amice), a large shield of six quarterings is
placed.[2]   On the brass of Bishop Bernhard de Lippe,
1340, at Paderborn, the orphrey of the chasuble bears
five-petalled roses in reference to his arms, and in the
Schwerin brasses the arms of de Bulowe occur in a similar
position, in one case also on the amice.   On the latter
vestment at Posen on the brass of Bishop Vrielis de Gorka,
1498, the letters P A T and I V S occur, which Creeny

---

[1] Crosses occur on the maniple of Archbishop Grenefeld, 1315, in York
Minster; that of Abbot Leonardus Betten, 1607, at Ghent, has three
crosses.

[2] The description of the brass of Bishop Lewis de Beaumont given in
the Durham Book of Rites shows that his arms occurred on his chasuble,
"his owne armes of France, being a white lyon placed uppon the breast
"of his vestment, beneath his verses of his breast with flower de luces
"about the lyon."   His seal shows a similar heraldic chasuble (see, with
engravings, Proc. Soc. Ant., Series II., Vol. XIII.)

supposed to be the first and last three letters of "Pater,
Spiritus, Filius." [1]   Figures of saints on chasubles are
rare. [2]   The Waltham brass, 1395, at Westminster, with
the Virgin and child, the arms of the See of Salisbury,
furnishes an English instance, which is shown alternately
with a cross on the vertical orphrey of the bishop's
chasuble.   Palimpsest brasses at Upminster, Essex, and
Bayford, Herts, show, when reversed, portions of the same
brass of an abbot or bishop, probably of fifteenth-century
Flemish work, whose finely-embroidered chasuble has an
orphrey with saints. [3]   The chasuble orphrey of Leonardus
Betten, 1607, Abbot of St. Trond, on his brass, now in
Ghent Museum, shows figures of SS. Quentin, Trond,
Peter, Paul, and James.   In each case the orphrey is
vertical.   Across the chasuble of Laurence de St. Maur,
1337, at Higham Ferrers, Northants, is written, "Fili dei
miserere mei."   Across that of Thomas Ouds, 1500,
Great Musgrave, Westmorland, "Reposita est spes mea
in sinu meo." [4]

---

[1] In "Inventories of Christchurch, Canterbury, etc., edited by J.
Wickham Legg, F.S.A., and W. H. St. John Hope, M.A., 1902, quoted
p. 165, Vol. I., *Hierurgia Anglicana*, 1902, occurs the following :—"Item
"j [albe] of red welvet embrodered w^t the Image of St. Laurence and St.
"Stephens ye amyse whereof is imbrodered w^t ye name of william hull in
"letters of golde."

[2] The apparel of the amice found in 1892 in Canterbury Cathedral on
the body of Archbishop Hubert Walter (*d.* 1205) was embroidered with
seven figures : Christ enthroned, the four evangelistic symbols, and the
archangels Michael and Gabriel.   *See* "Burial Places of the Archbishops
of Canterbury," by Canon Scott Robertson.   *Archæologia Cantiana*, Vol.
XX., 1893, p. 276.

[3] Another example (fifteenth-century Flemish) is on the reverse of a
man in armour, *c.* 1560, in the possession of Sir. M. Boileau, of Ketteringham Park, Norfolk.

[4] Bishop Beaumont "In pectore...Reposita est hæc spes mea in sinu
meo.   Domine miserere."   "Durham Book of Rites" (see *Proc. Soc. Ant.*,
Series II., Vol. XIII., p. 37).   The lost brass of Richard Stondon, priest
(early sixteenth century), formerly at St. Albans, showed him in a chasuble,
the orphreys of which were engraved with the inscription : "Jesu Christ,
Mary's son, Have mercy on the soul of Sir Richard Stondon, priest.   *See*
"The Brasses and Indents in St. Albans' Abbey," by William Page,
F.S.A.   *Home Counties Magazine*, Vol. I., 1899.

The PROCESSIONAL or CHORAL Vestments have now to be considered.   These, unlike the foregoing, cannot be said to possess a sacramental significance, but form the dress of dignity of ecclesiastics of rank, worn to show a temporal rather rather than a spiritual position.

First it will be convenient to mention a garment, by no means confined to the Processional Vestments proper, but worn by clergy as an ordinary course.

The CASSOCK (*camisia vestis, tunica talaris, cassacca, pellicium*) was the ordinary dress of the western ecclesiastic, worn beneath the eucharistic as beneath the processional vestments, though in the former case obscured by the alb, as we know was the case with the monastic habit.   It is well seen when worn with the surplice. Intended for warmth, we find it lined with fur (*pellis*), indications of which appear at the wrists on some brasses (*e.g.*, a Priest, *c.* 1520, St. Just-in-Roseland, Cornwall, a broad fur cuff).   Its form was that of a close-fitting garment, open in front, with sleeves. Its colour is usually black, though sometimes red, as in the west window of Cirencester Abbey, Gloucs., or purple for distinction of dignity.[1]   In the same church is a small brass (*c* 1480) representing the cassock with nothing worn over it.   Another instance is afforded by the second son, kneeling, on the brass of Nicholas Gaynesford, Esq., and wife, *c.* 1490, Carshalton, Surrey.   The bracket brass with the figure of John Whytton, 1420, Merton College, Oxford, shows it worn in conjunction with tippet and hood (*see* p. 104).   The tight-fitting buttoned sleeves,

---

[1] Professor E. C. Clark (in his account of English Mediæval Academical Costume in Vol. L., *Archæological Journal*) deals with the question of the significance of the scarlet cassock ; an eminent colour suitable for canons and cardinals ; but originally connected, in his opinion, rather with law than with divinity, though writers usually attribute it to doctors in the latter faculty, whose use of the scarlet gown is well known.   Archbishop Parker, at Morning Prayer on the day of his consecration (December 16th, 1559), wore a *toga talaris coccinea.*

prolonged over the hands, like mittens, seen in some effigies, may possibly be identified with those of the *subtunica*, mentioned by Professor Clark; for, as in the brass of Archdeacon Rothewelle, 1361, they appear to belong to a body-garment worn *under* the cassock.

SURPLICE (*superpellicium*), so named from being worn over the fur-lined cassock, is a loose-fitting vestment of white linen, as a rule unadorned, with long hanging sleeves. Not being of so great a length as the alb, it allows the cassock to appear beneath it, except in some early instances, such as St. Cross, Winchester (John de Campeden, 1382), or Cobham, Kent (Reginald de Cobham, 1402), in which the cassock is hidden by a long surplice. Not open in front, it is passed over the head, like the alb. On brasses it is frequently represented as crimped. Marriott points out [1] that the first mention of a surplice (*superpelliceum*) belongs to the twelfth century, when Stephanus, Bishop of Tournay, sent one to Cardinal Albinus with a sermon, "de mystica superpellicei confectione."

ALMUCE (*almutium, aumusse, amys, amess; muce*, Teutonic for cap or hood, to which is prefixed the Arabic article), originally a hood, worn to protect the head from the cold, the use of which was granted to various monastic, cathedral, and collegiate bodies, and as such appears in the arms of the Chapter of Laon.[2]

---

[1] *Vestiarium Christianum*, 1868, Appendix G., p. 227.

[2] *See* "The Black Scarf of Modern Church Dignitaries and the Grey Almuce of Mediæval Canons," by J. Wickham Legg, F.S.A., *Transactions of St. Paul's Ecclesiological Society*, Vol. III.

On an incised slab in Paris, engraved in Shaw's *Dresses and Decorations*, Vol. I., Iohn D......, Canon of Poitiers, and Chancellor of Noyon, 1350, is shown in *mass* vestments, wearing the almuce as a head covering. It is used as such on two small sepulchral effigies at Bitton, Gloucs., worn with cassock, surplice, and choral cope (illustrated p. 34, Vol. IV., 2nd series, 1878, *Transactions of Exeter Diocesan Architectural Society*, "The

THOMAS BUTTLER, 1494,
GREAT HASELEY, OXON.

This hood was made of dark cloth lined with fur, which in the case of canons and ecclesiastics of dignity was of a grey colour. About the end of the thirteenth century it appears to have assumed a cape form, by being allowed to fall back on the shoulders, whereby the fur lining became outermost, establishing the form of the garment, as the fur cape with a kind of roll-collar, with which we are familiar on brasses of priests in processional vestments. At first open in front and fastened with a morse or strings,[1] it later became closed, so that it had to be passed over the head. In the fourteenth century, we find it with two long pendent ends, hanging down in front, which are well shown on brasses, and must not be mistaken for the stole. One of the earliest brasses in processional vestments is that of Archdeacon Rothewelle, 1361, at Rothwell, Northants, in which the almuce seems to lack the cape-characteristic, so evident in later brasses, especially those in which the cope is not worn, as at Great Haseley, Oxon. (Thomas Butler, 1494) and at Christ Church, Oxford (James Courthope, 1557), in each of which appear the small pendent tails or tufts of the fur attached to the edge of the cape. Frequently the almuce is represented on brasses in a

Prebendal Church of St. Mary Bitton, Gloucestershire," by the Rev. H. T. Ellacombe, M.A., F.S.A." *See* also *Proceedings of the Society of Antiquaries*, Vol. II., 1849, p. 90. Bloxam writes: " In winter the " aumasse was worn as a hood as well as a tippet, and in the representations " of ecclesiastics of canonical rank on French incised monuments, we fre- " quently find the aumasse used as a hood, and worn on the head, but " in monumental brasses in this country we rarely find it otherwise than " . . . covering the shoulders and breast. In the fifth provincial " Council of Milan, held A.D. 1579, the aumasse is declared to be peculiar " to those of canonical rank, ' Almutia pellicea insigne canonicorum est.' " *Midland Counties' Herald*, Thursday, March 5th, 1846.

[1] The former can be seen at Cobham, Kent, William Tannere, 1418; the latter in sculptured figures of canons of the fifteenth century at Wells, and on the brass of Eberard de Rabenstain, 1505, at Bamberg (figured by Creeny).

white metal, engraved to resemble fur; the ends of the long pendants, unlike those of the stole, being of a rounded shape, though at Mawgan-in-Pydar, Cornwall, *c.* 1420, they are squared. In a few brasses, where the cope is seen, the almuce is omitted: (*e.g.*, 1438, John Lovelle, St. George's, Canterbury; 1458, William Kyrkeby, Theydon Gernon, Essex; *c.* 1460, a Priest, Temple Church, Bristol; 1508, Henry Wykys, All Saints', Stamford, Lincs; 1541, Thomas Dalyson, LL.B., Clothal, Herts; *d.* 1559, Bishop John White, Winchester College.)

COPE (*cappa, pluviale,* μανδύας). The necessity of protection from the weather in open-air processions at Rome[1] probably gave rise to the use of this vestment.[2] It is a large outer cloak, sleeveless, of semi-circular shape, worn over the surplice and almuce, and fastened in front by a brooch, called a *morse.* Originally a hood (*caputium,* diminutive of *cappa*) was attached to it, which could be drawn over the head; but when the cope became a costly vestment, made of silk (*cappa serica*) and cloth of gold, etc., and worn in church by high ecclesiastics, its use disappeared,[3] and in its place a flap was worn, which lent itself to the most elaborate embroidery. This flap is very rarely met with on brasses. The following are four examples:—

    1413.   William Langeton, canon, Exeter Cathedral (kneeling sideways).

    c. 1520.   A Priest, St. Just-in-Roseland, Cornwall (a plain cope).

---

[1] On the shape of the cope, resembling that of the ancient chasuble but for being cut up the front, see *The Chasuble; its Genuine Form and Size,* by Father William Lockhart, B.A., 1891.

[2] Its ancestor was, probably, the Roman *lacerna.*

[3] The use of the almuce may have rendered the hood of the cope unnecessary. Just as, later, the almuce was superseded by a cap as a head-covering, itself becoming a cape.

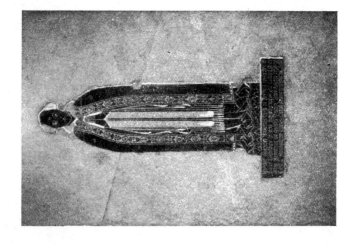

WALTER HYLL, M.A., S.T.S.,

WARDEN (1494), NEW COLLEGE, OXFORD.

RICHARD MALFORD,

WARDEN (1403), NEW COLLEGE, OXFORD.

1530.   Adam Graffton, Withington, Salop.
1550.   Thomas Magnus, archdeacon, Sessay, York-
         shire.

Hoods appear in a few instances on plain copes,
which, in all probability, form part either of the
monastic habit as at Dorchester, Oxon., 1510, or of
academical costume, as at All Souls, Oxford, 1461.
Along the straight sides of the cope, and sometimes,
to a less extent, as a border round the edge, are
placed orphreys of different degrees of richness; and
in some few cases the whole cope is represented as
richly worked, *e.g.* :—

1414.   Simon Bache, Knebworth, Herts.
1450.   Robert Thurbern, Winchester College,
         warden.[1]
1462.   John Blodwell, Balsham, Cambs.
1472.   Thomas Tonge, Beeford, Yorks.
1518.   Dr. Robert Langton, Queen's College,
         Oxford.
c. 1520. A Priest, Dowdeswell, Gloucs. (embroi-
         dered with *fleurs de lis* in lozenges, as is
         Langton's cope).
1529.   Edmund Frowsetoure, S.T.P., Dean, Here-
         ford Cathedral.
c. 1548. Bishop John White, warden, Winchester
         College (*d.* 1559).

But, as a rule, only the orphreys appear embroidered.
In the decoration of the cope, unlike that of the
chasuble, personal devices are not infrequently found.
At Fulbourn, Cambs., the cope of William de
Fulburne, 1391, bears the initials W.F.; at New
College, the orphrey on the cope of Richard Malford,
warden, 1403, has the initials R.M.; that of Walter
Hyll, warden, 1494, the letters W.H.   At Treding-
ton, Worcs., the orphrey on the cope of Richard

[1] With initials R.T. on orphreys and ihc on morse.

Cassey, Canon of York, 1427, "Inceptor legum," bears the initials R.C.; that of Thomas Mordon, 1458, at Fladbury, in the same county, the initials T.M.; that at Broadwater, Sussex (John Mapilton, 1432), has the letter M. and maple leaves. The name of "*Thomas Patesley*" is worked on the orphrey and morse of a cope at Great Shelford, Cambs., 1418. An instance of heraldic ornament on orphreys is furnished by the garbs on the brass of Thomas Aileward, at Havant, Hants, 1413.[1] An adaptation from Job xix. 25-26 is seen on the cope of William Prestwyk, 1436, Warbleton, Sussex. Figures of apostles or saints occur on the orphreys at Balsham, Cambs.; Castle Ashby, Northants; Bottesford, Leics.; Knebworth, Herts; Ringwood, Hants; Harrow, Middlesex; and Merton College, Oxford, all of the fifteenth century.

The *morse* is sometimes decorated with the contraction I$\overline{\text{H}}$S or I$\overline{\text{H}}$C (as at Winchester College, *c*. 1548, Bishop John White, where I$\overline{\text{H}}$S appears within a circle). The word "IESUS" occurs on that of the Magnus brass, 1550, at Sessay, Yorkshire. Heraldic morses are found at Castle Ashby, Northants, William Ermyn, rector, 1401 (ermine, a saltire gules; on a chief of the last a lion passant gardant or), and at Fulbourn, Cambs., William de Fulburne, 1391 (argent, a saltire sable between four martlets

---

[1] It is always well to obtain corroborative evidence before stating positively that such heraldic decorations represent the family bearings of the person commemorated. For, although such an assumption may be justifiable, as a rule, in the case of sepulchral monuments, this is by no means always the case with vestments, extant or mentioned in inventories, as concerning the donors. In the Havant brass the arms are probably those of the deceased: but an instance occurs at Flamstead, Herts, of the Beauchamp arms on the brass of John Oudeby, rector, *d.* 1454, who was canon of the collegiate church of Warwick, and chamberlain of the royal treasury for the Earl of Warwick. The arms of Thomas Arundel, Archbishop of Canterbury, are found on the brass of John Byrkhede, 1468, at Harrow.

gules). Sometimes the morse contains the initials of the deceased, as on the Aileward brass mentioned above. Sometimes the *Vernicle* or face of Christ is represented, as at Knebworth, Herts, Simon Bache, 1414, or at Tattershall, Lincs, *c.* 1510, or an emblem of the Trinity, as at Bottesford, Leics. (Henry de Codyngtoun, 1404). At Dowdeswell, Gloucs., *c.* 1520, the *rose-en-soleil* is seen.

CHORAL COPE.—The cope of dignity described above (*cappa serica*) must not be confused with the choral cope (*cappa nigra*) of plain cloth with a hood, but without ornament, worn in choir by canons and monks, or by the cantores, as at Westminster. Possibly the cope of Archdeacon Rothewelle, at Rothwell, Northants, 1361, may be a slightly ornamental form of this garment. Quite plain ones may be seen at Watton, Herts (an Ecclesiastic, *c.* 1380);[1] at Arundel, Sussex (Adam D'Ertham, 1382, half effigy); at Cottingham, Yorkshire (Nicholas de Louth, 1383); at St. Andrew's, Auckland, Durham (a Priest, *c.* 1400, whose cope is gathered about the shoulders, similarly to the mantle of the Garter, mentioned below); at Shillington, Beds (Thomas Portyngton, 1485); at Bampton, Oxon. (Robert Holcot, M.A., 1500); and at St. Just-in-Roseland, Cornwall (a Priest, *c.* 1520). The brass of Archdeacon Philip Polton, 1461, at All Souls' College, Oxford, may furnish an academical example. The monastic cope, as seen at South Creak, Norfolk (John Norton, 1509), and Dorchester, Oxon. (Richard Bewfforeste, 1510), is probably identical with the choral cope. As a rule, on brasses angels are represented in amice and alb, but on the Thornton Flemish brass (1429) at Newcastle, those supporting the cushions appear to wear choral copes; a like

---

[1] His feet rest on a lion couchant gardant. This is unusual. The feet of Mathew de Asscheton, 1400, Shillington, Beds, in processional vestments, rest on a dog.

garment is worn over the alb by the Archangel Gabriel on the brass of George Rede, rector, *c.* 1492, at Fovant, Wilts.

The MANTLE OF THE GARTER.—Three brasses remain of canons of St. George's, Windsor, wearing the mantle of the Order of the Garter,[1] which was of a purple colour, with a circular badge on the left shoulder, bearing argent, a cross gules :—

1. *c.* 1370.   Roger Parkers, North Stoke, Oxon. (half effigy with inscription; head lost).

2.   1540.   Roger Lupton, LL.D., Provost of Eton and Canon of Windsor, Eton College Chapel (mantle worn over fur-lined cassock; no surplice).

3.   1558.   Arthur Cole, S.T.B., President of Magdalen, at Magdalen College, Oxford, showing a very ornate almuce, worn over cassock and surplice.

The long cords which fasten the mantle are well represented at North Stoke and Magdalen College. On the Eton brass the mantle is fastened by a small morse, and in the two later examples it is gathered at the neck.

The lost effigy of John Robyns, *d.* 1558, of which the inscription remains in St. George's Chapel, Windsor, may have shown him wearing the mantle

---

[1] *See* "Brasses of Canons of Windsor," by the Rev. J. E. Field, *The Antiquary*, Vol. XV., 1887.   For military examples, *see* Ch. III.   Brasses of canons of Windsor are found vested in copes, without the Garter badge, as at Thurcaston, Leics. (John Mershden, 1425), and at Harrow (Simon Marcheford, 1442).   A brass was discovered in 1890 at Bennington, near Stevenage, Herts, showing a small mutilated effigy of a priest in a cope with a round badge (? a rose) on the left shoulder.   The cope has an orphrey.   This has been supposed to represent a canon of Windsor.   See *Transactions of the Cambridge University Association of Brass Collectors*, Vol. II., p. 24.

HENRY SEVER, S.T.P., 1471,
WARDEN, MERTON COLLEGE, OXFORD.

of the Order.   The effigy of William Boutrod (1522),
" Pety-canon of Windsor" at Eton, is vested in a
cope.

The following are good instances, showing the Processional Vestments.

(The brasses marked x have the orphreys of the cope
      embroidered with figures of saints.)

c. 1361.	William de Rothewelle, Archdeacon of Essex, Rothwell, Northants.
1382.	John de Campeden, St. Cross, Winchester, Hants.
1391.	William de Fulburne, Fulbourn, Cambs.
x *c.* 1400.	A priest, Boston, Lincs. ? John Strensall.
x 1401.	John de Sleford, Balsham, Cambs.
x 1401.	William Ermyn, Castle Ashby, Northants.
1402.	Reginald de Cobham, Cobham, Kent, on bracket.
x 1404.	Henry de Codyngtoun, Bottesford, Leics.
1413.	Thomas Aileward, Havant, Hants.
x 1414.	Simon Bache, Knebworth, Herts.
x 1416.	John Prophete, Ringwood, Hants.
1420.	Robert Wyntryngham, Cotterstock, Northants, on bracket.
1432.	John Mapilton, Broadwater, Sussex.
1436.	William Prestwyk, Warbleton, Sussex.
1450.	Robert Thurbern, Winchester College.
1454.	Robert Arthur, Chartham, Kent.
x 1462.	John Blodwell, Balsham, Cambs.
1464.	John Heth, Tintinhull, Somerset.
x 1468.	John Byrkhed, Harrow, Middlesex.
x 1471.	Henry Sever, Merton College, Oxford.
1498.	James Hert, Hitchin, Herts.
c. 1510.	Richard Wylleys, Higham Ferrers, Northants.
x *c.* 1510.	Walter Hewke, Trinity Hall, Cambridge.
x *c.* 1510.	A Provost, Tattershall, Lincs.
1518.	Robert Langton, Queen's College, Oxford.

1529. Edmund Frowsetoure, S. T. P., Hereford Cathedral.

1530. Adam Graffton, Withington, Salop.

1535. Warin Penhalluryk, Wendron, Cornwall (head lost).

1550. Thomas Magnus, archdeacon, Sessay, Yorkshire.

The following show the processional vestments *without* the cope, thereby fully exposing the almuce [1]:—

1413. John Morys, warden, Winchester College.

1418. William Tannere, Cobham, Kent (half eff.).

1419. William White, Arundel, Sussex.

1458. John Huntington, Manchester Cathedral.

1471. A son on the brass of Roger Kyngdon, Quethiock, Cornwall.[2]

1480. A Priest, Billingham, Durham.

1482. Henry Sampson, Tredington, Worcs.

1489. Thomas Teylar, Byfleet, Surrey.

1494. Thomas Buttler, Great Haseley, Oxon.

1508. Edmund Croston, St. Mary the Virgin, Oxford, kneeling before St. Katherine.

1508. Robert Sheffelde, M.A., Chartham, Kent.

1510. Ralph Elcok, Tong, Salop.

1514. John Fynexs, Archdeacon of Sudbury, Bury St. Edmunds, Suffolk.

1515. William Goberd, Magdalen College, Oxford.

---

[1] Possibly in some cases the almuce was worn over the surplice in summer, as a substitute for the cope, assumed in winter. *See* Du Cange, *Glossarium ad Scriptores mediæ et infimæ Latinitatis.* Frankfurt, 1710 (Vol. I., p. 158, Column 2, voc. ALMUCIUM) :—" Statuta Ecclesiæ Viennensis apud " Joan. Le Lievre, cap. 26 de Canonicis : A festo S. Martini usque ad " Pascha portabunt capas nigras supra pellicium, et a Pascha usque ad "festum omnium SS. portabunt superpellicium sine capa, et in capite " capellum de griso, quem vulgariter almuciam vocant."

[2] Other examples of children on brasses of parents in this costume are:—
  1487. Eldest son on brass of John Lambarde, Hinxworth, Herts.
  c. 1530. Son on brass of Richard Bulkley, Beaumaris, Anglesea.

ROBERT HACOMBLEYN, 1528,
KING'S COLLEGE, CAMBRIDGE.

1522. Richard Adams, East Malling, Kent.
1528. Robert Hacombleyn, King's College, Cambridge.
1528. Robert Sutton, Dean, St. Patrick's Cathedral,
        Dublin, kneeling.
1532. John Moore, M.A., Sibson, Leics.
1537. Geoffrey Fyche, Dean, St. Patrick's Cathedral,
        Dublin, kneeling.
1557. James Courthop, Christ Church, Oxford.
1558. Robert Brassie, King's College, Cambridge.

MONASTIC ORDERS (*Male*).

The scarcity of brasses of the Monastic Orders may be
accounted for either by the destruction of religious houses,
or by the comparative poverty of the monk. The memorials of mitred abbots show them, as a rule, in their
pontificals, similar to those of the bishops, described above.
Foremost among such is the Flemish brass of Abbot
Delamere, *c.* 1360, at St. Albans, in which church may be
seen a palimpsest, the obverse of which shows the lower
part of an abbot, *c.* 1490, similarly vested. The fragment
in the British Museum, *c.* 1350, has been already referred
to in the account of Flemish brasses, p. 48. At Westminster Abbey is the brass of Abbot Estney, 1498, and
at Burwell, Cambs, the reverse of the brass of Abbot
Laurence de Wardeboys of Ramsey, shows the pontificalia, whilst the obverse gives him in processional vestments, cassock, surplice, and almuce.[1] These brasses,
showing vestments similar to those of a bishop, do not
illustrate the monastic habit; but at Dorchester, Oxon.

---

[1] A brass to Hugo Price, Abbot of Conway, 1528, in cope with crozier
on right arm, formerly existed in Saffron Walden Church, Essex. *See*
illustration from Cole's MSS. in the British Museum, in *Transactions of
Essex Archæological Society*, N.S., Vol. VI. At Wendon Lofts, Essex, the
first son on the brass of William Lucas and wife, *c.* 1460, is clad in pontificalia, and has been supposed to represent John Lucas, Abbot of Waltham,
who died 1475. His right hand is raised in benediction; his left holds
a pastoral staff.

(Austin or Black Canons) is the brass of Richard Bewfforeste, *c.* 1510, wearing over the processional vestments,
instead of the orphreyed cope, a plain cope-like pallium or
cloak with a hood, and having a pastoral staff on the right
arm; a similar brass is that of John Norton, 1509, at
South Creak, Norfolk.   At Fountains Abbey, Yorkshire,
is the indent of a brass [1] of an abbot, described by Mr.
W. H. St. John Hope as wearing the Cistercian tunic and
cowl with a pastoral staff on the right arm, and a detached
mitre.   The matrix of the brass of Abbot Godfrey de
Croyland, 1329, at Peterborough, shows the indent of a
crozier, leaning on the right shoulder.   At Dorchester,
Oxon, there is a slab, commemorating John Sutton, Abbot,
c. 1349, containing the indent of a forearm with the hand
grasping a crozier.[2]   At Tilty, Essex, is an inscription to
Thomas of Takeley, Abbot of Tilty, *c.* 1450.

The earliest monastic habit was the Benedictine, consisting of a *tunica* or cassock, over which was worn
the *cucullus* or cowl, a large loose gown with hanging
sleeves and with a hood attached to it (*see* the plate
in Dugdale's *Monasticon*).   Examples of this habit
occur at St. Laurence's, Norwich (Geoffrey Langley,
d. 1437, prior of the Benedictine monastery of St. Faith
the Virgin, at Horsham, near Norwich), and at St. Albans'
Abbey (a half effigy of a monk, fifteenth century;
a monk, according to Haines, Reginald Bernewelt, 1443;
Robert Beauner, who held various offices in the Abbey,
c. 1460; and Thomas Rutland, sub-prior, 1521).   A
modern restored example is in Ely Cathedral (John de
Crauden or Crowden, prior, *d.* 1341).   The finest example
of a similar habit is that of Thomas Nelond, Prior of the
Clugniac Abbey of St. Pancras at Lewes, *d.* 1429, in

---

[1] Figured in Mr. Mill Stephenson's " Monumental Brasses in the West
Riding," in the *Yorkshire Archæological Journal*, Vol. XV.

[2] Engraved in Gough's *Sepulchral Monuments*, Vol. I., p. 101, and in
Haines, p. lvii.   Matrices of brasses of abbots are at Waltham, Byland,
Milton Abbas, etc.

ABBOT RICHARD BEWFFORESTE, *c.* 1510,
DORCHESTER, OXON.

MARTIN FORESTER, c. 1460.

On the Lectern, Yeovil, Somerset.

Cowfold Church, Sussex.[1] At Norbury, Derbyshire, the palimpsest brass of Sir Anthony Fitzherbert, 1538, and lady, shows on the reverse of the inscription part of the figure of a prior in cassock and cowl, *c.* 1440.

The Canons Regular of St. Augustine wore over a cassock a white rochet, girded, with close-fitting sleeves, and a plain cope or cloak with a hood. A good example occurs at Over Winchendon, Bucks, 1515 (John Stodeley, Canon of St. Frideswide's, Oxford).[2] Two palimpsest brasses show reverses of the fifteenth century, representing monastic attire[3] :—A bust at Halvergate, Norfolk, "ffrater Willm͞s Jernemu......" (Yarmouth); and at Denham, Bucks, John Pyke, wearing a gown with loose sleeves concealing the hands, girded with a knotted cord, hanging down in front; over this a tippet and hood covering the shoulders, similar to the Halvergate brass. The birch represented in saltire with a baton[4] on a shield may indicate a scholastic occupation for the deceased.

[1] The remains of the canopy of Abbot John Stoke, *d.* 1451, at St. Albans, show similar work and arrangement to that of Nelond. On the brass lectern in Yeovil Church, Somerset, is a figure of a monk (Frat^r Martin' Forester, *c.* 1460) habited in girded gown and hood ; illustrated in *Somerset and Dorset Notes and Queries*, Vol. IX., 1905, p. 71, "The Lectern, Yeovil Church," by W. H. H. Rogers. At Totternhoe, Beds, is a fifteenth century inscription for " Ffr Thom͞s greve q͞od͞a p'or isti' loci " ; another is at Boxgrove, Sussex, John Rykeman, " Monachi istius loci."

[2] At Warter Priory, Yorkshire (Augustinian), is the incised slab of Thomas Bridlington, 25th Prior, 1498, representing him in cassock, rochet, and *capa pluvialis* with hood. This is illustrated in *Proceedings of the Society of Antiquaries*, Vol. XVIII., 1900, p. 57, in "Account of Excavations lately carried out at Warter Priory, Yorks, by W. H. St. John Hope, M.A.," who writes : "Effigies of Black Canons similarly vested, "but with the hoods of their cloaks drawn over the head, occur at "Cartmel and Hexham. Brasses of Black Canons occur at Dorchester "(Oxon), and South Creak (Norfolk), both abbots, and at Over-Win- "chendon (Bucks). One of a prior was formerly at Royston, Herts, but " is now lost ; the Society fortunately possesses a rubbing." The Warter slab is illustrated in *Transactions of the East Riding Antiquarian Society*, Vol. VIII., 1900, p. 48, in paper by the same author.

[3] Each is engraved in *Transactions of Monumental Brass Society*, Vol. IV.

[4] This may be a ferule. See *Archæologia Cambrensis*, IV. Series, Vol. XII., 1881, on a scholastic ferule found in Melverley Church.

MONASTIC ORDERS (*Female*).

The costume of abbesses and their subordinates resembled the mourning habit of widows, who, as is well known, often retired to end their days in a convent.[1]

Abbesses are represented by but two existing examples:—

1. Elizabeth Hervey, elected Abbess of Elstow (Benedictine) in 1520, at Elstow, Beds.

2. Agnes Jordan, Abbess of the Bridgetine Convent of Syon, 1544, at Denham, Bucks.

The latter wears a long gown or cowl, bound at the waist by a girdle, with loose sleeves, beneath which appear the tight-fitting sleeves of the undergarment; a *barbe* or chin-cloth; a cope-like mantle, and a veil: rings are shown on some of her fingers, the largest appearing on the first finger of the right hand. The Elstow Abbess' costume differs from this in having a *plaited* barbe, and on the right arm a pastoral staff; the sleeves of the gown, which is ungirded, are looser; there is no ring.

There remain a few representations of nuns on brasses. The three following are members of the Order of Vowesses, *i.e.*, widows who have vowed never to remarry: Dame Iuliana Anyell, *c.* 1500, "votricis," Witton (Blofield), Norfolk; Dn̄a Johanna Braham, 1519, "vidua ac deo dicata,"[2] Frenze, Norfolk; Dame Susan Kyngeston, "vowess," 1540, Shalston, Bucks.

At Nether Wallop, Hants, is the brass of Maria Gore, Prioress, 1436.[3] At Dagenham, Essex, on the brass of

---

[1] *See* "Widows and Vowesses," by J. L. André, F.S.A., *Archæological Journal*, Vol. XLIX., p. 69.

[2] Her mantle has long cords, and she wears a strap-like girdle.

[3] In *Somerset and Dorset Notes and Queries*, Vol. III., 1893, p. 55, the Rev. C. H. Mayo gives the will of Elizabeth Martyn, 1584, last Prioress of Wyntney, Hants. She desires to be buried in Hartly Wintney Church. "I would that a stone should be layde over my graue wth a "picture made of a plate of a woman in a longe garment wth wyde "sleves her handes joyned together," etc.

Sir Thomas Urswyk and lady (1470), the eldest daughter is habited as a nun; as is one of the daughters, probably Cecily, on the brass of Thomas and Agnes Mountford, 1489, at Hornby, Yorkshire; and the third daughter, kneeling, on the brass of Sir Thomas Barnardiston, 1503, Great Cotes, Lincs.[1]   At Minchinhampton, Gloucs., the small figure of Dame Alice Hampton, probably a Syon nun,[2] c. 1510 (represented as a child on the brass of John Hampton, gent, 1556, and wife), has a rosary hanging from a girdle and a ring on the third finger of the right hand.   The mantle is lacking in the effigy of Margaret Dely, 1561, Treasurer of Syon, at Isleworth, Middlesex; which peculiarity is shared by one of the children on the reverse of the palimpsest brass of Nicholas Suttherton (1540), c. 1460, at St. John Maddermarket, Norwich. At St. Mary's, Kilburn, is a fragment, considered c. 1380, showing the head of a nun, which was found on the site of the Priory.   The wimple or barbe, in this instance, seems to be attached to the veil by a short string.

A Note on the Chalice-brass.

The Chalice, with or without the Wafer or Host is frequently found, either alone with an inscription, as a memorial for a priest, or held in his hands, when shown in mass vestments.   The representation of this symbol on ecclesiastical monuments fell into disuse at the Reformation, but has been revived in the nineteenth century. For convenience sake we may treat of this class of brass in two divisions :—

1. The chalice with or without the wafer, with an inscription, but no effigy.

2. Effigies supporting the chalice, with or without the wafer.

---

[1] The two daughters of Margaret Hyklott, whose effigy is lost (probably wife of William Hyklott), 1502, Althorne, Essex, may be additional examples.

[2] On the same brass her eldest brother is shown as a monk.

1. Norfolk possesses the greater number of these brasses, mostly of the sixteenth century; but in Yorkshire are four examples of the fifteenth century, consisting of chalices without wafers, and with inscriptions. These are :—

1429. Richard Kendale, M.A., rector, Ripley, West Yorks.
1460. Peter Johnson, vicar, Bishop Burton, East Yorks.
1466. William Langton, rector, St. Michael Spurrier-gate, York.
1469. Thomas Clarell, vicar, St. Peter's, Leeds.

Examples of the sixteenth century (chalice with wafer :—

1502. Richard Grene, rector, Hedenham, Norfolk.
1508. Robert Northen, vicar, Buxton, Norfolk.
1515. Robert Wodehowse, rector, Holwell, Beds (accompanied by two woodhowses or wild men).
c. 1520. Robert Wythe, chaplain, North Walsham, Norfolk.
c. 1525. Geo. Cunynggam, vicar, Attlebridge, Norfolk.
1540. William Curtes, South Burlingham, Norfolk.

At Bawburgh, Norfolk, is a chalice with wafer (William Richers, vicar, 1531), in which the chalice is upheld by two hands, of which the thumbs only are seen, issuing from clouds. A similar brass is at Little Walsingham (William Weststow, c. 1520), in the same county. At Blockley, Worcs., the brass of Philip Warthim, M.A., vicar, 1488, shows him in cassock, tippet, and hood, kneeling beside a chalice incised in the slab. At Aldbourne, Wilts, Henry Frekylton, chaplain, 1508, in mass vestments, lies beside a chalice, the bowl of which is lost. At Fishlake, in the West Riding, was formerly the brass of Richard Marshall, vicar, 1505, having the chalice with wafer, shown on each side of his effigy. Above the effigy of Sir Arthur Vernon, M.A., 1507, at Tong, Salop (*see*

JOHN FRYE, S.T.S, 1507,
NEW COLLEGE. OXFORD.

CHALICE BRASS—WILLIAM WESTSTOW, c. 1520,
LITTLE WALSINGHAM, NORFOLK.

p. 136) is a chalice with wafer. A chalice and missal are shown on the altar, before which St. Gregory kneels, in the brass of Roger Legh and wife, 1506, at Macclesfield, Cheshire.

2. Examples of the second division (in mass vestments).

(a) Without Wafer.

c. 1400.	A Priest, Stanford-on-Soar, Notts.
1429.	Roger Godeale, Bainton, E. Yorks.
c. 1470.	A Priest, Broxbourne, Herts.
1531.	John ap Meredyth, Bettws, Montgomeryshire.

(b) With Wafer.

1461.	Robert Lond, St. Peter's, Bristol.
1498.	Henry Denton, Higham Ferrers, Northants.
1504.	Alexander Inglisshe, Campsey Ash, Suffolk.
1507.	John Frye, S.T.S. Fellow, New College, Oxford, (half eff.).
1507.	John Scolffyld, Brightwell, Berks.
c. 1510.	A Priest, Littlebury, Essex.
1512.	William Bisshop, Wiveton, Norfolk.
1521.	Radulph Babyngton, Hickling, Notts.
1531.	John Athowe, Brisley, Norfolk.
1531.	Richard Bennett, M.A., Whitnash, Warwickshire.
1535.	Thomas Westeley, Wyvenhoe, Essex.

The Chalice is shown on the two Flemish brasses, c. 1360, at Wensley, Yorks, and North Mimms, Herts, (see p. 49) lying on the breast, in the former case above, in the latter below the hands. At Walton-on-Trent, Derbyshire, a priest, c. 1490, with Chalice and Host, is represented in the act of blessing them. Another instance, c. 1520, is supposed to have come from the dismantled chapel of North Weston, Oxon.[1]

---

[1] See illustration, p. 85, Vol. II., No. 2, December, 1900, *Journal of O.U.B.R.S.*

In the cope, worn with amice, there is one instance :—

1478. William Langley, rector, Buckland, Herts.
       (chalice with wafer).

In processional vestments without the cope :—

1522. Richard Adams, vicar, East Malling, Kent.[1]
       (chalice with wafer).

In academicals :—

c. 1480. A Priest, with a chalice, Barking, Essex.

1518. Thomas Coly, Bredgar, Kent (chalice with
       wafer).

1519. John Bowke, M.A., Merton College, Oxford.
       (chalice with wafer), half-eff.

John Yslyngton, S.T.P., c. 1520, Cley-next-the-Sea,
Norfolk, of whose costume we treat below, wearing
apparently a scarf over a fur-lined cassock, and a cap, holds
a chalice with wafer.

The chalices differ considerably in shape and size, and
sometimes have feet (e.g., 1500, William Abell, Coleshill,
Warwickshire; 1522, Edmund Assheton, Middleton,
Lancs., each in mass vestments).

The wafers are usually engraved, either with $\overline{ihs}$, as in
the two brasses just mentioned, or on that at Littlebury,
Essex, c. 1510; or $\overline{ihc}$, as at Tong, Salop, 1507, and
Brisley, Norfolk, 1531, each of which wafers is rayed; or
on that of Dr. Yslyngton, c. 1520, mentioned above;[2] or
with a cross-crosslet as at Higham Ferrers, Northants,
1498; Campsey Ash, Suffolk, 1504; East Malling, Kent,
1522; or Wyvenhoe, Essex, 1535. An instance of a plain
wafer[3] occurs on the brass of John Stokys, Rector, 1500,
Wimington, Beds.

---

[1] Prebendary "magne misse" in the monastery of West Malling.

[2] The wafer at Holwell, Beds, 1515, has in addition to IHC a small
spray of foliage.

[3] *The First Prayer Book of Edward VI.*, 1549, directs that the wafers be
"unleavened and round, as it was afore, but without all manner of print" :
the Injunctions of Queen Elizabeth, 1559, direct that the sacramental

ECCLESIASTIC ? 1372,
MERTON COLLEGE, OXFORD.

Before considering the dress of post-reformation ecclesiastics, a small class of brasses claims our attention. These show neither the mass nor processional vestments, and it is doubtful whether the garments bear any academical significance. Probably they represent the *habitus clericalis* worn when out of church, the chief characteristic of which was the cassock (*vestis talaris*). By the time when any such costume is met with in brasses, the *habit* seems to have become firmly established, though there appears to have been some difficulty in making it so in the thirteenth century, when the laity was shocked "de habitu clericorum, qui non clericalis videtur, sed potius militaris."[1] A possible early instance of a clerical habit may be afforded by the small brass, in the head of a cross at Merton College, Oxford, representing a tonsured figure, ?1372; though this may be an early instance of academicals.[2] At Cardynham, Cornwall, is the brass of Thomas Awmarle, rector, *c.* 1400 (figured in Dunkin), showing the tonsure and clad in a girded cassock, having twelve buttons, in pairs below

---

bread, which is to be similar to wafers or singing cakes, "be made and "formed plain, without any figure thereupon." See *Hierurgia Anglicana*, New Ed., Part II., 1903, pp. 129, 130.

[1] See "The Ecclesiastical Habit in England," by the Rev. T. A. Lacey, M.A., in *Transactions of the St. Paul's Ecclesiological Society*, Vol. IV., 1900, p. 126, wherein evidence is produced of the wearing of the clerical habit, cassock and gown, down to the nineteenth century; the latter is considered a modification of the *cappa clausa*. See *The Constitutions of Cardinal Otho*, 1237, XIV. "De habitu clericorum. Quoniam de habitu clericorum, "qui non clericalis videtur, sed potius militaris, grave scandalum laicis "generatur." Wilkins' *Concilia*, Vol. I., 1737, p. 652.

[2] But *see* account of fourteenth century civilian costume, Chap. IV. The Merton effigy wears a garment much like the longer *cote-hardie* worn by Nichole de Aumberdene, Taplow, Bucks, *c.* 1350, though without liripipes, but with lappets or bands at the neck, not unlike those of Thomas Rolf, S.L., 1440, Gosfield, Essex, where they are probably connected with the Coif (*see* Chap. V.). In Paul Lacroix's *Manners, Customs, and Dress during the Middle Ages, and during the Renaissance Period*, London, 1874, will be found similar lappets from *Fourteenth Century MS.* p. 6, and of *Fifteenth Century*, p. 370.

the waist, an anelace (*see* Chap. IV.) hanging from the girdle on the left side.

In a few instances, in some of which we find a figure kneeling before a saint, the cassock is worn supplemented by tippet and hood. In the absence of information establishing the degrees of the persons so represented, it would be unsafe to call this costume academical; at the same time it seems probable that some connection exists between the two. We find, however (*see* pp. 139-40), two instances of LL.B., wearing this dress (1) at Great St. Helen's, Bishopsgate, 1482, and (2) at All Souls' College, Oxford, 1490. Other examples are as follows :—

1405.   Magister John Strete, Upper Hardres, Kent, kneeling at the base of a bracket on which stand SS. Peter and Paul. He wears a pointed pileus, (*see* p. 128).[1]

c. 1410.   A Priest, Aspley Guise, Beds, kneeling on the dexter side of a cross (lost); on the sinister side of which stands St. John Baptist.

c. 1410.   Sir William Calwe, Ledbury, Herefordshire, kneeling before an effigy (lost) of St. Peter.

1420.   John Whytton, Merton College, Oxford, standing on a bracket.

1422.   John Lewys, rector, Quainton, Bucks, kneeling.

c. 1430.   A Priest, Melton, Suffolk, standing.

c. 1450.   Half Effigy, Harrow, Middlesex (?Robert Kyrkeham).

1474.   John Child, M.A., rector, Cheriton, Kent, standing.

c. 1480.   A Priest, Strethall, Essex, standing.

c. 1485.   The eldest son, kneeling, Clavering, Essex,

---

[1] The matrix of a similar figure, probably without pileus, is at Wotton-under-Edge, Gloucs, (Richard de Wotton, rector, *c.* 1320). A brass lost from Cirencester, Gloucs., probably John Avenyng and wife, *c.* 1500, showing the second son kneeling behind his father in cassock, tippet and hood, is illustrated, p. 209, *The Monumental Brasses of Gloucestershire*, by Cecil T. Davis, London, 1899.

JOHN YSLYNGTON, S.T.P., c. 1520,
CLEY-NEXT-THE-SEA, NORFOLK.

WILLIAM GEDDYNG? 1512,
WANTAGE, BERKS.

(part of the brass of — Songar, civilian, and wife, much mutilated).[1]

1488. Philip Warthim, M.A., vicar, (see p. 138), Blockley, Worcs, kneeling.

1489. Henry Mountford, "clericus," standing, Hornby, N. Riding ; one of the group of sons on the brass of Thomas and Agnes Mountford.

c. 1492. George Rede, rector, Fovant, Wilts, kneeling before a representation of the Annunciation, with his beads on his left arm.   Here we have no hood, and the tippet seems closely related to the scarf-like garment, about to be described.

? 1512. William Geddyng? vicar, Wantage, Berks, standing.

In a few brasses of the first quarter of the sixteenth century we find a curious short scarf (fastened to one shoulder by a rosette, and passed behind the neck on to the other), replacing the tippet and hood, above mentioned: though it would be difficult to tell whether it were a modification of either one or of both of them.   It seems to be more closely connected with the tippet, and may possibly be a form of almuce, though the latter was still in use.[2] An early stage in the development of this scarf is illustrated by the brass of an ecclesiastic (c. 1500, at North Creak,

---

[1] Another instance may have been at Crishall, in the same county, c. 1530, see *Transactions of the Essex Archæological Society*, New Series, Vol. VIII., 1903 : "Some interesting Essex Brasses," by Miller Christy and W. W. Porteous, pp. 15-54.

[2] In Seroux d'Agincourt's *Histoire de l'Art par les Monumens*, 1823, (Peinture, Planche CXLVII.) is an engraving after Masaccio (Fifteenth Century), showing a church dignitary standing behind a kneeling bishop, and wearing a cap, a gown with two slits for the arms, and a scarf, fastened to the right and passed round the neck on to the left shoulder.

In *The Reliquary and Illustrated Archæologist*, Vol. VII., 1901, p. 39, are reproduced two paintings on Norfolk rood-screens, showing John Schorne, at Cawston, clad in cassock, tippet, hood and pileus ; but at Gateley, wearing the scarf-like tippet of which we are treating.   *See the*

Norfolk, supporting a model of a church on his right arm), who wears a cassock, from the girdle of which hang his purse and beads, and round the neck a scarf, the ends of which are fastened together in front by a button, giving a cape-like appearance to the garment. Another probable example represents William Warham, afterwards Arch-bishop of Canterbury, and buried there in 1532, the eldest of four sons shown standing on the brass of Robert and Elizabeth Warham, 1487, at Church Oakley, Hants. In other examples the extremities are not fastened together, but the scarf is usually attached by one end to the left shoulder, the other end lying loose on the right shoulder.

Examples :—[1]

1501.   The second of thirteen sons on the brass of Robert and Elizabeth Baynard, Laycock, Wilts, with rosary.

1503.   The second son, kneeling, on brass of Sir Thomas Barnardiston, Great Cotes, Lincs.

1510.   William Smyght, Ashby St. Legers, Northants (head lost).

1518.   Richard Bethell, Shorwell, Isle of Wight.

c. 1520.   One of four sons, kneeling, Worlingworth, Suffolk (parents and inscription lost).

c. 1520.   John Yslyngton, S.T.P., Cley-next-the-sea, Norfolk, wears besides the scarf,[2] a fur-lined cassock, turned back towards the feet, and a

---

paper *John Schorne, a Mediæval Worthy*, by T. Hugh Bryant, pp. 37-44. Other papers dealing with this ecclesiastic are *Master John Shorne*, by the Rev. W. Hastings Kelke, *Records of Bucks*, Vol. II., 1863, p. 60, and Vol. III., 1869; *Master John Schorn*, by the Rev. W. Sparrow Simpson, M.A., F.S.A., p. 354; and by the same author in *Journal of the Brit. Arch. Association*, Vol. XXIII., 1867, pp. 256, 370; Vol. XXV., 1869, p. 334; and Vol. XLI., 1885, p. 262.

[1] A doubtful example represents a tonsured son kneeling behind Raffe Caterall, Esq., 1515, Whalley, Lancs., with wide-sleeved cassock.

[2] The Rev. N. F. Robinson in his *Pileus Quadratus*, (*see* p. 121, *note* 1) describes the cap as the canon's *pileus rotundus* without tuft or apex, and considers the scarf to be a veil for chalice or paten, with an embroidered cross (p. 5).

large cap with no point.   He holds a chalice
with wafer (*see* p. 102).

1522.   Robert Godfrey, LL.B., East Rainham, Norfolk.

c. 1530.   William Lawnder, Northleach, Gloucs., kneeling
in cassock and surplice before the Virgin and
Child (lost).

1534.   Thomas Leman, Southacre, Norfolk, in cassock
and surplice, kneeling before the Virgin and
Child.   This effigy is remarkable as affording
the earliest instance on a brass of a priest
without the tonsure.

POST-REFORMATION ECCLESIASTICS.

The religious disturbances of the sixteenth century
were the cause of much alteration in ecclesiastical costume.
The mass vestments practically disappeared in Edward
VI.'s reign,[1] becoming superseded by other garments, which
excepting in those cases in which a calvinistic influence is
seen to predominate, are pre-reformation in origin and
character, though partaking more of the nature of clerical
habit than of sacred vestment.   The First Prayer-Book of
Edward VI. (1549) prescribed for Holy Communion a
white alb plain (*alba pura, i.e.* without apparels) with a
vestment or cope; assistant priests or deacons wearing albs
with tunicles; a cope to be worn with a plain alb or surplice,
instead of a vestment, on Wednesdays and Fridays when
there was no Communion; a bishop to wear besides rochet
a surplice or alb, and a cope or vestment "and also his
pastoral staff in his hand or else borne or holden by his
chaplain."   In other ministrations the minister was to use

---

[1] The three last instances, given on pp. 80-1, of bishops in pontificalia,
can hardly be said to illustrate a post-reformation use of these vestments.
For the two first died in Queen Mary's reign, and the third, Bishop
Pursglove, refused to take the Oath of Supremacy to Elizabeth, and was
described as "stiff in papistry."   Some valuable remarks on the post-
reformation use of vestments may be found in *Vestments: what has been said
and done about them in the Northern Province since the Reformation*, by James
Raine, M.A., London, Rivington, 1866.

a surplice.   The Second Prayer-Book of 1552 prohibited alb, vestment and cope to the minister, allowing only a surplice, and to the archbishop or bishop a rochet.   But the Act of Uniformity of the first year of Queen Elizabeth upheld the ornaments rubrick of the First Prayer-Book of Edward VI., which rubrick has never since been superseded.[1]   Unfortunately brasses throw but little light on the observance of this rubrick; that of Archbishop Harsnett, 1631, at Chigwell, Essex, shows the mitre, pastoral staff, and cope; but there is abundance of independent evidence for the continuous use of these ornaments.[2]

The garments not already described are as follows :—

ROCHET (*rochetum*, It. *rochetto*, from word of German origin *rock*), a kind of modified alb, of white linen, either, as originally, sleeveless (*sine manicis*[3]) like the *colobium*, or with close-fitting sleeves.   We are concerned only with its use by bishops, who wear the *chimere* over it.[4]   The abnormal size to which the sleeves, familiar to us as lawn sleeves, attained, led to their removal from the rochet, to be fastened to the properly sleeveless chimere, thereby solving the difficulty of passing the chimere over these huge sleeves without soiling them.

---

[1] *See* Haines, p. ccxxviii.; also Marriott's *Vestiarium Christianum*, p. 223, *seq.*

[2] The sculptured effigy of Bishop Creyghton, 1672, at Wells, shows cope, mitre, and pastoral staff.   Other instances of the use of the two last on monuments of the last part of the seventeenth century, may be found cited in *Hierurgia Anglicana*, New Ed., Part I., 1902, pp. 232-3.   *See* also the *Reliquary*, Vol. XXII., 1881-2, p. 65, "The Mitre and Crozier of Bishop Wren at Pembroke College, Cambridge," by W. B. Redfarn. (Matthew Wren, D.D., Bishop successively of Hereford, Norwich and Ely, born 1585, died 1667).   This mitre is reproduced in *Hierurgia Anglicana*, Part III., p. 335, 1904.   Also in the *Connoisseur*, Vol. VII., p. 158 (Nov., 1903).

[3] So defined by Lyndewode, possibly owing to the fact that sleeves were an impediment "in baptizando pueros."

[4] When worn uncovered, the rochet is said to denote episcopal jurisdiction.

CHIMERE (It. *zimarra*, Fr. *simarre*), a sleeveless gown of black satin or silk,[1] open in front, with arm-holes, possibly derived from the gown with two slits (*taberdum talare*), the alternative for the *cappa clausa* (*see* under *Academical costume*, p. 123, as also the Rev. T. A. Lacey's paper, p. 128, referred to above, p. 103, *note* 1). If so, it has become open in front, as did the surplice to accommodate the wig, which form is still preserved at the Universities. We have already noted that the chimere became, in a manner, sleeved by the transference to it of the lawn-sleeves of the rochet. The Rev. N. F. Robinson (*Pileus Quadratus*) illustrates the *habitus episcopalis* of a fifteenth century bishop, from a MS. French Pontifical (fifteenth century) in the British Museum (Egerton MS. 1067, fol. 12), in which a bishop wears a rochet under a taberdum talare, and a pointed pileus. Were this tabard but slit up the front, it would bear a striking resemblance to the chimere.

SCARF or TIPPET.[2] The theories of the origin of this garment are as full of interest as of difficulty. Dr.

---

[1] Its colour has varied; scarlet being sometimes found. *See* the Rev. N. F. Robinson's *The Black Chimere of Anglican Prelates, etc.*, referred to on p. 121, *note* 1. At Methley, in Yorkshire, St. Jerome is depicted in glass, wearing over his rochet a *blue taberdum talare* with white lining. *See* "On the Painted Glass at Methley," by James Fowler, F.S.A., Part II., *Yorkshire Archæological Journal*, Vol. II., 1873, p. 226.

[2] "Tippet, a kind of kerchief for womens Necks (commonly of Furs). Also a long scarf which Doctors of Divinity wear over their gowns."— Bailey's *Universal Etymological Dictionary*, London, 1721. 1549.—"Whit-"sundaie the cannons and petie canons in Paules left of their grey and "calabre amises and the cannons wore hoodes on their surpleses after the "degrees of the Universities and the petie cannons *tipittes* like other "priestes."—*Wriothesley*, II., 14, quoted by the Rev. Mackenzie E. C. Walcott, in paper on "Old St. Paul's": *Transactions of St. Paul's Ecclesiological Society*, Vol. I., p. 177. The use of a scarf as an *insigne* was not confined to the clergy. Up to about the middle of the nineteenth century the Mayor of Christchurch in Hampshire, wore a broad scarlet-silk scarf with a narrow border of black velvet, over his gown, to distinguish him from the councillors.

Wickham Legg in his paper *The Black Scarf of Modern Church Dignitaries and the Grey Almuce of Mediæval Canons* (referred to above, p. 86, *note* 2) derives it from the latter, as does Bloxam,[1] traced through the tippet of sables as worn in the sixteenth century, by Cardinal Wolsey, Archbishops Warham and Cranmer, and Bishops Fox, Ridley and Fisher, and later by Archbishop Parker, immediately after his consecration, December 16th, 1559.[2] The Rev. N. F. Robinson considers this fur tippet, as also the black tippet, referred to on p. 104, to be a different garment altogether from the almuce (see *The Black Chimere*, etc.), and in his *Pileus Quadratus* produces evidence, that seems to make it probable that the black scarf is derived from the mediæval hood of the clergy, worn turban-wise, with the liripipe hanging down in front. Another author[3] considers the black scarf a contracted form of the *cappa nigra* or canon's cope; an origin that seems to us, to say the least, improbable. From its being considered a kind of stole, it became superseded in many places in the nineteenth century by a

---

[1] "The scarf, which is in reality the tippet answering to the ancient "aumasse, and is not, as some have considered, perhaps from the pendant "bands hanging down in front on each side from the shoulders, derived "from the fanon or stole, a vestment nowhere prescribed as such by the "Anglican Church. For the ancient aumasse, or tippet of sable or fur "continued to be worn by bishops and other dignitaries of the Church "of England in the reign of Elizabeth, during which it was in a great "measure superseded by a similar habit of silk, the precursor of the present "scarf, which continued to be called a tippet down to the last century." —"Monuments in St. Martin's Church, [Birmingham], Letter II.," by Matthew Holbeche Bloxam, Rugby, March 2nd, 1846, in *The Midland Counties' Herald*, Thursday, March 5th, 1846.

[2] "circa collum vero collare quoddam ex preciosis pellibus sabellinis "(vulgo 'sables' vocant) consutum," worn with episcopal alb, surplice and chimere.

[3] The Rev. George Smith Tyack in his *Historic Dress of the Clergy*, London, 1897, p. 29.

black stole,[1] and by some Doctors of Divinity a broad
stole has been substituted for the scarf.   Its use by
the prelates, mentioned above, as part of their ordinary
dress in which they went 'abroad,' seems to militate
against any connection with the eucharistic stole.   We
have already noted, p. 105, a peculiar kind of scarf
that occurs on a few brasses of the first quarter of
the sixteenth century.   The form in which we now
find it is that of a broad silk or sarcenet scarf worn
round the neck, with the ends hanging down in front.
This was worn by doctors of divinity, heads of
colleges, members of cathedral bodies, and chaplains of noblemen.[2]   At South Pool, in Devonshire,

---

[1] "It was retained by dignitaries, who wore it as they still do, in quire.
"Bishop Blomfield, of London, for some reason wished all his clergy to
"use it, and from them it spread to other dioceses.   Then it came to be
"called a stole, and that soon led to its being made like one.   Thus it
"comes that the stole is now generally used, though sixty years ago it was
"as obsolete as the chasuble was."—"The Ornaments of the Rubric," by
J. T. Micklethwaite, F.S.A., *Alcuin Club Tract I.*, London, Longmans,
1897, p. 59.
[2] The Rev. F. G. Lee, in *Directorium Anglicanum*, p. 359, states that the
scarves of chaplains should be of the colour of their patrons' livery.   On
this Professor J. C. Robertson comments as follows :—"In the *Directorium
"Anglicanum*, p. 359, it is said that the scarf of chaplains 'is made of silk
"of the colour of the nobleman's livery to whom the cleric is chaplain.'
"As the editor of the *Directorium* describes himself as chaplain to a noble-
"man, this is probably not to be interpreted as satire; but I do not know on
"what ground it is said."—*How shall we Conform to the Liturgy of the Church
of England?* 3rd Ed. revised, London, Murray, 1869, p. 108 (footnote).
   The Rev. Percy Dearmer in the *Parson's Handbook*, London, 1899,
interpreting Canon LVIII., 1604, says, "the tippet should be worn by all
"the clergy ; of stuff by non-graduates (and presumably also by Bachelors);
"of silk by Masters and those above that degree"—p. 86 ; and p. 85,
"There is no known authority for confining the use of the tippet to
"dignitaries and chaplains ; that custom grew up in the days when the
"direction of the canons as to copes also fell into abeyance, and is paral-
"leled by the general disuse of the hood among the parish clergy at the
"same time."   .   .   .   "At Court the youngest curate is still required to
"wear the tippet with his cassock and gown" (footnote).   For an interesting reference to the wearing of "graduates hood, tippet and square cap,"
1604, at Badelsmere, *see* "Some East Kent Parish History," *The Home
Counties Magazine*, Vol. VII., p. 213 (July, 1905).

is a stone effigy representing a priest, without tonsure, of the sixteenth century, wearing cassock, surplice and scarf.[1]

Three forms of gown are met with on brasses, chiefly in the seventeenth century :—

1. A gown open in front with false hanging sleeves, after the manner of the Oxford M.A., the arm of the doublet coming through near the shoulder ; practically identical with the civilian gown of the period.

2. A gown, open in front, with surplice-like sleeves, like the Oxford B.A.[2]

3. The preaching gown, the sleeves of which were narrower, and close at the wrists.[3]

The *pileus quadratus* or square cap is found on a few

---

[1] Plate xxii., illustrating " The Sepulchral Effigies in the Parish Churches of South Devon," by W. H. H. Rogers, *Transactions of the Exeter Diocesan Architectural Society*, 2nd series, Vol. II., 1872. At Ruthyn, Denbigh-shire, Gabriel Goodman, D.D., Dean of Westminster, is shown on the brass of his father and mother (Edward and Ciselye Goodman, 1560), in close-sleeved gown, and a scarf.

[2] Canon LXXIV., 1604, prescribes for ordinary dress "gowns with " standing collars, and sleeves straight at the hands, or wide sleeves, as is " used in the Universities "—" togis cum collaribus erectis manicisque ad " manum contractioribus, vel laxioribus, prout in academiis usitatum est." Wilkins' *Concilia*, Vol. IV., p. 393.

[3] " The clerical gown is described in the Canon, as having a ' standing " collar,' that is, not falling back in a lappet like the civilian's gown, and " ' straight at the hands,' that is, with a narrow wristband : modern custom " having, however, tucked up the full sleeve to the elbow, the narrow " wristband no longer appearing. This gown has been objected to as not " so regular a dress as the other ; as adopted from the Puritans, and as less " distinctive, since dissenting teachers use it. But, in reality, it is more " regular, as marking the clerical order, which the academical gowns do " not. It is not adopted from the Puritans, since the Geneva gown or cloak " was in fashion altogether different : and the dissenters may rather be " regarded as having usurped an ancient clerical dress. Old pictures, etc., " will fully bear out these observations. It is always worn at the Court " of the Sovereign. In fact, the whole tendency of our times has been, " especially at the Universities, to mark the academical rank, rather than " the order of the Church." *The Choral Service of the United Church of England and Ireland*, by the Rev. John Jebb, M.A., London. Parker, 1843

EDMUND GESTE,
BISHOP OF SALISBURY, 1578,
SALISBURY CATHEDRAL.

brasses. Its origin is dealt with by the Rev. N. F. Robinson, who appears to derive it, as well as the scarf, from the mediæval hood.

The following list, which, except in the case of episcopal brasses, makes no attempt at completeness, gives some characteristic examples of the garments mentioned :—

1578. *Edmund Geste*, S.T.P. Cantab.,—Bishop of Salisbury, in Salisbury Cathedral, wears rochet, lawn-sleeves, chimere and scarf, holding in his right hand a curious short pastoral staff with no head, and but for its pointed extremity, more like a walking-stick, possibly corresponding to the πατέρεσσα or pastoral staff of the Greek Church ; in his left hand a book or Textus.[1]

1616. *Henry Robinson*, SS.T.D.—Bishop of Carlisle (where he is buried, and where a similar brass is erected to his memory), Queen's College, Oxford, clad in rochet, chimere, lawn-sleeves, and scarf, and a skull-cap, with ruffs at the neck and wrists, and a curious pastoral staff (surmounted by a crane, holding a stone in one claw), the inscriptions on which have been given above, page 77. In the background is a representation of Carlisle Cathedral, in the doorway of which three bishops, similarly vested, appear to be ordaining a kneeling figure, wearing a gown with false sleeves. In front of Queen's College, also represented, stand three figures in square caps, two of them in gowns with false sleeves, and a third in one with surplice-like sleeves.

1631. *Samuel Harsnett*, S.T.P.—Archbishop of York,

---

[1] Bishop Geste, when Archdeacon of Canterbury, was one of the two chaplains (the other being Nicholas Bullingham, Archdeacon of Lincoln), who officiated as Epistoler and Gospeller, vested in *cappæ sericæ*, at the consecration of Archbishop Parker, 1559.

I

Chigwell, Essex,[1] wears a slightly ornamented rochet, a chimere, and a fine cope embroidered throughout, mitre and pastoral staff. This is the only brass of a post-reformation bishop in a cope. At Winchester College is the headless palimpsest brass of John White, Warden, died 1559, shown wearing cassock with undergarment, surplice, and rich cope embroidered throughout with pomegranates, marguerites, and Tudor roses and with $\overline{\text{IHS}}$ on the morse, but without almuce. This brass was probably engraved before he was consecrated Bishop of Lincoln in 1554, from which see he was translated to Winchester in 1556, but was deprived on refusing to take the oath of Supremacy to Elizabeth.

The mitre, without effigy, is used in three instances as a memorial for a bishop. These are :—

1626. Arthur Lake, D.D., Bishop of Bath and Wells, in Wells Cathedral.

1650. John Prideaux,[2] D.D., Bishop of Worcester, at Bredon, Worcs.

1661. Henry Ferne, S.T.D., Bishop of Chester, in Westminster Abbey.

---

[1] Illustrated in Waller. Also in *A Catalogue of the Harsnett Library at Colchester*, by Gordon Goodwin, 1888, which latter is reproduced in *Hierurgia Anglicana*, Vol. III., 1904, p. 229. *See* also the illustrated edition of Green's *Short History of the English People*, Macmillan, Vol. III., 1903, p. 1056.

[2] The celebrated Rector of Exeter, and Regius Professor of Divinity at Oxford. He married Anna, daughter of William Goodwin, Dean of Christ Church. She died 1627, and a brass inscription at St. Michael's church, Oxford, commemorates her and two children. At Harford, near Ivybridge, Devon, is a painting on copper representing John Prideaux and wife Agnes, with seven sons and three daughters, erected by their fourth son in 1639, who is depicted kneeling, wearing a black cassock and over it a scarlet sleeveless doctor's gown or academical cope (closed in front), with black armholes, and small black hood, a black skull-cap on his head, and a square cap lying beside him.

In Holy Trinity Church, Guildford, is the mural brass of Maurice and Alice Abbot, 1606. Of the six sons, shown kneeling, the third is Robert Abbot, D.D., Bishop of Salisbury, *d.* 1617/18, and buried at Salisbury; the fourth is George Abbot, D.D., Archbishop of Canterbury, *d.* 1633, who lies buried in this church. Each wears a gown with close sleeves, probably the cassock and a hood.[1]

At St. John's College, Oxford, is preserved a small plate with arms and inscription. "In hac cistula conduntur exuviæ Gullielmi Laud." Beheaded 1644/5.[2] A brass inscription commemorating Samuel Rutter, Bishop of Sodor and Man, 1662, is in St. Germain's Cathedral, Peel, Isle of Man.[3]

In the following examples, where not otherwise mentioned, the gown with false hanging sleeves is worn,[4] the ruff is usual, and moustache and beard become common:—

1560.　Leonard Hurst, Denham, Bucks, in cassock and scarf. (Lost, see *Trans. Monumental Brass Society*, Vol. V., p. 75.)

1561.　William Bill, S.T.D., Dean, Provost of Eton, Master of Trinity, Westminster Abbey, in cassock and hood lying loosely on the shoulders.

---

[1] *See* "Remarks on a brass plate formerly in the Church of the Holy Trinity at Guildford, and now remaining in the Hospital there," by Thomas William King, F.S.A., York Herald.—*Surrey Archæological Collections*, Vol. III., 1865, p. 254.

[2] Buried in All Hallows, Barking, London, but his body removed to St. John's College, Oxford, July 1663; see Le Neve's *Fasti Ecclesiæ Anglicanæ*, edited by T. Duffus Hardy, Vol. I., p. 27, 1854.

[3] It was found in 1844, in a well in Peel Castle (see *Arch: Cambrensis*, series III., Vol. XI., 1865, p. 430) and in 1875 was restored to its slab. *See* "Monumental Brass to Bishop Rutter, Peel, Isle of Man," by A. Knox, *Transactions of the Monumental Brass Society*, Vol. II., p. 100. At Cawood, Yorkshire, is a brass inscription to George Mountain, Archbishop of York, 1628. At Croydon, Surrey, the brass coffin-plate of William Wake, Archbishop of Canterbury, 1737, was placed in the pavement after the fire in 1867.

[4] At Christ Church, Oxford, are three brasses of Masters of Arts, wearing this gown.—1584, Thomas Morrey; 1587, Stephen Lence; 1613, Thomas Thornton. Other examples are known.

1566. John Fenton, Coleshill, Warwickshire, in preaching gown, with tight wristbands and full sleeves, holding in left hand a Bible inscribed 'verbū dei.' 'Bachelor of Law.'

1567. William Dye, parson of Tattisfylde, Westerham, Kent, in cassock, surplice and narrow scarf.[1]

1582. Nicholas Asheton, "sacre theologiæ Bacchalaureus Cantabr." Rector, Whichford, Warwickshire, chaplain to the Earl of Derby, wearing over doublet a gown open in front with wide sleeves and scarf.

1587. Richard Woddomes, (with wife and seven children) Ufton, Warwickshire, "Parson and pattron and vossioner," (occupying his own advowson).

1589. John Garbrand, 'Doctor in Divinity,' Crawley, Bucks, kneeling in close-sleeved gown, probably the cassock, and hood.

1595. Thomas Reve, D.D., Monewden, Suffolk, kneeling in close-sleeved gown like the last, and hood; a senior fellow of Gonville and Caius College, Cambridge.

1596. Griffin Lloyd, Rector, Chevening, Kent. Doublet.

1602. William Lucas, 'Maister of Arte,' Clothall, Herts.

1608. Erasmus Williams, Tingewick, Bucks, gown edged with fur; doublet.

1608. John Burton, Burgh, Norfolk.

1610. Peter Winder, Whitchurch, Oxon. "Hujus ecclesiæ Curatus." Kneeling.

1610. Isaia Bures, Northolt, Middlesex, M.A., kneeling.

1614. Humfrey Tyndall, D.D., Dean, Master of Queens' College, Cambridge. Ely Cathedral. Wearing over doublet the gown with false sleeves, scarf and skull-cap.[2]

---

[1] Illustrated in *Hierurgia Anglicana*, Vol. III., 1904, p. 143.

[2] A somewhat similar brass was sold at Newark, 1904, and is now in private possession.

WILLIAM DYE, 1567,
WESTERHAM, KENT.

1614. John Torksay, B.D., Barwell, Leics., shown in a pulpit,[1] wearing preaching gown.

1615. John Wythines, D.D., Battle, Sussex, scarf and square cap.

1616. Henry Airay, D.D., Provost, Queen's College, Oxford, (an allegorical plate similar to that of Bishop Robinson) shown kneeling on an altar-tomb; wearing scarf, hood and skull-cap; doublet.

1619. Henry Mason, M.A., Camb. Eyke, Suffolk. Doublet.

1627. Thomas Stones, Acle, Norfolk, (half-eff.). Doublet; skull-cap.

1627. William Procter, Rector, Upper Boddington, Northants. Doublet; skull-cap.

1632. Edward Naylor, (and family) Bigby, Lincs., "a faithfull and painefull Minister of Gods word."

1648. Rice Jemlae, Husband's Bosworth, Leics.; cassock, gown with false sleeves, and skull-cap.

---

[1] At Hackney, Middlesex, is another example. The half-effigy of Hugh Johnson, 1618, wearing the false-sleeved gown.

CHAPTER II.

Of Academical Costume on Brasses

THOMAS HYLLE, S.T.P., 1468,
NEW COLLEGE, OXFORD.

OF ACADEMICAL COSTUME ON BRASSES

THE subject of mediæval academical costume, as shown on brasses, presents many difficulties, owing, in some measure, to the absence of colour and to the inability of the brass engraver to depict the quality of the silk or fur linings indicated. Professor E. C. Clark, in his learned essay contributed to the *Archæological Journal* for 1893 (Vol. L.) has examined the available evidence.[1] The use of the same term to indicate different articles of costume is, in itself, productive of much confusion; but, in connection with monumental brasses, we can but classify similar examples together, deducing therefrom the dress appropriate to different degrees, holding that, in all likelihood, the deceased, when represented in academicals, is shown in the most dignified costume agreeable to his

---

[1] The following, also, throw light on the subject :—

The same author's "College Caps and Doctors' Hats," *Archæological Journal*, Vol. LXI., 1904, p. 33.

The University of Cambridge from the Earliest Times to the Royal Injunctions of 1535, by James Bass Mullinger, M.A., St. John's College, Cambridge. Cambridge, at the University Press, 1873 : and the same author's *The University of Cambridge from the Royal Injunctions of* 1535 *to the Accession of Charles the First.* 1884. *The Universities of Europe in the Middle Ages*, by the Rev. Hastings Rashdall, M.A., Oxford, at the Clarendon Press, 1895. Vol. II., Part II., pp. 636-644.

"The Ecclesiastical Habit in England," by the Rev. T. A. Lacey, M.A., p. 126, Vol. IV., *Transactions of the St. Paul's Ecclesiological Society*, 1900, in which volume (p. 313) may be found :—"The Hood as an Ornament of the Minister at the Time of His Ministrations in Quire and elsewhere," by E. G. Cuthbert F. Atchley, and (p. 181) "The Black Chimere of Anglican Prelates : A Plea for its Retention and Proper Use," by the Rev. N. F. Robinson. "The Pileus Quadratus : An enquiry into the Relation of the Priest's Square Cap to the Common Academical Catercap and to the Judicial Corner-Cap," by the same author, p. 1, Vol. V., *Transactions* of the same Society, Part I., 1901. The "Habitus Academici singulis gradibus proprii" of the Seventeenth Century were engraved by David Loggan in his *Oxonia illustrata*, 1675, Plate X., and in *Cantabrigia illustrata*, 1688, Plate VII.

degree. That this costume, as indeed universities generally, must be of ecclesiastical origin, there can be but
little doubt.[1]   Moreover, the conferring of *insignia* proper,
as distinguished from costume, on the Doctor (the chair,
the hat, the book, ring and kiss of peace) would indicate
a religious significance.   Some alteration of dress was, in
all probability, made to distinguish the Regent or teaching
Master or Doctor from the Non-Regent; but it is uncertain
whether brasses throw light on the point.   The terms
Professor, Doctor, and Master, seem to have been used,
interchangeably, of the highest degree; but the term
Professor, confined to the higher faculties, seems to imply
teaching; *Doctor* and *Master* to have been applicable to
Regent and Non-Regent, the latter term becoming specially
connected with the Faculty of Arts.   The differences in
costume are as much a matter of quality of material as of
varying shape; the Bachelor being unable to use fur of so
costly a kind as that worn by his academical superiors, and
the dress appearing of a more or less sober and dignified
style as the degree, which it represented, was of a more or
less ecclesiastical nature.   The gown (*toga* or *roba talaris*,
possibly in accordance with the lesser or greater degree)
was in use in the fourteenth century.   Our examples are
mainly of the fifteenth and sixteenth centuries.   The
frequent representation of ecclesiastics of the higher
degrees in the ordinary processional vestments, almuce
and cope, leave us, comparatively speaking, but few
examples in academicals proper, and these, as is natural,
are to be found mostly at Oxford and Cambridge.

Broadly speaking, the articles of dress may be classed
as follows, in the order in which they were assumed :—

1. The UNDER or BODY GARMENT, appearing at the
   wrists, worn beneath the cassock.

---

[1] Anthony Wood considers it to be derived from the *tunica talaris* and
cucullus of the Benedictine habit.

2. The CASSOCK, probably fur-lined, and usually with fur cuffs.

3. The GOWN, which is represented by at least four distinct varieties :—

    a. A loose, full, sleeveless garment reaching to the feet, which must have been passed over the head, with one slit in front varying in size, through which both arms pass. Haines tentatively calls this a *rochet.* Professor Clark considers it to be the *cappa clausa*, or closed cope (prescribed by Stephen Langton, Archbishop of Canterbury, in 1222 as a decent garb for archdeacons, deans and prebendaries),[1] under which name we shall refer to it.

    b. A gown differing from the last in having two slits, usually showing a fur lining, through which the arms pass, but closed in front. This is Haines' "rochet with two slits."[2] Professor Clark considers it to be the *sleeveless tabard.* Its length may identify it with the *taberdum talare*, a view taken by the Rev. N. F. Robinson.[3]

---

[1] Council of Oxford, 1222, XXVIII. "De vita et honestate clericorum. "Ut clericalis ordinis honor debitus observetur, concilii præsentis auctori-"tate decrevimus, ut tam archidiaconi quam decani, et omnes alii in "personatibus et dignitatibus constituti, item omnes decani rurales, et "presbyteri decenter incedant in habitu clericali, et cappis clausis utantur." Wilkins' *Concilia*, Vol. I., 1737, p. 589.

[2] The Rev. T. A. Lacey calls it an alternative form of the *cappa clausa* and identifies it with the chimere (*Transactions of St. Paul's Ecclesiological Society*, Vol. IV., 1900, p. 128).

[3] *Transactions of St. Paul's Ecclesiological Society*, Vol. IV., 1900, p. 211. An example of this gown (*taberdum talare*), worked in gold thread (as is the cassock), and showing a blue lining, with which are worn a tippet of the same material edged with white, a red hood and a red pileus (no point visible), is afforded by the figure of a Doctor on the orphrey of a cope of the fifteenth century, belonging to the Pro-Cathedral of the Apostles, Clifton. This was shown at the Exhibition of English Embroidery Executed Prior to the Middle of the Sixteenth Century, held by the Burlington Fine Arts Club, 1905.

    c. A shorter gown than the cassock, not reaching to the ground, and, as Haines describes it, "with loose sleeves, lined with fur, reaching to the wrists and falling to a point behind." Following Professor Clark we shall call it the *sleeved tabard.*[1]

    d. Haines' "shorter gown sleeveless with slits at the sides edged with fur, for the passage of the arms,"[2] considered by him, though by no means conclusively proved, to represent M.A. costume in the latter half of the fifteenth century. Probably a form of sleeveless tabard. The Rev. N. F. Robinson considers it the *taberdum longum* or *ad medias tibias,*[3] as worn by the Warden in a drawing in the Chandler MS. at New College, representing that society, *c.* 1464.

4. The TIPPET,[4] a cape made of fur or of cloth edged or lined with fur, in accordance with degree, derived probably from the almuce, as being a dress of dignity and not worn inside the plain cappa or gown as the almuce was worn with the ecclesiastical cope, but outside; one reason for this being that it would be completely concealed if worn beneath such a garment as the *cappa clausa.*

5. The HOOD (*caputium*), originally worn by all members, graduate and undergraduate; but after it had ceased to be worn by the latter, it became an indication

[1] The Rev. N. F. Robinson calls it '*capa manicata*' *i.e.* sleeved cope, *ibid.* The Rev. H. W. Macklin considers it a surplice. *See* p. 44, *Monumental Brasses,* by the Rev. Herbert W. Macklin, London, 1898.

[2] A similar gown of red worn over a black cassock, and under a white fur tippet is seen in the figure of an ecclesiastic, 1595, Plate 100, Vol. III. Hefner-Alteneck's *Trachten des christlichen mittelalters.*

[3] *Transactions of St. Paul's Ecclesiological Society,* Vol. IV., 1900, pp. 210-1.

[4] The Tippet and Hood, doubtless, originally formed one garment. *See* account of Chaperon in *Faurteenth Century Civilian Costume,* Chapter IV.

of degree.   The undergraduate's hood was probably of cloth unlined, whereas the graduate's was *penulatum* (furred) or otherwise lined; the Bachelor being confined to the use of less costly fur.   The hood was early supplanted by a cap as a head-covering; but the peak, or tip of the hood, fell down behind, and became more or less exaggerated.   This *liripipium* was worn longer by undergraduates, probably for the sake of distinction.   The position in profile of the effigies of Dr. Billingford, 1442, St. Benet's, Cambridge, and of William Blakwey, 1521, Little Wilbraham, Cambs., well shows the manner of wearing and the shape of the hood; as a rule only the part worn round the neck appears.   In some cases in which the *cappa clausa* figures, but no hood, the latter possibly may be worn beneath the tippet, and so hidden.

6. PILEUS.[1]   Of this, broadly speaking, we find two kinds, though it must be remembered that there is a considerable diversity of shape shown in brasses.

  a. A plain skull-cap without any point, as, apparently, worn by Dr. Billingford and Dr. Hautryve.

  b. A round, brimless cap, with a point in the centre, called by Prof. Clark *"pointed pileus,"* which appears to have been a prerogative of the Doctorate, judging from its representation on

---

[1] *See* The Rev. N. F. Robinson's *Pileus Quadratus* for an account of the development of this cap.   The Laudian Oxford Statutes, 1636, ordained: 1, The common pileus quadratus or catercap for graduates, foundation scholars and choristers: 2, the pileus rotundus for commoners and those not on the foundation: 3, the pileus quadratus for Doctors in Theology: and 4, the pileus rotundus, probably the "John Knox laical cap" for Doctors of Civil Law, Medicine, Music, etc., instead of the quadratus (p. 14).   *See also* "College Caps and Doctors' Hats," by Professor E. C. Clark, LL.D., F.S.A., *Archæological Journal*, Vol. LXI., p. 33, 1904.

brasses.[1] Sometimes we find it worn as an
indication of degree with the costume of a church
dignitary, as at St. Cross, Richard Hayward,
1493, Decretorum Doctor, who wears the processional vestments without the cope; or at
Hereford, Dean Frowsetoure, S.T.P. 1529, who
wears a splendid cope;[2] but it is not shown on
the brass of Henry Sever, S.T.P. 1471, Warden,
Merton College, Oxford.

In giving examples we follow Professor Clark's arrangement in accordance with an ordinance of Archbishop
Chichele, 1417, thinking it necessary merely to mention

---

[1] An incised slab was found at St. Mary's Abbey, York, representing
William Seford or Sever (Abbot, 1485, Bishop of Durham, 1502, *d.* 1505)
clad in pontificals, with mitre, and holding crosier in right hand, and
book in left; a round doctor's cap being incised on each side of the
head (see *Proceedings of the Society of Antiquaries*, 2nd Series, Vol. XIX.,
p. 264 (March 26th, 1903). Wood describes the brass, now lost, at New
College of Thomas Gascoigne, 1457, as depicting a doctor's cap held over
the head of the effigy by two hands issuing from clouds. *See* "A Catalogue of the Brasses in New College, both Past and Present," by H. C.
Dobrée, *Journal of O.U.B.R.S.*, Vol. I., No. 2, June, 1897.

[2] The Rev. N. F. Robinson calls Dean Frowsetoure's cap, the Canon's
Pileus Rotundus. That Canons wore a Pileus may be proved by some
Continental Brasses, figured by Creeny: *e.g.*, 1464 Glorius Count of
Lewenstein, at Bamberg; 1505, John de Heringen, canon, "in decretis
licenciatus," at Erfurt; 1505, Eberard de Rabenstain, canon, at Bamberg;
1560, Eobanus Zeigeler, canon, at Erfurt; but he was Doctor Juris.
Deans seem to have worn a more elaborate variety; *e.g.*, 1460, Eghardus
de Hanensee at Hildesheim; or among the weepers on the brass of
Bishop Peter, 1456, at Breslau. A Manuscript in the Cotton Library
(British Museum) may possibly afford an early instance of an ecclesiastic
wearing a pointed pileus. *See* illustrations on pages 132 and 134, of an
article on "Pictures of English Dress in the Thirteenth Century," in *The
Ancestor*, No. V., April, 1903—but its significance at so early a period is
doubtful. In the Bodleian Library is an illuminated parchment roll
(Ashmole Rolls, No. 45) showing the procession of Abbots, Bishops and
Temporal Peers to the Parliament of February 4th, 3 Henry VIII., from
which are reproduced the Abbots of Reading, St. Mary of York, Ramsey,
and Peterborough, at p. 66 of *Reading Abbey*, by Jamieson B. Hurry,
M.A., M.D. London: Elliot Stock, MCMI. Each abbot wears a
tippet and hood and *pointed pileus.*

JOHN ARGENTEIN, D.D., M.D., 1507,
KING'S COLLEGE, CAMBRIDGE.

ROBERT BRASSIE, S.T.P., 1558,
KING'S COLLEGE, CAMBRIDGE.

that as at Paris the order of precedence of the Faculties was: Theology, Canon and Civil Law, Medicine and Arts, and that the *Licentiati* were those Bachelors, who held the Chancellor's licence, but had not yet completed the formalities necessary for the full degree.[1]

SACRÆ THEOLOGIÆ PROFESSOR (*Doctor Sacræ Theologiæ; Magister in Theologia*),[2] usually clad in girded cassock, beneath which is an under garment, *cappa clausa*, fur tippet, and pointed pileus.[3] If worn, the hood does not appear. Where not otherwise mentioned, the following six examples conform to this style:—

1442.   Richard Billingford, D.D., Master of Corpus. St. Benet's Church, Cambridge: a kneeling

---

[1] In the lists following will be found included some examples, in other than academical costume, but of which the degrees are known.

[2] At Greatham Hospital Chapel, Durham, is an inscription on a marginal fillet, in Lombardic characters, to Magister William de Middiltoun, "*sacre Pagine Doctor*," Warden of the Hospital, *c.* 1350. The inscription to William Hawkesworth, 1349, Provost of Oriel, in St. Mary's, Oxford, describes him as "*sacre pagine quondā p'fessor*." That to Geraldus Borell, Archdeacon of Chichester, 1508, at Cuckfield, Sussex, as "*sacre Theologie P'fessor*." The fine Lombardic uncial inscription on the margin of Prior Borard's slab, 1398, at Christchurch, Hants., reads "Tumba Johannis Borard *Magistri Theologie* Prioris Decimi Noni Huius Ecclesie." The matrix of the demi-effigy does not show the indent of a pileus.

[3] A possible example of this costume is to be seen in a French Fifteenth Century Boccaccio in the British Museum (Rothschild MS., XII.). A red cassock with black girdle is surmounted by a blue *cappa clausa*, over which a white fur tippet is worn, turned up over the shoulders so as to show the blue cloth lining, with a white hood. A high grey cap is on the head.—The illustration here referred to, has been reproduced in the *Burlington Magazine*, Vol. VII., No. 27, June, 1905: "The Rothschild MS. in the British Museum of Les Cas des Maltheureux Nobles hommes et femmes," by Sir Edward Maunde Thompson, K.C.B. A similar manner of wearing the tippet (but without hood), is shown on a brass (formerly in the possession of Mr. Wilson, Tuxford Hall, Notts., sold at Newark, 1904), representing an ecclesiastic clad in fur-lined cassock, fur tippet and possibly a pileus. Two appendages, which resemble short fur-edged liripipes belonging to the tippet, rather than pockets, are engraved on the cassock below the forearms.

figure, differing from the above description by having a fur-lined hood, but no tippet, and on the head a round skull-cap with no point.

1468.   Thomas Hylle, P.S.T., New College, Oxford: holding a Tau cross on which the five wounds are represented.

c. 1480.   A Doctor, St. Mary the Less, Cambridge: not showing garment under cassock, nor a point to the cap.   The buckled belt of the cassock is well shown.

1496.   William Towne, Doctor in Theologia, King's College, Cambridge.

c. 1500.   A Doctor, Great St. Helen's, Bishopsgate, London: attributed to John Brieux, Rector of St. Martin Outwich, 1459, though probably of later date.

1507.   John Argentein, D.D. (1504), King's College, Cambridge: Physician to Arthur, Prince of Wales; shows strap-girdle of cassock.

Besides the above, the following Doctors of Divinity should be noticed:—

1361.   John Hotham, Provost of Queen's College, Oxford, Rector, Chinnor, Oxon., Magister in Theologia (half effigy): apparently wearing a cassock, the gown with two slits (probably *taberdum talare*), tippet, and pointed pileus.

1405.   Magister John Strete, Upper Hardres, Kent: wearing undergarment buttoned over the hands, cassock, tippet, hood, and pointed pileus. It is just possible that the latter indicates a Doctor's degree, but it may have been an *insigne* of prebendarial rank in this case.

1471.   Henry Sever, S.T.P., Warden, Merton College, Oxford: in processional vestments; no cap.

1489.   Thomas Barker, S.T.P., Vice-Provost, Eton College Chapel: in processional vestments *without* cope; a round cap.

WILLIAM HAUTRYVE,
DECRETORUM DOCTOR, 1441,
NEW COLLEGE, OXFORD.

1501. William Heyward, S.T.D., Vicar, St. Helens, Abingdon, Berks. (now on the wall): in Haines' M.A. I. costume (see below), cassock, sleeved tabard, tippet and hood, with the addition of a pileus.

1529. Edmund Frowsetoure, S.T.P., Dean, Hereford Cathedral: in processional vestments (the cope embroidered throughout), and pointed pileus.

1558. Robert Brassie, S.T.P., Provost, King's College, Cambridge: in processional vestments *without* cope, with pointed pileus.

The brass of John Yslyngtone, S.T.P., Cley-next-the-Sea, Norfolk, *c.* 1520: is dealt with on p. 106.

The brass at Christ's College, Cambridge, *c.* 1540, attributed to Edward Hawford, D.D., shows cassock, sleeved tabard, tippet and hood; *no* pileus.

Haines, p. cxxxii., gives an illustration of a brass formerly at Hitchin, Herts., to John Sperehawke, D.D., 1474, wearing a cassock, a very loose chasuble-like garment without ornament,[1] a tippet and pointed pileus. In Creeny's *Continental Brasses* is an illustration of the brass of Magister Jacobus Schelewaerts, " parisiensis sacre theologie doctoris," 1483, in Bruges Cathedral. He was Professor in Theology at the University of Louvain, 1472-76, and is shown seated, giving a lecture to a class of seven sitting at desks before him. He appears to be wearing a cap, with his hood drawn over his head, a cassock with fur cuffs, and a loose gown with two slits (*taberdum talare*) through which his arms pass.

Decretorum or Juris Canonici Doctor. A similar costume to that given for S.T.P.—perhaps the tippet is

---

[1] Possibly this curious vestment was an instance of the chasuble-shaped surplice. For a description of the latter, *see* "On Two Unusual Forms of Linen Vestments," by J. Wickham Legg, F.S.A. *Transactions oj St. Paul's Ecclesiological Society*, Vol. IV., 1900, p. 141.

not always fur throughout, but of cloth, with a border of fur—is worn by :—

1441. William Hautryve, Decretor' doctor, New College, Oxford: undergarment, cassock, *cappa clausa*, fur tippet, pileus without point.[1] The tippet is turned up slightly over the shoulders, showing the cloth lining. (*See* footnote above, p. 127.)

1476. Richard Rudhale, Decretor' doctor, Archdeacon of Hereford, Hereford Cathedral: in processional vestments (the cope embroidered throughout), and a round pileus with point.

1493. Richard Hayward, Decretorum doctor, Master of the Hospital, St. Cross, Winchester: wearing a pointed pileus with processional vestments *minus* the cope.

1517. Walter Hewke, D.Can.L., Trinity Hall, Cambridge: wearing a fine cope with "sainted" orphreys, with a curious, flat, round cap; restored in 1895 from a similar brass at Tattershall, Lincolnshire, representing a Provost of Tattershall College, *c.* 1510.

1521. Dr. Christopher Urswick, Rector, Hackney, Middlesex: in processional vestments, with pointed pileus.[2]

1545. Thomas Capp, Juris ecc. doctor, St. Stephen's, Norwich: wearing processional vestments, but no pileus; no tonsure.

---

[1] The engraving in Waller gives the pointed pileus; the reproduction in the *Journal of Oxford University Brass Rubbing Society*, Vol. I. No. 2, June, 1897, shows no point.

[2] See "The Monumental Brasses of Hackney, Middlesex," by the Rev. J. F. Williams, M.A., *Transactions of the Monumental Brass Society*, Vol. V., pp. 62-4.

JOHN LOWTHE,
Juris Civilis Professor, 1427,
New College, Oxford.

LEGUM, or JURIS CIVILIS DOCTOR.

1412. Eudo de la Zouch, St. John's College, Cambridge:[1]
with the exception of the pointed pileus, this
effigy shows the costume, cassock, sleeved
tabard, tippet and hood, to be associated below
with the degree of M.A.

1427. John Sowthe, Juris Civilis Professor, New College, Oxford: wearing undergarment, cassock,
the gown with two slits (*taberdum talare*), a
tippet with fur edge, a hood and pointed
pileus, and a very curious development consisting of two pendants or liripipes, whether
attached to the tippet or to the gown (more
probably the latter) it would be difficult to
determine.[2]

1517. William Lichefeld, LL.D., Willesden, Middlesex,
Canon of St. Paul's: in processional vest-
ments, with cap similar to that worn by Dr.
Urswick.

1529. Bryan Roos, Childrey, Berks, "doctor of Lawe
sumtime p'son of this church": wearing
cassock, with wide sleeves (Haines' "ordinary
civilian's gown," p. lxxxii.), tippet, hood, and
pileus with small point.

1589. Edward Leeds, Legum doctor, Master of Clare
Hall, Cambridge; Croxton, Cambs.: wearing
a long gown open in front, where it appears to
be edged with fur, with false sleeves, of the
type met with in civilian costume, beneath

---

[1] It is to be regretted that the College has not replaced this brass in its
slab, which should be properly protected from the weather. At present,
the brass is fastened to the wall of a room beneath the organ in the new
chapel: the slab, the matrix of which is the only proof of a pointed pileus
(the head being gone from the brass) lies on the site of the old chapel.

[2] *See* Professor Clark's "English Academical Costume," *Archæological
Journal*, Vol. L., 1893, p. 188 (Reprint, 1894, p. 52).

which the sleeves of the doublet are shown. There is no cap.[1]

1601.   Hugh Lloyd, Juris Civilis Doctor, Canon of St. Paul's, New College, Oxford: shown kneeling in a long open gown with false sleeves.

A similar costume to that of John Sowthe, though without cap, and with differently shaped liripipes, may be seen on the brass of William Goche, rector, 1499, Barningham, Suffolk, and on a brass, *c.* 1530, at Trinity Hall, Cambridge, the liripipes worn with a *taberdum ad medias tibias*. It is uncertain what degree it indicates; possibly that of B.D., as there is no doctor's cap. The half effigy of John Whelpdall, "legum doctor," 1526, Greystoke, Cumberland, shows him in almuce, and without a pileus, as does that of Robert Honywode, LL.D., kneeling, Archdeacon of Taunton and Canon of Windsor, in St. George's Chapel, Windsor.

UTRIUSQUE JURIS DOCTOR.

c. 1510.   Edward Sheffeld, Luton, Beds., Canon of Lichfield: wearing processional vestments, without the cope, but with pointed pileus.

1515 (died 1524).   Robert Langton, Queen's College, Oxford: in processional vestments, with pointed pileus.

At Linwood, Lincs., beneath the effigies of John Lyndewode and Alice his wife, 1419, are the effigies of four sons and three daughters. The figure in the centre (fourth son) appears to be wearing a cassock and the gown with two slits (*taberdum talare*), and possibly tippet and hood. The state of the brass makes it impossible to state positively what kind of head-dress, if any, is worn. This

---

[1] The sculptured effigy of David Lewis, D.C.L., Judge of the High Court of Admiralty, *d.* 1584, in Abergavenny Church, shows false-sleeved gown and round cap. See the photograph in *Some Account of the Ancient Monuments in the Priory Church, Abergavenny*, by Octavius Morgan, Newport, 1872.

BRYAN ROOS,
DOCTOR OF LAWE, 1529,
CHILDREY, BERKS.

probably represents William Lindewode, *Utriusque Juris Doctor*, author of the "Provinciale," who became Bishop of St. David's in 1442, and died in 1446. The brass at Offord Darcy, Hunts., of William Taylard, *c.* 1530, who appears to have held this degree, shows him, kneeling, in a wide-sleeved gown (possibly a cassock), tippet, hood, and pileus.

MEDICINÆ DOCTOR.

1503. Master John Martok, Banwell, Somerset, a very doubtful example: wearing full processional vestments, but no pileus.

1507. John Argentein, King's College, Cambridge, Physician to Arthur, Prince of Wales: wearing the D.D. costume, already mentioned, *see* p. 128.

To these may be added the following Post-Reformation Doctors of Medicine, each wearing the false-sleeved gown:—

1592. Walter Bailey, M.A. 1556, B.Med. 1551, Prebendary of Wells 1561, Professor of Physic in the University, and Physician to Queen Elizabeth, New College, Oxford.[1]

1599. Richard Radcliff, "in medicina doctor," St. Peter-in-the-East, Oxford.

1613. Duncan Liddel, "Doctor medicus," Old or West Church, Aberdeen: half effigy seated at table and wearing a cap.

1619. Anthony Aylworth, "Medicinæ Doctor et Professor Regius sub Elizab. Reg," New College, Oxford: a hood and cap.

---

[1] *See* "A Catalogue of the Brasses in New College, both past and present," by H. C. P. Dobrée in the *Journal of the Oxford University Brass Rubbing Society*, Vol. I., No. 2, June, 1897.

LICENTIATI. The two following, "in decretis Licentiati," at Girton, Cambs., are shown in processional vestments:—

1492. Magister William Malster, rector, Canon of York.
1497. Magister William Stevyn, rector, Canon of Lincoln.

At Great Ringstead, Norfolk, is the brass of Richard Kegell, "arciū et decretor' inceptor," rector, 1482: in mass vestments, without stole or maniple.

SACRÆ THEOLOGIÆ BACCALAUREUS. The costume proper to this degree seems to have been the undergarment, cassock, sleeveless gown with two slits (*taberdum talare*), tippet edged with fur, and hood, but no pileus. Of this we have three examples:—

1387. John Bloxham, Merton College, Oxford (probably engraved 1420).
c. 1450. John Darley, Herne, Kent. The feet rest on a lion; an unusual feature.
c. 1535. Unknown; Queens' College, Cambridge; much worn.

In other costume there are several brasses of Bachelors of Divinity; such as the following:—

1420. William Fryth, S.T.B., New College, Oxford, whose effigy is concealed by the stalls.
1456. William Moor, "Sacre Scripture bacularius arte pbatus," Tattershall, Lincs., 2nd Provost of Tattershall College, Canon of York: in mass vestments, head bare.
1480. William Tibarde,? S.T.B., First President, Magdalen College, Oxford, in processional vestments. Haines assigns this brass to a later date and person, *c.* 1530.
1498. Jacob Hert, "in Theologia Baccalaureus" (inscription lost), Hitchin, Herts., in processional vestments.

JOHN BLOXHAM, S.T.B., AND JOHN WHYTTON,
c. 1420,
MERTON COLLEGE, OXFORD.

1505. Thomas Tyard, S.T.B., Vicar, Bawburgh, Norfolk : in shroud.

1517. John Spence, B.D., Ewelme, Oxon. : in cassock, sleeved tabard, tippet and hood.

1519. Thomas Swayn, S.T.B., Wooburn, Bucks. : in processional vestments.

1521. John Rede, S.T.B., Warden, New College, Oxford : in processional vestments.

1524. William Porter, S.T.B., formerly Warden of New College, Canon, Hereford Cathedral : in mass vestments, holding chalice with wafer stamped with a cross-crosslet.

1530. Hugo Humfray, " magistri arcum nec non in sacra s̄c̄a theologie bachelerii," Barcheston, Warwickshire : apparently in cassock, sleeveless tabard,[1] tippet and hood.

1558. Arthur Cole, S.T.B., President, Magdalen College, Oxford : wearing the processional vestments, with the Mantle of the Garter instead of a cope.

ARTIUM MAGISTER.—Much doubt exists as to the right costume for this degree. Haines cites an engraving in Montfaucon, Vol. III., plate xvii., p. 68, which represents " Jean Perdrier Prête, maître ès Arts", 1376, wearing a cassock, over which is a long gown with sleeves, and hood lined with fur ; the sleeves falling to a point behind. Haines considers that the M.A. and B.A. dresses were worn interchangeably ; that in the fifteenth century Bachelors of Arts and Scholars of Divinity wore a cassock, over which was a shorter gown, with loose sleeves lined with fur, reaching to the wrists, and falling to a point behind (*sleeved tabard*), a cape or tippet edged with fur and a hood ; but that after the middle of the fifteenth century Masters of Arts wore a cassock, a shorter gown,

---

[1] If intended for the *taberdum ad medias tibias,* it is wrongly engraved ; as its skirt covers the cassock, being " *talare.*"

sleeveless, with slits at the sides edged with fur for the passage of the arms (sleeveless *taberdum ad medias tibias*), a tippet and hood.   A good number of examples of the former costume exists, but it is difficult to tell in every case to which degree it belongs.   The following list will, we hope, be found trustworthy.[1]

<table>
<tr><td rowspan="13">Haines' M.A.,
I. sleeved
tabard.</td><td>1445.</td><td>John Kyllyngworth, "Magist' in Artibus," half effigy, Merton College, Oxford.</td></tr>
<tr><td>c. 1450.</td><td>A Priest, Thaxted, Essex.</td></tr>
<tr><td>1451.</td><td>Magist' William Snell, Boxley, Kent.</td></tr>
<tr><td>1451.</td><td>Magister Richard Folcard, half effigy, Pakefield, Suffolk.</td></tr>
<tr><td>1460.</td><td>Magister John Alnwyk, Surlingham, Norfolk.</td></tr>
<tr><td>1475.</td><td>Thomas Mareys, rector, Stourmouth, Kent.</td></tr>
<tr><td>c. 1480.</td><td>Half effigy (John Goolde, M.A. ?) Magdalen College, Oxford.</td></tr>
<tr><td>c. 1490.</td><td>John Westlake, Welford, Berks.</td></tr>
<tr><td>c. 1500.</td><td>George Jassy, half effigy, Magdalen College, Oxford.</td></tr>
<tr><td>1507.</td><td>Dn̄s Arthur Vernon, "in Artibus magri univ'sitatis Cantibrigie," Tong, Salop. This example differs from the rest in the cassock only appearing at the wrists; the tabard reaching to the feet.[2]</td></tr>
<tr><td>1515.</td><td>John Trembras, parson, "maist of arte," St. Michael Penkivel, Cornwall.</td></tr>
</table>

---

[1] In order to save space we shall refer to the costume showing the former gown as Haines, M.A., I., to that showing the latter, which is comparatively rare, as Haines, M.A., II.—At Harpswell, Lincs., is a sculptured effigy showing Haines, M.A., I. costume, and in addition a *pileus*, see *The Antiquary, A Fortnightly Medium*, etc. Vol. III., January to June, 1873, p. 247.   (Illus.)

[2] A similar example is at Barking, Essex, c. 1480 (?Robert Waleis, died before 1486), holding chalice without wafer.   This costume is seen in two miniatures of the fifteenth century Pontifical of Bishop Richard Clifford (died 1421) (MS. 79 Corpus Christi College, Cambridge) reproduced in the *Alcuin Club Collections*, IV., "Pontifical Services, Illustrated from Miniatures of the Fifteenth and Sixteenth Centuries, with Descriptive

JOHN BOWKE, M.A., 1519,
MERTON COLLEGE, OXFORD.

JOHN KYLLYNGWORTH, M.A., 1445,
MERTON COLLEGE, OXFORD.

1518. Thomas Coly, Bredgar, Kent, holding chalice with wafer.

1519. John Bowke, M.A., Merton College, Oxford, half effigy, holding chalice with wafer.[1]

The effigy of William Taberam, *c.* 1421, at Royston, Herts., is in this costume. The inscription, now lost, described him as "Legista pbatus." Another example is at Broxbourne, Herts., *c.* 1510.

c. 1480. Unknown. Magdalen College, Oxford.

1501. Thomas Mason, M.A., fellow, Magdalen College, Oxford.

1521. William Blakwey, M.A., Little Wilbraham, Cambs.: shown kneeling.

1523. Nicholas Goldwell, M.A., fellow, Magdalen College, Oxford: no tonsure.

Haines' M.A., II. sleeveless *taberdum ad medias tibias.*

At Chartham, Kent, is the brass of Robert Sheffelde, "artium magist'," 1508, in processional vestments without the cope. Examples of M.A.'s in mass vestments may be seen at Fladbury, Worcs., Wm. Plewme, 1504; at Whitnash, Warwickshire, Richard Bennett, 1531, with chalice and wafer; and elsewhere.

Notes and a Liturgical Introduction," by the Rev. W. H. Frere, 1901. Fig. 10, Presentation of the Bishop-Elect, two tonsured figures in red and ermine and blue and ermine respectively (?Proctors), and Fig. 13, the Installation of an Abbot, who wears a cope over amice and alb; a tonsured figure in red and ermine (?Archdeacon or Bishop's Commissary).

[1] The brasses of Thomas Coly and John Bowke, together with that mentioned above, of John Spence, B.D., 1517, Ewelme, Oxon., and the brass of Walter Charyls, M, A., 1502 ($\frac{3}{4}$ eff.) Magdalen College, Oxford, show on the tabard in addition to the sleeves two slits which may possibly be liripipia, but which it is not unreasonable to suppose may be intended for pockets. Haines (p. lxxxv.), considers that they "present apparently a combination of the dresses of the Bachelor of Arts, and Master of Arts." These lappets (or pockets?) are shown on the brass of Walter Smith, M.A., Fellow, 1525, Eton College, whose dress consists of a fur-lined cassock, the shorter gown with full sleeves, tippet and hood. In the same chapel the brass of Thomas Edgcomb, Vice-Provost, 1545, shows cassock, wide-sleeved gown and large hood.

Thomas Wilkynson, 1511, "Arcium magistri," Orping-
ton, Kent, wears full processional vestments. Ralph
Vawdrey, M.A., 1478, Magdalen College, Oxford, wears
cassock, tippet, and hood (half effigy), as does Philip
Warthim, M.A. (1488), Blockley, Worcs.

SACRÆ THEOLOGIÆ SCHOLARIS. Probably those of
this degree were already Masters of Arts.

Haines' M.A.,
I. sleeved
tabard.

1447.   Geoffrey Hargreve, S.T.S., fellow, New College,
        Oxford.[1]

1451.   Walter Wake, S.T.S., fellow, New College,
        Oxford, half effigy.

1478.   Thomas Sondes, S.T.S., Magdalen College, Ox-
        ford.

Haines' M.A.
II. sleeveless
taberdum ad
medias tibias.

1508.   John London, M.A., S.T.S., New College,
        Oxford, scribe of the university.

1494.   Walter Hyll, M.A., S.T.S., Warden, New Col-
        lege, wears processional vestments, with his
        initials on the orphreys of the cope.

1507.   John Frye, S.T.S., fellow, New College, half
        effigy, wears mass vestments, holding chalice
        with wafer.

JURIS CANONICI or IN DECRETIS BACCALAUREUS.

1461.   Magister Philip Polton, "Baccallr̄i Canon,"
        Archdeacon of Gloucester, All Souls' College,
        Oxford, kneeling (head gone), showing pro-
        file: undergarment, cassock, surplice, and
        ? almuce; over all a plain cope with academi-
        cal hood.

---

[1] Two fragments, forming the reverses of two palimpsest shields at
Tolleshunt Darcy, Essex, show a similar costume to that of Hargreve, with
the exception that the mitten sleeves of the undergarment appear. *c.* 1420.
Illustrated in *Transactions of the Monumental Brass Society*, Vol. IV., p. 112.

GEOFFREY HARGREVE, S.T.S., 1447,
NEW COLLEGE, OXFORD.

1419.   John Desford, " Juris Canonici Bacallari," Canon
        of Hereford, New College, Oxford: in pro-
        cessional vestments.

1421.   William Dermot, Kinnersley, Herefordshire,
        half effigy: in mass vestments.

c. 1456. Roger Gery, "in decretis bacularius," Rector,
        Whitchurch, Oxon.: in mass vestments,
        holding chalice with wafer.

1458.   John Huntington, " Baccalaureus in decretis,"
        Manchester Cathedral: in processional vest-
        ments, without the cope.

c. 1500. Stephen Hellard, " in decretis Bacallarius," died
        1506, Canon of St. Asaph, Rector, Stevenage,
        Herts.: in processional vestments.

1518.   John Aberfeld, "in decretis bac̄c̄," Great Cress-
        ingham, Norfolk: in processional vestments
        without the cope.

1519.   John Wryght, " clīcus in decretis bacalarius,"
        formerly Master of Trinity Hall, Cambridge,
        Rector, Clothall, Herts.: in mass vestments,
        holding chalice with wafer.

1535.   Warin Penhallinyk, Wendron, Cornwall, "in
        decretis baccallareus": in cope (head lost).

At Duxford, Cambs., is an inscription to Thomas
Wyntworth, vicar, 1489, "Baccalari in jure Canonico."

JURIS CIVILIS OR LEGUM BACCALAUREUS. The three
following wear the sleeved tabard. (Haines' M.A., I.
costume.)

1420.   John Mottesfont, LL.B., Lydd, Kent.
1478.   Richard Wyard, " [Bacca]larii Juris," fellow,
        New College, Oxford, holding a Tau cross.
1510.   David Lloyde, LL.B., All Souls' College, Ox-
        ford, half effigy.

1482.   Nicholas Wotton, " baccalarii legis," Great St.
        Helen's, Bishopsgate, London, removed from

St. Martin, Outwich), wears cassock, tippet
with fur edge, and hood. Similar to which is

1490. Richard Spekynton, LL.B., fellow, "commissary
and official of Buckyngham," All Souls'
College, Oxford.

To these may be added the following, not in academicals :—

1448. William Skelton, LL.B., "prepositus" of Wells,
Ashbury, Berks.: in processional vestments.

1458. Thomas Mordon, LL.B., Fladbury, Worcs.,
half effigy: in processional vestments.

1472. Thomas Flemyng, LL.B., fellow, New College,
Oxford, an emaciated effigy in shroud.

c. 1490. Thomas Tylson, B.C.L., vicar, Aylsham, Norfolk: in processional vestments, without cope.

1501. Thomas Worsley, LL.B., Wimpole, Cambs.: in
processional vestments.

1541. Master Thomas Dalyson, "bachelor of lawe
and sumtyme parson of this church," Clothall,
Herts: in processional vestments, without
almuce.

1631. Jerome Keyt, "Legum baccalaureus," Woodstock, Oxon., kneeling: wearing over doublet
gown with false sleeves and hood.

UTRIUSQUE JURIS BACCALAUREUS.

1456. Richard Drax, priest, "in utroq' jure Baculari,"
half effigy, Brancepeth, Durham: wearing the
sleeved tabard (Haines' M.A., I.).[1]

c. 1500. William Jombharte (?), kneeling: in mass vestments, Blockley, Worcs.

PHYSICÆ BACCALAUREUS.

c. 1480. John Perch, M.A., "Bacallarius Physice,"

---

[1] An inscription is at Walthamstow, Essex, commemorating Henry
Crane, vicar "quondā Bacallari' utriusque Juris." 1436.

JOHN PALMER, B.A., 1479,
NEW COLLEGE, OXFORD.

Chaplain to the Bishop of Winchester, formerly at Magdalen College, Oxford: in processional vestments.

Artium Baccalaureus.

1479. John Palmer, B.A., fellow, New College, Oxford: in sleeved tabard (Haines' M.A., I.).
1524. John Barratte, B.A., fellow, Winchester College: in sleeveless tabard (Haines' M.A., II.).

1515. William Goberd, B.A., Archdeacon of Salop, Magdalen College, Oxford: in processional vestments, without cope.
1613. Nicholas Roope, B.A., of Broadgates Hall, St. Aldate's, Oxford: wearing over doublet a long gown with false sleeves, and a hood.

Student of Civil Law.

1510. Thomas Baker, All Souls' College, Oxford, half effigy, wearing a belted tunic, a fur-sleeved gown with a mantle fastened on the left shoulder, with the front part thrown over the right arm, and a hood.

The brass of an undergraduate may be seen in St. Mary the Virgin, Oxford, representing Edward Chernock, of Brazenose College, 1581, in his sixteenth year, wearing the false-sleeved gown, and kneeling in a panelled room.

Schoolboys.[1] The following instances of schoolboys may be noted:—

1430. John Kent, scholar of Winchester, Headbourne

---

[1] In *The Antiquary*, Vol. I., January to June, 1880, p. 277, is given a school-boy's bill, A.D. 1547 (in Navy Accounts, Exch. Q.R., Bundle 616 B.) showing that Raphe Lyons' equipment consisted of: coat, two shirts, two pair of hose, doublet, two dozen points, girdle, cap, purse and pair of knives.

Worthy, near Winchester: wearing gown with full sleeves, close at the wrists.

1512.   John Stonor, scholar of Eton, Wyrardisbury, Bucks., wearing a long gown fastened on the right side, with tight sleeves, girded, and faced with fur, and a peculiar cap, with flaps covering the ears.

1512.   Thomas Heron, Little Ilford, Essex, aged fourteen, wearing a cassock-like tunic or gown, with a waistbelt from which hang his penner and inkhorn.

NOTE.—*Doctor of Music.*   A brass to Robert Fairfax, Doctor of Music (Cambridge, 1504; Oxford, 1511), died 1521, organist of St. Albans, formerly existed in St. Albans Abbey.   *See* "The Brasses and Indents in St. Albans Abbey," by William Page, F.S.A., *The Home Counties Magazine,* Vol. I., 1899, page 160.

JOHN STONOR, 1512,
WYRARDISBURY, BUCKS.

CHAPTER III.

Of Military Costume on Brasses

SIR ROGER DE TRUMPINGTON, 1289,
TRUMPINGTON, CAMBS.

CHAPTER III.

OF MILITARY COSTUME ON BRASSES

In the following account of arms and armour we do not propose to trace their origin and development prior to the time when they appear on brasses. These may be studied in the great works on Costume, which are mentioned in the list of books appended to this volume, especially in Meyrick's *Critical Inquiry.* The development of defensive armour is, naturally, found to correspond with that of the weapons opposed to it; and the ultimate superiority of the latter, due to the introduction of fire-arms, led, as naturally, to the abandonment of the former. We are fortunate in the survival of a very fine series of brasses from the reign of Edward I. to the final disuse of armour in the seventeenth century, which illustrate the different changes which necessity or fashion introduced.

The earliest brasses in England representing armour consist of four full-length and two half-effigies. These, with the exception of the Croft brass, belong to the reign of Edward I., and from a prominent characteristic, have been classed as the Surcoat Period. They are :—

1277.	Sir John D'Aubernoun, Stoke d'Abernon, Surrey.
1289.	Sir Roger de Trumpington, Trumpington, Cambridge.
1302.	Sir Robert de Bures, Acton, Suffolk.
c. 1306.	Sir Robert de Setvans, Chartham, Kent.[1]
c. 1290.	Sir Richard de Boselyngthorpe, Buslingthorpe, Lincs. (half effigy).
c. 1310.	A half effigy, Croft, Lincolnshire.

---

[1] A palimsest fragment, *c.* 1300, on reverse of the half-effigy of a lady, *c.* 1360, at Clifton Campville, Staffs, shows a portion of a knight, somewhat similar to the Setvans brass.

Chain mail is the chief defence of all these. They are usually described as belonging to the COMPLETE MAIL Period, although we find *genouillières* or *poleyns*, possibly of plate, covering the knees. The mail (Fr. *maille*) is represented in two ways, either *interlaced*, as at Stoke d'Abernon, Acton, Chartham, and Buslingthorpe; or *banded*, that is, apparently sewn to a foundation in parallel rows or bands, as at Croft and Trumpington; though in the latter the lines separating the rows of links are not engraved.

Of chain mail were worn :—

HAWBERK[1] on the body and arms; the gloves, not divided into fingers, being of one piece with the sleeves, and fastened by a leather strap round the wrists.

COIF DE MAILLES, or hood, covering the neck and drawn over the head, thereby encircling the face and covering the chin; kept in place by an interlaced strap across the forehead. Under it a scull-cap or *cervelière* was worn.

CHAUSSES, or stockings, covering the feet and legs; over which were worn :—

    1. GENOUILLIÈRES or POLEYNS, protections for the knees (*knee-cops*), often much ornamented, made either of a prepared leather, called *cuir-bouilli*, or of steel-plate.

    2. SPURS, consisting of single points, goads, or "*pricks*," fastened by a strap across the instep and under the foot.

Beneath the hawberk was worn the HAUKETON or *gambeson*, a quilted leathern garment, usually stitched in parallel vertical lines and stuffed with cotton, to prevent

---

[1] The hawberk, covering body and arms, and reaching to the knees, with hood and gloves all of one piece, is well shown in a MS. of the Apocalypse in the British Museum (Royal MS., 19. B. xv.) *See* Plate IV., " The loosing of the Four Angels which are bound in the Great River Euphrates," illustrating " English Costume of the Early Fourteenth Century."—*The Ancestor*, No. VII., October, 1903.

the mail hawberk, which in the case of Sir Robert de Setvans appears to be unlined, from chafing the skin. It may be seen both beneath the skirt of the hawberk and on the wrists of the Setvans effigy.

Over all was worn the SURCOAT or *bliaus*,[1] probably to screen the mail of the knight from the sun's heat and from the rain, and also, when embroidered with his arms, as on the Setvans brass, to distinguish him, as did the shield. This was made of linen or silk, with a fringed border, and hung loosely to below the knees, being slit up before and behind for convenience in riding. In our examples it is without sleeves, being laced up either at the side or back, and confined at the waist by a narrow cord.

On the shoulders were strapped AILETTES; rectangular pieces of leather covered with silk and fringed; often bearing the arms of the wearer.

The SHIELD, which was either *heater*-shaped as on the D'Aubernoun brass, or concave to the body, as at Trumpington, Acton, and Chartham, bore the arms of the wearer, and was worn on the left shoulder, being fastened by a *guige*, often much ornamented,[2] passing over the right shoulder, either above the *coif de mailles* as on the D'Aubernoun brass, or beneath it as on that of Sir Robert de Bures.

The large SWORD, with cross-piece (*quillons*) and ornamented *pommel*, was worn in front, inclining to the left, and fastened to a broad belt buckled over the hips. The scabbard was often finely worked, as at Trumpington, with the wearer's arms, or at Chartham.

---

[1] Vol. VI. of *Vetusta Monumenta* illustrates and describes a fragment of the surcoat of William de Fortibus, 3rd Earl of Albemarle (*d.* 1260), whose wife was Isabel, sister and heir of Baldwin de Redvers, Earl of Devon. "It consists of a coarse lining, on which fine linen has been "laid; and on this are worked, with coloured linens sewed on, and em- "broidery, coats of arms; in the centre is a shield displaying, or, a lion "rampant azure, Rivers; on each side a cross patonce vairé, Albemarle."

[2] With roses and fylfot crosses on the D'Aubernoun brass.

Besides the above, the following points should be noted :—

1277. *Sir John D'Aubernoun* is not cross-legged, and has no ailettes. His is the only instance of the principal effigy on a brass bearing the *lance*, which rests on the right shoulder, bearing beneath its head a *pennon* or *gonfanon* charged with his arms. The lion at his feet grasps the staff of the lance in its mouth. The shield bears :—Azure, a chevron or ; the blue enamel of which still survives (*see* p. 8). The Lombardic inscription on the edge of the slab, has lost its brass lettering, but reads :—

   + SIRE : IOHAN : DAVBERNOVN : CHIVALER : GIST
    : ICY : DEV : DE : SA : ALME : EYT : MERCY.

1289. *Sir Roger de Trumpington's* head rests on his *tilting helm* (a feature not shared by the other effigies). This is large and conical,[1] and is made fast by a chain to the girdle of the surcoat. At the apex is a staple, to which the *cointisse*—a silk scarf, originally worn over the armour, as a lady's favour, was attached. The shield and scabbard bear :—Azure, crusily and two trumps in pale or ; which coat, with the addition of a label of five points, is seen on the ailettes. A dog, on which the feet rest, holds the *bouterolle* or *chape* of the scabbard in its mouth. The inscription, which no longer exists, was on a fillet of brass, on the edge of the altar tomb, which is surmounted by a canopy.

1302. *Sir Robert de Bures* has no ailettes. The shield

---

[1] The *aventaille*, or piece to protect the face, in which slits were made to admit the air and light (*ocularia*), is hidden. These slits, in the sugar-loaf helm, were usually cruciform.

BRASS TO SIR JOHN D'AUBERNOUN, A.D. 1277.
STOKE D'ABERNON CHURCH, SURREY.

bears :—Ermine on a chief indented sable, two
lioncels or. Below the hawberk are seen,
covering the legs above the knees, costly
chauçons or breeches (*cuisseaux gamboisés*)
ornamented with *fleurs-de-lis*, etc., in what
was called *ouvrage de pourpointerie*. The
fringed ends of these breeches appear below
the genouillières. The feet rest on a lion
couchant. The Lombardic inscription is
given by Waller as follows :—

+ SIRE : ROBE[RT : DE : BVRES] : GIST : ICI :
DEV : DE : SA : ALME : EYT : MERCY : KIKE :
PUR : LALME : P[RIER]A : QVARA[V]NTE : IOURS :
DE : PA[R]DVN : AVERA.

1306. *Sir Robert de Setvans* differs from the foregoing in
having his head bare, exposing his flowing
curled hair, and showing the *coif de mailles*
falling loose about his neck. The hands, too,
are bare, the gloves hanging from the wrists,[1]
which show a buttoned garment, probably
the sleeves of the *hauketon*, which appears
beneath the mail hawberk. The surcoat and
ailettes are charged with winnowing fans,[2]
which also appear on the shield bearing :—
Azure three winnowing fans or; the *guige* of
which passes over the left shoulder instead of
the right. The feet rest on a lion couchant,
much mutilated.

Each of these knights appears to be clean-shaven, and
has the hands clasped in prayer. All but the first are
cross-legged : but as to any crusading significance in this
attitude, Sir Roger de Trumpington affords the only
evidence.

---

[1] A later example of this is illustrated in Shaw's *Dresses and Decorations*,
Vol. I., 1843. "Effigy of Charles, Comte d'Etampes, in the Royal
Catacombs at St. Denis. *d.* 1336."
[2] The motto of this family was "Dissipabo inimicos Regis mei ut
paleam."

Of the two half-effigies :—

c. 1290.   *Sir Richard de Boselyngthorpe* wears plain ailettes, and on his hands, which clasp a small heart, gloves formed of fish-scale-like overlapping plates,[1] attached to leather.   The strap fastening the coif is well shown.   There is no shield. The head rests on two cushions.   The Lombardic inscription runs :—

+ ISSY : GYT : SIRE : RYCHARD : LE : FIZ : SIRE : IOHN : DE : BOSELYNGTHORPE : DEL : ALME : DE : KY : DEVS : EYT : MERCY.

c. 1310.   The *Croft effigy* ends below the elbows, and has neither shield nor ailettes.   The most noticeable point is the banded mail.   The Lombardic inscription reads :—

ICI GIST SIR......BY, PUR DEU PR[IEZ PUR LUI KE DEU DE] SA ALME EYT MERCI.

Matrices of brasses of the Surcoat Period may be seen at :—

Emneth, Norfolk; Sir Adam de Hakebech, *c.* 1290-1300.
Norton Disney, Lincs.; Sir William d'Iseni, *c.* 1300 (the matrix appears to show rowell spurs).
Linwood, Lincs.; Sir Henry.........on bracket, *c.* 1300.
Hawton, Notts.; Sir Robert de Cumpton, 1308.
Aston Rowant, Oxon.; Sir Hugh le Blount, 1314.
Stoke-by-Neyland, Suffolk; Sir John de Peytone, ? 1318.

Two brasses of cross-legged knights, of the reign of Edward II., may be said to mark a transitional period. They have both lost pedimental canopies, shields, and inscriptions :—

---

[1] Compare the vambraces of Sir John de Northwode, *c.* 1330, at Minster, Kent, and the sollerets of Sir Adam de Clifton, 1367, Methwold, Norfolk, and of William Cheyne, Esq., 1375, Drayton Beauchamp, Bucks.

c. 1320.   Sir......Fitz Ralph, Pebmarsh, Essex.[1]
c. 1320.   Sir......de Bacon, Gorleston, Suffolk; lacking
              legs below the knees.

These conform to the costume above-mentioned, but
wear plate armour in addition, viz. :—

DEMI-PLATES, fastened by *arming-points* for the protection
   of the arms (*brassarts*), and consisting of REREBRACES
   (*arrière bras*) on the upper arms, and VAMBRACES
   (*avant-bras*) on the fore-arms.

COUTES or COUDIÈRES at the elbows (also called *cubitière*,
   elbow-cop).

ROUNDELS, circular plates with spikes or knobs, at the
   shoulders and in front of the elbows.

JAMBS or JAMBARTS, plates protecting the shins (sometimes
   called *bainbergs*).

SOLLERETS, overlapping oblong plates, or *lames*, riveted
   together, worn on the upper part of the foot, and
   fastened by straps over the mail.

The Pebmarsh knight wears interlaced mail, embroidered chauçons above the knees, and a curved shield,
much mutilated, which bore :—Or three chevrons gules,
each charged with as many fleurs de lis argent.   The surcoat is fringed, but otherwise plain.   The feet rest on a
dog.   There are no ailettes.

The Gorleston effigy shows banded mail, ailettes,[2] placed
lozenge-wise, and charged with a cross, and a heater-shaped
shield, bearing :—......a bend lozengy......on a chief two
mullets pierced.[3]

---

[1] Three fragments exist of the Lombardic uncial inscription on marginal fillet.   See *The Essex Review*, Vol. X., 1901, p. 87.   *See* also "Notes
on the Brass of Sir William Fitz Ralph in Pebmarsh Church, Essex," by
John Piggot, F.S.A., *The Reliquary*, Vol. IX., 1868-9, p. 193.

[2] Ailettes may be seen on sculptured effigies at Clehongre, Herefordshire; Great Tew, Oxon.; Ash, Kent, and St. Nicholas, Newcastle-on-
Tyne.

[3] The arms of Bacon, of Redgrave, Suffolk, are :—Gules, on a chief
argent two mullets pierced sable.

The MIXED MAIL AND PLATE Period is well illustrated on three brasses, which show the *cyclas* taking the place of the surcoat, and are, therefore, said to belong to the CYCLAS Period.[1]   These are :—

1325.   Sir John de Creke (with lady), Westley Water-less, Cambs.

1327.   Sir John D'Aubernoun II., Stoke D'Abernon, Surrey (son and heir of the knight above-mentioned).

c. 1330.   Sir John de Northwode (with lady), Minster, Kent.

The CYCLAS was an outer garment, closer-fitting than the surcoat, and much shorter in front than behind, where it reached to the knees.   This curtailment was due, pro-bably, to the greater convenience in riding thereby ob-tained.   It was laced up at the sides, and the slits were at the sides, instead of in front and behind as on the surcoat. In the mail, which is banded, we note the following differ-ences.   The hawberk is shaped to a point in front, and the sleeves end just below the elbows.   The coif de mailles is superseded by the *camail*, fastened to a pointed bascinet by means of a lace passing through staples called *vervelles*.

Steel vambraces are seen at the wrists, passing beneath the sleeve of the hawberk, and encircling the fore-arm.

Sir John de Creke wears rowell spurs, roundels at elbow and shoulder, representing lions' heads,[2] and plain coutes.

---

[1] Good examples of the Cyclas period in sculptured effigies are afforded by the following monuments : A knight of the Pembridge family, Clehongre, Hereford ; Humphrey de Bohun, Earl of Hereford, Hereford Cathedral, 1321 ; John of Eltham, Earl of Cornwall, 1334, in St. Edmund's Chapel, Westminster Abbey ; Sir John de Ifield, Ifield, Sussex, *d.* 1317 (probably engraved later) ; Sir Oliver de Cervington, Whatley, Somerset, *c.* 1348.   The sinister half of a brass shield, which may have belonged to the monument of John of Eltham, was presented by Sir Alexander Campbell, Bart., to the Museum of the Society of Antiquaries of Scotland.   See their *Proceedings*, Vol. VI., 1868, p. 204.

[2] Leopard-faced mammelières are seen on a stone effigy of a knight at St. Peter's, Sandwich, Kent.

His cyclas is confined by a narrow girdle at the waist. His heater-shaped shield, held in place by a guige passing over the right shoulder beneath the camail, bears :—Or on a fess gules three lozenges vair. The curtailment of his cyclas in front makes visible the hauketon and hawberk. Immediately above the latter a rich dress appears embroidered with rosettes, and with escalloped and fringed border, called the *pourpoint*.[1] Waller gives the inscription, now lost, which was engraved on a brass fillet :—

+ ICI : GIST : LE : CORPS : SIRE : IOHAN : DE : CREK : ET : DE : DAME : ALYNE : SA : FEME : DE : QVY : ALMES : DIEV : EYT : MERCY.

Sir John D'Aubernoun wears prick spurs and plain roundels. The guige of his shield is not visible ; nor is there a waist-belt over the cyclas. The arms on the heater-shaped shield are those of his father, whose brass is described above. The inscription was in Lombardic lettering.

The effigy of Sir John de Northwode differs much in style from the other two, showing pecularities which have caused it to be attributed to French workmanship (*see* p. 56). The part below the genouillières is a late and incorrect restoration. The border of the camail is engrailed. The bascinet is of a more swelling form than the fluted head-pieces of Creke and D'Aubernoun. There are no rerebraces, and the vambraces are of scale-work. On the left breast is a *mammelière*[2] (a steel plate fastened beneath the cyclas to the hawberk or to the *plastron de fer*, an early form of breastplate), to which is attached a chain passing over the left shoulder, and probably sustaining

---

[1] On the Creke brass some consider this *pourpoint* to be in reality two garments, owing to the presence of both fringe and escalloped border.

[2] The use of mammelières is well shown on the brass of Willem Wenemaer, 1325, at Ghent (illustrated in *Archæological Journal*, Vol. VII., 1850, and in Creeny), where the mail hawberk to which they are attached, is seen through slits in the surcoat. They secure by chains the sword and dagger. *See* also stone effigy of a member of the Salaman family, *c.* 1320, Horley, Surrey.

the tilting helm. The large shield rounded to the body hangs on the hips from a long guige passing under the camail on the right shoulder, and bears:—Ermine a cross engrailed gules.[1]

A short period of transition is represented by the following :—

1347.   Sir Hugh Hastings, Elsing, Norfolk. (Flemish, *see* p. 43).
1347.   Sir John de Wantyng or Wanton (with lady), Wimbish, Essex.
1348.   Sir John Giffard, Bowers Gifford, Essex.

These wear close-fitting *jupons*, which, however, still retain the loose skirt of the cyclas, but of equal length before and behind.

The brass of Sir Hugh Hastings is the most important of the three; for, in addition to the central figure, the sides of the canopy contained eight historic personages (of which two are lost), all wearing this early kind of jupon.   Sir Hugh Hastings wears a rounded bascinet with a moveable vizor, a steel collar or *gorget* over the camail, genouillières with spikes, and rowell spurs.   The cuffs of the hawberk hang down, showing the hauketon below.   Above the knees appear pourpointed cuisseaux. The hands are bare.   There are no jambs.   The heater-shaped shield and the jupon each bear the Hastings arms :— Or, a maunche gules, with a label of three points azure. The maunche is richly embroidered.

The figures in the side shafts are in mixed mail and plate armour, varying somewhat in detail; some having more, some less plate defences.   *Epaulières* or shoulder-plates appear; the spurs are of the prick kind, and the coutes and genouillières have spikes.

---

[1] Possibly this should be blazoned : A cross engrailed between twelve chestnut leaves ; for Northwood Chataigniers.

I.

SIR HUGH HASTINGS, 1347,
ELSING, NORFOLK.

II

KING EDWARD III.
FROM THE HASTINGS BRASS,
ELSING, NORFOLK.

III.

RALPH, LORD STAFFORD.
FROM THE HASTINGS BRASS,
ELSING, NORFOLK.

IV.

ALMERIC, LORD ST. AMAND.
FROM THE HASTINGS BRASS,
ELSING, NORFOLK.

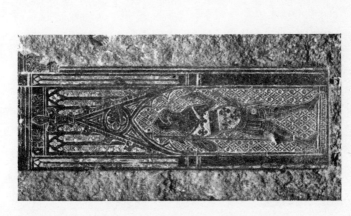

THOMAS BEAUCHAMP,
EARL OF WARWICK.

FROM THE HASTINGS BRASS, ELSING, NORFOLK.

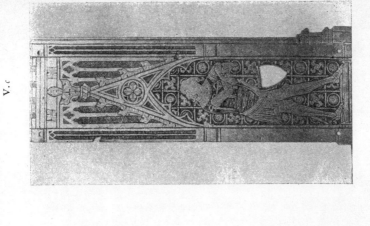

HENRY PLANTAGENET,
EARL OF LANCASTER.

FROM THE HASTINGS BRASS, ELSING, NORFOLK.

ROGER GREY,
LORD GREY DE RUTHIN.

FROM THE HASTINGS BRASS, ELSING, NORFOLK.

V. a

V. b

V. c

On the dexter side :—

1. Edward III., wearing a crown, but no shield. His jupon bears:—France and England quarterly. 1 and 4, az. semée of fleurs de lis or; 2 and 3, gules three lions passant gardant in pale, or; which coat he assumed in 1341.

2. Thomas Beauchamp, Earl of Warwick, wearing a pointed bascinet with vizor up, and holding a lance with pennon in the right hand, but without shield. His jupon bears :—Gules a fess between six crosses-crosslet or.

3. Lost. A member of the Despencer family.

4. Roger Grey, Lord Grey de Ruthin. The arms crossed, the head bare; the shield hanging at the hip bears :—Barry of six arg. and az., in chief three torteaux. In 1905 this figure was restored to Elsing by the Fitzwilliam Museum, Cambridge.

On the sinister side :—

1. Henry Plantagenet, Earl of Lancaster, holding in the right hand his tilting helm, on which is a lion for crest, and in the left a short lance with pennon. His jupon bears :—Gules three lions passant gardant or, a label of three points az., each charged with as many fleurs de lis or.

2. Lost. Lawrence Hastings, Earl of Pembroke, whose shield, bearing :—Hastings quartering Valence, Barry of ten, argent and azure, an orle of martlets gules, is quoted as one of the earliest examples of a subject quartering arms.

3. Ralph, Lord Stafford, holding in the left hand a lance with pennon ; the shield, hanging on the left hip, and the jupon bear :—Or a chevron gules.

4. Almeric Lord St. Amand, wearing the *chapelle de fer*, or kettle hat, over his bascinet (an unique occurrence on a brass) and a gorget of plate. His shield and jupon bear:— Or fretté sable, on a chief of the second three bezants.

In the pediment of the canopy is St. George on horseback, spearing the dragon, his shield and the horse-trapper bearing a cross.[1]

The effigy at Wimbish is placed in a much-mutilated, floriated cross, of which scarce more than the matrix remains. *Epaulières* appear, overlapping plates, here three in number, protecting the shoulders. The feet are lost; but there are jambs over the mail chausses. There is no shield.

The effigy of Sir John Giffard lacks the head. The cuisseaux end in points below the genouillières. The straight edge of the jupon has an ornamented border. There are no plate defences over the banded mail below the knees, nor are there brassarts. The heater-shaped shield borne over the left arm, with the guige passing over the right shoulder, bears:—Sable, six fleurs de lis, 3, 2, and 1 or. The field is finely diapered. On the hands are *gauntlets* with small plates of steel, protecting the fingers, sewn on a leather foundation.

Hitherto we have dealt with styles of armour, each represented by but two or three examples in brasses, but we now come to a period, extending over the second half of the fourteenth, and the first years of the fifteenth century, during the reigns of Edward III., Richard II., and Henry IV., in which the armour, much less variable in style, is represented by a fine series of brasses. These,

---

[1] Effigies on horseback in the pediments of their canopies may be seen in Westminster Abbey on the tombs of Edmund Crouchback, Earl of Lancaster, 1296, and Aymer de Valence, Earl of Pembroke, 1324. Armour for horses is described as follows by Mr. R. C. Clephan in his *Defensive Armour, etc.*, p. 54 : "Bards comprised the chamfron or chanfrien "for the face, worn sometimes with a crest; picière, breast; flanchière, "flanks; croupière, hinder parts; estivals, legs. The crinet, neck, "appears first in England on the seal of Henry V. The horses were "gaily caparisoned. The emblazoned housings were often made of "costly material, such as satin embroidered with gold or silver." The *trapper* of the horse corresponded to the surcoat of the knight. *See* "Horse Armour," by Viscount Dillon, P.S.A., *Archæological Journal*, Vol. LIX., 1902, pp. 67-92.

FROM THE HASTINGS BRASS,
ELSING, NORFOLK.

VII.

FROM THE HASTINGS BRASS,
ELSING, NORFOLK.

VIII.

FROM THE HASTINGS BRASS,
ELSING, NORFOLK.

from one of the chief characteristics, are said to belong to the CAMAIL Period.[1]

Mail armour worn :—

HAWBERK, sometimes called the *habergeon*, shorter than hitherto, with a straight-edged skirt, showing beneath the *jupon*; the sleeves gradually disappeared, *gussets* of mail at the arm-pits and inside the elbows taking their place. The *hauketon* was still worn beneath the hawberk, though it seldom appears; but may be seen at the wrists of Ralph de Knevynton, 1370, at Aveley, Essex, and beneath the skirt of the hawberk of Sir John de St. Quintin, 1397, Brandsburton, Yorkshire.

CHAUSSES, which gradually disappear, are worn by William de Aldeburgh, *c.* 1360, at Aldborough, Yorkshire. A *gusset* of mail protecting the instep is usually seen. Another sometimes appears at the knee, *e.g.*, Sir Morys Russel, 1401, Dyrham, Gloucestershire.

CAMAIL, already noticed, at first is seen passed under the jupon, but is usually found overlapping it. It is secured to the bascinet by a cord passing through *vervelles*, the earlier instances of which are carried up on either side of the face and end in tassels; but later examples encircle the forehead, the cord running in a groove for greater safety.

The mail is usually either banded or made of rings set on their edges; but that of William de Aldeburgh is of the interlaced kind, which we find on some of the later examples, *e.g.*, the Knight at Laughton, Lincs., *c.* 1400.

Of plate defences we find :—

BASCINET, which, but for the groove for the cord of the camail, is usually plain, and is acutely pointed.

---

[1] The bronze effigy of Edward the Black Prince (died 1376) in Canterbury Cathedral shows this style of armour. It is interesting, also, to note that a stone effigy of Henry IV. is to be seen on Battlefield Church, Shrewsbury, built about 1408, wearing a jupon.

REREBRACES and VAMBRACES, consisting of two plates, encircling the arms; *roundels* sometimes in front of the shoulders to protect the arm-pits (*vif de l'harnois* or *defaut de la cuirasse*).

COUTES at the elbows, with circular or heart-shaped hinges.

EPAULIÈRES, of three or more overlapping plates on the shoulders.

CUISSES on the thighs, in earlier examples often covered with studded work[1] or *pourpointerie*.

GENOUILLIÈRES, usually small and plain; but in some early instances (*e.g.*, Sir John de Cobham, 1354, Sir Thomas de Cobham, 1367, Cobham, Kent, and Thomas Cheyne, Esq., 1368, Drayton Beauchamp, Bucks) resembling pot-lids. In some cases plates appear above and below the knees.

JAMBS—as already described.

POINTED SOLLERETS, jointed, enclosing the feet (*à la poulaine*).

ROWELL SPURS.

GAUNTLETS of leather or steel, on the fingers of which are often found small knobs or spikes of steel called *gadlings*. The wrist part frequently is jointed. Sir John de St. Quintin, 1397, Brandsburton, Yorkshire, wears a kind of steel over-cuff, richly engraved, a form of the shell-backed gauntlet.

Over the body-armour is worn the JUPON, laced up at the side, as seen on some sculptured effigies,[2] tight-fitting, and made of leather or of some stout material covered with

---

[1] An example worn over mail chausses in relief on a marble tombstone of the fourteenth century at the Certosa, Florence, is given in *Ancient Sepulchral Monuments*, by Brindley and Weatherley, Plate 126. 1887. The jupon of the knight has a dagged border in the shape of leaves.

[2] As, for example, that of Sir John Leverick, Ash-next-Sandwich, Kent, or a Knight, St. Peter's, Sandwich.

silk or velvet, usually plain, but sometimes, as at Aldborough, c. 1360, and Southacre, 1384, etc., embroidered
with the arms of the wearer. The lower edge, beneath
which the skirt of the hawberk appears, is usually escalloped, or otherwise decorated. In some cases it is cut
into the form of leaves, as at Laughton, Lincs., c. 1400,
or Blickling, Norfolk, Sir Nicholas Dagworth, 1401.
This form of ornamentation was called "dagging" (barbes
d'écrevisses).

The BAWDRIC or knightly belt, worn horizontally on the
    hips, over the jupon, is usually finely ornamented, and
    probably was enriched with metal work. Sometimes
    it takes the form of a buckled belt, the end falling
    down in front, e.g., Sir John D'Argenteine, 1382,
    Horseheath, Cambs. At others it is fastened by a
    large clasp in front.

To the bawdric on the left side is attached the SWORD,
which usually hangs straight at the side; but in some
cases passes behind the left leg (e.g., 1382, Sir Nicholas
Burnell, Acton Burnell, Salop). The scabbard is usually
plain except at the top. The hilt is often corded, and has
straight crossguard and round, octagonal, or pear-shaped
pommel.

The BASILARD or MISERICORDE, a short dagger, not
always represented, hangs in its case on the right, attached
to the bawdric. It has no guard.

The TILTING HELM, surmounted by a crest, and with
lambrequins hanging behind, sometimes appears, used as a
pillow beneath the knight's head.

William de Aldeburgh, c. 1360, is the last instance on
a brass of a knight wearing a shield. The feet of the
knight usually rest upon a lion, but in some cases (e.g.,
Ralph de Knevynton, 1370, Aveley, Essex) on a dog.

It seems to have been the fashion to wear a beard and
moustache, but the former is hidden by the camail. It
appears, however, on the brass of Sir William Tendring,

1408, Stoke-by-Nayland, Suffolk, who is shown bare-headed.

It seems probable that in the latter part of this period the hawberk gave place to *breast* and *back-plates* and *taces* (described below), and that a skirt of mail was fastened either to the breast-plate or the lowermost *tace*. The shape of the figure, over which the jupon fits tightly, is an argument in favour of this view.

In some of the later examples the jupon has escalloped or fringed arm-holes, the plate-armour has invecked edges, and the camail and skirt of the hawberk show an orna-mental fringe of mail, probably composed of brass rings. In one or two instances (*e.g.*, *c.* 1400, Robert Albyn, Hemel Hempstead, Herts), as well as the horizontal bawdric, a diagonal belt is worn supporting the sword, as in the Complete Plate Period.

The following are some of the brasses of this period :—

1354. Sir John de Cobham, Cobham, Kent ; studded cuisses, no misericorde.

c. 1360. John ?Bodiham, Esq., Bodiam, Sussex ; arms on jupon.

c. 1360. William de Aldeburgh, Aldborough, near Boroughbridge, Yorkshire ; on a small bracket. The pourpoint appears between the jupon and the hawberk ; cuisses covered with pourpointerie. The misericorde appears for the first time ; the jupon and semi-cylindrical shield, worn on left arm, bear :— (Az.) a fess per fess indented...and..., between three crosses botony (or), the dexter cross charged with an annulet...for difference.

1361. Sir Philip Peletoot, Watton, Herts ; restored.

c. 1367. Sir John de Cobham (*d.* 1407), Cobham, Kent ; as founder holds church ; studded cuisses, no misericorde.

1367. Sir Thomas de Cobham, Cobham, Kent.

SIR JOHN DE COBHAM, *c.* 1367,
COBHAM, KENT.

1368. Thomas Cheyne, Esq., Drayton Beauchamp, Bucks[1]; shield-bearer to Edward III.

1370. Ralph de Knevynton, Aveley, Essex. Flemish. Hawberk-skirt pointed; both jupon and cuisses are pourpointed. From the former hang two chains to secure the sword and misericorde.

1375. William Cheyne, Esq., Drayton Beauchamp, Bucks; studded cuisses, sollerets of fish-scale pattern,[2] no misericorde.

1382. Sir Nicholas Burnell, Acton Burnell, Salop. The sword passes behind the left, the misericorde to the front of the right leg.

1382. Sir Iohn D'Argenteine, Horseheath, Cambs.; studded cuisses, no misericorde.

1384. Sir John Harsick (with lady), Southacre, Norfolk; holds sword with left hand, and with right hand clasps that of his lady. Arms on jupon :—Or, a chief indented sable.

1388. Sir William de Echingham, Etchingham, Sussex; no misericorde.

1390. Sir Andrew Luttrell, Irnham, Lincs.

1391. Sir William de Kerdeston, Reepham, Norfolk (lower part mutilated).

1392. Thomas, Lord Berkeley (d. 1417) with lady (d. 1392), Wotton-under-Edge, Gloucs.; on

---

[1] The jambs on this brass are noteworthy, consisting, apparently, of narrow vertical bands, the alternate ones studded. It is difficult to determine the materials of which these were composed. Haines (Introduction, p. clviii., note e) says: "The jambs . . . are either strips "of steel, sewed on cloth, or some similar material, or perhaps are of "pourpoint, fluted by strips of steel inlaid with the studs arranged in "rows in the depressions." The lost effigy of Sir Miles Stapleton (1364-5), formerly at Ingham, Norfolk, showed similar jambs and studded cuisses and jupon. A vandyked fringe appears below Thomas Cheyne's genouillières, which probably is connected with the cuisses. See also the effigy of Sir John Giffard mentioned above, p. 156.

[2] Similar sollerets appear on the mutilated brass of Sir Adam de Clifton, 1367, at Methwold, Norfolk.

altar tomb. Over the camail a collar of mermaids, a badge of this family.

1400. Sir John Mauleverere (with lady), Allerton Mauleverer, Yorkshire. Early example of a rectangular plate. The bascinet has a vizor shaped like a bird's beak. The jupon bears :— (Gu.) three levriers or greyhounds, courant in pale (arg.), collared and belled (or). His feet rest on a greyhound.

c. 1400. A Knight, Laughton, Lincs.; edges of plate armour invecked; the camail-cord surrounds the forehead; both diagonal and horizontal belt.

1401. Sir Nicholas Dagworth, Blickling, Norfolk; head rests on tilting helm.

1406. Thomas de Beauchamp, Earl of Warwick (with countess), St. Mary's, Warwick; jupon bears the Beauchamp arms, the charges finely diapered. The staff-ragulé appears on the rim of the bascinet, on roundels at elbows, and on sword-scabbard. The feet rest on a bear.

1407. Sir William Bagot (with lady), Baginton, Warwickshire; jupon bears arms. Collar of SS.

c. 1410. Sir Thomas Burton (d. 1382) (with lady), Little Casterton, Rutland. Collar of SS.

A transitional period, overlapping the later instances quoted, is found in the early part of the fifteenth century, in which the mail defences gradually give way to plate armour, but the camail is still retained, though sometimes worn below a steel GORGET or STANDARD of plate. The most noticeable change is the absence of the jupon, which enables to appear

1. The BREASTPLATE or CUIRASS;
2. The skirt of TACES, overlapping plates, shaped to the figure, varying in number, and fastened to the breast and back plates, from which they extend to the

A BRASS FORMERLY IN INGHAM CHURCH, NORFOLK.

ENGRAVED C. 1400.

From Impression preserved in the Brit. Mus.

SIR WILLIAM DE ECHINGHAM, 1388,
ETCHINGHAM, SUSSEX.

C.B.]

middle of the thighs.[1] To the lowermost *tace* a
fringe of mail is attached, taking the place of the
skirt of the hawberk, now probably abandoned.
When the jupon is retained, the lines of the taces
appear on it.

Examples:—

1401.   Sir Thomas de Braunstone, Wisbeach, Cambs.;
        horizontal bawdric.

1403.   Sir Reginald de Cobham, Lingfield, Surrey;
        orle or wreath round the bascinet; horizontal
        bawdric; head rests on tilting helm, feet on
        dog.

c. 1405. Robert de Freville, Esq., Little Shelford, Cambs.;
        feet on greyhound; horizontal bawdric.

1405.   Thomas de Freville, Esq., Little Shelford,
        Cambs.; similar to the last.

1408.   Thomas Seintlegier, Esq., Otterden, Kent (dis-
        covered September 7th, 1894); horizontal
        bawdric; feet on greyhound.

1408.   John Hauley, Esq. (with two wives), Dart-
        mouth, Devon; horizontal bawdric.

1410.   Sir John Wylcotes (with lady), Great Tew,
        Oxon.[2]; wearing a livery collar ? of SS.

c. 1410. William Loveney, Esq., Wendens Ambo, Essex;
        diagonal sword-belt; feet on lion.

c. 1410. A Knight (with lady) of D'Eresby family,
        probably William, 4th Baron Willoughby
        D'Eresby, Spilsby, Lincs.; *orle* round bas-
        cinet, gorget over camail; both diagonal and
        horizontal belts.

---

[1] The manner of fastening the taces at the sides does not appear on
brasses, but may be observed on sculptured effigies, as, for instance, on
the alabaster effigy, *c.* 1450, at Christchurch, Hampshire, supposed to
represent Sir John Chidiock, whose taces are hinged on the left and
buckled on the right side.

[2] An account of this family may be found in the *Berks Bucks and Oxon.
Archæological Journal*, Vol. III., No. 4, January, 1898, p. 97, "The
Wilcotes Family," by F. N. Macnamara.

1412. Sir Thomas Swynborne,[1] Little Horkesley, Essex; wearing gorget, under which the camail or a fringe of mail attached to the gorget appears; collar of SS.; roundels at shoulders; diagonal sword-belt.

The COMPLETE PLATE period, beginning under Henry IV., lasted during the reign of Henry V. and the first part of that of Henry VI., or in other words, during the ascendancy of the Lancastrians. The characteristic of this period, as its name denotes, is the absence of mail defences, except for a short fringe attached to the lowermost tace in some of the earlier examples.[2]

The plate armour worn consisted of the following pieces :—

BASCINET more rounded in shape than formerly; usually resting on the tilting helm.

GORGET or STANDARD of plate, superseding the camail.

BREASTPLATE (with corresponding *back-plate*) as in the transitional period.

SKIRT OF TACES, varying in the number, which increases. To the centre of the lowermost tace is sometimes attached a *baguette*, consisting of one or more small plates.

EPAULIÈRES, more of which appear than formerly, owing to the different shape of the gorget from that of the camail.

BRASSARTS (rerebraces and vambraces).

COUTES, either with roundels (*e.g.*, Sir John Lowe, 1426,

[1] Represented with his father, Sir Robert Swynborne, 1391, beneath a double canopy. Sir Robert wears the armour of the camail period. The initials R.S. occur on his horizontal bawdric.

[2] Exceptions to this rule may be cited, in the brass of Robert Hayton, Esq., 1424, Theddlethorp, Lincs., who wears the camail instead of a gorget, and in the rare appearance of a fringe of mail below the gorget (*e.g.*, Thomas Walysch, Esq., *c.* 1420, Whitchurch, Oxon.).

SIR THOMAS CHEDDAR, 1442-3,
CHEDDAR, SOMERSET.

Battle, Sussex); fan-shaped (*e.g.*, Sir Arnald Savage, 1420, Bobbing, Kent); or buckle-shaped (*e.g.*, Thomas Chaucer, Esq., 1434, Ewelme, Oxon.).

ROUNDELS in front of the arm-pits, instead of which, in later examples, we find

PALETTES, oblong plates, sometimes charged with a cross (*e.g.*, Sir Simon Felbrigge, 1416, Felbrigg, Norfolk). In a few cases these palettes appear to have the upper and lower edges curved outwards (*e.g.*, Thomas Salle, Esq., 1422, Stevington, Beds; Nicholas Manston, Esq., 1444, St. Laurence, Thanet); and in some a palette of this kind is worn on the left side, and a roundel on the right (*e.g.*, Sir Thomas de St. Quintin, 1418, Harpham, Yorkshire).

GAUNTLETS, sometimes not divided into fingers, but jointed (*e.g.*, John Launceleyn, Esq., 1435, Cople, Beds). In later examples the cuffs are often pointed (*e.g.*, Sir Thomas Cheddar, 1442, Cheddar, Somerset).

CUISSES and JAMBS, plain.

GENOUILLIÈRES, often with plates above and below, sometimes pointed, for additional protection.

SOLLERETS, as before.

ROWELL SPURS, either open (*e.g.*, Valentyne Baret, Esq., 1440, Preston near Faversham, Kent), or guarded (*e.g.*, Sir Thomas Brounflet, 1430, Wymington, Beds.).

The SWORD hangs on the left side by a belt crossing the taces diagonally, and often ornamented with quatre-foils, etc. On the brass of Sir John Phelip, 1415, Kidderminster, the belt has a fringe and bears the initials I.P.

The MISERICORDE is attached to the taces on the right side. The strap fastening it may be seen at Routh, E. Yorks. (Sir John Routh, *c.* 1410) and Brabourne, Kent (William Scot, Esq., 1433).

TUILLES, two tile-like plates fastened to the lowermost tace, and hanging over the thighs, begin to appear. Some instances are cited below.

HERALDIC TABARDS occur in one or two instances, though it is long before they become general on brasses. An early form may be that on the brass of John Wantele, 1424, Amberley, Sussex, which shows a kind of loose vest embroidered with the wearer's arms,[1] and with tight, short sleeves. But on the brass of William Fynderne, Esq., 1444,[2] Childrey, Berks., the tabard is of the form found later, and familiar as that worn by Heralds.[3] On the two

---

[1] Vert three lions' faces argent langued gules. An effigy with similarly-shaped tabard charged with three crescents is engraved in Millin de Grandmaison's *Antiquités Nationales*, Vol. III., 1791, No. 32, Plate 3, p. 19 (Pierre Des Essarts, 1413, Eglise des Mathurins, Paris).

[2] The style of this effigy accords more with that of the succeeding period. It is not improbable that it was engraved some twenty years later, on the death of the wife.

[3] No brasses of Heralds survive. A rubbing is in existence of the brass of Thomas Benolte, or Benold, Clarencieux King of Arms (to whom the earliest known commission for a Visitation was given in 1528-9), with his two wives, 1534, lost from St. Helen's, Bishopsgate, London, showing him in his tabard. In *The History and Survey of London, etc.*, by William Maitland, Vol. II., 1756, p. 1158, occurs the following (cited by Haines, p. cxxviii.) : "In the middle Isle of St. Olave's, Hart-"street, upon a flat Stone, inlaid with Brass, the Figure of a King of "Arms in his Coat and Crown, and underneath was formerly this "Inscription, of which the Date of the Year was lately remaining in the "old black Letter: *Orate pro anima Johannis Clarenseux Regis Armorum,* "*qui obiit vi.to die Mensis Februarii An. Dom. MCCCCXXVII.* It is not "mentioned by Stow what was the Sirname of this Clarenceux; but it "is supposed to have been Arundell; for there is this Entry in the "Office of the Chamberlain of London, 16 Henry VI. *viz.* Richardus "Arundell, filius Johannis Clarenseux Regis Armorum, venit hic coram "Camerario, et cognovit se esse Apprenticium Robert Asheley, Civis & "Aurifabri, &c." At Broughton Gifford, Wilts, is a brass to Robert, second son of Henry Longe, Esq., 1620, showing an altar tomb with a Herald in tabard, and Death standing behind it. At Middle Claydon, Bucks, the inscription of Roger Gyffard, Esq., 1542, and wife, when reversed revealed an inscription for Walter Bellingham, "Alias dicti Walteri Irelonde Regis Armor' in Hybernia," and wife Elizabeth, 1487.

SIR WILLIAM MOLYNS AND WIDOW MARGERY, 1425,
STOKE POGES, BUCKS.

short sleeves and on the breast the arms are seen, in this case:—Argent a chevron between three crosses patté fitché sable, an annulet for difference. The effigy of Sir Ralph Shelton, 1424, Great Snoring, Norfolk, is cited by Haines, as wearing a tabard (*See* Cotman, Vol. I., Pl. xix., ed. 1839), but only the head has survived.

In a few cases the head is bare (*e.g.*, 1424, John Wantele, Amberley, Sussex; 1441, Sir Hugh Halsham, West Grinstead, Sussex; 1444, William Fynderne, Esq., Childrey, Berks.). The fashion seems to have been for the face to be cleanshaven.[1] The feet usually rest on a lion, but sometimes on a dog (*e.g.*, Peter Halle, Esq., *c.* 1420, Herne, Kent), and in one or two instances on a representation of the ground sown with flowers (*e.g.*, John Peryent, Esq., junior, 1442, Digswell, Herts.).

Examples:—

1411. Thomas de Cruwe, Esq., Wixford, Warwickshire; oval palettes charged with cross; no swordbelt.

1412. Robert, Lord Ferrers, Merevale, Warwickshire; mail fringe below taces.

1414. Geoffrey Fransham, Esq., Great Fransham, Norfolk.

1415. John Peryent, Esq., Digswell, Herts.; feet on leopard.

c. 1415. Walter Rolond, Esq., Cople, Beds.; no animal beneath feet.

c. 1415. Sir Robert Suckling, Barsham, Suffolk; Collar of SS.; initials R. S. on scabbard.

c. 1415, *eng.* Sir John de Erpingham, Erpingham, Norfolk; *d.* 1370, mail fringe, feet on lion.

1416. Sir Simon Felbrigge, K.G., Felbrigg, Norfolk; mail fringe below taces, palettes charged with

[1] John (?) Knyvet, Esq., ?1417, Mendlesham, Suffolk, wears a large forked beard hanging over the gorget (illustrated in the Rev. Edmund Farrer's *List of Suffolk Brasses*, 1903, p. 43).

a cross. On left arm rests a staff to which a banner is attached, bearing the arms of Richard II., to whom he was standard-bearer.[1]

1418. Sir Thomas de St. Quintin, Harpham, Yorks.; *orle* round bascinet; waved edge to mail-skirt below taces; horizontal bawdric.[2]

1420. Sir William Calthorpe, Burnham Thorpe, Norfolk; feet on two dogs; collar of SS.

c. 1420. Sir John Lysle, Thruxton, Hants (*d.* 1407).

c. 1420. Peter Halle, Esq., Herne, Kent; feet on dog; no misericorde nor gauntlets; left hand on breast, right holding his wife's right hand.

c. 1420. Thomas Walysch, Esq., Whitchurch, Oxon.; fringe of mail below gorget.

1422. Thomas Salle, Esq., Stevington, Beds.; the tilting helm surmounted by a *panache* of nine feathers.

1422. Thomas de Coggeshall, Esq., Springfield, Essex; feet on ground.

1424. Thomas, Lord Camoys, K.G., Trotton, Sussex (*d.* 1419).

1424. John Poyle, Esq., Hampton Poyle, Oxon.; tuilles.

1425. Sir William Molyns, Stoke Poges, Bucks.

1426. Sir John de Brewys, Wiston, Sussex; no misericorde; slab powdered with scrolls.

1426. John Cosyngton, Esq., Aylesford, Kent; skirt of nine taces.

1430. Sir Thomas Brounflet, Wymington, Beds.; no misericorde; palettes.

---

[1] The arms attributed to Edward the Confessor (Azure a cross flory within an orle of martlets or) impaling France and England, quarterly.

[2] Sir Thomas' gorget runs up into a peak or ridge on either side of the face. A similar peculiarity is seen on the brass of a knight (? of Hansard family), *c.* 1410, at South Kelsey, Lincs. Compare also the stone effigy of Michael de la Pole, Earl of Suffolk, 1415, at Wingfield, Suffolk, who wears a jupon. *See* "Some Peculiarities and Omissions in Brasses," by Viscount Dillon, in No. 1 of the *Journal of the Oxford University Brass-Rubbing Society*, February, 1897.

THOMAS BROKILL, ESQ., AND WIFE JOAN (?), 1437,
SALTWOOD, KENT.

SIR JOHN HARPEDON, 1457,
WESTMINSTER ABBEY.

1433. Sir John Leventhorpe, Sawbridgeworth, Herts.; tuilles; feet rest on dog; round the neck a livery collar.

1434. Thomas Chaucer, Esq., Ewelme, Oxon.; palettes; skirt of ten taces; feet on unicorn.

1435. John Launceleyn, Esq., Cople, Beds.; tuilles; no misericorde.

1437. Thomas Brokill, Esq., Saltwood, Kent.

1437. Roger Elmebrygge, Esq., Beddington, Surrey; tuilles; feet on dog.

1440. Richard Malmaines, Esq., Pluckley, Kent.

1442. Sir Thomas Cheddar, Cheddar, Somerset; palettes.

1444. Sir William Echyngham, Etchingham, Sussex.

1445. Sir Giles Daubeney, South Petherton, Somerset; palettes; feet on dog.[1]

1457. Sir John Harpedon, Westminster Abbey.

A good example of the Complete Plate Period was the brass of Sir Brian de Stapilton, 1438, formerly at Ingham, Norfolk. Under his right foot was a lion, beneath his left a dog with label " Jakke."

The YORKIST Period of armour covers the latter part of the reign of Henry VI., and the reigns of Edward IV. and Richard III. It is distinguished from the previous period, which, of course, it overlaps, by various additional plate defences, made necessary or fashionable by the Wars of the Roses. But, however splendid or useful these pieces of plate may have been, the general effect of the armed knight is less pleasing than in the Lancastrian period, when the armour, simple and dignified, adhered more closely to the lines of the figure. This unwieldly appearance increases as the years advance;

---

[1] The diagonal swordbelt is ornamented with small cinquefoils—possibly in allusion to his arms: Azure three cinquefoils between six crosses crosslet argent.—Illustrated in *Somerset and Dorset Notes and Queries*, Vol. I., 1890, p. 241.

there is less uniformity than we have hitherto encountered, and the armour is often worked into ribs and curves, much elaborating the design.

The armour for the breast is formed of two or more pieces, overlapping for flexibility's sake, and known as *placcates* or *placcards*, or *demi-placcates* or *demi-placcards*. Various re-inforcing plates were added for tournaments, which do not occur on brasses. The place of the *roundels* or *pallets* of a former date is either supplied by the *pauldrons*, or by separate plates, fastened with spring-pins fitting into staples (*e.g.* 1445, Sir John Throckmorton, Fladbury, Worcs.). These plates were of different shape, that over the left or bridle arm being larger than that over the sword arm, which was called a *moton*, and was curved so as not to incommode the wearer when using a lance (*e.g.*, 1440, a Knight, Addington, Kent). The principal additional defences, therefore, were :—

DEMI-PLACCATES or DEMI-PLACCARDS, curved plates, some-
    times of two or more pieces, covering the lower part
    of the breast and backplates proper and narrowing
    as they near the gorget. Fastened to the cuirass by
    a buckle and strap, hidden, owing to the attitude of
    the hands clasped in prayer.[1]

PAULDRONS, shoulder-plates with ridges, worn over or in
    lieu of the *epaulières*, and serving a similar purpose.
    Frequently that worn on the left arm is further pro-
    tected by a larger ridge than that on the right. In
    some cases a pauldron is seen only on the left arm
    (*e.g.*, 1470, Robert Watton, Esq., Addington, Kent).

GARDES DE BRAS, additional plates attached to the coutes,
    varying in shape in accordance with their position on
    the right or left arm.[2] The *coutes* or *coudières* them-
    selves become much larger.

---

[1] An instance, showing the buckle, is to be found, a few years beyond the period, at West Harling, Norfolk (William Berdewell, Esq., *c.* 1490).

[2] Possibly the up-turned edge of the *vambrace* may sometimes be mistaken for a *garde de bras*. *See* Planché's comment on Fairholt, *sub nom.*

Instead of a gorget, a HAUSSE-COL, *standard*, or collar of
mail, sometimes vandyked (*e.g.*, 1454, William
Ludsthorp, Esq., Warkworth, Northants; 1478,
Richard Quartremayns, Esq., Thame, Oxon.) is
found in many cases.

The *tuilles* have their lower ends pointed as a rule, and
as they increase in size the *taces* decrease in number.
The latter are frequently curved or escalloped, and sometimes, as at Isleworth, Middlesex, *c.* 1450, are composed
of many small plates. In some of the later examples
smaller *tuilles* (or *tuillettes*) are seen at the sides, and a
small skirt of mail appears between them, to develop
under Henry VII. into the conspicuous *mail skirt*. A
baguette, or *brayette* (cod-piece), consisting of a lappet of
mail, supersedes that composed of steel plates.

The *epaulières* often take a *splint*-like form, as worn by
the Knight, *c.* 1450, Isleworth, Middlesex. The *cuirass* in
some late examples has a perpendicular ridge down the
centre, called a *tapul* (*e.g.*, 1479, Thomas Playters, Esq.,
Sotterley, Suffolk).

In a few brasses the *lance-rest* appears screwed into the
cuirass on the right side, *e.g.*,

1462. Sir Thomas Grene, Green's Norton, Northants.;
feet on dog.
1466? Henry Parice, Esq., Hildersham, Cambs.; feet on
lion; no gauntlets nor misericorde; wears
what is probably the *hauketon*; tuilles have
but one buckle each, attaching them to the
third tace.
1467. John Bovile, Esq., Stokerston, Leicestershire.

The *genouillières* become larger, and have plates behind
them protecting the back of the knees (*e.g.*, 1467, Sir
William Vernon, Tong, Salop). One or more plates,
those below pointed, occur above and below them.

Gussets of mail sometimes appear protecting the right
armpit, where a *moton* is not worn, and more rarely at the
knees (*e.g.*, 1483, Henry Bourchier, Earl of Essex, Little

Easton, Essex), and at the insteps (*e.g.*, 1458, Thomas Shernborne, Esq., Shernbourne, Norfolk).

The gauntlets often have a plate, of the shape of a tortoise-shell, on the back of the hands, hence called *shell-backed*, and the fingers protected by little overlapping plates (*e.g.*, 1467, Sir William Vernon, Tong, Salop).

The globular bascinet seen in early examples gradually goes out of use, many effigies having bare heads resting on tilting-helms, with elaborate crests and lambrequins, and showing the buckle which fastened down the rim in front, when worn. The hair is represented as cut short, in a roll-like conventional manner; later it becomes long and flowing. When head-pieces are worn they are of the form known as the SALADE, with a piece protecting the back of the neck, and with vizors which, when lowered, met a plate covering the chin (*mentonière*). Three brasses of the Yorkshire School well illustrate this, viz.:—

1459. Sir John Langton, St. Peter, Leeds; feet on ground.

1466. Richard Ask, Esq., Aughton, East Yorks.; feet on dog.

1474. William Fitzwilliam, Esq., Sprotborough, Yorks.; feet on lion.

Heraldic tabards are rarely found, and appear closer-fitting than later, *e.g.*—

1458. William Stapleton, Esq., Edenhall, Cumberland; wearing salade; arms on tabard:—Argent three swords conjoined at the pommel gules Stapleton impaling Or six annulets 3, 2, 1, gules for Veteripont or Vipont.

1473. Sir John Say, Broxbourne, Herts.; bearing:— Party per pale azure and gules, three chevronels or, each charged with another humetté, counterchanged of the field.

1477. John Feld, Esq., Standon, Herts.; Gules a fess or

MILITARY COSTUME 173

between three eagles displayed argent gutté de sang.

The Yorkist Collar of Suns and Roses is sometimes found, see p. 191.

The lion under the feet gradually becomes less common, the dog being more frequent than hitherto; but a representation of the ground, heraldically termed a *mount*, is more usual. The sword, which is large, often with fretted handle, the quillons usually curving towards the blade, at first hangs as before, but later it is suspended by a belt diagonally in front of the body. The misericorde hangs on the right side. Sir Thomas Grene, 1462, Green's Norton, Northants, has a large *anelace* hanging in front perpendicularly, the sword being at the left side.

Examples:—

1435. Richard Delamere, Esq., Hereford Cathedral.
1438. Richard Dixton, Esq., Cirencester, Gloucs.; feet on dog.[1]
c. 1440. Sir William Wadham, Ilminster, Somerset; feet on lion.
c. 1440. Thomas de Mohun, Esq., Lanteglos-juxta-Fowey, Cornwall; feet on lion; no misericorde.
1441. Reginald Barantyn, Esq., Chalgrove, Oxon.; feet on greyhound.
1445. John Throckmorton, Esq., Fladbury, Worcs.; feet on lion.
1445. John Daundelyon, "Gentilman," Margate, Kent; feet on mount.
1445. Thomas de St. Quintin, Esq., Harpham, Yorks.; feet on mount; livery collar.

The above, except for the additional defences, much resemble in style the brasses of the Lancastrian period.

---

[1] The pommel of the sword has a shield bearing:—Or, a pile azure, over all a chevron gules.

The sword hangs straight on the left side. Gorget and bascinet are retained.

The London school of engravers furnishes some examples that are peculiar, the taces being composed of several small pieces. No tuilles; the head bare; *e.g.*,

c. 1442.   Thomas Torrell, Esq., Willingale Doe, Essex; feet on dog.

1447.   John Maltoun, Esq., Little Waltham, Essex.

c. 1450.   A Knight, Isleworth, Middlesex; feet on dog.

1451.   Thomas Reynes, Esq., Marston Morteyne, Beds.; feet on collared greyhound.

1454.   Thomas Stathum, Esq., Morley, Derbyshire; kneeling on helm.

c. 1456.   Walter Grene, Esq., Hayes, Middlesex; feet on griffin.

Examples showing more marked characteristics of the period, such as the sword in front, the head bare, with the hair cut close, are as follows:—

1455/6.   Ralph, Lord Cromwell, K.G., Tattershall, Lincs. (head and left shoulder gone); mantle; feet on two wodehouses.

1458.   Thomas Shernborne, Esq., Shernbourne, Norfolk; head on helm; feet on lion; one buckle each for the tuilles.

1458.   Sir Robert Staunton, Castle Donnington, Leics.; salade; sword hanging straight on left side; feet on collared greyhound.

1459.   William Mareys, Esq., Preston, near Faversham, Kent. (The ground beneath the feet curiously worked.)

c. 1460.   Sir Robert del Bothe, Wilmslow, Cheshire; feet on dog; gussets at right armpit and insteps; neither misericorde nor gauntlets. Lady on dexter side; her right hand held in his, his left hand on his breast.

c. 1460.   A Knight, Adderbury, Oxon.; head on helm; feet on dog; collar of —(?).

Diete pro Animabus Thome Peyton Armigeri et Margarete ac Margarete
Vxores Eius Jm quidem Thomas obijt xx die mensis July Anno
Domini Millimo CCCCLxxxiiii quom Animabus propiciet De Amē

THOMAS PEYTON, ESQ., AND WIVES
MARGARET AND MARGARET, 1484,
ISLEHAM, CAMBS.

1461.   William Brome, Esq., Holton, Oxon.; (now mural); salade; feet on mount.

1462.   William Prelatte, Esq., Cirencester, Gloucs.; salade; feet on mount.

c. 1465.   John Anstey, Esq., Quy, Cambs.; feet on mount; sons kneeling in heraldic tabards.

1470.   Henry Unton, Esq., Sculthorpe, Norfolk; kneeling; no gauntlets; skirt of hauketon (?) appearing.

c. 1475.   A Knight (of the Lacon family?), Harley, Shropshire; head on helm turned with vizor outwards, and showing both buckles which fastened it when worn; sword hangs straight on left side; feet on greyhound.

1478.   Richard Quartremayns, Esq., and ? Richard Fowler, Esq., Thame, Oxon.; feet on mount.

1484.   Thomas Peyton, Esq., Isleham, Cambs.; feet on mount.

The following show some signs of transition to the next period. Where not stated, the hair is long, the feet rest on the ground, and a very short skirt of mail is seen.

1467.   Sir William Vernon,[1] Tong, Shropshire; head on helm; hair short.

c. 1470.   — Aubrey, Esq., Clehongre, Herefordshire; head on helm; feet on lion.

1472.   Robert Ingylton, Esq., Thornton, Bucks.; hair short.

1479.   Thomas Playters, Esq., Sotterley, Suffolk.

1480.   Sir Anthony Grey, St. Alban's Abbey, Herts.; . Collar of suns and roses; head on helm.

c. 1480.   A Knight, Howden, Yorkshire; hair short.

c. 1480.   A Knight of the Northwode family, Milton-next-Sittingbourne, Kent; feet on greyhound.

---

[1] In Millin de Grandmaison's *Antiquités Nationales*, Vol. III., 1791 (No. 26, Pl. 4, p. 18) is an engraving of a similar brass commemorating this knight and his lady, formerly at Vernon, in Normandy.

1482. Thomas Wayte, Esq., Stoke Charity, Hants.;
the sollerets in this and the next instance
have a curiously transitional appearance.
1483. Thomas Hampton, Esq., Stoke Charity, Hants.;
feet on collared greyhound.
1483. Henry Bourchier, Earl of Essex, K.G., Little
Easton, Essex; Collar of suns and roses;
mantle of Garter, feet on eagle.
1485. John Seyntmaur, Esq., Beckington, Somerset;
feet on greyhound.

Some military brasses existing in Norfolk and Suffolk
belong in date to this and the succeeding period, but show
the peculiarities of treatment of a local school of engravers,
which, in all probability, had its headquarters in Norwich.
With divergence in detail, much similarity of style is to
be observed in the following examples; among the more
striking characteristics being the chevron-like lines or
ridges engraved on the jambs, etc., the peculiar treatment
of pauldrons, coutes and tuilles, and the position of the
sword, hanging perpendicularly in front of the body.

c. 1470. Peter Rede, Esq., St. Peter Mancroft, Norwich;
died 1568; wears salade; the pointed sollerets
are long and narrow.
1471. Sir John Cursun, Belaugh, Norfolk; feet on
lion.
1475. Ralph Blen'haysett, Esq., Frenze, Norfolk.
c. 1480. Christopher Playters, Esq., Sotterley, Suffolk;
feet on dog; sword hangs on left side.
1484. Thomas Gybon, Gent., Whissonsett, Norfolk;
mentonière.
1488. Edmund Clere, Esq., Stokesby, Norfolk; feet
on dog; large salade; the plates on the feet
show mail beneath. He wears a kind of collar
of roses.
c. 1500. A Knight, Assington, Suffolk; wears sabbatons.
1510. John Blen'hayset, Esq., Frenze, Norfolk.

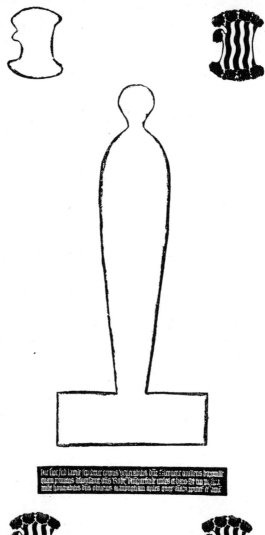

MATRIX OF SHROUD EFFIGY OF ALIANORE MULLENS,
c. 1476,
STOKE POGES, BUCKS. WITH TILTING SHIELDS.

The EARLY TUDOR Period of armour, sometimes called from its chief characteristic the MAIL SKIRT Period, may be said to have lasted from the accession of Henry VII., in 1485, to that of Elizabeth in 1558. Of this style many examples remain; but unfortunately the quality of the engraving shows a rapid deterioration. The armour differs from that lately described in the following particulars.

There is not the exaggerated appearance of the Yorkist period. The *coutes* are of moderate size, and are not encumbered by *gardes de bras*. The *demi-placcates*, where found, are simple in form. The *pauldrons* have the per-pendicularly-projecting plates, *pike-guards*, usually called *pass-guards*,[1] attached to them to ward off blows; that on the left shoulder being, as a rule, larger than that on the sword arm. The *cuirass*, to which a *lance-rest*[2] is some-times attached on the right side (*e.g.*, 1500, John Tame, Esq., Fairford, Gloucs.), usually has the *tapul* or ridge down the centre, and becomes more globular in shape. The neck is protected either by a steel gorget, or more frequently by the *standard* of mail. The skirt of taces varies much in shape and composition. In a few cases it is made of many small plates, possibly intended for the skirt of *lamboys*, or *bases*, consisting of laminated hoops, fastened together by "almayne," or sliding rivets, as worn in the sixteenth century (*e.g.*, James Peckham, Esq., *c.* 1530, Wrotham, Kent, and Sir William Scot, 1527, Brabourne, Kent, the latter having curious defences at the elbows, resembling roundels). In some late examples (*e.g.*, 1559, John Dauntesay, Esq., West Lavington, Wilts.) the taces have an arched opening in the centre, a

---

[1] The term *passguard* is probably misapplied to the upright shoulder pieces. *See* Lord Dillon's paper, "The Passguard, Garde de Cou, Brech-Rand, Stoss-Kragen or Randt, and the Volant Piece," pp. 129 and 433, *Archæological Journal*, Vol. XLVI., 1889.

[2] The tilting-shield, rare on brasses, had a cavity, (*à bouche*) cut in the dexter chief corner, acting as a lance-rest. Two shields of this shape may be seen at Rainham, Essex, *c.* 1475.

mark of transition to the *Tasset* period.   The *tuilles* vary
much in number, size, and shape.   Two large ones are
worn by Sir Humphrey Stanley, 1505, Westminster
Abbey.   Three (one in the centre) are seen at Nether
Heyford, Northants. (Sir Walter Mauntell, 1487), and in
the British Museum ("A man in armour," *c.* 1510).   Four
appear on some examples, two being worn at the sides
(*e.g.*, 1488, Henry Covert, Esq., North Mimms., Herts.).
Those worn at the back, called *culettes*, do not often
appear (*e.g.*, 1505, Morys Denys, Esq., Olveston, Gloucs.,
in tabard, kneeling).

The SKIRT or PETTICOAT OF MAIL is worn beneath the
tuilles,[1] and usually exceeds them in length, though sometimes the reverse is the case (*e.g.*, 1529, Sir Robert Clere,
Great Ormesby, Norfolk).   Its lower edge is found
straight (*e.g.*, 1510, John Leenthorp, Esq., Great St.
Helen's, Bishopsgate, London), or vandyked (*e.g.*, 1559,
John Dauntesay, Esq., West Lavington, Wilts.), and it
is often slit up the centre (*e.g.*, 1513, John Toke, Esq.,
Great Chart, Kent).   The armour for the legs (cuisses,
genouillières (sometimes ornamented with rosettes) and
jambs) presents but little change.   Gussets of mail appear
at the right armpit and at the insteps   Pointed *sollerets*
are replaced by broad-toed SABBATONS of inelegant shape,[2]
and frequently of clumsy proportions, to which the spurs
were often screwed (*e.g.*, 1500, John Tame, Esq., Fairford,
Gloucs.).   The sword and misericorde, each usually of
large size, hang straight at the sides, or pass diagonally
behind the body.   The belt for the former is often
omitted (*e.g.*, 1528, Henry Stanley, Esq., Hillingdon,
Middlesex).   The scabbard, worn in front, by Sir William

---

[1] The representation of the tuilles worn *beneath* the mailskirt, as,
c. 1500, a Knight, Chedzoy, Somerset; *c.* 1500, a Knight of the
Compton (?) family, kneeling, in the possession of the Surrey Archæological Society; or, 1517, Anthony Hansart, Esq., March, Cambs.,
kneeling, may be due to the engraver's error.

[2] Called "bear-paw," or "cow-mouth," "bec de cane."

THOMAS GOLDE, Esq., 1525,
CREWKERNE, SOMERSET.

Peeche, 1487, Lullingstone, Kent, is handsomely decorated. The hair is worn long, and the face is clean-shaven, except in a few cases, where beard and moustache are worn (e.g., 1545, Sir Robert Demoke, Scrivelsby, Lincs.). The head and hands are usually bare; but a small helmet appears, worn at Swallowfield, Berks., 1554, Christopher Lyttcot, Esq., and at Broxbourne, Herts., 1531, John Borrell (Sergeant-at-Arms, with mace). This helmet was sometimes provided with flaps to defend the ears, called *oreillettes*. An example occurs on the brass of Philip Mede, Esq., c. 1475, at St. Mary Redcliff, Bristol. Gauntlets are well shown at Hunstanton, Norfolk, 1506, (Sir Roger l'Estrange), whose hands are uplifted so as to show the palms. The head rests in many cases on the tilting helm, surmounted by crest and mantling. On two Bedfordshire brasses (1527, William Cokyn, Esq., Hatley Cockayne, and 1528, John Fysher, Esq., Clifton) the helm bears a triple plume. The feet, as a rule, rest on a mount, but lions and dogs are also found. Many effigies, especially those in tabards, are represented kneeling on cushions at prayer desks. Chains, usually supporting a Tau cross, are worn by some figures round the neck (e.g., 1508, John Mohun, Esq., Lanteglos-juxta-Fowey, Cornwall; 1528, Henry Stanley, Esq., Hillingdon, Middlesex). Ruffs and frills appear in some late examples at the neck and wrists (e.g., 1559, Sir Edward Greville, Weston-upon-Avon, Gloucs., in tabard). The space between the legs of the effigy is often not cut away (e.g., 1500, Richard Conquest, Esq., Houghton Conquest, Beds.). A large proportion of the knights and esquires represented during this period held office in the Royal Household. Examples :—

1485. Thomas Halle, Esq., Thannington, Kent; feet on dog.
1496. John Hampden, Esq., Great Hampden, Bucks.
1496. John Payn, Esq., Hutton, Somerset; feet on dog.

1497.   John Trenowyth, Esq., St. Michael Penkivel, Cornwall; feet on greyhound; head on helm.

c. 1500.   Sir Hugh Johnys, Swansea, Glamorganshire.

1503.   Robert Borrow, Esq., Stanford Rivers, Essex.

1507.   William, Viscount Beaumont, Wivenhoe, Essex; head on helm; feet on elephant.

1509.   John le Strange, Lord Strange of Knokyn, d. 1477, Hillingdon, Middlesex.

1511.   Richard Gyll, Esq., Shottesbrooke, Berks.

1521.   Richard, Lord Grey de Wilton, Eton College Chapel, Bucks.; Page of Honour to Henry VIII.

1523.   Thomas Boynton, Esq., Roxby Chapel, York-shire.

1527.   Sir Peter Legh, Winwick, Lancs.; wearing chasuble over his armour.[1]

1529.   Sir Thomas Brooke, Cobham, Kent; cross hanging by chain round neck.

c. 1530.   Henry Bures, Esq., Acton, Suffolk; head on helm; wearing gauntlets, and tuilles (two in number) at the sides of the thighs.

1531.   John Horsey, Esq., Yetminster, Dorset; cuirass decorated with scroll work.

1538.   Sir Thomas Bullen, K.G., Earl of Wiltshire, Hever, Kent; head on helm; feet on gryphon.

1546.   William Thinne, Esq., All Hallows' Barking, London; Master of the Household to Henry VIII., editor of Chaucer in 1532.

1551.   Peter Coryton, Esq., St. Mellion, Cornwall; head on helm.

1553.   Nicholas Saunder, Esq., Charlwood, Surrey; kneeling.

---

[1] At Merton, Norfolk, there is a shield with inscription to Thomas de Grey, Esq., 1556, and his wife, Elizabeth, died c. 1514, daughter of Sir Richard Fitzlewes, "who, after her decease made himself preast, and so lyved xli yeres."

SIR THOMAS BROOKE, LORD COBHAM, AND
WIFE DOROTHY, 1529,
COBHAM, KENT.

1553.   Sir John Hampden, Great Hampden, Bucks.;
        ruff; chain round neck.

1558.   Thomas Harlakynden, Esq., Woodchurch, Kent;
        kneeling.

1567.   (eng. *c.* 1520) John White, Esq., Southwick,
        Hants.

1577.   Hugh Starky, Esq., Over, Cheshire; head on
        helm; in armour of this period.

The *Tabard of Arms* frequently occurs in the first half
of the sixteenth century.   When represented on the same
monument as her husband, the wife usually wears an
heraldic mantle.   Examples :—

1485.   Piers Gerard, Esq., Winwick, Lancs.; feet on
        lion.   The mail-skirt and tuilles are hidden.

1499.   Thomas Heveningham, Esq., Ketteringham,
        Norfolk; kneeling; coloured.

c. 1500.   A Knight of the Scarisbrick family, Ormskirk,
        Lancs. ; head on cushion ; feet on lion ; chains
        round the neck.   The tabard shows the taces
        at the side.

1501.   Robert Baynard, Esq., Lacock, Wilts.

1506.   Sir Roger le Strange, Hunstanton, Norfolk;
        head on cushion, above which is a helm with
        huge mantling ; the coutes and genouillières
        have curious knobs ; the hands are upheld,
        showing the inner side of the gauntlets ; the
        whole rests on a low bracket enclosed within
        a fine triple canopy, the side shafts of which
        contain eight ancestors in tabards.

1516.   Thomas Knyghtley, Esq,, Fawsley, Northants;
        head on helm.

1526.   John Shelley, Esq., Clapham, Sussex.

1534.   Sir Edmond Tame, Fairford, Gloucs.; head on
        helm ; wearing chain with Tau cross.

1539.   Sir John Clerk, Kt., Thame, Oxon.; kneeling
        on cushion.

c. 1540.   Sir William Gascoigne, Cardington, Beds.; head

on helm; feet on greyhound. Comptroller
of the household to Cardinal Wolsey.

1546/7. Sir Ralph Verney, Aldbury, Herts.; head on
helm; ruffs at wrists.

1546. Sir John Greville, Weston-upon-Avon, Gloucs.;
head on helm; frill at neck; bearded; arched
opening in front of the taces.

1548. Sir Humphrey Style, Beckenham, Kent; kneeling.

1556. Sir John Russell, Strensham, Worcs.; kneeling;
wearing chain and mail skirt vandyked.

1559. Sir Edward Greville, Weston-upon-Avon,
Gloucs.; vandyked mail skirt; bearing much
resemblance to the effigy of his father, 1546.

Several brasses exist showing a transitional stage, in the
retention of the mail skirt, often vandyked, worn beneath
tassets; the rest of the armour corresponding to that
described in the next period. Examples:—

1545. Sir John Arundell, Kt., St. Columb Major, Cornwall; head on helm.

1548. Sir William Molyneux, Sefton, Lancs.; wearing
an antiquated *coif de mailles* (*see* p. 146), over
which is a livery collar. The cuirass is engraved with a cross moline.

1552. Robert Cheyne, Esq., Chesham Bois, Bucks.;
wearing helmet.[1]

1559. John, Lord Williams, Thame, Oxon.; head on
helm; feet on collared greyhound; long
mantle, fur lined, fastened on left shoulder.

1561. Sir John Arundell of Trerice, Kt., Stratton, Cornwall; wearing helmet and plate gorget.

1565. John Toke, Esq., Great Chart, Kent.

1565. Sir Edward Warner, Little Plumstead, Norfolk;
head on helm; feet on collared greyhound.

[1] Another instance of the helmet worn is at Burgh Wallis, Yorkshire,
1554 (?), Thomas Gascoigne, Esq.

1568.   Sir Richard Molyneux, Sefton, Lancs.

1571.   Richard, Ralph and Edward Blondevile, Esquires, Newton Flotman, Norfolk; kneeling.

1572.   Ralph Jenyns, Esq., Churchill, Somerset.

1572.   Anthony Daston, Esq., Broadway, Worcs.

1573.   Sir William Harper, St. Paul's, Bedford; head on helm; wearing civic mantle.

1576.   Richard Tomynw, Esq., Boxley, Kent; head on helm.

The TASSET Period of armour is the latest, including the reign of Elizabeth and those of the Stuarts, till armour fell into disuse. Its characteristic is the substitution of *tassets* for the skirt of taces and tuilles, the mail skirt disappearing except in some transitional instances just mentioned. The *tassets*, overlapping plates, taking the place of the *taces*, were fastened to the lower edge of the breast-plate, which became long-waisted and protuberant in the lower part (*peascod*). The tasset-ends were either rounded, obtusely pointed, or rectangular; but sometimes, usually in later examples (*e.g.*, 1590, Thomas Nevynson, Esq., Eastry, Kent), joined to the genouillières (*tassets à l'écrevisse*), which are frequently engraved with rosettes (*e.g.*, 1583, Hercules Raynsford, Esq., Clifford Chambers, Gloucs.). The pauldrons, often scroll-shaped, sometimes nearly meet in front, and frequently have escalloped edges, as have the *tassets*, caused by their lining. The latter are worn above trunk hose, puffed and often slashed, over which they are bound by straps. The sabbatons are smaller, the toes being rounded. Ruffs and frills are worn at neck and wrists. The sword assumes the modern guard, and sometimes has a tassel; the dagger is suspended by a small sash. The hair is cut short; but moustache and beard are worn. The head sometimes still rests on the helm (*e.g.*, 1575, John Cosowarthe, Colan, Cornwall; 1584, John Wingfield, Esq., Easton, Suffolk). Headpieces are seldom worn. A plumed instance occurs at Cardington, Beds. (Sir Jarrate Harvye, 1638).[1] Tabards are seldom found, *e.g.* :—

1561. Henry Hobart, Esq., Loddon, Norfolk ; in splint-like armour, and wearing gauntlets.

1562. Sir John Russell, Strensham, Worcs.

1562. Sir Gyles Strangwayes, Melbury Sampford, Dorset; head on helm.

1565. Sir John Tregonwell, D.C.L., Milton Abbas, Dorset.

The feet are usually on a chequered pavement or rounded pedestal. The brass is often not cut away between the legs and sword.

The following are some examples :—

1551. Edward Leventhorp, Esq., Sawbridgeworth, Herts.

1567. John Killigrew, Esq., Budock, Cornwall.

1576. Thomas Higate, Esq., Hayes, Middlesex.

1577. Francis Clopton, Esq., Long Melford, Suffolk ; head on helm.

1578. Sir Edward Baynton, Kt., Bromham, Wilts. ; kneeling ; his helmet, with vizor up, lying beside him.

1587. Thomas Hawkins, Esq., Boughton-under-Blean, Kent ; tassets joined to genouillières.

1591. Thomas Stoughton, Gent., St. Martin's, Canterbury.

1593. Humphrey Brewster, Esq., Wrentham, Suffolk.

1594. John Clippesby, Esq., Clippesby, Norfolk.

1597? John Browne, Gent., St. John de Sepulchre, Norwich.

1602. Christopher Septvans, *alias* Harflete, Esq., Ash-next-Sandwich, Kent.

c. 1608. Thomas Windham, Esq. (*d.* 1599), Felbrigg, Norfolk.

---

[1] An earlier example is at Norton Disney, Lincs., William Disney, Esq., *c.* 1556.

CHRISTOPHER SEPTVANS,
alias HARFLETE, ESQ., 1602,
Ash-next-Sandwich, Kent.

1618. Nicholas Wadham, Esq. (d. 1609), Ilminster, Somerset. Founder of Wadham College, Oxford.

c. 1620. Nicholas Poulett, Esq., Minety, Wilts.; kneeling on cushion; rectangular plate.

c. 1620. John Mallevorer, Esq., Laughton en le Morthen, West Yorks.

1625. Sir Arthur Gorges, Kt., St. Luke's, Chelsea; kneeling; his eldest son similar; on a rectangular plate.

1638. William Cleaybroke, Esq., Margate, Kent.

1680. Nicholas Toke, Esq., Great Chart, Kent; kneeling; has long hair.

Under the Stuarts large jack-boots with spurs and spur-leathers take the place of jambs and genouillières; the hair is worn long, and collars and cuffs supersede ruffs and frills. A minimum of armour may be seen worn by George Hodges, c. 1630, Wedmore, Somerset (engraved in Haines, p. ccxxxviii.). A buff coat with sash has taken the place of the body armour, a small steel gorget alone surviving; breeches and jack boots complete his suit. A sword hangs by a belt passing over the right shoulder; a small pike is held in the right hand.

Examples:—

1633. John Arundell, Esq., St. Columb Major, Cornwall.

c. 1634. John Boscawen, Esq. (d. 1564), St. Michael Penkevil, Cornwall; kneeling on cushion; the tassets do not reach to the knees.

1638. Sir Edward Filmer, Kt. (d. 1629), East Sutton, Kent; in finely engraved armour.[1] His eldest

[1] This brass is the work of Ed. Marshall (see above, Introduction, p. 14). In *The History and Antiquities of Tottenham High Cross*, by Richard Randall Dyson, London, 1792, pp. 43-44, is a description of a marble monument in that church to Mary, wife of Sir Robert Barkham, 1644, signed "*Ed. Marfhall. Sculptor.*" This fact will be found mentioned in *The History and Antiquities of the Parish of Tottenham*, by William

son, Sir Robert Filmer, stands below in similar armour, but wears in addition a short cloak with the arms hanging loose. He wears a collar, while Sir Edward has a fine ruff.

1650.   Ralph Assheton, Esq., Middleton, Lancs.; locally engraved.

1655.   Adam Beaumont, Esq., Kirkheaton, West Yorks.; wearing sword on the right side.

KNIGHTS OF THE GARTER.

Brasses of Knights of the Most Noble Order of the Garter,[1] founded by Edward III., 1349, are rare. The following occur. The Garter is worn just below the knee on the left leg.

1409.   Sir Peter Courtenay, Exeter Cathedral; in armour of the Camail period.

1416.   Sir Simon Felbrigge, Felbrigg, Norfolk; in complete plate armour.

1424.   Thomas, Lord Camoys, Trotton, Sussex; in plate armour, wearing collar of SS. (d. 1419).

1455/6.   Ralph, Baron Cromwell, Tattershall, Lincs.; Lord High Treasurer of England to Henry VI.; much injured; wearing the Mantle. The badge is not visible owing to the loss of the shoulder.

1483.   Henry Bourchier, Earl of Essex, Little Easton, Essex; in armour, with Collar of suns and roses; wearing the Mantle, with badge on the left shoulder.

Robinson, LL.D., F.S.A., 1818, p. 86 (2nd ed., 1840, Vol. II., p. 41), much of which work seems to have been derived from that of Dyson, though we fail to find any mention of the latter's name.

[1] A good article on this subject is "Garter Brasses," by John Alt Porter (in *The Antiquary*, Vol. XIV., November, 1886, p. 197), who writes in *Walford's Antiquary*, Vol. X., July to December, 1886, pp. 167; 253, on "Garter Knights Degraded."

1538. Sir Thomas Bullen, "Erle of Wilscher and erle of Ormunde," Hever, Kent; wearing a jewelled coronet or cap, and over his armour the full insignia: Surcoat, Mantle with badge on left shoulder, the *Humerale*, or Hood over the right shoulder, Collar of Garters, each enclosing a rose, and the Garter.

At Holy Trinity Church, Chester, is an inscription to Henry Gee, died 1545, which is palimpsest, the reverse showing part of a brass of a Knight of the Garter, *c.* 1520, from which it is evident that the knight wore over his armour the Mantle of the Order, and the Garter on his left leg.

A fine matrix remains at Pleshey, Essex, 1480, showing the outlines of the brass of Humfrey Stafford, 1st Duke of Buckingham, K.G., with Anne his wife, beneath a fine canopy. His head rests on his helm, and he wears the Mantle of the Garter, similarly to Henry Bourchier, Earl of Essex, 1483, at Little Easton, in the same county.

The lost brasses of Thomas, 2nd Duke of Norfolk, K.G., 1524, and Agnes his wife, are illustrated in *Norfolk Archæology*, Vol. VIII. (1879). The Duke wears the Mantle of the Order; the Duchess an heraldic mantle. Originally at Thetford Priory, Norfolk, these brasses were removed at the dissolution to St. Mary's Church, Lambeth. At Painswick, Gloucs., is the matrix of Sir William Kyngston, K.G., and Lady, 1540. He was depicted kneeling, in the Mantle of the Garter. His coat of arms was given enclosed in a Garter.[1]

---

[1] See pp. 216-217 *The Monumental Brasses of Gloucestershire*, by Cecil T. Davis; London, 1899. A few instances occurring on brasses of the coat-of-arms surrounded by the Garter, are as follows :—

1416 On the brass of Robert Hallum, Bishop of Salisbury, in Constance Cathedral; France and England quarterly.

1424 On the Camoys brass, at Trotton, Sussex, two shields bearing :— Argent on a chief gules three plates (Camoys).

c 1535 Lady Katherine Howard, *d.* 1452, Stoke-by-Nayland, Suffolk (illustrated by Cotman); the Howard arms within a Garter, the motto being in Roman capitals (lost).

The late Duke of Devonshire in 1867 laid down brasses in Skipton in Craven Church, Yorkshire, to replace those stolen in the seventeenth century, representing Henry Clifford, 1st Earl of Cumberland, K.G., and Margaret, daughter of Henry Percy, Earl of Northumberland, his Countess, 1542. The Earl is shown in armour of the *mail-skirt* period, and wearing the Garter; the Countess in a pedimental headdress surmounted by a coronet, and wearing an heraldic mantle. Four shields are each surrounded by the Garter.

LIVERY COLLARS ON MILITARY BRASSES.

Of the much-disputed meaning of the letters SS. worn collar-wise, we do not propose to treat.[1] That the collar of SS. was as much an *insigne* of the House of Lancaster, as that of suns and white roses was of the House of York, there seems no doubt. Of their use the late

---

1555 Lady Jane Guildford, Duchess of Northumberland, sole heiress to Sir Edward Guyldeford, K.G., St. Luke's, Chelsea; kneeling in heraldic mantle. Her arms enclosed in a Garter above.

1557 Mural; above sculptured effigies of Sir John Gage, K.G., "preclari ordinis Garterii," Constable of the Tower of London, and wife Phillipa, West Firle, Sussex.

c 1580-82 On brass to two sons of Arthur, Lord Grey of Wilton, in Christchurch Cathedral, Dublin. They died at the Castle.

At Woodrising, Norfolk, is an achievement for Sir Francis Crane, Chancellor of the Most Noble Order of the Garter, 1636; below the shield is a badge, consisting of a rose, encircled by the Garter motto. *See* illustration, p. 325, Vol. I., Farrer's *Church Heraldry of Norfolk*, 1885. In this connection we may mention the Stall Plates of the Knights of the Garter in St. George's Chapel, Windsor, of which over five hundred survive, made of copper, many of them finely enamelled and gilt, and a few palimpsest. *See* the illustrations of fifteenth century plates in *The Stall Plates of the Knights of the Order of the Garter, 1348-1485; A Series of Ninety Full-sized Coloured Facsimiles, with descriptive Notes and Historical Introductions,* by W. H. St. John Hope, M.A. Westminster: Constable, 1901.

[1] *See* "On Collars of the Royal Livery," by J. G. Nichols, *Gentleman's Magazine*, New Series, Vol. XVII., January to June, 1842, pp. 157, 250, 378, 477; Vol. XVIII., July to December, 1842, pp. 353, 595; Vol. XIX., January to June, 1843, p. 258. And the same author's "Notes

Mr. John H. Mayo wrote as follows[1]:—" Of the various
" collars which were in use in this country prior to the
" institution of the Collar of the Order of the Garter by
" Henry VII., the best-known is the Collar of SS., repre-
" sentations of which are seen in many monumental
" effigies and brasses, usually those of knights.   It is also
" met with on effigies of ladies, and in such cases the
" lady is nearly always beside her husband.   In its earlier
" form it consisted of a band or strip of leather or other
" material to which the SS. were affixed; at a later time
" the SS. were linked together, and the band disappeared.
" This collar was the livery of the Lancastrian kings.   It
" seems to have first made its appearance in this country
" in the latter half of the fourteenth century.   With the

---

in Illustration of the Wills of Joan, Lady Cobham, and Eleanor, Lady
Arundell, *Surrey Archæological Collections*, Vol. III., 1865, p. 354.

"Hackington, or St. Stephen's, Canterbury, Collar of SS.," by Edward
Foss, F.S.A., *Archæologia Cantiana*, Vol. I., 1858, pp. 73-93.

"Notes on Collars of SS.," by Albert Hartshorne, F.S.A., *Archæological
Journal*, 1882, Vol. XXXIX., p. 376.

"On the SS. Collar, and others," by H. K. St.-J. Sanderson, M.A.,
Transactions of the Cambridge University Association of Brass Collectors,
Vol. I., No. vii., February, 1890, p. 6.

"Seneschallus" seems the most probable meaning.   Other interpreta-
tions are "Souverayne," "Sanctus," "Souvenez," "Societas," "Silentium,"
"Signum," "Soissons" (Martyrs of: St. Crespin and St. Crespinian),
"St. Simplicius," "Countess of Salisbury," etc.   Whatever its origin its
decorative effect may have had something to do with the retention of
this collar.

If the explanation that the letter stands for "Souverayne," Henry IV.'s
motto, be correct, it is of interest to note that the word "Souverayne"
is repeated on the wooden canopy above the effigies of Henry IV. and
his Queen, Joan of Navarre, in Canterbury Cathedral, on which canopy
may be seen a device attributed to the Queen, and supposed by Gough
to represent a sable, by Sandford an ermine, collared, under a crown (*see*
Gough's *Sepulchral Monuments*, Vol. II., Part ii., p. 32).   Haines mentions
a brass of "a Man in armour, *c.* 1390," formerly at Mildenhall, Suffolk,
and engraved by Hollis (Part 3, No. 8, December 1st, 1840), whose
livery collar had as pendant a similar badge, supposed by Haines to be a
lion or a dog.   *See* Planché, *sub* Collar.

[1] *Medals and Decorations of the British Army and Navy*, by John H.
Mayo.   London: Constable; 1897.   Vol. I., pp. xliv. to lii.

"accession of the Yorkists to power in 1461, their Collar
"of Suns and Roses came into use; but on the accession
"of Henry VII. in 1485, the Collar of SS. was revived.
"In the time of the Tudors their badge of the portcullis,
"a former badge of the Beauforts, was used in conjunc-
"tion with the letter S., as was likewise the Union rose—
"the collars thus combining the Lancastrian, the Yorkist,
"and the Tudor devices. In the reign of Henry VIII.
"the collar appears to have become, to some extent, a
"badge of civil office, and to have ceased to bear any
"political significance. At any rate, it is not met with on
"effigies of knights in armour in that period, and it may
"therefore be inferred that it had gone out of fashion as
"a military badge."[1]

The following brasses show the SS. collar (where the
lady is mentioned she also wears it):—

1405.   Sir Thomas Massyngberde and Lady, Gunby,
        Lincs.
1407.   Sir William Bagot and Lady, Baginton, War-
        wickshire.
1410.   Sir John Routh and Lady, Routh, Yorks.
c. 1410.   Sir Thomas Burton (d. 1382), Little Casterton,
        Rutland.
1411.   Sir John Drayton, Dorchester, Oxon.
1412.   Sir Thomas Swynborne, Little Horkesley, Essex.
1415.   Sir Robert Suckling, Barsham, Suffolk.
1415.   Sir Thomas Peryent and Lady, Digswell, Herts.
1415.   Sir John Phelip, Walter Cookesey, Esq., and
        Lady, Kidderminster, Worcs.
1416.   Matthew Swetenham, Esq., Blakesley, Northants.
1420.   Sir Arnold Savage, Bobbing, Kent.
1420.   Sir William Calthorpe, Burnham Thorpe,
        Norfolk.
1424.   Thomas, Lord Camoys, and Lady, Trotton,
        Sussex.

---

[1] Vol. I., p. xlviii., with illustration of Camoys brass, Trotton, Sussex.

SIR JOHN DRAYTON, 1411,
DORCHESTER, OXON.

1426.   Sir Thomas le Straunge, Wellesbourne, War-
          wickshire.

1431.   Edward de la Hale, Esq., Oakwood, Surrey.

1435.   Thomas Wideville, Esq., Bromham, Beds.

1444.   John Frogenhall, Esq., Teynham, Kent.

1444.   Nicholas Manston, Esq., St. Lawrence, Thanet,
          Kent.

c. 1450. A man in armour, South Kensington Museum,
          London.

1451.   Sir John Bernard, Isleham, Cambs.

c. 1475. Nicholas Kniveton, Esq., Mugginton, Derby.

c. 1490. — Guise, Esq., Aspley Guise, Beds.

c. 1490. Sir William Pyrton, Little Bentley, Essex.

Collars of Suns and Roses.

1465.   John Theel, Esq., Arundel, Sussex.

1470.   Sir William Yelverton, Rougham, Norfolk.

1471.   Thomas Colte, Esq., and wife, Roydon, Essex.

1471.   Thomas Clarell, Esq., Lillingstone Lovell, Oxon.

1473.   Sir John Say, Broxbourne, Herts.

1478.   Robert Bothe, Esq., Sawley, Derbyshire.

1480.   Sir Anthony Grey, St. Alban's Abbey, Herts.

1483.   Henry Bourchier, Earl of Essex, and Countess,
          Little Easton, Essex.

c. 1490. Nicholas Gaynesford, Esq., Carshalton, Surrey.

Some effigies have collars, the nature of which it is
impossible to determine, such are :—

1410.   Sir John Wylcotes (d. 1422), Great Tew, Oxon.

1445.   Sir Thomas de St. Quintin, Harpham, Yorks.

c. 1460. A man in armour, Adderbury, Oxon.

c. 1465. A man in armour. Manners? Helmsley,
          Yorkshire (possibly collar of suns and roses).

Thomas, Lord Berkeley, 1392, Wotton-under-Edge,
Gloucs., wears a family collar of Mermaids.[1] A trefoil

---

[1] A curious collar, that of park palings, with a hart lodged, occurs on
the stone effigy of Sir Thomas Markenfield in Ripon Cathedral.

toret or clasp is sometimes found on collars of SS.   The
Countess of Essex (1483) at Little Easton, wears as
pendant the White Lion of March : which may be that
worn by Jenkyn Smyth, Esq. (*c.* 1480) St. Mary, Bury
St. Edmunds, Suffolk.

Two brasses of Serjeants-at-arms (*serviens ad arma*)
exist, showing the mace indicative of their office.[1]

1420.   Nicholas . . . . . Wandsworth, Surrey.
     " Serviens Regis Henrici quinti ad arma."
1531.   John Borrell, Sergeant-at-Arms to Henry VIII.,
     Broxbourne, Herts.

A third instance is at Shopland, Essex :—Thomas Stapel
(1371-2) in armour of the Camail period but without a
mace.   " Jadis Seriant d'Armes nostre Seigneur le Roi "
(*see* illustration, p. 218, Vol. V., 1896, *Essex Review*).
Thomas Broke, Esq., Serjeant-at-arms to Henry VIII., at
Ewelme, Oxon., 1518, wears armour of the Mail-skirt
period, with sword and misericorde.   At Bray, Berks., is
an inscription to William Smyth, Esq., Serjeant-at-arms to
Queens Mary and Elizabeth, 1594.

The brass of Bishop Robert Wyvill, 1375, in Salisbury
Cathedral, affords an instance of the *croc, baton,* or
martel-de-fer[2] (*fustis cornutus*) held by Richard Shawell,
champion of the Bishop in his suit against William
de Montacute, Earl of Salisbury, for the recovery
of Sherborne Castle, Dorset.   The champion is represented standing at the gate of the outer ward, in

---

[1] *See* Planché, *sub* Mace, who mentions French stone examples of the
fifteenth century.   These are engraved in Willemin's *Monuments Français
Inédits,* 1839, and there dated 1314.   Pottier states that they were
taken to St. Denis from the Musée des Monuments français, and that
they were formerly at the Church of Sainte Catherine du Val des
Écoliers, Saint Antoine, Paris.   *See* " On a brass in Wandsworth Church,"
by Mill Stephenson, B.A., F.S.A., *Surrey Archæological Collections,* Vol. X.,
1891, p. 293.

[2] An instance of this pickaxe-like weapon may be seen held by a
sculptured effigy in Great Malvern Abbey, Worcs.

front of the portcullis, wearing tight-fitting hose and leathern jack. Round his neck is suspended a shield, with a hole in the centre. The Bishop obtained possession of the castle on payment of 2,500 marks.[1] (*See* Kite's *Monumental Brasses of Wiltshire*.)

Halberds are found held by the soldiers in representations of the Resurrection, connected with tombs used as Easter Sepulchres, at Hedgerley, Bucks, *c.* 1500, on reverse of palimpsest shield of brass of Margaret, wife of Edward Bulstrode, Esq., 1540; at Swansea, Glam., Sir Hugh Johnys and lady, *c.* 1500, on which also appear a spiked mace, or *morning star* (*morgenstern*), a *holy-water sprinkler*, or *military flail*, and a *scimitar*; at Cranley, Surrey, 1503, from the destroyed monument of Robert Hardyng and wife; and at Narburgh, Norfolk, 1545, Sir John Spelman and lady. Other examples are at Great Coates, Lincs., 1503; All Hallows Barking, London, *c.* 1510; and Slaugham, Sussex, 1547.[2]

---

[1] " From the time of Bishop Wyvil his successors held Sherborne un-"disturbed till the Reformation, when the castle was granted first to " the Paulets by Edward VI. and afterwards by Elizabeth to Sir Walter " Raleigh, who built the adjacent house, and probably fitted up the Castle "itself for a residence in the meantime. The estate was wrenched by " chicane by James I. from the son of Sir Walter, and finally it came to " Digby, Earl of Bristol." "Sherborne Castle," by Mr. G. T. Clark, p. 31, Vol. XX., 1874, *Proceedings of the Somersetshire Archæological and Natural History Society*.

[2] *See* "The Resurrection as represented in Monumental Brasses," by Rev. J. E. Field, p. 130, Vol. I., *Journal of the Oxford University Brass Rubbing Society*, May, 1898.

CHAPTER IV.

Of Civilian Costume on Brasses

NICHOLE DE AUMBERDENE, *c.* 1350,
TAPLOW, BUCKS.

CHAPTER IV.

OF CIVILIAN COSTUME ON BRASSES

THE costume of Civilians in the fourteenth century is illustrated by a few, but important brasses, containing in their number four of the fine Flemish class, already mentioned (*see* above, p. 43). Two of the earlier examples are placed in the heads of floriated crosses :—

c. 1325. Iohan de Bladigdone (with wife Maud), small half effigies, East Wickham, Kent, with inscription in Lombardic lettering on stem of cross :—

+ IOHAN DE BLADIGDONE ET MAVD S......

c. 1350. Nichole de Aumberdene, Taplow, Bucks.

The large Flemish brasses at St. Margaret's, Lynn :—

1349. Adam de Walsokne (with wife Margaret),
1364. Robert Braunche (with wives Leticia and Margaret),

and at Newark, Notts, 1361, Alan Fleming, show the costume excellently. The most conspicuous feature is the COTE-HARDIE, which term appears to have been given to garments of somewhat different shapes. On the three Flemish brasses and that at Taplow it fits the body somewhat loosely. Its skirt, prolonged nearly to the ankles, is slit up in front like a military surcoat, and at Newark and Taplow shows two pocket-holes in front. The sleeves terminate at the elbows, from which depend *liripipia,*[1] or lappets of varying length. On the fore-arms

---

[1] Mr. Mill Stephenson, in his description of the Hampsthwaite brass (in the *Yorkshire Archæological Journal,* Vol. XV., p. 21, 1898), considers these liripipes to belong to the tippet. But there seems to be reason for connecting them with the sleeves, since in examples of this class the *chaperon* would have but one liripipe formed by the tip of the hood ; the fashion of wearing it turban-wise produced the *two* ends. The illuminations of contemporary MSS., such as the famous Luttrell Psalter

appear the tight-fitting sleeves of an under-tunic or vest, each sleeve bearing on the underside a long row of buttons. Similar sleeves are found on the shorter form of the *cote-hardie* described below. Round the neck and over the shoulders is worn the CHAPERON, consisting of tippet and hood in one piece. On the legs are tight hose, over which on the feet are worn pointed shoes, fastened by a strap across the instep at Newark, and by laces on the inside of the foot at Lynn. To wear the hair long and wavy seems to have been the fashion, and beards and moustaches, the former sometimes bifurcated, are usual. Adam de Walsokne, however, and Alan Fleming are clean-shaven.

The other form of *cote-hardie*, with which we are concerned, was shorter, not reaching to the knees, fitted the body closely (*just au corps*), and was, usually, buttoned down the front.[1] A good instance of this, with tight mitten sleeves without liripipes, is seen on the kneeling effigy of Robert de Paris, *c.* 1379, Hildersham, Cambs. He wears the mantle, described below, and a horizontal *bawdric* sustaining an anelace.[2] Other instances are:—

(reproduced in *Vetusta Monumenta*, Vol. VI.), throw valuable light on the shape of the *chaperon* and on the different modes of wearing it. *See* also Planché, *Cyclopædia of Costume*, sub nom. Hood.

[1] The lost brass of Simon Walshe (with wife Joan), *c.* 1370, St. Alkmund, Shrewsbury, showed this costume with liripipes, as do tiles found at the Abbeys of Strata Florida and Strata Marcella. *See* illustration in *The Cistercian Abbey of Strata Florida, its History, and an account of the recent excavations made on its site*, by Stephen W. Williams, F.R.I.B.A., London, 1889. The same pattern is on tiles from Shrewsbury and Haughmond Abbeys. *See* "On Encaustic Tiles," by Llewellyn Jewitt, *Journal of British Archæological Association*, Vol. II., 1847, p. 261.

[2] A very beautiful instance of an embroidered short *cote-hardie* with horizontal bawdric, worn with a mantle, fastened on the right shoulder, the edges dagged in the form of leaves, is to be seen at York Minster, on the sculptured effigy of the young prince, William of Hatfield, second son of Edward III. Other examples of the costume are afforded by the sculptured effigy of William of Windsor, another young son of Edward III., in St. Edmund's Chapel, Westminster Abbey, and by the figures of the children of Edward III. on his tomb, and of those of Elizabeth, Lady Montacute, at Christ Church, Oxford.

c. 1325. Iohan de Bladigdone, East Wickham, Kent, half effigy with liripipia.

c. 1350. A Civilian, Hampsthwaite, W. Yorks, with liripipia. Attached to the left side of a buckled belt worn horizontally is a *gypcière*, or purse (from Fr. *gibier*), with an *anelace* secured by being passed through the lappets which fasten the gypcière to the girdle.[1]

c. 1350. A Civilian on reverse of inscription to William Wolstonton, 1403, Great Bowden, Leicester-shire. Flemish; same costume as last, but without gypcière or anelace.[2]

c. 1350. A Civilian (with wife), Upchurch, Kent, half effigies, each wearing a cote-hardie with plain sleeves, reaching half-way between elbow and wrist; buttons only on the sleeves of the undertunic which end at the wrists; no liri-pipia.

c. 1360. Raulin Brocas (with sister), Sherborne St. John, Hants, half effigy, a clean-shaven boy, wearing a cote-hardie like the last, except that it has buttons down the front. The buttoned sleeves of the undertunic end in mittens; no liripipia.

c. 1360. The bust of a Civilian at Blickling, Norfolk, showing the chaperon, worn by a man with flowing hair and pointed beard.

c. 1360. John de Walden, Ashbury, Berks, half effigy.

c. 1360. Beneit Engliss', Nuffield, Oxon., half effigy;

---

[1] A similar mode of wearing gypcière and anelace is illustrated by Waller from a Flemish brass, *c.* 1350, of a civilian in Bruges Cathedral.

For some account of gycières, see *Journal of the British Archæological Association*, Vol. XIV., 1858, p. 131, "History of Purses," by H. Syer Cuming.

[2] Illustrated in *Transactions of Monumental Brass Society*, Vol. IV., p. 160, described p. 161. The feet rest on a dog. The edge of the chaperon is "pinked." The beard is bifurcated. There is a fine diapered background.

buttons under fore-arm of cote-hardie; no
liripipia.

c. 1370.   John de Faversham? (with mother), Graveney,
Kent, half effigy similar to the last, but with
buttons in front.

c. 1370.   A Civilian, Deddington, Oxon., half effigy.

c. 1370.   A Civilian, Cheam, Surrey, mutilated; under-
tunic has mitten sleeves with buttons; no
liripipes to the cote-hardie; small hood; forked
beard; hair cut close.

c. 1370.   A Civilian, Cheam, Surrey, half effigy; the
cote-hardie had liripipes, but their length is
not discernible owing to the half-effigy; the
undertunic sleeves have buttons; there is
a beard, but the hair is cut close.

c. 1370.   John de Kyggesfolde (with wife, Agnes), Rusper,
Sussex, half effigy; short hair; clean shaven.

c. 1370.   Richard de Heylesdone (with wife, Beatrice),
Hellesdon, Norfolk, three-quarter effigy;
wearing a looser garment than the foregoing,
with no buttons. The mitten sleeves of the
undertunic appear.

Some brasses, belonging for the most part to the last
quarter of the century, show a costume differing somewhat from the foregoing. The tunic or *cote* is long and
full, reaching below the knees, has tight sleeves, and is
confined at the waist by a girdle from which, usually on
the left side, hangs the *anelace* or *basilard*, a large *couteau
de chasse*, in its sheath. The open character of the tunic
is indicated by the appearance of buttons down the front
(as at Shottesbrooke, Berks, *c.* 1370). Over this *cote-
hardie* is worn a loose mantle, fastened by buttons, of
which two or three are seen, on the right shoulder;—
a shape which we find associated, later on, with Judges
and Civic Dignitaries. Worn round the neck, perhaps
attached to the mantle, is a *chaperon*, sometimes showing
buttons (*e.g.*, Kings Sombourne, Hants, *c.* 1380), the

PRIEST AND FRANKELEIN, *c.* 1370,
SHOTTESBROOKE, BERKS.

tippet part of which does not appear owing to the presence of the mantle. The mitten sleeves of the undertunic frequently appear. The hair, as a rule, is worn shorter than in the previous examples. The forked beard is retained. The feet rest on the ground. The following are noted by Haines:—

c. 1370. A Frankelein (with Priest), Shottesbrooke, Berks.

c. 1380. Two Civilians, Kings Sombourne, Hants; the one with beard, the other clean-shaven.

c. 1380. Simon de Felbrig, Felbrigg, Norfolk; long hair, anelace on right side.

1391. Thomas de Topclyff (with wife), Topcliffe, Yorks.; Flemish; anelace on right side.[1]

1391. John Curteys (with widow), Wymington, Beds.; Mayor of the Staple of Calais; feet on dog.

1398. Walter Pescod, Boston, Lincs. The left side of his tunic semée of peascods: possibly a rare example on a brass of the fashionable parti-coloured garments of the period. No anelace is visible.

c. 1400. A Wool Merchant (with wife), Northleach, Gloucs. The pendent end of the girdle has the letter T.; feet on wool-pack.

1401. William Grevel (with wife), Chipping Campden, Gloucs.: "quondm' Ciuis London' & flos m'cator' lanar' tocius Anglie."

A Frankelein, c. 1370, at Cheam, Surrey, has no mantle, which omission is shared by the following:—

c. 1380. John Pecok (with wife), St. Michael's, St. Alban's, Herts.

1391. John Corp (with granddaughter on pedestal), Stoke Fleming, Devon; wavy hair; the *cote*

---

[1] The lost brass of Robert Attelath, 1376, formerly at St. Margaret's, Lynn, was a fine example of this class. No anelace appeared. The feet rested on two lions addorsed. A Civilian (lost) c. 1400, St. Alkmund, Shrewsbury, was another instance, showing mantle and anelace.

is fur-edged.   The bawdric holding the anelace
passes over the right shoulder.

c. 1400.   A Civilian, Ore, Sussex; similar to the last.

A long, loose tunic, like a night-gown, with a hood, is
worn by the following :—

1356.   Richard Torrington (with wife), Great Berk-
             hampstead, Herts.; the sleeves turned back
             from the wrists.
c. 1380.   A Civilian (? Robert de Brentyngham), East
             Horsley, Surrey, half effigy.
1396.   A Civilian, Temple Church, Bristol, half effigy.
c. 1400.   William Overbury (with wife), Letchworth,
             Herts, half effigy.
c. 1400.   Thomas Somer (with wife), Ickleford, Herts,
             half effigy.
c. 1400.   John de Estbury (with wife), Lambourn, Berks,
             half effigy.
c. 1400.   John Covesgrave, Eaton Socon, Beds.

The brass of a Civilian, *c.* 1390, once in the head of a
floriated cross, cited by Haines, in Hereford Cathedral,
shows a tunic sleeve indicating the transition to the bag-
sleeve of the next period.   The feet rest on a dog.
    The small figures on the Walsokne, Braunche, and
Fleming brasses, above mentioned, give additional illustration of the costume of the period.   At Harrow, the reverse
of the inscription commemorating Dorothy Frankishe, 1574,
shows the side shaft of a canopy of Flemish work, *c.* 1370,
containing two figures in chaperons, the long liripipe of
that of the small person reading, in a sitting posture, being
very distinct.

    In the reign of Henry IV. we find a change in the
tunic.   It is long and loose, with a buttoned collar, high
in the neck, and the skirt partly slit up from the bottom.
But the most distinct difference from the tunic, lately described, is in the sleeves.   These become very full and

bag-like in the arms,[1] but are tight at the wrists, which have an edging of fur, and in early examples (*e.g.*, *c.* 1400, a Civilian, Tilbrook, Beds) have a single button beneath the wrist. From beneath these sleeves appear those of the under-tunic, sometimes prolonged into mittens. The tunic, confined at the waist by a girdle, is often lined and edged with fur. Over this is worn the hood, and, more rarely, the mantle and hood. The hair is usually treated, as already described, brushed back and kept short on the head. Moustache and small forked beard are worn. Pointed shoes are seen over the hose, or the hose appear alone, without shoes. Examples :—

1400. John Mulsho, Esq., Newton-by-Geddington, Northants, kneeling at the base of a floriated cross, in the head of which stands St. Faith ; no girdle.

c. 1400. A Civilian, Tilbrook, Beds. ; the hair wavy ; a large anelace suspended in front ; feet on dog.

c. 1400. A Civilian in head of octofoiled cross, St. Michael's, St. Alban's ; no hood ; anelace hanging from girdle on left side.

c. 1400. A Wine Merchant, Cirencester, Gloucs. ; head lost ; tunic reaching to the feet ; letter T on end of girdle ; feet on wine-cask.

1402. Richard Martyn, Dartford, Kent, *wearing mantle;* feet on ground ; girdle, if any, hidden.

c. 1405. Herry Notingham, Holm-by-the-Sea, Norfolk ; wearing anelace ; similar in style to the civilian at Tilbrook.

1409. Robert de Haitfeld (*d.* 1417) with wife, Owston,

---

[1] "The anonymous writer of a life of Richard II. (a monk of Evesham) "speaks of gowns with deep wide sleeves, commonly called *pokys,* shaped "like a bagpipe : 'Maxime togatorum cum profundis et latis manicis "vocatis vulgariter *pokys* ad modum *bagpipe* formatus ;' they are also, "he says, rightly termed, 'devils' receptacles'—receptacula dæmoniorum "recte dici—for whatever could be stolen was put into them."— Planché, *Cyclopædia of Costume,* 1876, Vol. I., "Dictionary," p. 466, *sub* Sleeve.

Yorks; wavy hair; anelace hanging from girdle on left side. He holds the end of girdle in his left hand, and with his right the right hand of his wife, who occupies the dexter side. Each wears a collar, possibly of SS.[1]

1411. Hugo de Gondeby, Supervisor to Ralph, Lord Cromwell, Tattershall, Lincs.; anelace.

c. 1411. John Barstaple, Founder, Trinity Almshouses, Bristol; anelace on left side.

1414. The seven small head-and-shoulders effigies of the brothers of Philippa Carreu, Beddington, Surrey.

1416. Thomas Stokes, Esq., Ashby St. Legers, Northants; early instance of roll-shaped hair, worn with forked beard.

1417. Geoffrey Barbur, half effigy, St. Helen's, Abingdon, Berks.

1418. Thomas Polton, half effigy, Wanborough, Wilts.; hood.

1419. John Lyndewode, woolman, Linwood, Lincs.; *wearing mantle;* girdle not visible; feet on wool-pack. His three sons below wear similar tunics, but no mantles. For the fourth son, *see* p. 132.

1420. John Urban, Southfleet, Kent; waved hair; no beard; without hood.

---

[1] An instance of a brass of a civilian, wearing collar of SS., is afforded by that of Sir Thomas Brook (*d.* 1419), Thorncombe, Devon (mentioned below p. 206). The sculptured effigy of John Gower, *d.* 1402, at St. Saviour's, Southwark, shows a collar of SS., with swan badge. At Ashby de la Zouch, Leics., is the alabaster effigy of Ralph Hastings, late fifteenth century, clad as a pilgrim and wearing a collar of SS. (see *Archæological Journal*, Vol. XXXVI., 1879, p. 102). The stone effigy of William Staunton (?) *c.* 1500, at Elford, Staffs., is not in armour, but has collar of SS. (illustrated in *The Monumental Effigies and Tombs in Elford Church, Staffordshire, with a Memoir and Pedigree of the lords of Elford*, by Edward Richardson, Sculptor, The Restorer and Illustrator of the Temple Church Effigies, etc. London: George Bell, 168 Fleet Street, and of the Author, Melbury Terrace, Harewood Square. 1852. Folio).

c. 1420 (Haines).   A Civilian, Furneaux Pelham, Herts.;
            anelace; feet on dog (? John Barloe with wife
            Joan).

1421.   John Lyndewode, woolman, Linwood, Lincs.
            (son of above); anelace; feet on wool-pack
            bearing a merchant's mark.

1425.   William Chichele, Higham Ferrers, Northants;
            wearing mantle; no girdle; feet on dog.   Sheriff
            and Alderman of London.

1425.   Roger Sencler, Erith, Kent; the tunic only
            reaching just below the knees.

c. 1425.   Hugo atte Spetyll, Luton, Beds.; tight sleeves;
            hood; no girdle.   (Wife lost; son John in
            mass vestments.)

1427.   William Bayly, half effigy, Berwick Basset,
            Wilts.; hood; similar to Thomas Polton,
            above.

1429.   Roger Thornton, All Saints', Newcastle-on-
            Tyne; Flemish; hair wavy; tunic reaching to
            feet; very long anelace hanging from girdle
            on left side, with ornamented scabbard; feet
            on dog gnawing a bone.   The seven sons
            beneath have shorter tunics and no anelaces.

1430.   William West, marbler, Sudborough, Northants;
            small, standing next to John West, priest (*see*
            pp. 68, 71).

1431.   Nicholas Canteys, Margate, Kent; long beard;
            anelace on left side; boots embroidered with
            stars, and laced up on the inner side.

At Baldock, Herts., is a Civilian, dated by Haines
c. 1420, attired as a hunter, possibly William Vynter,
1416.   He wears a girded tunic, reaching to the knees,
with tight sleeves, and a hood; flowing hair and forked
beard; a horn hanging on his right side by a strap passing
over the left shoulder.   On his left side an anelace, the
scabbard of which sheathes two smaller knives ("*bastardeau*"), hangs from the girdle, and a coil of rope, one

end of which seems to have been fastened to a dog at the feet; but the part below the knees of the effigy is lost.

Towards the middle of the century some changes are observable. The hood goes out of use. The fur-lined tunic has a shorter skirt, and less " baggy " sleeves. The undergarment appears at the wrists, and sometimes at the neck. The hose often are seen on the feet without half-boots. The hair is cut close, assuming a roll-shaped form. The face is clean-shaven. The anelace is rarely worn. A fur-lined, girded tunic, with surplice-like hanging sleeves, probably the "*houppelande*," is worn by Sir Thomas Brook, 1437 (*d.* 1419),[1] Thorncombe, Devon, whose feet rest on a hound. A similar tunic, but with broad, falling collar, showing the under-tunic at the neck, is seen at Trotton, Sussex, on the small figure of Sir Richard Camoys, standing beside his mother on the brass of Lord and Lady Camoys, 1424.[2]

A few of the numerous extant examples of the ordinary costume are as follows :—

c. 1430.   A Civilian (with priest and lady), Melton, Suffolk; wearing a hood; feet lost.

---

[1] He wears Collar of SS.

[2] Similar gowns are worn with turban-wise chaperons by small figures on the sides of the alabaster altar-tomb of Sir Thomas Arderne, Kt. *c.* 1400, and Matilda, his lady, Elford, Staffs. See *Monumental Effigies and Tombs in Elford Church, Staffordshire*, by Edward Richardson, cited above, p. 204 *note*. *See* also illustration in Planché from Royal MS. 15, E 6, in which John Talbot, Earl of Shrewsbury, wearing a houppelande, presents a book to Henry IV. and his Queen. *See* also "The Miniatures in Harleian MS. 1,319," reproduced in the *Burlington Magazine*, May and June, 1904, "A Contemporary Account of the Fall of Richard the Second," by Sir Edward Maunde Thompson, K.C.B. An example of similar arrangement to that on the Camoys brass (son on mother's skirt) is afforded by an incised slab at Longforgan, Perthshire, *c.* 1420, Johanes de Galychtly and Mariota, his wife (the son, like the father, in armour). *See* "Notice of an Incised Sepulchral Slab found in the Church of Longforgan, Perthshire," by A. H. Millar, F.S.A. Scot., *Proceedings of the Society of Antiquaries of Scotland*, Vol. XXXIV., 1900, p. 463 (illus. p. 464).

SIR THOMAS BROOK AND WIFE JOAN, 1437,
THORNCOMBE, DEVON.

c. 1430. John Todenham, St. John Maddermarket, Norwich.

1432. Nicholas Carew, Beddington, Surrey; feet on dog.

1435. John Ailmer, Erith, Kent; wearing half-boots.

c. 1435. Hugo Bostock, Wheathampstead, Herts.; father of John de Whethamstede, Abbot of St. Alban's.

1437. Robert Skern, Kingston-on-Thames, Surrey; girdle ornamented with rosettes hanging down on left side (no anelace, as supposed by Haines).

1437. John Bacon, woolman, All Hallows' Barking, London; feet on wool-pack; boots laced up on the inner side.

1439. Edmund Forde, Esq., Swainswick, Somerset; *anelace* hanging on left side.

1440 (?) Robert Pagge, Cirencester, Gloucs.; feet on wool-pack with merchant's mark; boots laced up on inner side.

1441. John Parker, Margate, Kent; feet on dog; boots like Pagge's.

1442. Peter Stone, Margate, Kent; similar to last, but wearing *anelace* on left side.

1447. Thomas Fortey, woolman, and William Scors, tailor, Northleach, Gloucs.; their boots fastened in front; between Scors' feet a pair of shears.

1449. John Quek (and son), Birchington, Kent; wearing anelace on left side. Each wears boots like Pagge's.

1450. William Welley, merchant, Chipping Campden, Gloucs.

c. 1450. A Wool Merchant, Lechdale, Gloucs.; feet on wool-pack.

1451. John Younge, woolman, Chipping Norton, Oxon.; feet on two wool-packs.

1454. Roger Felthorp, Blickling, Norfolk; his nine sons similarly clad.

1455.　Richard Manfeld (with brother and sister), Taplow, Bucks.

1458.　John Fortey, woolman, Northleach, Gloucs.; right foot on sheep, left on wool-pack.

1459.　Richard Quek, Birchington, Kent.

c. 1460.　Sir Edward Courtenay, Christ Church, Oxford; feet on dog; boots like Pagge's; anelace hanging on left side, the scabbard containing two small knives (bastardeau).

1467.　John Lethenard, merchant, Chipping Campden, Gloucs.; wearing boots.

A period of transition may be remarked in some effigies, *e.g.* :—

1470.　John Wynter, St. Margaret's, Canterbury.

c. 1470.　A Civilian, with sons, Abingdon Pigotts, Cambs.

c. 1480.　Jenkyn Smith, St. Mary's, Bury St. Edmunds, Suffolk.

The two former wear the fur-lined tunic, but with sleeves of equal breadth; the collar of the under-dress appearing at the neck. A trefoil is seen between the feet, which are shod in pointed boots. The third is kneeling, has no girdle to his tunic, which falls loosely round him, and wears a collar (?Yorkist) with a pendant (?the white lion of March). All three have the hair cut short, and roll-shaped. Similar to the last, but with a girdle and without a collar, is the kneeling effigy of a civilian, *c.* 1480, Chrishall, Essex. Roger Kyngdon, *c.* 1471, Quethiock, Cornwall, wears the long civilian tunic, next described, with a rosary at his belt; but his hair is in the roll form.

In the last quarter of the century a distinct change is visible. The hair is worn long. The tunic or gown assumes a cassock-like appearance, and though open in front, does not, as a rule, appear so on brasses. The pointed shoes become modified, and are soon to be rounded or square-toed, like the change from *sollerets* to *sabbatons*,

RICHARD MANFELD AND SISTER, ISABEL, 1455,
TAPLOW, BUCKS.

JENKYN SMYTH AND WIFE MARION, *c.* 1480,
ST. MARY, BURY ST. EDMUND'S, SUFFOLK.

WILLIAM WALROND AND WIFE
ELIZABETH, *c.* 1480,
CHILDREY, BERKS.

noticed in our account of armour. The feet usually rest on the ground, on which is often a conventional plant or slipped trefoil. From the girdle hangs a gypcière, frequently with a rosary, usually of twelve beads. To this costume is sometimes added the hood, worn on the shoulder, as a rule the right one. This hood is the descendant of the *chaperon*, which we have noticed in the attire of fourteenth-century civilians. But it has passed through a curious transition. It became the fashion in the latter part of the fourteenth century to wear it horizontally, that is, with the crown of the head inserted in the opening, which formerly enclosed the face. The ends were then tucked in turban-wise, and this coiffure was called a *bourrelet*. We now see it in the form of a cap with a long streamer or scarf, representing the liripipe of the hood, the tippet part hanging on the back[1]:—a shape that was retained by the Knights of the Garter, as seen on the Bullen brass at Hever (1538).

Examples are numerous.[2] The following may easily be supplemented:—

c. 1475.   A Notary, St. Mary Tower, Ipswich; hood on left shoulder; penner (or pen-case) and inkhorn hanging to girdle on the right; an inscribed roll on his breast; a skull and bones on the ground at the feet.

c. 1475.   A Civilian, Littlebury, Essex; hood on right shoulder; gypcière and rosary.

c. 1475.   A Civilian, Hempstead, Essex; similar to the last.

---

[1] *See* Planché, *Cyclopædia of Costume*, *sub nom.* Hood, and the Rev. N. F. Robinson's "Pileus Quadratus, etc," *Transactions of St. Paul's Ecclesiological Society*, 1901, Vol. V., Part I. The *bourrelet* in many of its forms may be seen in the Hardwicke Hall Tapestries. *See* "The Fifteenth Century English Tapestries at Hardwicke Hall," by W. Harvey, *The Connoisseur*, Vol. III., p. 39.

[2] Children in this costume are frequently found on the brasses of their parents. Two Essex examples are: *c.* 1495, the four sons of Edward Sulyard, Esq., High Laver, and 1501, the five sons of Sir William Pyrton, Little Bentley.

1479.   Thomas Selby, East Malling, Kent.

c. 1480.   A Civilian, British Museum; hood on left shoulder; gypcière and rosary.

1483.   Geoffrey Kidwelly, Esq., Little Wittenham, Berks; hood on left shoulder; gypcière and rosary.

1484.   William Gybbys, Chipping Campden, Gloucs.; rosary on right.

1485.   William Goldwell, Great Chart, Kent.

c. 1485.   Thomas Kyllygrewe, St. Gluvias, Cornwall; wearing hood on right shoulder, remarkable in that the cap assumes a hat-like appearance, and the scarf or liripipe seems to be attached to it by two bands.

1488.   William Mond and John Sayer, Newington, Kent; the former wearing a cap on the right shoulder, and a gypcière; round shoes.

1488.   John Hertcombe, kneeling, Kingston-upon-Thames, Surrey; head lost; gypcière and rosary on right; round shoes.

1493.   John Ceysyll, Tormarton, Gloucs.; gypcière and rosary.

1496.   John Beriffe, Brightlingsea, Essex; gypcière and rosary.

1497.   John Camber, Sevenhampton, Gloucs.; hood on right shoulder; gypcière and rosary.

1497.   William Maynwaryng, Ightfield, Salop; head gone; rosary, gypcière, and *anelace* with *bastardeau*.[1]

In the last decade of the fifteenth century the fur-lined robe resembles a dressing-gown in shape, turned back down the front to show the fur, and with broad fur collar and cuffs. This robe either hangs loose, or is confined by a

---

[1] Another late instance of a knife worn by a civilian is afforded by the brass of Henry Jarmon, c. 1480, Geddington, Northants, who wears a small knife and rosary hanging from his girdle.

GEOFFREY KIDWELLY, ESQ.,
1483,
LITTLE WITTENHAM, BERKS.

girdle to which a gypcière and rosary are found attached. In the former case, the gypcière is sometimes seen fastened to the girdle of the under-tunic and worn beneath the outer gown. The shoes are broad-toed, and become clumsy and loose in appearance. This costume continued to the middle of the sixteenth century, becoming gradually superseded by the gown with long, false sleeves about to be described, and was worn by young as well as old, frequently figuring on the effigies of boys on the brasses of their parents. Examples are common :—

1498.   John Rusche, All Hallows Barking, London.

1498.   John Stokys, Seend, Wilts.

1500.   John Sedley, Southfleet, Kent.

c. 1500.   Richard Wakeherst, Esq. (1457), Ardingley, Sussex.

1506.   John Colman, Little Waldingfield, Suffolk.

1506.   Robert Wymbyll, Notary, St. Mary Tower, Ipswich ; pen-case and ink-bottle on the left.

1510.   John, son of Sir John Seymour, Great Bedwyn, Wilts.

1510.   Ralf Rowlat, Merchant of the Staple, St. Alban's, Herts.

c. 1510.   A Notary, New College, Oxford ; pen-case and ink-bottle on right.

1517.   Thomas Goddard, Ogbourne St. George, Wilts ; gypcière worn beneath gown.

c. 1520.   A Civilian, St. Breock, Cornwall.

1526.   William Freme, Berkeley, Gloucs. ; head lost. His gown has a fur cape. He holds a heart inscribed " m'cy."

1529.   William Bloor, Gent., Rainham, Kent. The under-tunic is seen reaching to the knees with embroidery at the neck and edge of the skirt. The gypcière is beneath the furred gown ; the broad shoes are tied with bows. In the inscription Henry VIII. is described as " Fidei defensoris."

1535. Andrew Evyngar, All Hallows, Barking, London; Flemish. The long under-tunic is well shown.
1564. Pawle Yden, Gent., Penshurst, Kent.

About the year 1520 a change in the form of the gown is seen. It is without girdle, open down the front. The arms, instead of passing through the whole length of the sleeves, are carried through openings below the shoulders, producing the effect of long, false sleeves, hanging as pendants.[1] This fashion is no novelty, but is not found on brasses before this time. The lost effigy, however, of Christopher Elcok, draper, 1492, formerly at St. Mary Magdalene's, Burgate, Canterbury, showed the arms passing through short, false sleeves attached to the cassock-like tunic (described p. 208), to the girdle of which a rosary and gypcière were fastened. Instances occur of the slit in the sleeve appearing, although the arm passes through the whole length of it (*e.g.*, *c.* 1520, a Civilian, Brown Candover, Hants; *c.* 1520, a Civilian (mutilated), Euston, Suffolk; 1521, William Cheswryght, Fordham, Cambs.; 1524, John Terry, and 1525, John Marsham, St. John Maddermarket, Norwich). Beneath the gown are worn the square-skirted doublet, usually girded, the sleeves of which come through the openings in the gown-sleeves, and long hose. On the feet are low, broad shoes. The hair is worn long, but the face remains clean-shaven. The rosary disappears in the religious disturbances.

The following are some examples:—

1525. Thomas Pownder, St. Mary Quay, Ipswich, Suffolk; Flemish.
1531. Thomas Potter, Westerham, Kent.
1532. Robert Goodwyn, Necton, Norfolk.
1533. Henry Hatch, Faversham, Kent.
1535. Richard Sawnders, Pottesgrove, Beds.

---

[1] This gown was much affected by the clergy. *See* above, pp. 115-117.

GYLES PENNE, GENT., AND WIFE ISABELL, 1519,
YEOVIL, SOMERSET.

1542.   Thomas Fromond, Esq., Cheam, Surrey; kneeling.

1542.   Sir Thomas Nevell, Kt., Mereworth, Kent; a cross hanging by a long chain round the neck; kneeling.

1546.   Robert Barfott, Lambourne, Essex.

1558.   John Selyard, Edenbridge, Kent; small gypcière fastened to girdle of doublet.

1558.   Edward Crane, Stratford St. Mary, Suffolk.

1561.   Robert Swift, kneeling, Rotherham, Yorks. (rectangular plate).

c. 1565.   A Civilian, Southminster, Essex.

In civil as in military costume the reign of Queen Elizabeth introduced some alterations. The hair was worn short, and moustaches and pointed beards became the fashion. The square-cut doublet became shorter, though longer in the waist, and was buttoned down the front, fitting the body tightly, and having a short, pointed skirt below a waistband or sash. Over the long hose were worn trunk hose, stuffed or "bombasted like beer-barrels," which in their turn gave way to stuffed breeches, the hose becoming two articles of dress:—the "upper stocks" or breeches, and the "nether stocks" (our stockings), the garters for which, usually tied in bows, are visible on some brasses. The long gown with false sleeves became modified in some particulars, the false sleeve becoming a mere strip, often elaborately slashed or striped, hanging from behind the shoulder. This gown, frequently without fur-edging or lining, continued in use during the seventeenth century, but seems to have been worn more by "reverend signors" than by their children; the latter and the younger gallants generally seeming to have preferred a short, open cloak, often of rich materials, which we find worn towards the end of the sixteenth and throughout the seventeenth century. The shoes lost their clumsy appearance, and were small and round-toed, a feature noticed in the military brasses of the period.

Ruffs and frills were worn at the neck and wrists. This costume, with but slight alteration, lasted to the end of James I.'s reign. The effigies are often represented standing on a chequered pavement. Examples are exceedingly numerous.

Examples in the long gown :—

1567.   Thomas Noke, Esq., Shottesbrooke, Berks. ; crown-keeper's badge on the left shoulder.[1]

1570.   John Webbe, St. Thomas', Salisbury, Wilts.

1574.   Richard Payton, Isleham, Cambs.

1576.   Edward Bell, Writtle, Essex.

1586.   Edward Arundell, Mawgan in' Pyder, Cornwall.

1587.   Michael Fraunces, St. Martin's, Canterbury.

1590.   Laurence Hyde, Esq., Tisbury, Wilts. ; rectangular plate.

1591.   Robert Whalley, Gent., Queen's College, Cambridge.

1592.   Roger James, All Hallows Barking, London.

1600.   Richard Thornhill, Bromley, Kent.

1607.   Jacob Verzelini, Esq., Downe, Kent.

1615.   James Hobart, Esq., Loddon, Norfolk.

1616.   John Darley, Gent., Rawmarch, Yorks. ; kneeling.

The short cloak, under which a rapier was frequently worn on the left side, obviously gives a better opportunity than the gown for seeing the doublet and breeches or trunk hose, often slashed or embroidered. These latter are well depicted worn by sons on the brasses of their parents. Good examples, though they wear a kind of

---

[1] Other examples of this badge are :—1471, a son of Roger Kyngdon, Quethiock, Cornwall ; a brass belonging to the Society of Antiquaries c. 1480 ; and 1519, James Tornay, Slapton, Bucks. Instances of brasses of Yeomen of the Guard, with the badge of the Rose and Crown on their breasts are known, e.g., William Payn, 1568, East Wickham, Kent ; Robert Rampston (with sword), 1585, lost from Chingford, Essex ; John Kent, 1592, Aston, Herts. ; Thomas Mountague, holding halberd, and giving bread to two poor men, 1630, Winkfield, Berks. See Haines' Introduction, p. cxxvii.

WILLIAM STRACHLEIGH, ESQ., WITH WIFE ANNE AND
DAUGHTER CHRISTIAN, 1583,
ERMINGTON, DEVON.

long open gown, are afforded by the two boys on the brass of Lady Norton, 1580, Newington, Kent; and without cloak or gown, by Henry Baynton, Esq., kneeling, on the brass of his father, Sir Edward Baynton, Kt., 1578, Bromham, Wilts.

The following are some examples in short cloaks:—

1582. Edward Bugge, Gent., Harlow, Essex.
1584. Edward Wiot, Esq., Tillingham, Essex; kneeling.
1585/6. Humphrey and Humphrey Heies, West Thurrock, Essex; the son a good example.
1587. George Clifton, Esq., Clifton, Notts.
1592. John Lyon, Harrow, Middlesex, founder of the school.
1594. George Duke, Gent., Honington, Suffolk.
1606. Effigy in private possession, probably Arthur Crafford, Gent., from South Weald, Essex; the cloak has an embroidered border.
1609. Thomas Garland, Todwick, Yorks.; kneeling.
1610. John Cremer, Snettesham, Norfolk, and sons.
1615. John Gladwin, Harlow, Essex.

The mutilated effigy (lacking head and legs) of William Hyldesley, 1576, at Crowmarsh Giffard, Oxon., shows a short cloak with false sleeves, worn over a doublet, to the girdle of which hangs a large gypcière on the right side. Trunk hose were worn.

The reign of Charles I. introduced collar and cuffs in preference to ruffs. The doublet sometimes ends below the waist in two peaks, not joining. The knee-breeches are much reduced in size; the hair is worn long; the large jack-boot appears; rapiers are worn below the short cloaks.

Examples in long gowns with false sleeves:—

1624. Richard Gadburye, Eyworth, Beds.; wearing a broad-brimmed hat; the gown curiously braided and with many loops and buttons.

1626. John Gunter, Cirencester, Gloucs.

1630. John Kent, Esq., St. John's, Devizes, Wilts.

1631. Robert Coulthirst, Kirkleatham, Yorks.; book in right hand, stick in left.

1636. Henry Gibbes, St. James', Bristol; kneeling.

1638. William Jones, Gent., St. Mary's, Dover, Kent.

1639. Thomas Covell, Esq., St. Mary's, Lancaster.

1647. John Morewood, Bradfield, W. Yorks.; kneeling; skull-cap; rectangular plate.

Examples in short cloaks :—

c. 1630. A Civilian, Croydon, Surrey.

1631. Richard Chiverton, Quethiock, Cornwall; locally engraved.

1632. William Gardiner, Daylesford, Worcs.; right hand holding book; jack-boots and spurs.

1634. John King, Gent., Southminster, Essex.

c. 1635. The sons on the brass of Sir John Arundel, Knt., St. Columb Major, Cornwall; jack-boots. (The sons of John Arundel, Esq., 1633, at the same place, are similarly attired.)

1638. The sons on the brass of Sir Edward Filmer, Kt., East Sutton, Kent, except the eldest. The short cloaks have sleeves, but the arms are not inserted in them ; all but the youngest wear jack-boots; the latter has rosettes at his knees.

1639. Robert Alfounder, East Bergholt, Suffolk; jack-boots and spurs. The breeches terminate at the knees in nebulé-shaped *cannons*.

1641. William Randolph, Biddenden, Kent.

1642. William Septvans (*alias* Harflet), Esq., Ash-next-Sandwich, Kent; the cloak longer than usual.

A curious local engraving at Heigham, Norfolk, represents a cavalier, " Thomas Holl, second son of Thomas Holl, Esq.," 1630. His hair has a periwig-like appearance. His collar is trimmed with lace. The sword sash

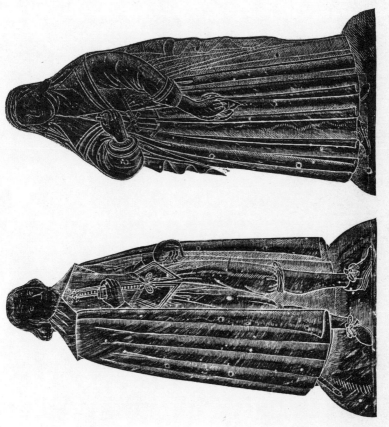

WALTER SEPTVANS (*alias* HARFLETE), ESQ., AND WIFE JANE, 1642,
ASH-NEXT-SANDWICH, KENT.

passes over the right shoulder, from which a scarf hangs. He wears jack-boots.

Eighteenth-century civilian costume is represented on the brass of Benjamin Greenwood, 1773, St. Mary Cray, Kent, who wears a large coat, the cuffs of which are turned back, a long waistcoat, knee-breeches, stockings, shoes, and a wig.

The graceful mantle (doubtless descended from the classical *chlamys*) fastened by buttons on the right shoulder, which we have remarked worn in the fourteenth century, continued in use, as an *insigne* of civic dignitaries, mayors, and aldermen, worn over the gown of the period, long after it had gone out of fashion. Such a qualification is, probably, the cause of its appearance on most of the following effigies. Haines remarks (pp. ccxl.-i.) that the dress of mayors and aldermen of the sixteenth century "consisted of a red gown, a black or brown mantle, and "a short black scarf, which last appears in some instances "to have been worn by mayors only."[1] Some examples, a large proportion of which are in Norwich, are as follows :—

1432.	Robert Baxter, St. Giles', Norwich.
1433.	Simon Seman, Barton-on-Humber, Lincs.
1436.	Richard Purdaunce, St. Giles', Norwich.
1436.	John Asger, St. Laurence, Norwich.
c. 1450.	John Arderne, Esq., Leigh, Surrey.
c. 1460.	John Browne, All Saints', Stamford, Lincs.
c. 1460.	William Browne (*d.* 1489), All Saints', Stamford, Lincs.
1472.	William Norwiche, St. George Colegate, Norwich.

---

[1] *See* footnote 2, p. 109. The brass of Edward Goodman, Burgesse and Mercer of Ruthin, 1560, Ruthin, Denbighshire, shows him wearing over a long doublet a fur-lined gown with false sleeves, a cap, and a *short scarf.* Reproduced in *A Memoir of Gabriel Goodman, D.D., Dean of Westminster,* etc., by the Rev. Richard Newcome. Ruthin, 1825.

c. 1472.	Ralph Segrym (?), St. John Maddermarket, Norwich.
1474.	John Feld, Standon, Herts.
1475.	John Brown, junr., All Saints', Stamford, Lincs.
1477.	John Croke, All Hallows Barking, London.
1478.	Thomas Rowley, St. John, Bristol.
1487.	John Lambarde, Hinxworth, Herts.
1496.	Henry Spelman, "Hospes" and Recorder of Norwich, Narburgh, Norfolk.
c. 1500.	Robert Gardiner (?), St. Andrew, Norwich.
1513.	Richard Brasyer and son, St. Stephen, Norwich.
c. 1513.	Robert Brasyer, St. Stephen, Norwich.
1524.	John Terry, St. John Maddermarket, Norwich.
1525.	John Marsham, St. John Maddermarket, Norwich.
1529.	John Cooke, St. Mary de Crypt, Gloucester.
1539.	Nicholas Leveson, St. Andrew Undershaft, London.
1540.	John Semys, St. John Baptist, Gloucester.
1558.	Robert Rugge, St. John Maddermarket, Norwich.
1573.	Sir William Harper, in armour, St. Paul's, Bedford.
1574.	Richard Atkinson, St. Peter-in-the-East, Oxford.
	From this design was copied :—
1826.	William Fletcher, Yarnton, Oxon. (Mayor of Oxford, Antiquary).

CHAPTER V.

Of Legal Costume on Brasses

NICHOL ROLOND AND WIFE PERNEL, *c.* 1410,
COPLE, BEDS.

CHAPTER V.

OF LEGAL COSTUME ON BRASSES

For centuries *les gens de robe* have retained a costume appropriate to their respective functions. On the origin of this costume, as to whether or not it illustrates the *"quasi-sacerdotium"* of Judges and their ecclesiastical origin, we do not propose to enlarge. It is a subject involved in much uncertainty. That ecclesiastics often exercised judicial functions there can be no doubt; but that they did so by virtue of their Orders is by no means proved. At any rate, by the time when we find the costume of a judge engraved on a brass, the law had renounced any allegiance which it may ever have owed to the Church. Largely from Mr. Serjeant Pulling's work, *The Order of the Coif*,[1] surveying the position of the Serjeants-at-law from early times to the present day, the following notes have been drawn, for the purpose of illustrating the costume which we find on brasses.

It would appear that the following classes existed in the legal profession:—

Attornati et apprenticii ad legem (apprentices de la ley), who "came to form two very distinct classes, the class of ap- "prenticii ad legem coming first, and gradually embracing "not only the learners, but the *learned*, the sages gentz, "the counsellors, the apprenticii *ad Barros*, who consti- "tuted with the older order of the Serjeants, the *Bar*, "whilst the Attornati came to occupy a prominent place "for many ages subordinate to the Bar and governed by "no system of regulation, except those which from time

---

[1] *The Order of the Coif*, by Alexander Pulling, Serjeant-at-law. London: William Clowes & Sons, Limited, 27 Fleet Street, 1897. A letter by George Bowyer on the history of the degree of Serjeant-at-law will be found in *Proceedings of the Society of Antiquaries*, 1st Series, Vol. I., p. 178 (February 25th, 1847).

"to time special statutes, or the *regulæ generales* of the
"Judges, prescribed."[1]

From the ranks of the *Apprenticii ad Barros* (or Utter
Barristers, corresponding to the modern Barrister) were
chosen the *Servientes ad legem*, or Serjeants-at-law; and
from the King's Serjeants (*Servientes Regis ad legem*) were
chosen the Judges of the one bench and the other (King's
Bench and Common Pleas), and the Chief Baron of the
Exchequer, who, with the Serjeants, constituted the Order
of the Coif.[2]

The Serjeants-at-law (Serjeant Counters, Serjeants of
the Coif) formed a far more exclusive and privileged class
than the King's Counsel, who, in modern times, have to
so large an extent usurped their position.   Their permanent rank placed them immediately after Knights
Bachelor, and they may be compared in degree to the
Doctors in the higher faculties.   "Under the old system
"at Westminster Hall," writes Mr. Serjeant Pulling,
". . . the Serjeants-at-law not only had the precedence
"and preaudience, but constituted the whole Common
"Pleas Bar,"[3] in which court they had the right of exclusive audience.

The Coif[4] (*tena*,[5] *birettum album*), which gave its name
to the Order, being described by Fortescue as the "prin-
"cipal and chief insignment of habit wherewith Serjeants-
"at-law on their creation are decked," was a close-fitting
kind of skull-cap, tied beneath the chin, made of white

---

[1] *The Order of the Coif*, p. 112.

[2] "Sir E. Coke describes the ordinary gradation of members as first,
"*Mootmen* or Students" [sometimes called Gentlemen under the Bar or
"Inner Barristers, constituting legal undergraduates]; "secondly, Utter
"Barristers" [who had *passed* the Bar or graduated]; "thirdly, Ancients;
"fourthly, Readers and Double Readers; and fifthly, Serjeants-at-law,
"the King's Serjeants and the Judges."—The same, p. 171.

[3] The same, p. 210.

[4] Called "houve" by Langeland, *Vision of Piers Ploughman, c.* 1369.

[5] Doubtless so called from the strings, *tenæ* or *infulæ*, which tied it
beneath the chin, the ends of which may be the origin of bands.

lawn or silk, frequently with a band down the centre. The origin of this coiffure is lost in obscurity, such explanations as that it was worn to conceal the tonsure, or the latter's absence, whether right or wrong being incapable of proof. We must be content with an admission of ignorance as to its original significance, and with a statement that it constituted as much a part of the *insignia* of the Serjeant-at-law, as the pointed pileus formed a part of those of the Doctor in Theology (*see* p. 125).

Over this coif the judges sometimes wore a skull-cap of black silk or velvet, the remains of which, as of the coif, were to be seen in the small circular white patch with black centre shown on the top of the serjeant's long wig. This black skull-cap is quite distinct from the judge's black, square, or corner cap, known as the sentence cap, worn, according to Mr. Serjeant Pulling's supposition, to veil the coif, but, possibly, merely as a symbol of dignity and authority; for it was ordered to be worn in church, when on circuit.[1]

Chief Justice Fortescue states[2] that "a Serjeant-at-law

---

[1] *See* the "Solemn Decree and Rule made by all the Judges of the Courts at Westminster bearing date the fourth day of June, An. 1635," in Dugdale's *Origines Juridicales*; also "English Academical Costume (Mediæval)," by Professor E. C. Clark, LL.D., F.S.A., *Archæological Journal*, Vol. L., 1893, pp. 142-3; and the "Pileus Quadratus, etc," by the Rev. N. F. Robinson, *St. Paul's Ecclesiological Society's Transactions*, Vol. V., Part I., 1901. At Weekley, Northants, the monument of Sir Edward Montagu (*d.* 1556) shows him in judge's robes, and wearing over the coif a pileus quadratus; engraved in *Sepulchral Memorials, consisting of engravings from the Altar Tombs, Effigies, and Monuments, ancient and modern, contained within the County of Northampton*, from the pen-drawings of W. H. Hyett. London: Nicholls, 1817. At Wroxeter, Salop, the alabaster effigy of Sir Thomas Bromley (S.L. 1540, C.J. of King's Bench, *d.* 1555) shows scarlet gown lined with light green, a red mantle, and a black square cap. (See *Transactions of Shropshire Archæological and Natural History Society*, 2nd series, Vol. I., 1889, p. 15.)

[2] *De Laudibus Legum Angliæ*, C. li.: " Roba longa ad instar sacerdotis "cum capicio penulato circa humeros ejus et desuper collobio cum duobus "labellulis qualiter uti solent doctores legum in universitatibus quibusdam " cum supra descripto birreto vestiebatur."

"is clothed in a long robe not unlike the sacerdotal
"habit, with a furred cape, about his shoulders, and a hood
"over it, with two lapels or tippets such as the Doctors
"of Law use in some universities, with a coif as is above
"described."

This bears much similarity to academical costume, there
being a striking resemblance in the dress of Thomas Rolf,
S.L., 1440, "legi pfessus" at Gosfield, Essex, who appears
to wear a tabard over his "long robe," to that of the
Master of Arts, described p. 135. Indeed, it is well-nigh
identical but for coif and bands.[1] (*See* Professor Clark,
Vol. L., *Archæological Journal*, pp. 203-4.)

The "long robe" is best described as being "cassock-
like," worn without girdle. Over this is seen a fur cape
or tippet,[2] lined and edged with lambs' wool (budge), and
a hood. On the colour of these garments much light is
thrown by four illuminations from a MS. (*temp* Henry VI.)
described and illustrated in the *Archæologia*, Vol. XXXIX.,
1863.[3] Here the Serjeants are seen standing by their
clients, and wearing parti-coloured robes (Chaucer's
"medlee cote") of blue and green, rayed or striped, as

---

[1] At the Exhibition of English Embroidery executed prior to the
middle of the Sixteenth Century, held at the Burlington Fine Arts Club,
1905, were shown two copes, *c.* 1500 (Case R., Nos. 2 and 4), lent by
Oscott College, Birmingham, on the orphreys of which figures, holding
rolls in the left hand, appear in robes, possibly those of a serjeant:—a
long robe (*roba talaris*) ; over it a shorter gown with surplice-like sleeves
(*taberdum*) of a colour lighter than that of the long robe ; a green hood
and white coif.

[2] Langeland's "pelease."

[3] "Observations on four Illuminations representing the Courts of
Chancery, King's Bench, Common Pleas, and Exchequer at Westminster,
from a MS. of the time of King Henry VI., in a letter from G. R. Corner,
Esq., F.S.A., to Frederic Ouvry, Esq., Treasurer." Read December 6th,
1860, pp. 357-372, Vol. XXXIX., *Archæologia*, 1863.

At Faversham, Kent, was found, in 1851, a fourteenth-century wall-
painting of a kneeling figure (? Robert Dod), wearing red cassock-like
robe, tippet, and hood (apparently combined), and white coif. *See*
"Faversham Church, Kent," by Thomas Willement, Esq., F.S.A.,
pp. 150-153, *Archæologia Cantiana*, Vol. I., 1858.

though they had accepted some patron's livery in accordance with the practice of the age. Sir William Dugdale,
in his *Origines Juridicales*, says : " The robes they now
" use do still somewhat resemble those of the justices of
" either bench, and are of three distinct colours, viz.,
" murrey, black furred with white, and scarlet; but the
" robe which they usually wear at their creation only is of
" two colours, viz., murrey and mouse-colour ; whereunto
" they have a hood suitable, as also a Coif of white silk or
" linen."[1]

Unfortunately the few brasses, which we possess, of
Serjeants-at-law, give no indication of colour.

The illuminations, just mentioned, amply illustrate the
scarlet colour of the robes of the Judges. In form these
are the same as those of the Serjeants, as members of the
same Order :—a long robe (supertunic or surcoat) with or
without girdle, cape, hood, and coif, with the exception
that the hood is worn over a mantle fastened on the right
shoulder, in the manner prevalent in the fourteenth century. " After he [the Serjeant] is made a Judge, instead
" of the Hood he shall be habited with a cloak fastened
" upon his right shoulder. He still retains the other
" ornaments of a Serjeant, with the exception that a Judge
" shall not use a parti-coloured habit, as the Serjeants do ;

---

[1] " In the *Liber Famelicus* of Sir James Whitelocke, edited by John
" Bruce, Esq., F.S.A., and published by the Camden Society, 1858, he
" relates that on the occasion of his being created a serjeant, June 29th,
" 1620, after taking his leave of the Society of the Middle Temple, they
" attended him to Serjeants' Inn in Fleet Street ; where, his party-coloured
" robe being put upon him in his chamber, he was conducted into the
" hall by the tipstaves, his scarlet hood and his coif laid upon it being
" carried before him by his man. And, after recording the expenses of his
" creation and robes, he adds : ' Memorandum : I made no black robe,
" nor purple, because I was not to need them, but only a party-coloured
" and a scarlet; the party-coloured, a robe, a hood, and tabard ; the
" scarlet, a robe and hood,' He says further : ' I rode circuit in summer,
" 1620, Serjeant-at-law, and practised in my party-coloured robe on
" Sundays and holidays, both in the circuit and in the term.'"—"Observations on Four Illuminations, etc," *Archæologia*, Vol. XXXIX., 1863,
p. 370.

" and his cape is furred with minever, whereas the Serjeant's " cape is always furred with lambs' wool."[1]

From this we see that more costly fur, minever, was used,[2] and that the robes were not to be parti-coloured.

The Barons of the Exchequer (*Scaccarium*), except the Chief, and the Masters in Chancery, were not, necessarily, of the Coif, and, accordingly, were of lower rank. The illuminations cited show four Barons,[3] each either wearing or holding a curious high cap (or chaperon), not unlike that worn by John Edward, 1461, Rodmarton, Gloucs. (*see* below). The four Masters in Chancery are tonsured. In each case these robes are of mustard colour, in the case of the Exchequer of the same shape as the Judge's; but the centre figures are in scarlet.

The following are the brasses of Judges remaining :—

1400.   Sir John Cassy, Kt., Deerhurst, Gloucs., Chief Baron of the Exchequer; wife on dexter side; mantle lined with vair; cape does not appear; the sleeves of the under-tunic end in buttoned mittens; feet rest on lion, facing sinister.

---

[1] Fortescue, *De Laudibus*, C. li., quoted by Serjeant Pulling, p. 223-4. *See* also Stow's *Survey*: " And now, in some Things, his former Habit " of a Serjeant is altered. His long Robe and Cap, his Hood and Coif " are the same. But there is besides a Cloak put over him, which is " closed on his right shoulder; and his *Caputium* is lined with *Minever*, " that is, divers small Pieces of white rich Furr. But the Two Lord " Chief-Justices, and the Lord Chief Baron, have their Hoods, Sleeves " and Collars, turned up with Ermine." Ed. 1720, Book I., p. 122.

[2] The Orders of 1635 prescribe as follows :—"The facing of their " Gowns, Hoods, and Mantles, is with Changable Taffata; which they " must begin to wear upon Ascension Day, being the last Thursday in " Easter Term; and continue those Robes until the Feast of Simon and " Jude: And upon Simon and Jude's day the Judges begin to wear their " Robes faced with white furs of Minever; and so continue that facing " till Ascension Day again." *See* Pulling, p. 225.

[3] " Mr. Corner suggests that they are the other Barons of the Exchequer; " but I doubt it, as the robes issued to them appear to have been always " similar in colour to those of the chief."—Planché, *Cyclopædia of Costume*, 1876, *sub* Robe.

SIR WILLIAM LAKEN, 1475,
BRAY, BERKS.

1415. Sir Hugh de Holes, Kt., Watford, Herts., Justice of the King's Bench; feet gone. (Placed on the wall in 1871.)

1419. William Lodyngton, Gunby, Lincs., Justice of the Common Pleas to Henry V., S.L. 1410; wearing anelace;[1] feet on leopard.

1420. Richard Norton, Wath, N. Yorks., Chief Justice of the King's Bench, S.L. 1406; much worn; feet on lion.

c. 1430. John Staverton (?), Eyke, Suffolk, Baron of the Exchequer; head gone. Probably did not wear the coif.

1436. John Martyn, Graveney, Kent, Justice of the King's Bench, S.L. 1415; holding heart inscribed, "Ihu mcy"; feet on lion.

1439. Sir John Juyn, Kt., St. Mary Redcliffe, Bristol, Chief Justice of the King's Bench, S.L. 1403; feet rest on ground.

1439. John Cottesmore, Brightwell Baldwin, Oxon., Chief Justice; mural, kneeling. Commemorated by two brasses, one mural, the other on the floor.

c. 1465. Nicholas Assheton, Callington, Cornwall, "one of the Kynges Juges," "Secundarie" of the Common Pleas; feet on ground.

1467. Sir Peter Arderne, Kt., Latton, Essex,[2] Chief Baron of the Exchequer, Judge of the Common Pleas, S.L. 1443; tunic covering his feet.

1475. Sir William Laken, Kt., Bray, Berks., Justice of the King's Bench, S.L. 1453; rosary and anelace hanging from girdle.

---

[1] An anelace and gypcière are worn by Sir William Gascoigne, Chief Justice of the King's Bench *temp.* Henry IV. (stone effigy), Harewood, Yorks. The latter is seen on the alabaster effigy of Sir Richard Newton (S.L. 1424), Chief Justice of the Common Pleas, c. 1448, at Yatton, Somerset.

[2] *See* paper entitled, "Arderne's Chantry at Latton, Essex," by C. E. Johnston, *The Home Counties Magazine*, Vol. IV., 1902, pp. 222-5.

1476. Sir Richard Bingham, Kt., Middleton, Warwickshire, Justice of the King's Bench, S.L. 1443; wearing fur-lined gown open in front, over which is mantle; feet on ground.

1479. Sir Thomas Urswyke, Kt., Dagenham, Essex, Chief Baron of the Exchequer, 1472, formerly Recorder of London; became S.L. 1479, in which year he died. An early date of engraving may account for the absence of the coif. Neither tippet nor hood show; wearing rosary; feet on dog.

1481. Sir Thomas Billing, Kt., Wappenham, Northants, Chief Justice of the Common Pleas, S.L. 1448. The slab was *semée* of scrolls, "Ihu mercy" and "lady helppe." Originally at Biddlesden, Bucks.

1494. Brian Rouclyff, Cowthorpe, W. Yorks., third Baron of the Exchequer; no coif. The monument has been much injured.

1513. Sir William Greville, Kt., Cheltenham, Gloucs., Justice of the Common Pleas, S.L. 1504; worn.

1538. Sir Anthony Fitzherbert, Kt.,[1] Norbury, Derbyshire, Justice of the Common Pleas, S.L. 1510; much mutilated, head gone; casting hood on right shoulder; holding roll in right hand.

1544/5. Sir Walter Luke, Kt., Cople, Beds., Justice of the Common Pleas, S.L. 1531; mural in stone frame; kneeling; scarlet mantle and hood; wearing gypcière. The traces of colouring matter are visible.

1545. Thomas Holte, Esq., Aston, Warwickshire, Justice of North Wales; the head is lost, but

---

[1] For "The Will of the celebrated Judge, Sir Anthony Fitzherbert," by the Rev. R. H. C. Fitzherbert (proved 26th August, 1538), see *The Reliquary*, Vol. XXI., 1880-1, p. 234.

probably no coif, as he was not a Serjeant;
holding scroll in hands; a gypcière attached
to girdle on right; broad shoes.

1553.   Henry Bradschawe, Esq., Halton, Bucks., Chief
Baron of the Exchequer; kneeling; head
bare; gypcière.

1553.   William Coke, Esq., Milton, Cambs., Justice of
the Common Pleas, "communi banco," S.L.
1547; casting hood hanging on right shoulder;
gypcière.

1556.   Sir John Spelman, Kt., Narburgh, Norfolk,
secundary justice of the King's Bench, S.L.
1521; kneeling at prayer-desk.

1563.   Nycholas Luke, Esq., Cople, Beds., Baron of
the Exchequer; no coif; similar in design to
that of Sir Walter Luke, above; gypcière.

1567.   Sir Anthony Browne, Kt., South Weald, Essex,
Chief Justice of Common Pleas, S.L. 1555;
kneeling at prayer-desk; only lower part of
effigy left.

1598.   Hen. Bradshawe (ob. 1553), Noke, Oxon.,
Chief Baron of the Exchequer; no mantle.

c. 1470.   Sir William Yelverton, Kt., Rougham, Norfolk,
Justice of the King's Bench, S.L. 1440; wearing armour, over which mantle, hood, and
collar of suns and roses; on his head a coif.

1570.   Sir Clement Heigham, Kt., Barrow, Suffolk,
Chief Baron of the Exchequer to Queen
Mary, S.L. 1555; kneeling; in armour.

At Writtle, Essex, are three shields, belonging to the
altar-tomb of Richard Weston, Justice of the Common
Pleas, 1572 (S.L. 1559).

At Sedgebrook, Lincs., is the matrix of the brass of
John Markham, Lord Chief Justice temp Edward IV.

The few brasses of Serjeants-at-law vary more in type
than those of the Judges:—

1404. John Rede, Checkendon, Oxon., S.L. 1401, "Serviens domini Regis ad legem," or King's Serjeant; wearing the cassock-like gown, from beneath the sleeves of which appear the buttoned mitten-sleeves of the under-tunic; hood and pointed shoes; no coif nor girdle; the hair flowing; feet on ground.

c. 1410. Nichol Rolond, Cople, Beds., possibly S.L.; wearing robe with tight sleeves, tippet, hood, and *coif.* The wife occupies the dexter side.

1440. Thomas Rolf, Gosfield, Essex, S.L. 1418, "legi pfessus"; wearing cassock-like gown, tabard (as described p. 135), tippet, hood, bands, and coif; "inter iuristas quasi flos enituit." Somewhat similar to this, though without cape or hood, is a recumbent stone effigy of the fourteenth century at Pembridge, Herefordshire.[1]

1519. Thomas Pygott, Whaddon, Bucks., S.L. 1503.

1522. John Brook, St. Mary Redcliffe, Bristol, Serjeant-at-law to King Henry VIII., Justice of Assize in the west parts of England,[2] Chief Steward

---

[1] Engraved in *Transactions of the Bristol and Gloucestershire Archæological Society,* Vol. XVIII., 1893-4, illustrating a paper, "The Dress of Civilians in the Middle Ages from Monumental Effigies," by Mrs. M. E. Bagnall-Oakeley, pp. 252-270. On brass of Thomas Rolf, *see* Professor Clark's "Mediæval Academical Costume," Vol. L., *Archæological Journal,* pp. 203-4. Sculptured effigies of Serjeants-at-law, of a later date, exist, *e.g.,* 1622, Edward Drew, Esq. (S.L. 1589), Broadclyst, Devon, "qui Reginæ Elizab. serviens erat ad legem"; 1640, John Darcy, Serjeant-at-law, died 1638/9, St. Osyth, Essex, above which is a mural brass inscription in Roman capitals engraved by Fr. Grigs. In the *Proceedings of Somerset Archæological and Natural History Society,* Vol. XXXVIII., 1892, is a paper by H. C. Maxwell Lyte, C.B., on the Lytes of Lytescary, with an illustration from a pedigree compiled in 1631 by Thomas Lyte, of glass formerly in Charlton Makerel Church, depicting William Lyte, Serjeant-at-law, *temp* Edward I., kneeling in his robes.

[2] *See* Pulling, p. 4, note 3. "Assizes may be taken before any justices of the one Bench or the other, or Serjeant le Roi juré, *i.e.,* every Serjeant-at-law.—4 Edw. III., c. 16." He quotes, p. 4, Chaucer's :—

"Justice he was ful often in assise,
By patent, and by pleine commissiun."

JOHN BROOK, SERJEANT-AT-LAW, AND WIFE JOAN, 1522,
ST. MARY REDCLIFFE, BRISTOL.

of Glastonbury Abbey ; wearing coif, tippet, hood, and round-toed shoes, gown, and tabard.

15—.   John Newdegate, Harefield, Middlesex, S.L. 1510 (wife died 1544); no cape; holding a scroll.

1681.   Edmund West, Marsworth, Bucks., S.L. 1679; represented in armour and lying on his left side, a book in right hand, a sword in left.

At Brampton, Norfolk, is an inscription for Guybon Goddard, Serjeant-at-law, 1671, remarkable for its ending "cujus animæ propitietur deus" at so late a date.

At Great Bardfield, Essex, was formerly the effigy of William Bendlowes, 1584 (S.L. 1555).

Barons of the Exchequer and Masters in Chancery are occasionally mentioned on brasses :—

BARONS OF THE EXCHEQUER.

1448.   Nicholas Dixon, rector, Cheshunt, Herts., "pipe subthesaurarius," Baron of the Exchequer; in cope.

1460.   Inscription, Outwell, Norfolk, to Margaret, wife of Gilbert Haultoft, one of the Barons of the Exchequer to King Henry VI.

c. 1520.   Inscription, Attlebridge, Norfolk, William, son and heir of William Elys, Baron of the Exchequer.

MASTERS IN CHANCERY.

1561.   John Eyer, Esq., Narburgh, Norfolk ; in armour ; mural.

1565.   Sir John Tregonwell, D.C.L. and a Master of the Chauncerye, Milton Abbas, Dorset; in heraldic tabard.

1586.   Nicholas West, Marsworth, Bucks. ; in armour.

Barristers are represented by a few brasses.   The terms
in lege peritus and *Apprenticius ad legem* or *ad leges* are occasionally found, and probably denote this degree[1] :—

1437.   Robert Skerñ, Kingston-upon-Thames, Surrey,
"lege peritus"; in civilian tunic.

1461.   John Edward, Rodmarton, Gloucs., " ffamosus
apprenticius in lege peritus"; wearing the
civilian tunic of the period, but on his head
a curious high cap of velvet or some soft
material with an edging of fur.[2]

c. 1460.   An Effigy, St. Peter's, Chester, wearing a high-
crowned cap with vandyked base, and the
civilian bag-sleeved gown, without girdle.
The inscription is lost, but the similarity to
the last-mentioned brass may justify its in-
clusion in this class.

1472.   Robert Ingylton, Esq., Thornton, Bucks.,
in armour ; Chancellor of the Exchequer.
Browne Willis gives a lost inscription, " qui
quondam erat juris peritus, et totius virtutis
amicus."

1501.   Robert Baynard, Esq., Laycock, Wilts., " vir
egregius et legis peritus, etc."; in armour
with heraldic tabard.

1507.   William Eyre, Esq., Great Cressingham, Norfolk, " juris peritus "; in civilian gown.

1514.   Robert Southwell, Esq., Barham, Suffolk,

---

[1] In the *Calendar of the Freemen of Norwich from* 1317 *to* 1603
(Edward II. to Elizabeth inclusive), by John L'Estrange, and edited by
Walter Rye (London : Elliot Stock, 1882), occur the names of Edmund
Grey, Esq., Juris Peritus, and Nicholas Hare, Esq., Legis Peritus, each
admitted 28 Hen. VIII.

At Preston Bagot, Warwickshire, is the brass of Elizabeth, wife of
Wm. Randoll, "*legis consiliarius*," 1637.

[2] "In the church of Norton St. Philip, Somersetshire, is a stone effigy
surmounted by a similar cap."—p. 61, *The Monumental Brasses of
Gloucestershire*, by Cecil T. Davis, 1899.

"apprenticius ad leges": wearing civilian fur-lined gown.

1574. Richard Payton, Isleham, Cambs., "In Greys Inne student of the lawe, wheare he a Reader was"; in false-sleeved gown; holding a book in right hand.

1585. Francis Saunders, Welford, Northants, "legum Anglie apprenticius"; in armour.

1596. Robert Trencreeke, St. Erme, Cornwall, "coūseler at lawe"; kneeling in false-sleeved gown.

1621. Thomas Palmer, Epping, Essex, "A Professor of that illustrious and flourishing Scyence of ye common Lawe, and an utter Barrester of that Right Worshipfull Socyetie of Lincolnes Inne"; in false-sleeved gown and ruff.

1668. Robert Shiers, Great Bookham, Surrey, "of the Inner Temple, London, Esq."; called to the Bar 1641, Bencher 1660, Lecturer 1667; in civilian costume; holding open book in right hand.

INSCRIPTIONS.

1531. Robert Fulwode, Tamworth, Warwickshire, "Excellentissiē doctrinat' siue litterat' in cōīe lege Anglie."

1585. Nicholas Pury, Esq., Sanderstead, Surrey (a palimpsest reverse of the brass of Nicholas Wood, 1586, and probably a spoilt plate), "Templi que medii socius erat."

1604. John Clarke, Bennington, Herts., "Councill at lawe."

1613. James Mott (?), Mattishall, Norfolk, four English verses, "He professed the lawe."

1614. Andrew Gray, Esq., Hinxworth, Herts., "double reader of ye Lawe in ye Inner Temple in London."

STUDENTS.

1483.　Wm. Crofton, Gent., B.C.L. of Grey's Inn,
　　　　Trotterscliffe, Kent; civilian gown.

1581.　William Saxaye, Stanstead Abbotts, Herts.,
　　　　"late of Graīs In gentlemā," aged 23.

1596.　Inscription, William Bramfeilde, Gent., Wal-
　　　　kern, Herts., "sumtym student of Grayes
　　　　Inn."

1612.　Arthur Strode, St. Aldate's, Oxford, of Broad-
　　　　gates Hall, "in medio templo Londinensis
　　　　legum studiosi," aged 23; wearing gown with
　　　　false sleeves.

The following are some brasses of other legal function-
aries and officials :—

1470.　Hen. Unton, Sculthorpe, Norfolk, "Gentilman
　　　　Cirographorius" (engrosser) of the Court of
　　　　Common Pleas; in armour, kneeling; restored.

c. 1470.　Inscription to John Colard, Halling, Kent, for
　　　　thirty-seven years one of the King's Clerks of
　　　　the Exchequer.

1492.　Bartholomew Willesden, Willesdon, Middlesex,
　　　　"comptroller of the great roll of the Pipe";
　　　　inscription lost; cap with pendent scarf on
　　　　shoulder.

1512.　John Muscote, Gent., Earls Barton, Northants,
　　　　a prothonotary of the Court of Common
　　　　Pleas.

c. 1520.　John Sedley, Southfleet, Kent, "an auditor of
　　　　the King's Exchequer."

1552.　Mr. Wm. Fermoure, Esq., Somerton, Oxon.,
　　　　"Clarke of the Crowne in the Kyng' Benche."

1586.　Henry Dynne, Esq., Heydon, Norfolk, "an
　　　　auditor of the Court of Exchequer."

1588.　William Tooke, Esq., Essendon, Herts., kneel-
　　　　ing; Auditor of the Courte of Wardes and
　　　　Liveries.

1590. William Death, Gent., Dartford, Kent, "once Prynsipall of Staple Inne, and one of the Attorneys of the Comon Pleas at Wesminster"; gown with false sleeves.

1612 (?) Richard Symonds, Esq., Great Yeldham, Essex, a Cursitor in Chancery; kneeling; gown with false sleeves.

1630. Inscription to Richard Fittz, Letheringsett, Norfolk, "one of the Cursitors of the Court of Chancery."

Besides the Notaries mentioned on pp. 209, 211, we have the following:—

1499. William Curteys, Necton, Norfolk, "notarius," with pen-case and ink-pot. (Wrongly stated by Cotman and Boutell to be at Holme Hale.)

1500. Rich. Foxwist, Llanbeblig, Carnarvonshire; ? Notary; in bed holding a shield charged with the Stigmata; pen-case and ink-bottle.

INSCRIPTIONS.

1474. Robert Aldrych, Sall, Norfolk, public notary; fragment.

156–. Robert Garet, Hayes, Kent, Rector of Hayes and Chiselhurst; notary public.

1580. John Bossewell, Gent., Kingsclere, Hants, "notarye publique."

At Great Bircham, Norfolk, was formerly the effigy of Master John Wattys, c. 1470, notary.

CHAPTER VI.

Of Female Costume on Brasses

SIR JOHN DE CREKE AND WIFE
ALYNE, *c.* 1325,
WESTLEY WATERLESS, CAMBS.

CHAPTER VI.

OF FEMALE COSTUME ON BRASSES

MORE from a sense of convenience than of chivalry we have given precedence in this account of costume to knights and civilians; for the dress of the ladies, whether of the fourteenth or of the nineteenth century frequently shows a marked tendency to imitate that of their husbands. It is well, therefore, to have some knowledge of the latter before discussing the former.

The earliest brass of a lady, which survives in England, is that of Margarete de Camoys, c. 1310, at Trotton, Sussex. She wears a long and flowing COTE-HARDIE, the sleeves of which end a little below the elbows, thereby exposing the tight-fitting buttoned sleeves of the KIRTLE, which end at the wrists. Round the throat is a WIMPLE, covering the chin and carried up the sides of the face, to which it gave a triangular appearance.[1] On the head is the COVRECHEF, *kerchief,* or veil, falling upon the shoulders, and held in place by two pins on either side of the forehead, which, probably, also help to sustain the wimple. The hair is bound by a narrow fillet across the forehead, allowing a small curl to appear on either side. Pointed shoes cover the feet, at which lies a small dog. The hands are clasped in prayer. Originally the cote-hardie was *semée* of nine enamelled shields, which have been

---

[1] *See* the stone effigy of Aveline, Countess of Lancaster, *d.* 1269, Westminster Abbey (engraved by Stothard). At Gonalston, Notts., is the stone effigy of a lady, *c.* 1320, showing well the wimple and hair fillet. (engraved in the *Archæological Journal,* Vol. VI., 1849). A good MS. example is afforded in Royal MS. 19 B XV., British Museum, by "The Woman sitting upon the Scarlet-coloured Beast" (*see* Plate II. illustrating "English Costume of the Early Fourteenth Century."—*The Ancestor,* No. VII., October, 1903). She wears a cote with wide slits for the arms. Compare the military *coif de mailles.*

stolen.[1]   The slab also was sprinkled with flowers
(? marguerites) and held eight shields.   The effigy was
enclosed by an elegant crocketed canopy (lost), with
slender sideshafts.   Round the verge of the slab the
Lombardic-uncial inscription ran :—

MARGARETE : DE : CAMOYS : GIST : ICI :
DEVS : DE : SA : ALME : EIT : MERCI : AMEN.

A similar effigy is that of Lady Joan de Cobham, *c.* 1320,
Cobham, Kent.   The covrechef is somewhat differently
treated, curving outward at the sides and barely touching
the shoulders.   There is no dog at the feet.   The cote-
hardie is plain.   The effigy is surmounted by a fine
pedimental canopy, the earliest surviving on a brass in
England.   The marginal Lombardic inscription, of which
no brass letters remain, runs :—

+ DAME : IONE : DE : KOBEHAM : GIST : ISI :
DEVS : DE : SA : ALME : EIT : MERCI :
KIKE : PVR : LE : ALME : PRIERA :
QVARAVNTE : IOVRS : DE : PARDOVN : AVERA.

Two other effigies in this costume exist :—

c. 1320.   The reverse of the palimpsest brasses of Sir
Anthony Fitzherbert,[2] 1538, and Lady, at
Norbury, Derbyshire, shows a large portion
of the figure of a lady, possibly Dame
Matilda, wife of Sir Theobald de Verdun,
d. 1312, buried in Croxden Abbey.   The
long cote-hardie, over which is a mantle, is
tucked up under the right arm.   The feet
rest on a lion.

---

[1] The mantle on a sculptured effigy of the thirteenth century at
Worcester, is similarly adorned with the arms of Clifford.   *See* engraving
in Hollis and *Journal of the British Archæological Association*, Vol. VI.,
1851, p. 5, "On the effigy of a Lady in Worcester Cathedral," by J. R.
Planché.

[2] *See* among the Judges, p. 228.

c. 1350. At Upchurch, Kent, is the half-effigy of a lady
(for male effigy, *see* p. 199). The edge of the
covrechef is crimped.

Besides the above, a few effigies survive of the
middle of the fourteenth century, the costume of
which enables them to be classed together. The head is
still attired in covrechef and wimple, but the hair is shown
plaited on either side of the face, bearing some resemblance to ears of wheat. Over the close-fitting kirtle is
worn a sleeveless cote-hardie, an interesting stage in the
development of which toward the *sideless côte-hardie*, soon
to be noticed, may be seen in the costume of Lady Creke.
This low-necked cote-hardie was of great length. Consequently we find it gathered up under one arm, which,
besides exposing the skirt of the kirtle, afforded scope to
the engraver for a delicate treatment of the folds of the
drapery. Over this garment was worn a mantle, fastened
in front by a cord either passing through holes in the
mantle itself, or fastened to studs or brooches called
fermailes or *tasseaux*.

Examples, more or less conforming to the above
description, are as follows :—

A Lady, kneeling, Sedgefield, Durham, to which
Mr. J. G. Waller ascribes the date *c.* 1300-10.[1]
The *cote*, which is girded, is gathered up
under the left arm. Over all a mantle.

c. 1325. Alyne, Lady Creke, Westley Waterless, Cambs.,
on the dexter side of her husband.[2] The
cote-hardie (? *surcote overte*), gathered up under
the left arm, has large slits at the sides for
the arms, though not large enough for it to
be called "*sideless.*" Both mantle and cote-
hardie have an invecked pattern along their
borders. The feet rest on a small dog.

[1] See *Archæologia Aeliana*, Vol. XV.
[2] For whom, and inscription, *see* pp. 152-3.

c. 1325.   Maud, wife of Johan de Bladigdone (*see* p. 197), East Wickham, Kent.   Half effigy on dexter side of husband; wearing a cote-hardie with slits of similar size to those of Lady Creke's, but no mantle.

c. 1330.   Joan de Northwode, Minster, Kent (for husband, *see* p. 153).   Her chin, and the sides of her hair, which is plaited, are enclosed in a large gorget.[1]   Her head, which is without covre-chef, rests on a cushion.   Her hair is parted in the centre.   The sleeveless cote-hardie, gathered up under the right arm, has two curious pointed lappets hanging down in front from the neck, lined with fur, and with buttons on their inner edges.   The right foot rests on a dog with bell-collar.   This brass is probably of French workmanship[2] (*see* p. 56).

---

[1] Compare the stone effigy of A Lady of the Ryther Family, Ryther, Yorkshire,   Engraved by Hollis.

[2] The costume on this brass is thus described in Stothard's *Monumental Effigies of Great Britain*, new edition by John Hewitt, 1876, p. 91A.

"Lady Northwood wears a kirtle with tight sleeves, terminating in an "ornamental border at the wrists.   The hooded surcoat is lined with "vair, and bordered in the same pattern as the kirtle.   The hood, being "thrown off the head, shows us its fur lining in front of the figure. "When worn close, it was drawn over the back and sides of the head till "it reached the forehead in front, and was then fastened at the throat "by that row of small buttons which is seen at its edge, below the hands. "Armholes, for occasional use, add to the commodity of this garment. "No example of a surcoat exactly similar to that of Lady Northwood has "hitherto been observed in English monuments; but in Montfaucon's "'Monarchie Française' will be found two figures in which the resem-"blance is very close: that of Jeanne de St. Verain, 1297, 'gravée sur sa "tombe dans le Chapitre de l'Abbaye de Vauluisant' (ii., pl. 32) and "that of Marguerite de Beaujeu, 1336 (ii., pl. 52).   Of the latter, "Montfaucon observes that 'son habit est assez remarquable'; showing "that, even in French monuments, this dress was not of common occur-"rence.   In this resemblance of the Minster effigy with known French "examples is found an additional reason for believing it to have been of "foreign workmanship.   Over the neck and chin of the figure is seen the

1347. Ellen, Lady Wantone, Wimbish, Essex (for husband, *see* p. 156); wearing a plain mantle fastened by a broad band in front, over a flowing cote. The hair, which is uncovered, except for a fillet is curiously braided.

1349. Margaret de Walsokne, St. Margaret's, King's Lynn, Norfolk. Flemish (*see* pp. 46, 197); wearing wimple and covrechef, a finely-embroidered kirtle, over which is a sleeveless, almost *sideless*, cote-hardie gathered up under the right elbow, and a mantle, of which but little appears. Feet on a dog.

1364. Leticia and Margaret, wives of Robert Braunche, St. Margaret's, King's Lynn. Flemish (*see* pp. 46, 197); wearing wimple and covrechef, the latter concealing the hair, and over an embroidered kirtle a plain cote-hardie which has *liripipia* or lappets, lined with vair, hanging from the elbows, in shape like those of the male cote (*see* p. 197). On the skirt sits a toy-terrier.

In the second half of the century less uniformity of costume is found. The last brass mentioned introduces us to a form of the cote-hardie with which we became familiar in the male costume of the period. Its characteristic lies in the long liripipes or streamers, usually of a white colour, hanging from the elbows.[1]

"*gorget*, a variety of the wimple, which came into vogue in the reign of "Edward the First. It was 'poked up with pins'; but its difference "from the older wimple of the thirteenth century may best be seen by "comparing the effigy of the Countess of Lancaster (plate 40). Tresses "of hair are brought from the back of the head and fastened over the "flowing hair of the sides, in a manner by no means ungraceful. Beneath "the feet is a dog, with its collar of bells."

[1] Compare the sculptured effigy of Blanche de la Tour, daughter of Edward III., 1372, in Westminster Abbey, whose hands are in the pockets of the *cote*, and the small figures in Westminster Abbey, and Oxford Cathedral. *See* footnote, p. 198.

Another form is that known as the SIDELESS COTE-HARDIE,[1] in which the sides of the garment have been cut away, leaving narrow strips, often faced with fur, passing over the shoulders and down the body. Its skirt, sometimes with a fur border, is occasionally found slit up at the sides. From the neck to the waist large circular or lozenge-shaped ornaments frequently appear. Over it the MANTLE is usually worn, often with long pendent cords held together by a slide. Under the cote, or sometimes without it, is worn the KIRTLE with low neck and tight-fitting sleeves, the latter usually buttoned on the underside and terminating in mittens.[2]

Another tunic or cote, found worn over the kirtle at Great Berkhampstead, Herts., c. 1360; Hellesden, Norfolk, c. 1370; Chinnor, Oxon, c. 1380; Reepham, Norfolk, 1391; and Ore, Sussex, c. 1400, has tight sleeves with cuffs, and at Chinnor and Ore buttons from neck to feet.

The head-dress presents much variety. The braided style, with fillet already noticed, occurs; but, broadly speaking, the coiffures divide into two classes, the VEILED, and that known as ZIG-ZAG, NEBULÉ, or RETICULATED, according to the manner of engraving.

The first consists of two kerchiefs; the inner one fitting the head like a cap and enclosing the forehead and sides of the face, its edges being frequently crimped; the outer one falling on the shoulders, and corresponding to the *covrechef*, mentioned above. The *gorget*, or *wimple*, is rarely found, but occurs at West Hanningfield, Essex (Isabel Clonvill, half effigy, 1361), and at Topcliffe, York-

---

[1] Fine examples on brasses of the sideless cote worn over embroidered kirtle are at Ringstead in Zealand (Queen Ingeborg of Denmark, 1319), and at Thorn, in Prussian Poland (the Wife of Johan von Zoest, 1361), figured by Creeny.

[2] The kirtle is worn alone, and plain by Johane Plessi, c. 1360, Quainton Bucks (half effigy) and by Elyenore Corp, 1391, Stoke Fleming, Devon, with buttons from neck to waist and on the sleeves from shoulder to mitten.

shire (Mabel de Topcliff, 1391). But these effigies probably illustrate the garb of widows, in whose attire the
gorget or *plaited barbe* survived.

The second class of attire consisted of cauls or close
caps, enclosing the hair and forming a kind of frame to
the face. The *zig-zag*, or *nebulé*, appearance is probably
intended to represent frills[1]; the *reticulated* to portray
network, usually jewelled—a step towards the *crespine*
head-dress soon to be noticed. The natural hair was
probably supplemented by pads of false; as otherwise it is
difficult to account for the evident presence of a cap
beneath the coiffure. Sometimes a jewelled fillet, or
bandeau, crosses the forehead, as at Spilsby, Lincs., 1391
Later in the century the *nebulé* head-dress does not come
so low down the sides of the face as formerly, and resting
on the shoulders are shown two balls, or cushions, probably confining escaped tresses, between which and the
upper part of the head-dress the veil appears at the sides,
as at Cobham, Kent, 1395.

Two instances of young girls with flowing hair, in the
case of the latter enclosed in a simple jewelled fillet or
garland, may be seen at Quainton, Bucks. (Johane Plessi,
c. 1360), and Sherborne St. John, Hants. (Margaret
Brocas, *c*. 1360).

As a rule, a small toy terrier with a collar of bells is
seen at the lady's feet.

The following examples are arranged according to
coiffure. It may be understood that, where not otherwise
stated, the kirtle has mitten sleeves, buttoned beneath.

In veil head-dresses :—

c. 1370. Dame Elizabeth de Cornewaylle, Burford,
Shropshire ; lower part gone ; cote-hardie
with pockets in front, and tight sleeves ;

---

[1] These frills bear some resemblance to the bonnets, now sometimes
seen worn by elderly peasants. That they *are* frills is plainly shown on the
monument of Elizabeth, Lady Montacute, 1354, at Christ Church, Oxford.

mantle with short pendent cords; head resting on an embroidered cushion.

c. 1370.   A Lady, possibly Blanche Bradstone, Winterbourne, Gloucs.; similar, but without mantle or cushion.   The cote-hardie enfolds the feet.

c. 1370.   Dame Joan de Faversham (?), Graveney, Kent; half effigy, on dexter side of son John (?). The cote has tight sleeves like those of Lady Camoys.   The kirtle sleeves end at the wrists and are without buttons.   The outer veil, or covrechef, which is voluminous, alone appears.

c. 1370.   Beatrice, wife of Richard de Heylesdone, Hellesdon, Norfolk (three-quarter effigy).   Covrechef like the last.   The cote has close sleeves, and buttons down the front.

c. 1370.   Agneys, wife of John de Kyggesfolde, Rusper, Sussex (half effigy, on dexter side); in similar head-dress; the buttoned kirtle sleeves ending at the wrists.   A mantle with cords and slide is worn.

1379.   Alienora, wife of Robert de Paris, Hildersham, Cambs. (kneeling on sinister side of cross); the sleeves of the kirtle buttoned to the shoulder, over it a cote, buttoned from neck to feet, with short arm lappets.[1]

c. 1380.   Alice, wife of Simon de Felbrig, Felbrigg, Norfolk; mutilated; kirtle and mantle.

At St. Alkmund's, Shrewsbury, was formerly the brass of Simon and Joan Walshe, *c.* 1370.   The latter wore the cote-hardie with liripipes at the elbows, and the veil head-dress.

The costume of widows remained practically the same throughout three centuries, and was similar to that of the

---

[1] A similar coiffure is given in Strutt's *Dress and Habits*, Vol. II., Plate XCIX. "Mourning Habits of the Fourteenth Century."

nun (*see* p. 98), where the Order of Vowesses, or widows who had taken a vow of chastity, is referred to. This profession was known as "taking the mantle and ring."[1] Widows' weeds consisted of kirtle, mantle, veil head-dress, and plaited barbe or gorget, which was worn above or below the chin according to rank.[2]

c. 1360.	Half effigy of a widow, Clifton Campville, Staffs., on bracket, the stem of which is lost. Kirtle, with buttoned sleeves ending at wrists.
1361.	Isabel Clonvill (half effigy), West Hanning-field, Essex (son, a priest, lost). The buttoned kirtle sleeves end at the wrists. The *cote* sleeves are like those at Upchurch.
1383.	Philippa de Beauchampe (*née* Ferrers), Necton, Norfolk; two dogs fighting at her feet.
c. 1390.	A Lady, Stebbing, Essex; dog on skirt.
1391.	Mabel, wife of Thomas de Topclyff, Topcliffe, Yorks. Flemish. A hood attached to the fur-lined mantle; a dog gnawing a bone on her skirt.
1391.	Albreda, wife of John Curteys, Wymington,

---

[1] For further information see *Surrey Archæological Collections*, Vol. III., 1865, p. 208. "Thomas Burgh and Isabella, his wife; with a few words on the Benediction of Widows," by Francis Joseph Baigent; *Archæological Journal*, Vol. XLIX., 1892, p. 69. "Widows and Vowesses," by J. L. André, F.S.A.; *Antiquarian Communications, being papers presented at the meetings of the Cambridge Antiquarian Society*, Vol. I., 1859, No. XVII., p. 71. "The Vow of Widowhood of Margaret, Countess of Richmond and Derby (Foundress of Christ's and St. John's Colleges): with Notices of similar vows in the 14th, 15th, and 16th cen-turies," by C. H. Cooper, F.S.A.

[2] "Mentioned by Margaret, Countess of Richmond, mother of Henry "VII., in her 'Ordinance for the Reformation of apparell for great "Estates of Women in the tyme of Mourning.'—(Harleian MS. 6064). "The queen, and all ladies down to the degree of a baroness, are therein "licensed to wear the barbe above the chin. Baronesses, Lord's daughters "and knights' wives, are ordered to wear the barbe beneath it, and all "chamberers and other persons, 'below the throat goyle,' or gullet, that "is, the lowest part of the throat."—Planché *Cyclopædia of Costume, sub.* Barbe.

Beds., on dexter side; head on two cushions; feet on two bell-collared dogs.

1393/4. Elyne, wife of Sir Edward Cerne, Draycot Cerne, Wilts., on dexter side; holding her husband's right hand in hers; the kirtle sleeves ending at the wrists; the head resting on a cushion.

1399. Alianore de Bohun, Westminster Abbey, widow of Thomas of Woodstock, Duke of Gloucester,[1] youngest son of Edward III. A cote, or tunic, worn over the kirtle; head on two cushions; crimped edge to the inner veil.

The hair plaited at the sides, and bound with a fillet[2]:—

1384. Katherine (*née* Calthorpe), wife of Sir John Harsick, Southacre, Norfolk, on dexter side of husband, and holding his right hand in hers; kirtle, on which are their arms impaled,[3] and mantle; feet on dog.

1403. Joan and Alice, wives of John Hauley, Dartmouth, Devon; the husband, in the centre, holding in his right hand that of his first wife. Each wife wears a kirtle with sleeves buttoned to the shoulders, and a sideless cote-hardie with circular ornaments from neck to waist, and a veil added to the head-dress. At the feet of each are two dogs with bell-collars.

1407. Margaret, wife of Sir William Bagot, Baginton, Warwickshire (head restored by Waller); on dexter side; kirtle with girdle; sideless cote-hardie; vair-lined mantle; collar of SS.; two dogs on the skirt; head resting on two cushions.

---

[1] Who, also, was commemorated by a fine brass in the Abbey, now lost.

[2] Compare the sculptured effigy of Blanche de la Tour, 1372, daughter of Edward III., in Westminster Abbey.

[3] Geslingthorpe, assumed by Calthorpe (*see* Cotman):—Ermine a maunch gules impaling Harsick. *See* p. 161.

The lost effigy of Ioan, wife of Sir Miles de Stapelton, 1364, Ingham, Norfolk, showed her on the dexter side of her husband, holding his right hand in hers and wearing a cote-hardie with liripipes and buttons, and with pockets in front, over a kirtle. A veil hung behind the hair. At the feet was a dog.

The *zig-zag* head-dress, which is less frequently found than the *nebulé*, differs from the latter merely in the treatment of the lines. Examples of it are as follows:—

1. In the earlier form, framing the sides of the face, but not touching the shoulders.

c. 1370. Isabel Beaufo,[1] Waterpery, Oxon., mutilated. The kirtle sleeves end at the wrists. The cote-hardie has liripipes, and buttons to the waist. The crimped cap appears below the head-dress.

1372. Ismayne de Wynston, Necton, Norfolk. The kirtle skirt does not cover the feet, and is seen beneath that of the cote. Its sleeves end at the wrists. The cote-hardie has liripipes.[2]

2. In the later form, framing the face, but with veil and cushions of hair falling to the shoulders.

1376. Lady Elizabeth Cobham, daughter of Ralph, Lord Stafford, wife of Sir Reginald, 2nd Baron Cobham, of Sterborough, Lingfield, Surrey; in sideless cote-hardie, with button-like ornaments from neck to waist, and a broad flounce of fur bordering the skirt; mantle.

---

[1] At Wennington, Essex, is the matrix of an effigy (? Marjorie de Gildesburgh, *c.* 1380), which probably showed a similar costume.

[2] In Kite's *Monumental Brasses of Wiltshire*, is an illustration restored from a sketch by John Aubrey, of a lost brass, formerly at Draycot Cerne, Wilts., probably of Philippa de Cerne. Her costume is similar to that at Necton, except that the head-dress is *nebulé* instead of *zig-zag*.

1380.   Maud, wife of Sir Thomas Cobham, Cobham,
Kent; kirtle with buttons to waist, and
flounce of fur at the foot, over which is a
mantle. The feet rest on a dog of large
size, with bell-collar.

In *nebulé* head-dress, similar in form to the zig-zag
coiffure, last mentioned (2) :—

1356.   Margaret, wife of Richard Torrington, Great
Berkhampstead, Herts.; on dexter side of
husband and holding his right hand in hers;
cote-hardie with liripipes worn over kirtle;
two dogs with bell-collars at feet.

c. 1370. Joan (*née* Cobham), wife of Sir John de la Pole,
Crishall, Essex, holding her husband's right
hand in hers; over kirtle a cote with liripipes, and buttoned to the waist; feet on dog
with bell-collar.

1375.   Elizabeth (de Ferrers), wife of David de
Strabolgie, Earl of Athole, Ashford, Kent,
mutilated; wearing over kirtle a sideless cote-
hardie, with lozenge-shaped ornaments from
neck to waist; the skirt slit up at the sides.

1375.   Dame Margarete de Cobham, Cobham, Kent;
wearing a sideless cote-hardie similar to the
last; dog at her feet.

1378.   Matilda and Joan, wives of Sir John de Foxley,[1]
Bray, Berks. (on bracket, the stem of which
rests on a fox couchant), each wearing over
kirtle a cote-hardie, with long liripipes hanging from the elbows. Matilda's cote bears
the arms of Foxley (Gules two bars argent)
impaling Sable a lion rampant or (? Brocas);
that of Joan (*née* Martin) those of Foxley alone.

---

[1] He is in armour of the Camail period, with jupon bearing his arms.
For his will, see *Archæological Journal*, Vol. XV., 1858, p. 267. "The
will of Sir John de Foxle of Apuldrefield, Kent, dated November 5th,
1378." Communicated by the Rev. William H. Gunner, M.A.

SIR JOHN DE LA POLE AND WIFE JOAN, c. 1370,
CHRISHALL ESSEX.

DAME MARGARETE DE COBHAM, 1395,
COBHAM, KENT.

DAME MARGARETE DE COBHAM, 1375,
COBHAM, KENT.

c. 1380. ——, wife of Sir —— Dalyngrugge, Fletching, Sussex; wearing over kirtle, with buttons to the waist, a mantle; feet on dog.

c. 1380. Elizabeth, wife of Roger de Felbrig, Felbrigg, Norfolk; in kirtle and mantle.

c. 1380. The two wives of Reginald de Malyns, Chinnor, Oxon. The lady on the dexter side wears over a kirtle a long gown with close sleeves, and buttons from neck to feet, unbuttoned in the lower part. But the wife on the sinister side differs somewhat; her head-dress being square and with the zig-zag ornament, while the sleeves of the over-gown are not represented. This may be due to an engraver's error.

c. 1390. A Lady (? of the Roos family), Gedney, Lincs.;[1] over kirtle a sideless cote-hardie and mantle; at feet a dog with bell-collar.

1391. Cecilia, wife of Sir William de Kerdiston, Reepham, Norfolk; kirtle, tunic, and mantle.

In the later form of *nebulé* head-dress, in which the sides of the face are not enclosed:—

c. 1370. A Lady, probably the wife of Sir Henry Redford, Broughton, Lincs.; in kirtle and mantle, holding a heart in her hands.

1395. Dame Margarete de Cobham, Cobham, Kent; kirtle and mantle; head on embroidered cushion.

c. 1400. Wife of Civilian, Ore, Sussex; kirtle, over which tunic or cote, buttoned from neck to feet, with close sleeves and square-cut corsage.

1401. Isabel, wife of Sir Morys Russel, Dyrham, Gloucs., on dexter side of husband; in kirtle and mantle.

[1] Discovered 17th June, 1889.

1406.   Margaret, wife of Thomas de Beauchamp, Earl
        of Warwick (daughter of William, Lord
        Ferrers of Groby), St. Mary's, Warwick; in
        kirtle and mantle, beautifully diapered with
        arms: on kirtle:—Gules seven mascles 3, 3,
        and 1 (Ferrers); on mantle:—Gules a fess be-
        tween six crosses-crosslet gobony or, (Beau-
        champ).

Margaret, wife of Sir Henry Englissh, 1393, Wood
Ditton, Cambs., wears a kirtle and mantle, and her head,
now lost, was attired in this fashion.

The following wear the *reticulated* head-dress:—

1391.   Margaret, wife of Robert, Lord Willoughby
        D'Eresby, Spilsby, Lincs.; in kirtle, sideless
        cote-hardie with ornaments to waist, and
        mantle; jewelled fillet across forehead; head
        on two cushions; feet on two bell-collared
        dogs addorsed.

1393.   Katherine, wife of Sir Thomas Walsh, Wanlip,
        Leics., in similar costume.

1394.   Dionisia, wife of Sir Richard Attelese, Sheldwich,
        Kent; in kirtle and mantle.

1400.   Alicia, wife of Sir John Cassy, Deerhurst, Gloucs.;
        wearing over the kirtle a long gown reaching
        to the feet, with close sleeves, and buttoned
        high up round the neck; no girdle nor
        mantle. On the feet, which rest on a dog
        with bell-collar, called Terri, are embroidered
        shoes.

1400.   Elianor, wife of Sir John Mauleverere, Allerton
        Mauleverer, W. Yorks.; in a girded kirtle
        and flowing mantle.

1401.   Elizabeth ——, Goring, Oxon.; in kirtle girded
        and buttoned all down the front, and mantle;
        feet on dog with bell-collar.

The long close-sleeved gown worn by some ladies over
the kirtle (*e.g.*, 1400, Lady Cassy, mentioned above),
bears a close resemblance to the long tunic of the civilians.
Usually high in the neck, it is either buttoned up close,
or turned down forming a small collar. It is found both
with and without a girdle. Examples :—

c. 1400.   A Wool Merchant's Wife, Northleach, Gloucs.,
             on dexter side ; in mantle and veil head-dress,
             but without barbe ; a ring on the third finger
             of the right hand ; lap-dog on skirt.

   1401.   Marion, wife of William Grevel, Chipping
             Campden, Gloucs. ; in late form of *nebulé*
             head-dress. Buttons are seen from neck to
             feet on the gown.

c. 1405.   Wife of Herry Notingham, Holm-by-the-
             Sea, Norfolk ; in *nebulé* head-dress ; on dex-
             ter side ; wearing a girdle ; buttons from neck
             to waist.

   1410.   Alicia, wife of Sir John Wylcotes, Great Tew,
             Oxon, on dexter side ; no mitten sleeves to
             kirtle ; wearing a mantle and *nebulé* head-dress,
             with veil hanging in front of the shoulders ;
             a lap-dog on the skirt.

In the case of Margery, wife of Sir Thomas Burton,
Little Casterton, Rutland, *c.* 1410, the hair is confined in
reticulated cauls at the sides of the face, and is surmounted by a kind of coronet. Possibly this may form
a connecting link between the *reticulated* and *crespine*
modes.[1]

An early form of the *crespine* head-dress, soon to be
described, is seen on a few brasses taking the form
of ornamented network placed above the ears, and enclosing the hair on the top of the head, where a veil is
pinned which hangs behind. Examples :—

---

[1] Compare the sculptured effigy in Westminster Abbey, of Edward the
Third's Queen, Philippa of Hainault, *d.* 1369.

1391.   Elyenore Corp, Stoke Fleming, Devon, on short
        bracket on dexter side of her grandfather
        John Corp; wearing kirtle alone, buttoned to
        the waist, and on the arms from shoulders to
        mittens.

1392.   Margaret, wife of Thomas, Lord Berkeley,
        Wotton-under-Edge, Gloucs., on dexter side;
        in kirtle and mantle; head on two cushions;
        dog at feet.

1397.   Lora, wife of Sir John de St. Quintin, Brands-
        burton, Yorks.; wearing over kirtle a long,
        loose gown, high in the neck, and with wide
        sleeves, a step, possibly, toward the surplice-
        sleeve to be noticed below. From the head-
        dress hang strings of pearls looped up at the
        ears. She wears a necklace with pendant.
        Dog at feet.

1400.   Ele, wife of Richard Bowet, Wrentham, Suffolk;
        wearing over kirtle a wide-sleeved gown,
        similar to the last, but with buttons from
        neck to feet, and a girdle.

1401.   Margaret, wife of Sir Fulk Pennebrygg, Shottes-
        brooke, Berks.; wearing over kirtle a long
        gown with close sleeves and buttons from neck
        to feet. The head rests on two cushions. The
        gown is confined at the waist by a girdle, the
        end of which falls down in front.

At Great Berkhampstead, Herts., is the brass of a lady,
c. 1360, wearing over a kirtle a long, close-sleeved gown
low in the neck. On her head is an early crespine head-
dress, with a veil arranged so as to frame the sides of the
face. One of the latten effigies of the children of
Edward III., on his tomb in Westminster Abbey, shows
a similar head-dress.

The chief change in the fashions of the first part of the
fifteenth century was in the head-dress. The kirtle and
mantle (both occasionally heraldic, and the former with

mitten sleeves, buttoned underneath, until about the year
1420, when they ended at the wrists), and the sideless
cote-hardie preserve the forms with which we are already
familiar. These garments were worn by ladies of rank,
who sometimes, instead of the mantle, wore a long, loose
robe, probably fur-lined, with short, girded waist, surplice-
like sleeves reaching to the ground, and broad, falling
collar. This may be a form of the *houppelande*,[1] of which
we have noticed two probable specimens on p. 206. A
dress corresponding to the bag-sleeved tunic of the
civilian of the period (*see* p. 203), but with longer skirt,
seems to have become an ordinary female outer-garment,
worn more particularly, but by no means exclusively, by
the middle classes.

The head-dress worn is the CRESPINE, or *crestine*, composed by gathering up the hair into jewelled cauls or
nets, on each side of the face and over the forehead, with
a veil hung over the top, and falling behind. This head-
dress went through various changes, which may be traced
in the examples given below.

The following wear the earlier form of *crespine* head-
dress (the hair bunched at the sides above the ears, which
are visible; the veil falling gracefully in front), in conjunction with kirtle and mantle. Small lap-dogs, usually
with bell-collars, are found either on the skirt or at the
feet:—

1404. Maria, wife of a Le Moigne, Sawtry All
Saints', Hunts., on dexter side; head on two
cushions.

[1] Possibly introduced from Spain into France, and so into England,
where it was fashionable as early as the reign of Richard II. Claricia,
wife of Robert de Freville, Esq., Little Shelford, Cambs., c, 1405, wears
a modified form of houppelande, the sleeves of which bear some
resemblance to those of Lora, wife of Sir John de St. Quintin, 1397, at
Brandsburton, Yorks. They are fur-lined. She wears a girdle and holds
her husband's right hand in hers. Her hair is plaited at the sides and
bound by a fillet, the veil appearing on the top of the head only. At her
feet are two toy terriers with bell-collars.

1405.   Margery, wife of Sir Roger Drury, Rougham, Norfolk; head on two cushions; kirtle with button-like ornaments to the waist from neck.

c. 1405.   Iohanna(?), wife of Sir Thomas Massyngberde,[1] Gunby, Lincs.; collar of SS.

1407.   Margaret Brounflet, Wymington, Beds.; lozenge-shaped ornament on kirtle from neck to waist.

1409.   Margaret, first wife of Bartholomew, Lord Bourchier, Halstead, Essex, on dexter side.

1409.   Alianora, wife of Sir William de Burgate, Burgate, Suffolk.

1409.   Ada, wife of Robert de Haitfeld, Owston, Yorks., on dexter side, her right hand clasped in that of her husband; a collar possibly of SS.

1409/10.   Alicia, wife of William Snayth, Addington, Kent.

c. 1410.   A Lady, Hillmorton, Warwickshire; a scroll from the hands.

1411.   Juliana, wife of Thomas de Cruwe, Wixford, Warwickshire, on dexter side.

c. 1412.   Margaret, wife of Robert, Lord Ferrers of Chartley, Merevale, Warwickshire; head on two cushions.

1414.   Johanna, wife of John Urban, Southfleet, Kent, on bracket.

A similar attire for the head is occasionally found with the bag-sleeved gown worn over the kirtle, *e.g.* :—

c. 1400.   Wife of a Civilian, Tilbrook, Beds.; ungirded.

1420.   Johanna, wife of John Urban, Southfleet, Kent; with girdle. The second memorial of the same lady.

---

[1] For an account of this family, *see* "The Massingberds of Sutterton, Gunby and Ormsby," by the Rev. W. O. Massingberd.—*The Ancestor*, No. VII., October, 1903, p. 1.

The cauls of the *crespine* head-dress gradually became larger, assuming a square shape and covering the ears: the veil hung on the shoulders much as before:—

1416.   Margaret, wife of Sir Simon Felbrigge, K.G., Felbrigg, Norfolk; in kirtle and mantle.

1418.   Agnes, wife of Sir Thomas de Saint Quintin, Harpham, Yorks., on dexter side; in girded gown with voluminous bag-sleeves, with large cuffs, and broad collar.

The square cauls are more prominent, and are overlapped by the veil which hangs behind:—

c. 1410.   Agnes, wife of Sir John Routh, Routh, Yorks., on dexter side; in girded bag-sleeved gown like that at Harpham above, with inlaid collar and cuffs, and probably a collar of SS. like that of the knight, but owing to the destruction of the enamel only the pendant appears. The veil of the head-dress is gathered up on the top of the head, as in the case of Lady Phelip, 1415, at Kidderminster (see below).

1414.   Dame Philippa Byschoppesdon, Broughton, Oxon., in kirtle and mantle.

1423.   Alice, wife of Sir Ralph Shelton, Great Snoring, Norfolk; in kirtle and mantle; the former without mitten sleeves, and charged with her arms:—Argent a cross moline gules, Uvedale.

1424.   Elizabeth, wife of Thomas, Baron Camoys (previously of Henry Percy "Hotspur"), Trotton, Sussex; in kirtle with girdle; sideless cote with ornament from neck to waist; mantle and collar of SS. Her son (Sir Richard) stands on her skirt (*see* p. 206).

Similar head-dresses appear on the brasses of Millicent Meryng, *c.* 1415, East Markham, Notts, and of Margery Arundell, 1420, East Anthony, Cornwall, mentioned among those wearing the gown with surplice sleeves. A celebrated and enormous instance of this attire, surmounted by a large coronet, the veil wired on either side, is to be seen on the sculptured effigy of Beatrice, Countess of Thomas Fitz Alan, Earl of Arundel (*d.* 1439, Arundel, Sussex), who wears kirtle, sideless cote and mantle.

The next development shows the cauls curving outwards and upwards, and terminating above the head in a pair of horns. This form is called the HORNED, *lunar*, *mitre* or *heart* shaped head-dress, according to the shape which it assumes. This coiffure is said to have been made fashionable by Isabella of Bavaria, Queen of Charles VI. of France,[1] where it was known in this and its later developments as the HENNIN, *escoffion cornue* or *aux cornes*, and seems sorely to have wounded the susceptibilities of the clergy and of contemporary satirists, many of whom inveighed against it.[2]

In the following instances it is worn with kirtle and mantle, and except where otherwise stated, the cauls are richly worked[3] :—

1419.   Margaret, wife of William Cheyne, Hever, Kent ; plain cauls ; mitten sleeves to the kirtle ; head resting on a cushion supported by two angels clad in amices and girded albs.

c. 1420.   Elizabeth, wife of Peter Halle, Esq., Herne, Kent ; on dexter side, holding husband's right hand in hers ; the girdle of the kirtle showing beneath the sideless cote ; necklace with circular pendant.

---

[1] *See* Planché, *General History*, pp. 124-128, and *Dictionary*, *sub nom.* "Head-dress." In the former, facing p. 126, is a coloured plate, "Christine de Pisan presenting her Book to Isabel of Bavaria, Queen of Charles VI. of France. From the book itself now in the British Museum, Harl MS., 6431." The Queen and some of her ladies wear the wide-horned head-dress, exposing the ears, and the long surplice-sleeved, girded gown, fur-lined and with broad falling collar.

[2] The horned head-dress is caricatured on the carved woodwork of the stalls at Ludlow, Shropshire.

[3] A good instance was the brass of Cecilia, wife of Brian de Stapilton, 1438, lost from Ingham, Norfolk.

SIR WILLIAM ECHYNGHAM WITH WIFE JOAN
AND SON SIR THOMAS, 1444,
ETCHINGHAM, SUSSEX.

JOAN, WIFE OF SIR WILLIAM ECHYNGHAM, 1444,
ETCHINGHAM, SUSSEX.

1435. Isabella, wife of Richard Delamere, Esq., Hereford Cathedral; sideless cote; Collar of SS. (not worn by her husband).

1436. Anna, wife of John Martyn, Justice of the King's Bench, Graveney, Kent.

1437. Joan, wife of Robert Skerne, Kingston-upon-Thames, Surrey; on dexter side; wearing necklace with circular ornament.

1437. Joan, wife of Sir Thomas Brook, Thorncombe, Devon; Collar of SS.

c. 1440. The Lady Philippa, wife of John Halsham, West Grinstead, Sussex (d. 1395); plain cauls. She was daughter of David de Strabolgie, Earl of Athol. Her mother's brass at Ashford is cited on p. 250.

c. 1440. A Lady, (?) of Devenish family, Hellingly, Sussex (discovered 1869).

c. 1440. A Lady, Great Ormesby, Norfolk (three-quarter effigy), appropriated for Alice, wife of Sir Robert Clere, 1538. In her hands a heart circumscribed in black letter " Erth my body I give to the / on my soule Ihū have m'cy." Plain cauls.

1441. Joice, wife of Sir Hugh Halsham, West Grinstead, Sussex; on dexter side.

1444. Joan, wife of Sir William Echyngham, Etchingham, Sussex; between husband and son.

1444. Elizabeth, wife of William Fynderne, Esq., Childrey, Berks. The kirtle bears :—Argent a chevron between three crosses patté fitché sable, the chevron charged with an annulet of the field for difference—Fynderne. The mantle bears :—Quarterly 1 and 4 Argent a bend nebulé between two cotises gules (the arms of Sir John Kyngeston, her first husband); 2 and 3 Argent a whirlpool gules—Chelvey (her paternal coat). On the skirt of the kirtle is a lion couchant.

1445.   Joan, first wife of Sir Giles Daubeney, daughter
        of John, Lord Darcy, South Petherton,
        Somerset. The girdle of the kirtle appears
        from beneath the sideless cote. The girdle
        and head-dress cauls are ornamented with
        cinquefoils.[1]

1447.   Alice, first wife of William, Lord Zouch,
        Okeover, Staffs.; plain cauls (appropriated
        for Isabell, wife of Humphrey Oker, Esq.,
        1538).

The following are some instances of the surplice-sleeved
gown (described above, p. 255), possibly a form of the
houppelande, worn by ladies of position[2]:—

c. 1410.   Lucy, first wife of William, fourth Baron
           Willoughby d'Eresby, Spilsby, Lincs.; on
           dexter side. The gown has a standing collar.
           The crespine head-dress does not cover the
           ears, nor has it a veil; it is surmounted by a
           kind of coronet. The hands are held up, not

---

[1] Possibly in allusion to the Daubeney Arms (*see* p. 169 *note*). This effigy
lies on an altar tomb with that of Sir Giles. His second wife, Mary,
daughter of Simon Leek has a brass on the floor, 1442. Her costume is
similar to that of the first wife, except for the absence of girdle and
toy terrier. *See* illustration *Somerset and Dorset Notes and Queries*, Vol. I.,
1890, p. 241, accompanying description by Hugh Norris.

[2] A fine example of this costume on an incised slab is at East Horndon,
Essex, Alice, wife of Sir John Tyrell, Knight, 1422. The Flemish brass
at All Saints', Newcastle, 1429, representing Agnes, wife of Roger Thornton,
Esq., shows broad sleeves, but scarcely sufficiently so to be said to belong
to the houppelande. Mr. J. G. Waller in *Archæologia Aeliana*, Vol. XV.,
p. 78, writes: "It is not easy to describe the lady's dress, but it consists
"of a tunic flowing to the feet, confined at the waist by a girdle, having
"open hanging sleeves, plaited upon the chest, and buttoned about the
"neck. Over all is an ample mantle, and it seems to have an upright
"stiff collar, the wings of which are seen projecting on each side of her
"veil. [Compare Lucy, Lady Willoughby d'Eresby, c. 1410.] Her head-
"dress is curious. There is an inner covering, veil-like in form, over
"which is the veil proper, which seems to have projecting horns or pads
"from which it hangs down in the usual manner."

clasped. This brass belongs, as does the next instance, to a local school of engraving.

c. 1410. Wife of a Knight, South Kelsey, Lincs.; in early form of horned head-dress with large veil.[1]

1415. Ioan, wife of John Peryent, Esq., Digswell, Herts.; on dexter side; wearing Collar of SS. A swan is engraved on the left side of the collar; a hedgehog is represented on the skirt. The head-dress, to which no similar example is known on a brass, is triangular in form; the veil merely showing in folds on the top, after the manner of that worn by Lady Phelip (1415) Kidderminster, and by Lady Routh (*c.* 1410) Routh, Yorks.

1415. Matilda, wife of Sir John Phelip, Kidderminster, Worcs.; square cauls with veil folded on the top of the head; ? Collar of SS.

c. 1415. Mellicent, wife of Sir William Meryng, East Markham, Notts.; square cauls.

1418. Matilda, wife of John Fossebrok, Esq., Cranford St. Andrew, Northants; horned head-dress unornamented; wearing a Collar (?) of SS.

1420. Margery, wife of Thomas Arundell, Esq., East Anthony, Cornwall; square cauls.

1420. Isabella, wife of Iohn Doreward, Esq., Bocking, Essex; square cauls.

c. 1420. Katherine, wife of Thomas Quartermain, Thame, Oxon.

c. 1420. A Lady, Horley, Surrey (inscription added for Joan Fenner, 1516). The veil of the head-dress is tucked up behind, not falling on the shoulders. Collar (?) of SS.

c. 1420. A Lady, Brampton-by-Dingley, Northants; head gone. Possibly she may have worn a head-dress like that of Lady Phelip.

[1] Another Lincolnshire example was at Scrivelsby, *c.* 1430, Elizabeth, wife of Sir Thomas Dymoke. Illustrated in *Transactions of the Monumental Brass Society*, Vol. II., p. 108. *See* also Jeans' *List*, p. 58.

1430. Agnes, wife of Thomas Salmon, Esq., Arundel, Sussex; horned head-dress; a large Collar of SS. Principal woman to Beatrice, Countess of Arundel and Surrey (daughter of John I. of Portugal).

1433. Catherine, wife of William Rikhill, Northfleet, Kent; horned head.

c. 1440. Elizabeth, first wife of Sir Laurence Pabenham, Orford Darcy, Hunts.; in horned head-dress (lower half of effigy lost).

The following are among those who wear the girded *bag-sleeved* gown [1] with the horned head-dress, the cauls of which are usually unornamented :—

1414. Cristina, wife of John Cressy, Dodford, Northants; on dexter side.

1420. Cristina Bray, Felstead, Essex (half effigy).

1424. Elizabeth, wife of John Poyle, Esq., Hampton Poyle, Oxon.

1426. Sarra, wife of John Cosyngton, Esq., Aylesford, Kent.

1430. Alyanora, wife of John Pollard, St. Giles-in-the-Wood, near Torrington, Devon.

c. 1430. A Lady, in private possession, Wroxall Abbey, Warwickshire.

c. 1430. Johanna Kelly, Tintagil, Cornwall (three-quarter effigy).

c. 1430. Wife of a Man in Armour, Harlow, Essex.

1432. Isabelle, wife of Nicholas Carew, Beddington, Surrey.

1435. Elizabeth and Alice, wives of Thomas Wideville, Esq., Bromham, Beds.; ornamented cauls. The second wife has the rare addition

---

[1] Occasionally a girded gown with *tight* sleeves is found worn with the horned head-dress, *e.g.* :—

    1428. Maud, wife of John Norwiche, Yoxford, Suffolk.

    c. 1480. Anna, wife of Henry Jarmon, Geddington, Northants.

JOHN BACON AND WIFE JOAN, 1437,
ALL HALLOWS' BARKING, LONDON.

of the mantle worn with this gown. The brass was appropriated to commemorate Sir John Dyve, his mother and wife, 1535.

1435.   Margaret, wife of John Launcelyn, Cople, Beds.

1435.   Margery, wife of John Ailmer, Erith, Kent; on dexter side.

c. 1435.   Margaret, wife of Hugo Bostock, Wheathampstead, Herts.

1437.   Joan, wife of John Bacon, All Hallows' Barking, London.

c. 1440.   A Lady, Bigbury, Devon; a crescent in front of head-dress, the cauls of which are ornamented.

1441.   Elizabeth, wife of John Boteler, Mepshall, Beds.

1442.   Margaret and Joan, third and fourth wives of Reginald Spycer, Cirencester, Gloucs.

1447.   Joan, wife of Robert Hoton, Wilberfosse, Yorks.

Occasionally the veil head-dress is worn[1] with the bag-sleeved gown. Examples:—

1400.   Joan, wife of John Mulsho, Newton-by-Geddington, Northants; kneeling on sinister side of cross, in the head of which is the figure of St. Faith; no girdle.

1402.   ——, wife of Richard Martyn, Dartford, Kent.

c. 1410.   A Lady, St. Stephen's, Norwich; two bedesmen below the feet. Appropriated for Eel Buttry, "su'tyme pryores of Campese," 1546.

1416.   Elena, wife of Thomas Stokes, Ashby St. Legers, Northants.

1418.   Edith, wife of Thomas Polton, Wanborough, Wilts. (half effigy), parents of Archdeacon Polton, see p. 138.

c. 1425.   Margaret, wife of John Framlingham, Debenham, Suffolk (half effigy).

---

[1] Katherine Stoket, c. 1420, at Lingfield, Surrey, wears the veil head-dress with kirtle with mitten sleeves and mantle.

In a few cases the covrechef seems to have plain bands or frilling framing the forehead, *e.g.* :—

1415. Maria, wife of William West, Sudborough, Northants.

c. 1430. A Lady, with ecclesiastic and civilian, Melton, Suffolk,

c. 1440. Margaret, wife of Robert Pagge, Cirencester, Gloucs.

1442. Margaret, first wife of Reginald Spycer, Cirencester, Gloucs ; wearing gown with close sleeves.

A widow appears dressed in a kirtle, over which is a long close-sleeved gown, sometimes girded, and a mantle. The head-dress consists of the close-crimped cap and covrechef, and the plaited *barbe* or *chin-cloth*, which in some cases (*e.g.*, Tong, Salop ; Lowick, Northants, 1467 ; and Stretham, Cambs., 1497) covers the shoulders like a cape. Among palimpsest brasses may be mentioned the figure of a widow (*c.* 1440) in gown with long surplice sleeves on the reverse of the effigy of Bishop John White (*c.* 1548), Winchester College, and that of a widow (*c.* 1460) on the reverse of a priest in cope, of the same date, in the Temple Church, Bristol.

Instances of this costume, lacking the barbe, are rare. Of the three which we mention Lady Cobham was not a widow at the time of her death :—

1425. Beatrice, wife of William Chichele, Higham Ferrers, Northants ; mitten sleeves to kirtle.

1433. Katherine, wife of John Leventhorpe, Esq., Sawbridgeworth, Herts.

1433. Joan, Lady de Cobham, Cobham, Kent ; mitten sleeves to kirtle. She married (1) Sir Robert Hemenhale ; (2) Sir Reginald Braybrok ; (3) Sir Nicholas Hawberk ; (4) Sir John Oldcastle ; (5) Sir John Harpedon, who survived her, and whose brass is in Westminster Abbey (*see* p. 169).

JOAN, LADY DE COBHAM, 1433,
COBHAM, KENT.

SIR REGINALD BRAYBROK AND SONS
REGINALD AND ROBERT, 1405,
COBHAM, KENT.

SIR NICHOLAS HAWBERK AND SON JOHN, 1407,
COBHAM, KENT.

The following examples of widows throughout the
fifteenth century conform to the above costume except
where otherwise mentioned [1] :—

1405.   Margaret, wife of Thomas de Freville, Esq.,
          Little Shelford, Cambs.; on dexter side,
          holding husband's right hand in hers. [2]

1409.   Idonea, second wife of Bartholomew, Lord
          Bourchier, Halstead, Essex.

c. 1410. Pernel, wife of Nichol Rolond, Cople, Beds.;
          on dexter side.

1419.   Alice, wife of John Lyndewode, Linwood,
          Lincs.; mitten kirtle sleeves.

c. 1420. Johanna, wife of Sir Arnold Savage, Bobbing,
          Kent.

c. 1420. Widow of a Civilian (? Joan, wife of John
          Barloe) Pelham Furneaux, Herts.

c. 1420. Joan, wife of Thomas Quartermain, Esq.,
          Thame, Oxon.

1422.   Cecilia, wife of William Wylde, Esq., Dodford,
          Northants; dexter side (the mother of Cristina
          Cressy, mentioned above).

1425.   Margery, wife of Sir William Molyns, Stoke
          Poges, Bucks.

1427.   Margery Argentine (*bis viduata*) Elstow, Beds.

c. 1430. Alice, wife of Sir Edmund Bryan, Acton,
          Suffolk.

1430.   Joan, widow of Sir Wm. (?) Clopton, Quinton,
          Gloucs.; vowes " Que tibi sacrata clauditur
          hic vidua."

1432.   Cristiana, wife of Robert Baxter, St. Giles',
          Norwich; mitten kirtle sleeves.

1433.   Margery, wife of William Harwedon, Esq.,
          Harrowden Magna, Northants; on bracket.

---

[1] A good example, lost from Ingham, Norfolk, was that of Ela, wife
of Sir Miles Stapleton, *c.* 1425.

[2] " Postea sacre maiestatis amica professa."

1436. Matilda, wife of Thomas Chaucer, Esq., Ewelme, Oxon.; at feet a lion couchant queue fourchée (crest of Burghersh).

1436. Margaret, wife of Richard Purdaunce, St. Giles', Norwich.

1440. Matilda, wife of —— Clitherow, Ash-next-Sandwich, Kent; lower part gone.

1445. Alianora, wife of John Throckmorton, Esq., Fladbury, Worcs.

c. 1445. ——, wife or mother of Sir William Wadham, Ilminster, Somerset.

1446. Agnes, wife of Thomas Reynes, Esq., Marston Morteyne, Beds.

1454. Agnes, wife of Sir Thomas Molyngton, Dartford, Kent. Her first husband was William Hesilt, Baron of the Exchequer, whose brass was at Northfleet, Kent.

1459. Eufemia, wife of Sir John Langton, St. Peter's, Leeds, Yorks.

c. 1460. A Widow of the Forster family, Harpsden, Oxon.

c. 1460. A Widow, Great Thurlow, Suffolk.

c. 1460. Margaret, wife of Sir John Byron, Manchester Cathedral.

1462. Matilda, wife of Sir Thomas Grene, Greens Norton, Northants.

1462. Isabella, wife of George Langham, Esq., Little Chesterford, Essex.

1464. Anna, wife of Sir Henry Norbury, Stoke D'Abernon, Surrey; children on skirts.

1466. Margaret, wife of Richard Ask, Esq., Aughton, Yorks.

1467. Margaret, wife of Sir William Vernon, Tong, Salop; barbe covering shoulders; sideless cote; ermine-lined mantle; feet on elephant.

1467. Margaret, wife of Henry Grene, Esq., Lowick, Northants; head on embroidered cushion.

1474. Elizabeth, wife of William Fitzwilliam, Sprotborough, Yorkshire.

MATILDA CLITHEROW, *c.* 1440,
Ash-next-Sandwich, Kent.

ISABEL, WIDOW OF SIR THOMAS CHEDDAR, c. 1475,
CHEDDAR, SOMERSET.

1476.   Margaret, wife of Sir Richard Byngham, Justice
        of the King's Bench, Middleton, Warwick-
        shire; large rosary hanging from waist.

c. 1480.   A Widow, Grendon, Northants; between two
           men in armour.

c. 1480.   Anne, wife of Sir Thomas Tyrell, East Horndon,
           Essex.

1487.   Joan, wife of William Brokes, Esq., Pepper
        Harrow, Surrey; kneeling at desk; rosary
        hanging from right hand.

1489.   Agnes, wife of Thomas Mountford, Esq.,
        Hornby, North Yorks.

c. 1490.   A Widow, Luton, Beds.

1497.   Matilda, Lady Willoughby d'Eresby, Tatters-
        hall, Lincs. (? engraved c. 1460). 1st husband,
        Robert, sixth Lord Willoughby d'Eresby,
        K.G., d. 1454; (2) Sir Thomas Neville,
        d. 1460; (3) Sir Gervase Clifton, d. 1471.

1497.   Joan, wife of John Swan, Stretham, Cambs.

1501.   Catherine, wife of Sir William Pyrton, Little
        Bentley, Essex.

About the year 1460 we find a different form of gown
in use, worn over the kirtle, which latter garment appears
at the neck, and sometimes at the feet.   This gown, with
but small alteration, remained in fashion for three-quarters
of a century.   In the earlier examples it is distinguished
by being cut very low at the neck, where a fur border
appears.   The sleeves are tight-fitting, ending in cuffs
reaching to the knuckles, but usually turned back, showing
a fur lining, which, often probably, was extended to the
whole garment.   The gown appears to have had a fur-
edged opening, reaching to below the waist, and kept closed
by means of a girdle.

The horned head-dress becomes more acutely pointed,
the cauls usually being plain, and the veil either hanging
behind the shoulders or, more frequently, raised off the

shoulders in two folds. The following examples illustrate this change in the head-attire:—

(*a*) In kirtle and mantle, the veil falling behind the shoulders, except at Thame and Latton:—

1440. A Lady, Minehead, Somerset (ornamented cauls); sideless cote.

c. 1440. A Lady, Horton Kirby, Kent.

c. 1450. Elena, wife of Sir John Bernard, Isleham, Cambs. (ornamented cauls).

1458. Jamima, wife of Sir Thomas Shernborne, Shernbourne, Norfolk; sideless cote.

1460. Sybil, wife of Richard Quatremayns, Esq., Thame, Oxon.; sideless cote.

c. 1460. Margaret, wife of William Browne, All Saints, Stamford, Lincs.

c. 1460. Elizabeth, wife of ——— ———, Bigbury, Devon; ornamented cauls; sideless cote; head on cushion; a cross hanging by a chain round neck.

c. 1460. Elizabeth, wife of Roger Dencourt, Upminster, Essex; sideless cote; ornamented cauls.

1467. Catherine (?), wife of Sir Peter Arderne, Latton, Essex; ornamented cauls; sideless cote.

(*b*) In other costume, where not mentioned, the fur-cuffed gown:—

1454. Cecily, wife of Roger Felthorp, Blickling, Norfolk; bag-sleeved gown; five daughters similar.

1458. Agnes, wife of Sir Robert Staunton, Castle Donnington, Leics.; ornamented cauls; cross hanging by chain round neck; three daughters similarly dressed on her skirt.

1462/3. Agnes, wife of Oto Trevnwyth, St. Ives, Cornwall; bag-sleeved gown; kneeling before St. Michael.

Prey for the sowle of Jane Keriell
ye freendis alle that herbby passe
In endeles lyffe perpetuell
That god it grawnte mercy and grace
Roger Cletherowe hir fadir was
Thowgh erthe to erthe of kinde retorne
Prey that the sowle in blisse sowne

JANE KERIELL, c. 1460,
ASH-NEXT-SANDWICH, KENT.

1465. Margaret, wife of Nicholas Assheton, Callington, Cornwall.

1470. Dame Christina, wife of Matthew Phelip, Herne, Kent; ornamented cauls showing alternate suns and roses—the badge of the House of York; fur-lined mantle over fur-cuffed gown; large rosary; hands held outwards.

1470. Alicia, wife of Robert Watton, Addington, Kent.

c. 1470. Emma, wife of Sir Henry Grey, Ketteringham, Norfolk.

1471. Johanna, wife of Roger Kyngdon, Quethiock, Cornwall.

1472. Margaret, Clemens, and Isabella, wives of Robert Ingylton, Esq., Thornton, Bucks.

1478. Petronilla, wife of Richard Bertlot, Esq., Stopham, Sussex.

c. 1480. A Lady, Baldock, Herts., ? Margaret or Joan, wife of William Crane, 1483.

1485. Avice, wife of William Goldwell, Great Chart, Kent.

The horned head-dress seems to have become more of a mitre shape; witness the brass of Jane, wife of — Keriell (1460) Ash-next-Sandwich, Kent, wearing the fur-trimmed gown with broad sleeves, and a unique head-dress with a horseshoe ornament in front, but no veil.

Decorated cauls, surmounted by coronets, are seen in the two following instances:—

c. 1470 (eng.) Joice (d. 1446), daughter and heir of Sir Edward Charlton (Lord Powis) and Eleanor (daughter of Thomas Holland, Earl of Kent, and formerly wife of Roger Mortimer, Earl of March) and wife of Sir John Tiptoft, Baron Tiptoft and Powis, Enfield, Middlesex. Wearing kirtle, ermined sideless cote, heraldic mantle charged with Charlton impaling Holland, and a large necklace. The veil is curiously treated.[1]

1483.   Isabel Plantagenet, daughter of Richard, Earl of Cambridge, and wife of Henry Bourchier, Earl of Essex (whose mother, Anne, was daughter of Thomas of Woodstock, sixth son of Edward III.), Little Easton, Essex. Wearing kirtle, ermined sideless cote, mantle and Collar of Suns and Roses, with a pendant or *toret* of the lion couchant of March. The ears are concealed by two cauls, behind which is seen a veil. The head rests on a cushion upheld by two angels; the feet on an eagle, a Bourchier cognizance. A magnificent brass, retaining its colour.

The mitred head-dress without veil is sometimes found worn by groups of daughters below the effigies of their parents. Instances exist at South Weald, Essex, *c.* 1450, in a group of twelve children, six of them daughters, of whom the parents are lost; at Quy, Cambs., *c.* 1465, worn by four daughters of John Ansty, Esq.; at Abingdon Pigotts, Cambs., by eight daughters of a Civilian, *c.* 1470.

The transition from the *horned* form of head-dress to that known as the BUTTERFLY is interesting to note. As in the case of the chaperon or hood, noticed above, p. 209, the early kind of the butterfly head-dress seems to have been formed by wearing the horned head-dress horizontally instead of perpendicularly; in other words, the cauls confining the hair are removed from the sides to the back of the head, and the hair is strained off the forehead and

[1] For this manner of wearing the coronet, compare illustration, p. 273, Planché's *Cyclopædia of Costume*, 1876 (Vol. I., *Dictionary*): "Ladies, *circa* 1450, from a drawing in the portfolio of M. De Gagnières, Paris." The arms of Charlton, Lord Powys, are:—A lion rampant gules; those of Holland, Earl of Kent:—Three lions of England within a bordure argent.

JOICE, LADY TIPTOFT AND POWIS,
d. 1446, ENGRAVED *c.* 1470,
ENFIELD, MIDDLESEX.

confined behind. From the veil of the horned head-dress then was developed the winged appearance behind, which has given the name of *butterfly* head-dress to this style which prevailed in the reign of Edward IV. Examples of this transition, showing but slight traces of the veil and taking the form of square projections at the back of the head, are to be found on brasses chiefly amongst the effigies of daughters on the tombs of their parents, *e.g.* (all wearing the fur-lined gown, low in the neck) :—

1467. Three daughters on the brass of Sir William and Lady Vernon, Tong, Salop.

c. 1475. A Lady, Rainham, Essex.

1477. Three daughters on the brass of John Feld and son, Standon, Herts.

c. 1480. Five daughters on the brass of Civilian (lost) and wife, who wears the later horned-head with veil, Chelsfield, Kent.

Indeed, on the brass of Robert Ingleton and three wives (1472) Thornton, Bucks., one daughter is turned sideways showing the butterfly-head, whilst the others, *affronté*, wear the same head-dress as their mothers.

The later form of the " *hennin* " may be said to have taken two shapes, the *steeple* and the *butterfly*; the former consisting of " round caps gradually diminishing to the " height of half or three-quarters of an ell, with a loose " handkerchief atop, sometimes hanging as low as the " ground." [1] Of this no example occurs on a brass, unless the five daughters of Sir Thomas and Lady Urswyk (1470) Dagenham, Essex, are wearing a modified form without the veil.

Planché's description [2] defines the *butterfly* variety. Illuminations give a better idea of this head-dress than

---

[1] Planché's *Cyclopædia*, Vol. II., " General History," p. 127.

[2] " The bonnet or cap, the proper name for which was cornet, is seen " through the veil of gauze which is sustained, curiously folded, high " above its apex by wires so fine as to be invisible, instead of being loosely

brasses, though it must be admitted that the latter are sufficiently successful, considering the difficulty of the medium when employed to represent the diaphanous texture of the veil, which constituted one of the great elegancies of this attire.   It will be noticed that in order to give a due representation the engravers resorted to the expedient of drawing the head-dress *en profile*, thereby producing the effect from which this has been called the " *butterfly* " or " *wired* " head-dress.[1]

The following examples are noteworthy.[2]   Those at Ingrave, Harley, Melford and Crowan have a narrow veil in front, to be developed later into the frontlet of the pedimental head-dress.   Fine necklaces or carcanets occur. The girdles sometimes have pendent ends :—

1466.   Margaret, daughter of Sir Lewes John, Ingrave, Essex; in kirtle and mantle; dog with bell collar on skirt.

1470.   ——, wife of Sir Thomas Urswyk, Dagenham, Essex; mantle over fur-trimmed gown, the cuffs of which are not turned back; belled dog at feet; a fine necklace.

c. 1470.   ——, wife of —— Aubrey, Clehongre, Herefordshire.   The gown, instead of exposing a fur-lining, shows one of some diapered material.

c. 1470.   Agnes, wife of Sir William Yelverton, Rougham, Norfolk;   fur-trimmed gown and mantle; large necklace.

" thrown over it, or attached only to the top, and allowed to stream down " behind almost to the ground.   In the latter instance a smaller veil was " worn over the head beneath the cornet shading the face and neck." Planché, Vol. II., p. 127-8.   (*See* Woodcuts annexed, Front and side views of Hennins, from the *Traité de Tournois* of René d'Anjou, *c.* 1450, and also p. 275 of Vol. I. (*Dictionary*).)

[1] A similar attire called the *cauchoise* has survived in Normandy, in the Pays de Caux.   It is also worn by the Sisters of Charity of St. Vincent de Paul.

[2] It is easy to tell from a matrix, if the lost head-dress were of the *butterfly* variety.   *See*, for instance, the brass of Thomas Hampton, 1483, and Isabella, his wife, at Stoke Charity, Hants, of which the upper part of the lady's effigy is lost.

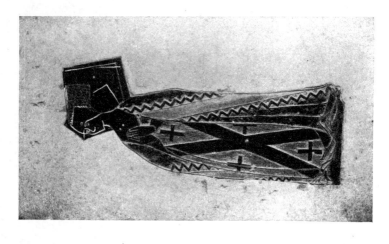

TWO LADIES OF THE CLOPTON FAMILY, *c.* 1480,

LONG MELFORD, SUFFOLK.

c. 1470.   Elizabeth, wife of William Culpeper, West Peckham, Kent.

1471.   Joan, wife of Thomas Colte, Roydon, Essex; kirtle, sideless cote, and mantle; collar of suns and roses.

1473.   Elizabeth, wife of Sir John Say, Knt., Broxbourne, Herts.; kirtle, sideless cote, and heraldic mantle, with her paternal coat (Cheyny); elaborate necklace.

c. 1475.   Wife of a Gentleman of the Lacon (?) family, Harley, Salop; fur-trimmed gown, the skirt tucked up under the left arm, thereby exposing the kirtle.

1479.   Anna, wife of Thomas Playters, Esq., Sotterley, Suffolk; fur cuffs not turned back; broad necklace.

1479.   Isodia, wife of Thomas Selby, East Malling, Kent; similar to the last.

1480.   Isabella and Iohanna, wives of John Cobleigh, Chittlehampton, Devon; fur-trimmed gown.

c. 1480.   Two Ladies of the Clopton family, Long Melford, Suffolk; heraldic kirtle and mantle.

c. 1480.   Two Ladies, Saffron Walden, Essex; fur-cuffs not turned back.

1484.   Margaret and Margaret, wives of Thomas Peyton, Esq., Isleham, Cambs.; the wife on the dexter side has fur-trimmed gown, embroidered throughout; that on the sinister wears one unornamented.

1485.   Isabella, wife of William Cheyne, Blickling, Norfolk; fine necklace; hands held out.

1485.   Anne, wife of Robert Herward, Aldborough, Norfolk; hands held out.

1485.   Elizabeth, wife of Sir —— Biconyll, Beckington, Somerset; fur-cuffs not turned back; necklace.

1487.   Issabella, wife of Sir Robert Strelley, Strelley, Notts.; cuffs not turned back; mantle.

1487.   Anne, wife of John Lambarde, Hinxworth,
            Herts. ; cuffs not turned back.

1490.   Margery, wife of Philip Bosard, Gent., Ditching-
            ham, Norfolk.

c. 1490.   Margaret, wife of Nicholas Gaynesford, Esq.
            Carshalton, Surrey (kneeling in mantle) ; the
            red colour is still preserved.

c. 1490.   Alicia, wife of Geoffry Seyntaubyn, Crowan,
            Cornwall ; cuffs not turned back.

A curious treatment of the butterfly head-dress with
decorated caul is found in Norfolk, showing some connection with its predecessor. A good example formerly
existed at Ingham, 1466, representing Katherine and
Elizabeth, wives of Sir Milo Stapleton.   Others are :—

1471.   Joan, wife of Sir John Curson, Belaugh, Nor-
            folk.

1483.   Margaret, wife of Rauf Wylloughby, Esq.,
            Raveningham, Norfolk ; cuffs not turned
            back ; collar of suns and roses ; dragon and
            dog at feet.   Her husband was " Squier for
            Kyng Rychard the thyrd's body."

A modified and much smaller form of butterfly head-
dress is seen in the following examples :—

c. 1480.   Marion, wife of Jenkyn Smyth,[1] St. Mary, Bury
            St. Edmunds ; kneeling.

c. 1480.   Wife of a Civilian, Chrishall, Essex ; kneeling.

c. 1480.   A Lady (unknown), St. Lawrence, Isle of
            Thanet.

1488.   Katherine, wife of John Hertcombe, Kingston-
            upon-Thames, Surrey ; kneeling.

1488.   Alice, third wife of Symon Brooke, Ufford,
            Suffolk.

c. 1490.   Two wives of — Paycock (?), Great Coggeshall,
            Essex.

---

[1] But *see* Farrer's *List of Suffolk Brasses*, 1903, in which this brass is
said more probably to belong to John Smyth, 1480, and wife Anne.

c. 1490. Agnes, wife of Edmund Grene, Hunstanton, Norfolk.

1496. Amia, wife of John Beriffe, Brightlingsea, Essex.

About 1490, soon after Henry VII. came to the throne, the butterfly head-dress gave way to that known as the PEDIMENTAL, *pyramidal*, *kennel*, or *diamond*-shaped head-dress. This development consisted in the amplification of the strip bordering the forehead, which we have noticed occurring on some of the butterfly head-dresses,[1] and in the depression or total abolition of the wing-like veil. The caul, or "*cornet*," into which the hair was strained, became a kind of bonnet or cap worn at the back of the head, and sometimes assuming a crown-like appearance (*e.g.*, 1488, Elizabeth, wife of Edmund Clere, Esq., Stokesby, Norfolk, and *c.* 1490, Elizabeth, wife of William Berdewell, Esq., West Herling, Norfolk). The band or "*frontlet*," framing the face and falling to the shoulders (to the shape of which the head-dress owes its designation), though sometimes represented as plain, is more often found engraved to represent embroidery and jewelled work. It was made of rich materials, velvet,[2] or sometimes fur, and in some cases may have had borders of pearls, *e.g.* :—

c. 1490. Elizabeth, heiress of the Barony of St. Amand, held by her husband William Beauchamp, Lord St. Amand, Bromham, Wilts.; kneeling in kirtle, ermine sideless cote, and mantle.

1499. Anne, wife of Thomas Hevenyngham, Esq., Ketteringham, Norfolk; kneeling in mantle charged with her husband's arms, worn over

---

[1] That at Crowan, Cornwall, *c.* 1490 (Alicia wife of Geoffry Seyntaubyn) shows evident signs of transition.

[2] "My Cosin Alice Storke shall have my best bonet and a frontlet of tawny velvet."—Codicil to will of Isabella, widow of Iohn FitzIames of Redlynch, Somerset, proved October 23rd, 1527. *Proceedings of Somerset Archæological and Natural History Soeiety*, Vol. XXIV. 1878, p. 35.

fur-cuffed gown charged with her own. (One of her five daughters kneeling behind her wears a similar head-dress.)

1520.   Mary and Grace, wives of William de Grey, Esq., Merton, Norfolk; kneeling.

Sometimes more strips or lappets are seen at the side of the head when represented in profile. A good instance is at Laycock, Wilts., 1501, Elizabeth, wife of Robert Baynard, Esq., wearing an heraldic mantle, Baynard quartering Ludlow. Instances of the retention of the veil are not uncommon, *e.g.*, *c.* 1500, Elizabeth, wife of Richard Wakeherst, Ardingley, Sussex, and, 1533, Joan, wife of Henry Hatche, Faversham, Kent. The Flemish brass at St. Mary Quay, Ipswich, 1525, shows Emma, wife of Thomas Pownder, wearing over a kirtle a fur-lined gown with loose sleeves, and pedimental head-dress with veil, the peaked form of which is explained by the netted cauls worn by the six daughters without veils.[1]

The gown worn with this head-dress is, as a rule, that with tight-fitting sleeves, fur-cuffs, and border, already noticed; but the aperture for the neck is not so large and is cut square. The kirtle sometimes appears at the neck, and also at the feet when, as at Ardingly, *c.* 1500 (just mentioned), the skirt of the gown is tucked up under the arm to give an air of greater convenience in walking. Although usually the mark of the opening in the gown extends to the waist, in some instances it appears to have been fastened from neck to feet (*e.g.*, Anne, wife of Thomas Asteley, Esq., 1512, Blickling, Norfolk). With this gown was worn a broad ornamental girdle,[2] fastened by various méthods, often by a buckle at the side, from which a long pendent end hangs, sometimes as low as the ground. At Hadley, Middlesex, 1500, Joan, wife of

---

[1] A rosary hangs from the centre of the girdle. Compare with the Evyngar Flemish brass, 1535, All Hallows' Barking, London.

[2] "to my daughter Lady FitzIames a girdle of gold harneysed with gold."—Will of Isabella FitzIames, *see* note 2, p. 275.

William Turnour, wears a girdle fastened at the back, and without pendent end.[1] Another form of girdle is fastened in front, and from the centre ornament, often consisting of three rosettes, hangs a chain supporting an ornament or a silver or gold pomander (*pomme d'ambre*), or perfume box for scents or disinfectants[2]; or a receptacle for *pommes chaufferettes*, the equivalent of the modern muff-warmer. Rosaries are found in the first half of the sixteenth century hanging from the girdle, and round the neck chains or necklaces with pendent crosses. Where shoes appear they are of the broad, rounded shape worn by civilians.

Some brasses show a veil instead of the pedimental head-dress, *e.g.* :—

1509. Jacquetta, lady of John, Lord Strange, Hillingdon, Middlesex, sister of Elizabeth Woodville, Queen of Edward IV.; in mantle.

c. 1520. A Lady, Dengie, Essex.

1526. Julyen Deryng, gentylwoman, Pluckley, Kent.

1535. Ellyn, wife of Andrew Evyngar, All Hallows' Barking, London; Flemish (rosary hanging from the centre of the girdle).

---

[1] A somewhat similar girdle of earlier date (after 1460) is worn by Elizabeth, wife of William Culpeper, West Peckham, Kent. She wears the butterfly head-dress.

[2] See *Archæological Journal*, Vol. XXXI., 1874, p. 337. "Notes on Pomanders," by R. H. Soden-Smith, M.A., F.S.A. A perfumed orange sometimes served a similar purpose; *see* the beautiful little picture by Sir John Gilbert, in the Art Gallery, Birmingham, illustrating the passage in Cavendish's *Life of Cardinal Wolsey*. "Of the manner of his going "to Westminster Hall." "He...came out of his Privy Chamber about "eight of the clock, ready apparelled and in red like a Cardinal; his "upper vesture was all of scarlet or else of fine crimson taffeta or crimson "satin engrained, his pillion of scarlet, with a black velvet tippet of sables "about his neck, holding in his hand an orange the meat or substance "thereof being taken out and filled again with a piece of sponge, with "vinegar and other confections against pestilent airs, the which he most "commonly held to his nose when he came to the presses, or when he "was pestered with many suitors." (*See* pp. 46, 47, Edition, London, 1901, by Grace H. M. Simpson).

Examples wearing the pedimental head-dress are very numerous, and a long list might be compiled. The following are some instances[1] :—

1492. Joyce, wife of Geoffrey Sherard, Stapleford, Leics. ; cuffs turned over hands.

1494. Margaret, wife of William Catesby, Esq., Ashby St. Legers, Northants; in heraldic mantle, wearing a cross.

c. 1495. (eng.) Margery, wife of Sir Hugh Calveley, Knt., Ightfield, Salop.

c. 1495. Myrabyll, wife of Edward Sulyard, High Laver, Essex.

1496. Ela, wife of Henry Spelman, Esq., Narburgh, Norfolk ; on dexter side ; large rosary.

1496. ——, wife of John Northwode, Milton-next-Sittingbourne, Kent.

1500. Elizabeth, wife of Richard Conquest, Esq., Houghton Conquest, Beds.

1500. Alice, wife of John Tame, Esq., Fairford, Gloucs.

1502. Elizabeth, wife of Robert Russell, Esq., Strensham, Worcs.

1505. Margaret, wife of John Burgoyn, Impington, Cambs. ; sideless cote ; heraldic mantle.

1506. Margaret, wife of Sir John Brooke, 5th Baron, Cobham, Kent ; in mantle.

1508. Anne, wife of John Mohun, Esq., Lanteglos juxta Fowey, Cornwall ; wearing a tau cross.

1510. Elizabeth, wife of Nicholas Culpeper, Esq., Ardingley, Sussex.

c. 1510. Wife of Man in Armour, ? of Compton family, in possession of the Surrey Archæological Society ; said to have come from Netley Abbey, Hants. ; mantle.

---

[1] The lost brass of Agnes, Duchess of Norfolk, 1524, formerly at Lambeth, was a fine example of heraldic mantle worn with pedimental head-dress surmounted by coronet.

MARGARET, WIFE OF SIR JOHN BROOKE,
LORD COBHAM, 1506, COBHAM, KENT.

REYNOLD PEKHAM, ESQ., AND WIFE
JOYCE, 1525,
Wrotham, Kent.

THOMAS PEKHAM, ESQ., AND
WIFE DOROTHY, 1512,
Wrotham, Kent.

1514. Ann, wife of Sir John Danvers, Dauntesay, Wilts.

1516. Katherine, wife of Sir William Huddesfeld, Shillingford, Devon; kneeling behind her husband, in heraldic mantle charged with Courtenay (daughter of Sir Philip Courtenay, of Powderham).

1517. Katherine, wife of Anthony Hansart, March, Cambs.; kneeling; heraldic mantle.

1518. Elizabeth, daughter of Sir William Knevet, Eastington, Gloucs.; in heraldic mantle.

1519. Jane, wife of Sir John Iwarby, Ewell, Surrey; in heraldic mantle.

1524. Margaret, wife of Henry Everard, Esq., Denstone, Suffolk; head on cushion; heraldic mantle.

1525. Joyce, wife of Reynold Pekham, Wrotham, Kent; in heraldic mantle.

1526. Elizabeth, wife of John Shelley, Esq., Clapham, Sussex; in heraldic mantle, Shelley impaling Michelgrove; round neck the *partlet* (*see* below).

1527. Ellen, wife of Sir Peter Legh, Winwick, Lancs.; ermined sideless cote girdled; heraldic mantle; wearing large Tau cross.

1528. Margaret, wife of William Bulkeley, Esq., Sefton, Lancs.; large Tau cross.

c. 1528. The four wives of Sir Richard FitzLewes, Ingrave, Essex,[1] wearing ermined sideless cotes like Lady Legh's, and large Tau crosses. The first (probably Alice Harlestone), the third (Elizabeth Sheldon), and the fourth (Jane Hornby), wear heraldic mantles. The mantle of the second is not heraldic.

---

[1] Ascribed by Haines to John FitzLewis and four wives, c. 1500, but *see* "FitzLewes of West Horndon, and the brasses at Ingrave," by Rev. H. L. Elliot, M.A., *Essex Archæological Society Transactions*, New Series, Vol. VI., 1898, p. 28.

c. 1535 (eng.) Lady Katherine Howard (*d.* 1452), Stoke-
by-Nayland, Suffolk; ermine-trimmed side-
less cote and heraldic mantle charged with
Howard arms.   Wife of Sir Thomas Howard,
K.G., created in 1483 Duke of Norfolk.
1540.   Margaret, wife of John Semys, St. John Baptist,
Gloucester.
1547.   Elizabeth, wife of Richard Covert, Esq., Slaugham, Sussex.

The next change is found about 1525, when the tight
sleeves of the gown are superseded by wide sleeves, richly
furred, ending near the elbows.   On the forearms full
sleeves of fine materials, embroidered or slashed, are
worn, probably attached to an undergarment, and confined
at the wrists, where frills are inserted, bearing some
resemblance to a bishop's lawn-sleeves.   At the neck is
worn the *partlet*, seen by the opening of the gown, and
usually of fine linen pleated and gathered in round the
neck.   The pedimental head-dress, though its older
variety is frequently found worn with the above dress,
now assumes the form with which we are familiar in
Holbein's portraits of the Queens and Court Ladies of
Henry VIII.[1]   The ends of the front lappets are turned
up, no longer falling on the shoulders as hitherto.   The
manner of fastening them is well shown on the stone
effigy of a lady of the Arden family at Aston, Warwickshire (engraved by Hollis).

---

[1] *See* Bartolozzi's engravings in "*Imitations of original Drawings by
Hans Holbein in the Collection of His Majesty, for the Portraits of illustrious
persons of the Court of Henry VIII., with Biographical Tracts.*   Published
by John Chamberlaine, Keeper of the King's Drawings and Medals, and
F.S.A., London, 1792, also *Portraits of Illustrious Personages of Great
Britain engraved from authentic Pictures in the Galleries of the Nobility and
the Public Collections of the Country, with biographical and historical memoirs
of their lives and actions,* by Edmund Lodge, Esq., F.S.A., London:
Printed for Harding and Lepard, 1835, 12 vols. (the last 5 vols. of later
period than that covered by this book).

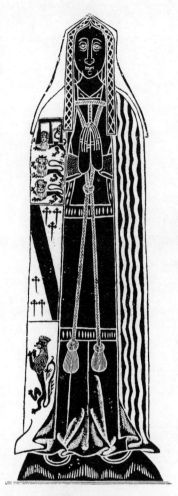

THE LADY KATHERINE HOWARD,
d. 1452, engraved *c.* 1535,
Stoke-by-Nayland, Suffolk.

The following examples illustrate this costume :—

1527.   Isabell, wife of Walter Curzon, Esq., Waterpery, Oxon. (palimpsest).

c. 1530.   ——, wife of —— Hutton, Dry Drayton, Cambs.

c. 1530.   A Lady, Messing, Essex; with rosary.

1533.   Anne, wife of Francis Yonge, Esq., Edgmond, Shropshire; gown tucked up in front; rosary and pomander.

1535.   Catherine, wife of Lord William Howard, St. Mary, Lambeth, Surrey; heraldic mantle.

1537.   Elizabeth, Countess of Oxford, Wivenhoe, Essex, second wife of John de Vere, Earl of Oxford, widow of William Viscount Beaumont, in ermined sideless cote and heraldic mantle (Scrope quartering Tiptoft); the head-dress surmounted by a coronet; chains round the neck; a pendent cross.

1538.   Mawde, wife of Sir Anthony Fitzherbert, Norbury, Derbyshire; in fur-cuffed gown, heraldic mantle and wimple. One of her daughters wears an heraldic mantle.

1539.   Ann, wife of Sir John Danvers, Dauntsey, Wilts.; kneeling, on quadrangular plate; gown open in front.

c. 1540.   Wife of a Man in Armour, Winestead, Yorkshire; over-gown short, wide sleeves lost; large rosary; at feet a greyhound.

1541.   Agnes, wife of Thomas Andrewes, Esq., Charwelton, Northants.

1542.   Elizabeth, wife of Thomas Fromond, Esq., Cheam, Surrey; kneeling.

1543.   Elizabeth, wife of Geo. Perepoynt, Esq., West Malling, Kent.

1545.   The Lady Elizabeth and Katherine, wives of Sir John Arundell, St. Columb Major, Cornwall; heads on cushions.

1545.   Elizabeth, wife of Sir John Spelman, Narburgh, Norfolk; heraldic mantle.

1546.   Katheryn, wife of Robert Barfott, Lambourne, Essex; in fur-cuffed gown.

1548.   Elizabeth, wife of Edward Chichester, Esq., Braunton, Devon; kneeling.

1551.   Jane, wife of Peter Coryton, St. Mellion, Cornwall; gown open in front.

1552.   Anne, wife of Richard Fermer, Esq., Easton Neston, Northants.

1553.   Alice, wife of Nicholas Saunder, Esq., Charlwood, Surrey; kneeling. Daughters similar with the exception that their head-dress is the *Paris head* (see below).

1560.   Ciselye, wife of Edward Goodman, Ruthyn, Denbighshire (daughters wearing the 'Paris head').

Brasses of ladies by provincial artists, especially in the eastern counties, exhibit various peculiarities of treatment, not observable in the average examples. The gowns are frequently pinned up at the sides or turned up in front. Some Norfolk examples have a narrow strip of fur down the centre of the gown from neck to feet. Rosaries are frequent, and large reticules are found. When the pomander is added, the effect of the three cannot fail to appear somewhat clumsy. A sash often takes the place of the girdle, and a small cape is sometimes worn on the shoulders. The following examples will suffice :—

c. 1500.   Wife of a Man in Armour (?Corbet), Assington, Suffolk.

1514.   Margaret, widow of — Pettwode, St. Clement's, Norwich.

1520.   Margaret, wife of Francis Mundeford, Esq., Feltwell, Norfolk.

c. 1520.   ?Jane and Thomasine, wives of John Goldingham, Belstead, Suffolk.

SIR JOHN BASSET AND WIVES HONOR AND ANN,
c. 1540,
ATHERINGTON, DEVON.

1521. Matilda, wife of William Cheswryght, Fordham, Cambs.

1524. Lettys, wife of John Terri, St. John Maddermarket, Norwich.

1525. Elizabeth, wife of John Marsham, St. John Maddermarket, Norwich.

1526. Mary, wife of Roger Appleton, Little Waldingfield, Suffolk.

1528. Elizabeth, wife of Edward Whyte, Esq., Shotesham St. Mary, Norfolk.

c. 1530. A Lady of the Drury family, Denstone, Suffolk.

c. 1530. Anne, wife of Thomas Underhill, Great Thurlow, Suffolk.

c. 1530. Wife of a Civilian, Lakenheath, Suffolk.

1532. Sabina, wife of Robert Goodwyn, Necton, Norfolk.

1551. Anne, wife of George Duke, Esq., Frenze, Norfolk.

1558. Elizabeth, wife of Robert Rugge, St. John Maddermarket, Norwich.

The following examples from Essex show similar peculiarities, and were probably executed by a school of engravers centred at Cambridge. A kind of *tam-o'-shanter* cap appears, and a short cape on the shoulders :—

c. 1530. Wife of a Civilian, Hempstead.

c. 1530. Two Wives of a Civilian, Elmdon.

c. 1530. Wife of a Civilian, Saffron Walden.

1532. Agnes, wife of William Holden, Great Chesterford.

1533. Joan, wife of John Paycock, Great Coggeshall.

1534. Agnes, wife of John Cracherood, Toppesfield.

In somewhat similar attire, but wearing an early form of 'Paris head,'[1] are :—

---

[1] Compare with a Holbein drawing of Queen Anne Boleyn among Chamberlaine's *Portraits*, 1792, engraved by F. Bartolozzi. (For title, *see* p. 280.)

1557.   Malyn, wife of Thomas Harte, Lydd, Kent.
1560.   Elizabeth, wife of Robert Stokys, Eton College, Bucks.

The reigns of Edward VI., Mary, and the first part of that of Elizabeth, produced but few changes in ladies' costume. Moreover, the accessibility of contemporary portraits, or of engravings of them, tends to decrease the value of evidence, important in earlier periods, which is afforded by brasses. The chief alteration is in the head-dress, the pedimental attire disappearing, and being super-seded by the PARIS HEAD, or FRENCH HOOD,[1] popularly known as the Mary Queen of Scots cap or bonnet.[2] This consisted of a close-fitting cap, stiffened by wires, and often depressed in the centre. A kind of lappet or jewelled fillet formed a border in front, concealing the ears; a veil fell behind. The hair appears on the forehead, parted down the centre. The gown[3] worn is opened in front below the waist, exposing the petticoat or under-gown, which soon became elaborately embroidered. The opening is partly closed by means of bows. On the arms appear the sleeves of the under-gown, usually striped. The over-gown has puffed sleeves ending just below the shoulders, or hanging down like the false sleeves of civilians (e.g., 1553, Alice, wife of Sir William Coke, Milton, Cambs.; 1554, Katherine, wife of Christopher Lytkot, Esq.,

---

[1] But see Planché, sub Head-dress and Hood.

[2] A possible connecting link between the two styles of coiffure may be seen at Herne, Kent, 1539, Elizabeth, wife of Sir John Fyneux.

[3] This gown is sometimes found worn with the old-fashioned pedi-mental head-dress, e.g., 1548, Jane and Elizabeth, wives of Sir William Molyneux, Sefton, Lancs. (low-necked gowns; no partlets), and c. 1556, Margaret, wife of William Disney, Esq., Norton Disney, Lincs. Again, the gown described as worn with the later form of pedimental head-dress is sometimes accompanied by the Paris head; e.g., 1557, Ursula, wife of Sir Edmund Knyghtley, Fawsley, Northants.

Swallowfield, Berks.[1]). The partlet fits the neck closely,
and is surmounted by frills, to develop into the well-
known Elizabethan ruff. In many cases, from the waist
an ornament hangs, or a book (*e.g.*, 1573, Isabel, wife of
George Arundell, Esq., Mawgan-in-Pyder, Cornwall), or
possibly a mirror (1577, Ann, wife of Peter Rede, Esq.,
St. Margaret's, Norwich). About 1570, the under-gown
or petticoat is embroidered, usually in diaper patterns,
but occasionally with arabesques, as later in Queen Elizabeth's reign. The over-gown is usually sleeveless, with
a stiff collar. The sleeves of the under-garment are
striped or slit down and refastened by bows.[2] At the
wrists are frills. The shoes, when seen, are of the small,
round-toed type. A few instances of ladies wearing
heraldic mantles are found, *e.g.* :—

1546/7.   Elizabeth, wife of Sir Ralph Verney, daughter
          of Edmund, Lord Bray, Aldbury, Herts. ; dexter
          Verney, sinister Bray. Her husband wears a
          tabard.
1552.   Brydgett and Elizabeth, wives of Sir Humfrey
          Style, Beckenham, Kent ; kneeling.
1555.   Lady Jane Guyldeford, Duchess of Northumber-
          land, St. Luke's, Chelsea ; kneeling ; widow of
          John Dudley, Duke of Northumberland.

An instance is known of a lady represented on a brass
wearing an heraldic tabard :—

1558.   Elizabeth, wife of Sir William Gorynge, Burton,

---

[1] Illustrated in Haines, p. ccxlv.

[2] " Some be of the new fashion, some of the olde, some of this fashion,
" and some of that, some with sleeves hanging down to their skirts, trayl-
" ing on the ground, and cast over their shoulders, like Cowtayles.
" Some have sleeves much shorter cut up the arme, and pointed with silk
" ribons, very gallantly tyed with true-looves knottes, for so they call
" them."—Phillip Stubbes' *Anatomie of Abuses*, 1583 (edited by Frederick
J. Furnivall for the New Shakspere Society, 1877-9).

Sussex; kneeling; arms, Gorynge and Covert impaled.[1]

Brasses showing the costume of this time are of frequent occurrence. The following selection may be enlarged at pleasure:—

1545. Anne, wife of Gregory Lovell, Esq., Harlington, Middlesex.

1554. Joan, wife of Edward Shelley, Esq., Warming-hurst, Sussex (showing traces of pedimental head-dress).

1558. Mary, wife of Vyncent Boys, Gent., Good-nestone, Kent.

1559. Jane, wife of John Corbet, Esq., Sprowston, Norfolk; kneeling.

c. 1560. Martha, wife of Richard Butler, Esq., North Mimms, Herts.

1561. Mary and Juliana, wives of Sir John Arundell, of Trerice, Stratton, Cornwall.

1561. Margaret, wife of John Eyer, Esq., Narburgh, Norfolk; kneeling.

1562/3. Alice, wife of William Heron, Esq., Croydon, Surrey.

1563. Margaret, wife of Sir William Dansell, Becken-ham, Kent.

1567. The three wives of Thomas Noke, Esq., Yeoman of the Crown, Shottesbrooke, Berks.

1570. Anne, wife of John Webbe, St. Thomas', Salis-bury.

1570. Anne and Anne, wives of Sir Clement Heigham, Knt., Barrow, Suffolk; kneeling.

1571. Jane, wife of Henry Bradbury, Gent., Little-bury, Essex.

[1] *See* illustration, Vol. II., *Transactions of the Monumental Brass Society*, p. 329, and in *Archæological Journal*, Vol. LVII., 1900, in paper, "Mis-cellanea Heraldica," by J. Lewis André, F.S.A., pp. 301-24, who men-tions a kneeling instance, once existing in glass at St. Michael Bassishaw, London, reproduced by Weever in his *Funerall Monuments*, p. 698, as Alice (*d.* 1579), wife of Adrian d'Ewes.

The lady Norton once she was whole Corpes is couched here
John Cobhams late and louuige wyfe of the Conntry of Kent Esqr
who in her lyfe dud well deserue to haue a future fame.
for that she was vnto the poore a good and gratins dame
Vnth Charitie and modestie and all the gyste of grace
Acquainted so she was to good to tarry in thys place.

She died y 9 daye of September 1580

ALICE, LADY NORTON, 1580,
NEWINGTON, KENT.

Here lieth y⁰ body of marie huddleston. Doughter of Sir william Barrentine knight & wief to Anthony Huddleston esquier. A gentlewoman of soche vertue wisedome & godlines. as wee have. great cause to thank god for her & to have sure hope y⁰ shee is exalted to A Crown of glorie. she died y⁰ xv⁰ daie of May. 1581

MARY, WIFE OF ANTHONY HUDDLESTON, ESQ., 1581,
GREAT HASELEY, OXON.

1571.   Avice, wife of Thomas Tyndall, Thornbury, Gloucs.

1572.   Jane, wife of Raphe Jenyns, Esq., Churchill, Somerset.

1573.   Margaret, wife of Sir William Harper, St. Paul's, Bedford.

1574.   The two wives of Richard Atkinson, St. Peter-in-the-East, Oxford.   The head-dress has a three-cornered appearance.[1]

1574.   Mary, wife of Richard Payton, Isleham, Cambs.

1577.   Margaret, wife of Humfrey Clarke, Kingsnorth, Kent.

1577.   Dorothe, wife of Sir Lawrence Taylare, Ewell, Surrey.

1578.   Thomasine, third wife of William Playters, Esq., Sotterley, Suffolk.

1578.   Agnes, wife of Sir Edward Baynton, Bromham, Wilts.; kneeling.

1580.   Lady Norton, wife of John Cobham, Esq., widow of Sir John Norton, of Northwood, Kent, Newington, Kent.

c. 1580.   Nele and Jane, wives of Richard Disney, Norton Disney, Lincs. (half effigies).

1581.   Wilmota, wife of George Cary, Tor Mohun, Devon.

1581.   Mary, wife of Anthony Huddleston, Esq., Great Haseley, Oxon.

1582.   Mistress Ann Sackville, widow, Willingale Doe, Essex.

1587.   Jane, wife of Michael Fraunces, Esq., St. Martin's, Canterbury.

During the latter part of the reign of Queen Elizabeth, about 1590, some changes were introduced which continued till the reign of Charles I.   The Paris head has the

---

[1] As has that of Joane, second wife of Valontyne Edvarod, Gent., St. Nicholas', Thanet, Kent, 1574.

lappet, hitherto falling behind, turned up over the top of
the head.   This flap may have been the *shadoe* or *bongrace*
used to protect the head from the sun.   This head-dress
is frequently surmounted by a hood (a precursor of the
calash (calèche) and *cardinal*) of ample proportions, falling
like a cape on the shoulders, and sometimes prolonged to
the ground behind.   The hair is brushed up and back in
the manner familiar to us in portraits of Queen Elizabeth,
and a jewel is often fastened in front.   The circular ruff
presents a stiffer and more formal appearance.   The
outer-gown is usually plain and open in front to show
a finely embroidered under-gown or petticoat.   The
bodice is conspicuous for its peaked or pointed stomacher,
often embroidered, and the skirt is distended by means of
a *farthingale* (vardingale, Fr. *vertugale*), the ancestor of the
eighteenth-century hoop-petticoat and of the nineteenth-
century crinoline.   Sometimes the flounces at the top of
the skirt assumed a wheel shape (whence the *wheel-
farthingale*).   Loose lappets or "wings" were worn,
flowing from the shoulders.   The large ruff,[1] the special
adornment of Queen Elizabeth, which was held up by a
framework of wires, called a *supportasse* or *underpropper*, is
seen on a few brasses, *e.g.* (wearing wheel-farthingales) :—

c. 1600.   Mary, wife of Edward Leventhorp, Esq., Saw-
                 bridgeworth, Herts.

   1601.   Anne, first wife of Gyfford Longe, Gent.,
                 Bradford-on-Avon, Wilts.

   1601.   Radcliff, wife of S[r] Thomas Wingfeld, Easton,
                 Suffolk.

   1614.   Margaret, wife of Sir George Chute, Marden,
                 Herefordshire, whose hair is dressed in a
                 wonderful manner, having nine peaks above

---

[1] Philip Stubbes is severe on "these cartwheeles of the divels charet
"of pride," and on the unfortunate medium of their stiffness, "a certaine
"kinde of liquide matter which they call Starch, wherin the devill hath
"willed them to wash and dive his ruffes wel, which, when they be dry,
"will then stand stiffe and inflexible about their necks."

the head, possibly upheld by a comb. The effigy of her little daughter Anne is similar.[1]

Hats frequently occur, worn by ladies, and are supposed to indicate Puritanical tendencies. They usually have broad brims and high, wreathed crowns, somewhat of the form associated with Welsh peasant women: that of Susan, wife of John Selwyn, Walton-on-Thames, Surrey, 1587, approximates to the shape of the modern felt hat (*vulgo* "bowler"). The shoes worn are small, with thick soles. The effigies are often represented standing on low, circular pedestals.

The following are good examples:—

1590.   Elizabeth and Anne, wives of William Death, Gent., Dartford, Kent; in hats.

1591.   Alice, wife of John Rashleigh, Fowey, Cornwall.

1594.   Julian, wife of John Clippesby, Esq., Clippesby, Norfolk.

1596.   Mary, wife of Robert Rust, Necton, Norfolk.

1598.   Dame Mary, widow of Henry Fortescue, Esq., Faulkbourne, Essex.

c. 1600.   Elizabeth, wife of Edward Leventhorp, Esq., Sawbridgeworth, Herts.

1602.   Mercy, wife of Christopher Septvans, *alias* Harflete, Ash-next-Sandwich, Kent.

1603.   Joan, wife of Thomas Buriton, Streatley, Berks.; hood.

1604.   Frances, wife of Richard Frankelin, Latton, Essex.

---

[1] Compare head-dress of "Catherine, Duchess du Bar, Sister of Henry IV., Died 1604." Planché, *General History*, p. 248. It is possible that this adornment may represent lace stiffened to form a half-hoop above the hair. *See* the portrait of Maria Schurmans, wife of Dirck Alewyn Dirckz, by Paul Moreelse (1571-1638, pupil of Mierevelt), engraved in the *Magazine of Art*, November, 1893, p. 23, in a description of the old masters in the collection of Mr. Joseph Ruston, of Monks Manor, Lincoln, by Claude Phillips.

1605. Aphra, wife of Henry Hawkins, Gent., Fordwich, Kent.

1606. Barbara, wife of Roger Eliot, rector, Sutton
Coldfield, Warwickshire; hood.

1606. Margaret, wife of Myles Dodding, Esq., Ulverstone, Lancs.

1607. Margaret, wife of Arthur Chewt, Ellough,
Suffolk; an extraordinary hood raised over
the head.

1607. Elizabeth, wife of Jacob Verzelini, Esq., Downe,
Kent; fine. The over-gown has an edging of
embroidery.

1609. Sybilla and Isabella, wives of Alban Butler, Esq.,
Aston-le-Walls, Northants; kneeling.

1610. Sessely, wife of Arthur Page, Gent., Bray,
Berks.; kneeling; hat.

1610. Barbara, wife of John Plumleigh, Dartmouth
S. Petrock, Devon; hood.

1610. Hester, wife of Francis Neve, Ham, Essex;
hat.

1610. Dorcas, wife of Thomas Musgrave, Esq., Cres-
sing, Essex; sitting; hood.

1611. Elizabeth, wife of John Carewe, Esq., Haccombe,
Devon.

1615. Elizabeth, wife of Henry Crispe, Wrotham,
Kent; hood.

1615. Frances, wife of James Hobart, Esq., Loddon,
Norfolk.

1616. Mary, wife of Richard Hatton, Long Ditton,
Surrey; large hood.

1618. Joan, wife of Sir Robert Brooke, Yoxford,
Suffolk (daughter of Sir Humphrey Weld).

1618. Dorothie, widow of Nicholas Wadham, Esq.,
Ilminster, Somerset.

c. 1620. Margaret, wife of Nicholas Poulett, Esq.,
Minety, Wilts.; kneeling.

1624. Margaret, wife of Richard Gadburye, Gent.,
Eyworth, Beds.

APHRA, WIFE OF HENRY HAWKINS, 1605,
FORDWICH, KENT.

THOMAS SMYTH, HIS WIFE MARY AND
DAUGHTER ELIZABETH, 1610,
NEW ROMNEY, KENT.

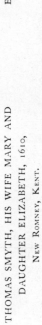

ELIZABETH, WIFE OF HENRY CRISPE, 1615,
WROTHAM, KENT.

HIC IACET SEPVLTA DOMINA IOHANNA
BROOKE VXOR ROBERTI BROOKE MILITIS
QVÆ FVIT PRIMOGENITA FILIARVM HVMFRIDI
WELD MILITIS VIXIT ANNOS TRIGINTA
OCTO ET OBIIT XXIJ DIE MAIJ AÑ᷄ DÑI.1618

JOAN, WIFE OF SIR ROBERT BROOKE, 1618,
YOXFORD, SOMERSET.

Soon after the accession of Charles I. changes appeared, gradually introducing that most elegant style, familiar to us in the portraits of Vandyke, by whose name it is frequently called. For, though ruff and farthingale are still found, the latter becomes exceptional, whilst the former is frequently superseded by *bands*,[1] either falling (*falls*) or upright, the broad, lace-trimmed collars or *fichus*, so conspicuous in contemporary portraits. Brasses, with but few exceptions, among which the Filmer monument at East Sutton holds a foremost place,[2] do not reproduce the dress of the times in a satisfactory manner, partly owing to the decay of the art, which became practically extinct before the Restoration, and partly to the increasing difficulty of portraying graceful gowns in so stubborn a medium. The plates of Hollar[3] form a complete guide to the female fashions of Charles' reign. The hair is allowed to escape in ringlets from beneath the Paris head or embroidered cap, over which the kerchief, hood (or calash) is still worn, sometimes of great length (*e.g.*, dated 1614, Mary and Roesia, wives of Richard Barttelot, Esq., Stopham, Sussex). Higher waists are worn, and the bodice or doublet often has a short vandyked skirt (*e.g.*, 1630, Mary, wife of John Kent, Esq., St. John's, Devizes, Wilts.). The sleeves are very full, striped, and often tied in at the elbows by a bow, which form was called a *virago* (*e.g.*, 1632, Dorothy, wife of Sir Francis Mannock, Bart., Stoke-by-Nayland, Suffolk, and the daughters of Sir Edward and Lady Filmer). Petticoats beautifully em-

---

[1] Whence the term " band-box."

[2] Reproduced by Waller; also in Vol. I., *Portfolio of Monumental Brass Society*, and in *Archæologia Cantiana*, Vol. XXV., 1902, p. lvii.

[3] " *Ornatus muliebris Anglicanus, or the severall habits of English Women* " *from the Nobilitie to the Contry woman as they are in these times* 1640. " Printed and sold by Robt. Sayer, Print & Map-Seller, No. 53, Fleet " Street. Wenceslaus Hollar, Bohemus, fecit. Londini, A°. 1640.
In 1643 was issued another set dealing with the costumes of Europe. " *Theatrū Mulierum sive Varietas atque Differentia Habituum Fœminei* " *Sexus diversorum Europæ Nationum hodierno tempore vulgo in usu.*"

broidered are at Ardingley, Sussex, and Stoke-by-Nayland, Suffolk, etc. The shoes have high heels, and sometimes rosettes (*e.g.*, 1638, Elizabeth, daughter of Thomas Rotton, Meriden, Warwickshire). A handkerchief is held by Jane Septvans, 1642, Ash-next-Sandwich, Kent. A feather fan hangs at the side of Sarah, wife of John Pen, Esq., 1641, Penn, Bucks. Rich necklaces are worn. Anne, wife of Eustace Bedingfeild, Esq., 1641, Darsham, Suffolk, wears a large, plain gown, similar to a modern masculine great-coat. She holds a handkerchief in her left hand.

Some other examples of brasses of this period are:—

1625.   The Lady Elizabeth, wife of Sir Arthur Gorges, Chelsea, Middlesex; kneeling.

1626.   Jane, wife of John Cradock, Gent., Ightham, Kent; high-crowned hat.

1633.   Ann, wife of John Arundel, Esq., S. Columb Major, Cornwall.

1633.   Mrs. Ann Kenwellmersh, Henfield, Sussex.

1633.   Frances, wife of Sir Thomas Hord, Bampton, Oxon.

1633.   Elizabeth, wife of Sir Edward Culpeper, Ardingley, Sussex.

1634.   Elizabeth, eldest daughter of Sir William and Jane Culpeper (aged seven), Ardingley, Sussex.

1635.   Elizabeth, wife of John Blighe, Finchampstead, Berks.

c. 1635 (*eng.*)   The Lady Ann, wife of Sir John Arundel, Knt., S. Columb Major, Cornwall.

1636.   Vahan and Elizabeth, wives of Richard Bugges, Esq., Harlow, Essex.

1636.   Ann, wife of Henry Gibbes, St. James', Bristol; kneeling; hat.

1638.   Elizabeth, wife of Sir Edward Filmer, Knt., East Sutton, Kent; in large ruff; her nine daughters wearing falling collars.

1640. Sarah and Eleanor, wives of George Coles, St. Sepulchre's, Northampton; in hats.

1642. Jane, wife of Walter Septvans, *alias* Harflete, Esq., Ash-next-Sandwich, Kent.

1647. Grace, wife of John Morewood, Bradfield, W. Yorks.; high-crowned hat.

1650. Elizabeth, wife of Ralph Assheton, Esq., Middleton, Lancs.

1655. Elizabeth, wife of Adam Beaumont, Esq., Kirkheaton, W. Yorks.; holding infant.

1656. Ann, wife of Thomas Carew, Esq., Haccombe, Devon; kneeling.

Two late examples of brasses, both in Kent, must be noticed :—

1. Three ladies of the Toke family, *c.* 1680, Great Chart, kneeling on cushions and holding books and flowers, show the low-necked, short-sleeved dress of the ladies of Charles II.'s reign, so well pictured by Lely and Kneller, of which Planché writes: "a studied negligence, an elegant déshabille, is the prevailing character."[1] The hair falls in curls on the neck.

2. Philadelphia, wife of Benjamin Greenwood, Esq., 1747, St. Mary Cray, gives a very poor idea of the costume of the eighteenth century :—a low-necked, tight-sleeved bodice, with neck-band above, open skirt with petticoat beneath, completed by an immense hood or veil (possibly a kind of *cardinal*), framing the head and figure.

The costume of widows found throughout the fifteenth, is not so frequently met with in the sixteenth century. Instances of widows wearing the ordinary dress of their

[1] *History of British Costume*, 3rd edition, 1874, p. 332.

period are not uncommon.[1] The following show the traditional costume already described (*see* p. 264) :—

1512. Elizabeth, widow of Henry Porte, Etwall, Derbyshire.

1519. Dame Joan, widow of John Braham, Esq., Frenze, Norfolk (*see* p. 98).

1529. Joan, wife of John Cooke, St. Mary de Crypt, Gloucester.

1536. Dame Alice Beryff, Brightlingsea, Essex; on bracket with daughter Margaret.

1540. Dame Susan Kyngeston, "vowess," Shalston, Bucks., widow of John Kyngéston, of Childrey, Berks. (*see* p. 98).

We have mentioned (p. 245) a very simple method of wearing the hair long and flowing, either completely unadorned, or encircled by a plain or jewelled fillet or by a chaplet of flowers. This is usually found in the case of young unmarried ladies, the wearing of a garland being supposed to be indicative of death in virginity.[2] Examples are uncommon. The following should be noted :—

[1] *e.g.*, 1521. Jane, second wife of John Blen'haysett, Esq., Frenze, Norfolk.

1582. Mistress Ann Sackville, widow, Willingale Doe, Essex.

1598. Dame Mary, widow of Henry Fortescue, Esq., Faulkbourne, Essex (quoted, p. 289).

Sometimes a veil alone would seem to denote the widowed state, as in more modern times :—

1587. Margery, wife of Richard Belassis, Houghton-le-Spring, Durham, kneeling.

1614. Julian, widow of — Osborne, Clyst St. George, Devon, kneeling and wearing a high-crowned hat.

[2] Maiden Garlands are found hung up in some churches, as memorials of the deceased; for example, at Minsterley, Shropshire, an illustration of which will be found, p. 237, of *Nooks and Corners of Shropshire*, by H. Thornhill Timmins, F.R.G.S. London : Elliot Stock, 1899. This practice seems to have been popular in Derbyshire, as at Ashover (see *Collectanea Topographica et Genealogica*, Vol. II., 1835, p. 99, in article entitled, "Notices of Dethick and Ashover, co. Derby, and the families

HERE LYETH BVRIED THE BODY OF MARY BROOKE,
ALIAS COBBVM WIDDO VNTO EDWARD BROOKE,
ALIAS COBBVM ESQVIER, WHOE DEPARTED THIS
LIFE THE XXIJTH DAYE OF IVLY A^NO DÑI. 1600,

MARY, WIDOW OF EDWARD BROOKE, ESQ., 1600,
NEWINGTON, KENT.

c. 1360.   Margaret Brocas, Sherborne St. John, Hants; wearing garland or jewelled fillet.

c. 1360.   Johane Plessi, Quainton, Bucks.

c. 1450.   A Maiden Lady, Lingfield, Surrey; with fillet.

1455.   Isabel, daughter of Robert Manfeld, Taplow, Bucks.

1458.   Cecilie, sister to Geoffrey Boleyn, Esq., Blickling, Norfolk (aged 50).

c. 1470.   A Maiden Lady, Bletchingley, Surrey.

1479.   Anna, daughter of William Boleyn, Esq., Blickling, Norfolk (aged three). Her hair appears to be short.

1479.   Elizabeth, daughter of Thomas Echyngham, and Agnes, daughter of Robert Oxenbrigg, Etchingham, Sussex. The former has a narrow fillet; the latter wears the hair plaited on the top of the head.

c. 1480.   A Lady, Felbrigg, Norfolk.[1]

1493.   Ursula, only daughter of Luke Gaspar, Low Leyton, Essex.

of Dethick and Babington"). Additional information may be found in the *Gentleman's Magazine*, May, 1803, p. 403 (Swanscombe, Kent); *Antiquarian Repertory*, Vol. IV., 1809, pp. 663-4 ; *Brand's Popular Antiquities of Great Britain*, Vol. II., 1870, p. 220. *See* also the *Journal of the British Archæological Association*, Vol. XXXI., 1875, p. 190, "On Funeral Garlands," by H. S. Cuming, F.S.A. Scot., and N.S. Vol. VI., 1900, p. 54, "Derbyshire Funeral Garlands," by T. N. Brushfield, Esq., M.D., F.S.A. ; *The Reliquary*, Vol. I., 1860-1, pp. 5-11, "On Funeral Garlands," by Llewellynn Jewitt, F.S.A., and Vol. XXI., 1880-1, an additional note on "Virgin Crants" or Garlands, by the same, p. 145 ; Vol. XXVI., 1885-6, p. 239, "Funeral Garlands at Astley Abbots, Shropshire" ; *Walford's Antiquary*, Vol. XII., July to December, 1887, p. 16, "Funeral Garlands," by J. Potter Briscoe, F.R.H.S. ; *The Antiquary; a Fortnightly Medium of Intercommunication for Archæologists, etc.*, Vol. III., p. 178, 207, by J. Perry ; *Wiltshire Notes and Queries*, Vol. IV., 1904, p. 519, "Funeral Garlands, an instance at Stockton, Wilts." *Transactions of the Shropshire Archæological and Natural History Society*, 2nd series, Vol. VII., 1895, p. 147, mentions maiden garlands formerly at Shrawardine.

[1] Compare two daughters on brass of Tomesina, wife of William Tendryng, Esq., 1485, Yoxford, Suffolk.

1508. Edith and Elizabeth, daughters of John Wylde, Esq., Barnes, Surrey; "dyed virgyns," with fillets.

1522. Elisabeth, daughter of George Fitz-William, Esq., Mablethorpe, Lincs.

1524. Constance, "meyden doughter," of John Berners, Esq., Writtle, Essex; wearing pedimental frontlet.

1536. Margaret, daughter of Dame Alice Beryff, Brightlingsea, Essex; on bracket with her mother.

1545. Amphillis, daughter of Sir Edmund Peckham, Denham, Bucks.; with pedimental frontlet.

1547. Wenefride Newport, Greystoke, Cumberland; in 'Paris head.'

1626. Grace Latham, "died a mayde," Upminster, Essex (aged 22); hair brushed back.

At Maids' Moreton, Bucks., in 1890, a brass was placed in the matrix of the lost original commemorating two maids, daughters of Thomas Pever, died c. 1480, representing them in kirtle and mantle with long hair and wreaths of roses.

Occasionally married ladies are represented wearing their hair long. The four examples following have the fillet :—

c. 1450. Isabel, wife of Sir Gervase Clifton, widow of William Scott, Esq., Brabourne, Kent.

1460. Douce, wife of Sir Robert del Bothe, Wilmslow, Cheshire.

1479. Joan, wife of Sir Robert Ratcliffe, widow of Humphrey Bourchier (Lord Cromwell), Tattershall, Lincs.

c. 1480. Joan, wife of Nicholas Kniveton, Esq., Mugginton, Derbyshire.

The palimpsest fragments of the brass of Elizabeth St. John, second wife of William, Lord Zouch, 1447, Okeover,

ELIZABETH ECHYNGHAM AND AGNES OXENBRIGG, 1480,
ETCHINGHAM, SUSSEX.

Staffs., show her in long hair, probably filleted, on the reverse of the Oker children.

Some peculiarities in head-dresses of simple form of the fifteenth century should be mentioned. They appear on effigies of daughters, as follows:—

The hair done in plaits at the sides above the ears, and bound by a fillet:—

1416. The twelve daughters, kneeling, on brass of Thomas and Elena Stokes, Ashby St. Legers, Northants.

1420. A daughter of Joan Waltham, Waltham, Lincs. (half effigy).

A kind of flat cap surmounting the hair, which is gathered up at the sides of the face:—

1414. Philippa Carreu, with her six sisters, Beddington, Surrey.

1429. Seven daughters of Roger and Agnes Thornton, All Saints, Newcastle-on-Tyne.

A fillet having a rolled appearance,[1] slightly raised at the sides:—

1433. Four daughters on the brass of Joan, Lady de Cobham, Cobham, Kent.

c. 1440. The daughters of Robert and Margaret Pagge, Cirencester, Gloucs.

c. 1440. Anna, Bridgett and Susanna, daughters of John and Elizabeth Arderne, Leigh, Surrey.

c. 1440-50. Susanna, daughter of the same, Leigh, Surrey.

At Long Melford, Suffolk, a lady of the Clopton family, c. 1420, wears a broad band or cap, ornamented

---

[1] A beautiful example of this head-dress, showing it in the form of a broad jewelled roll or fillet surrounding the head but exposing the hair in the centre, is given in Hefner-Alteneck's *Trachten des christlichen Mittelalters*, Plate 65, Vol. II.

with six estoiles of five points. Her bag-sleeved gown
has a broad, falling collar.

A cap-like head-gear, from which the hair escapes
behind, is seen worn by :—

c. 1480. Three daughters on the brass of John and Joan
          Jay, St. Mary Redcliffe, Bristol.
1483. Two daughters on the brass of Thomas and
          Isabella Hampton, Stoke Charity, Hants.

A Note on the Effigies of Children.

Effigies of children on the brasses of their parents, rare
in the fourteenth, become frequent in the fifteenth, and
are common in the sixteenth and seventeenth centuries.
The term " children " must not be taken to indicate youth,
but rather descent; for the persons represented as children on the brasses of their parents are often shown as
middle-aged. As a rule, the costume is a replica or
modification of that worn by the parents, and has been
already described. Sons are more usually in the civilian
than in the military habit of the period, but instances in
armour are occasionally found, and a few cases are known
of sons in holy orders being represented in vestments or in
clerical habit (see pp. 94, 95, 104, 106). The head-dress of
the daughter is, as a rule, simpler than that of her mother,[1]
long hair being frequently found (e.g., four daughters of
Roger Kyngdon, 1471, Quethiock, Cornwall). In brasses
of the sixteenth century the daughters sometimes wear
the Paris head, whilst their mothers show the older pedimental coiffure (e.g., 1542, Elizabeth, wife of Thomas
Fromond, Esq., and daughters, Cheam, Surrey, or the
daughters of Edward and Ciselye Goodman, 1560, Ruthyn,
Denbighshire). The early part of the fifteenth century

---

[1] For instance, the pedimental head-dress is shown with frontlet, but
allowing the hair to escape behind, e.g., the daughters of Edward Sulyard,
Esq., c. 1495, High Laver, Essex.

does not afford many examples of these effigies. A few exist, *e.g.* :—

1405. Reginald and Robert, sons of Sir Reginald Braybrook, Cobham, Kent; on small pedestals.

1407. John, son of Sir Nicholas Hawberk, Cobham, Kent; similar to the last.

1416. The Children of Thomas Stokes, Esq., Ashby St. Legers, Northants.

1419. The Children of John Lyndewode, Linwood, Lincs.; in small canopies beneath the larger effigies.

1429. The Children of Roger Thornton, Esq., All Saints, Newcastle-on-Tyne; similarly placed.

As a rule, the children are placed either standing or kneeling beneath the principal effigies; but when a rectangular plate is employed, they are usually found grouped, the sons behind their father, and the daughters behind their mother. Brasses commemorating young children do not become common till a late period. The following are some examples, in which seven of the boys wear the long skirts of childhood, giving to their costume a feminine appearance :—

1585. Peter, son of Nicholas Best, Merstham Surrey; with towel-like handkerchief tied to girdle.

1601. John Shorland, Woodbridge, Suffolk (aged seven).

1623. John, son of Francis Drake, Esq., Amersham, Bucks. (aged four).

1631. The Hon. Edward Saintmaur, fourth son of William, Earl of Hertford, Collingbourne Ducis, Wilts. (in his first year).

1633. William, eldest son of William Glynne, Clynnog, Carnarvonshire (aged two); a similar handkerchief to that of Peter Best.

1641. George Evelyn, Esq., son of Sir John Evelyn, West Deane, Wilts. (aged six).

1642. Arthur, only son of Philip, Lord Wharton,

Wooburn, Bucks. (aged nine months); recumbent.

1599.   William, son of George Brome, Holton, Oxon
(aged ten); in trunk-hose, doublet and short
cloak.
1606.   Ralph, son of William Wiclif, Wycliffe, Yorks.
(aged fourteen); kneeling in similar costume,
but without cloak.

1628.   Dorothy, daughter of John Turner, Gent., Kirkleatham, Yorks. (aged four); large standing
ruff or collar.
1630.   Ann, daughter of Barnard Hyde, Esq., Little
Ilford, Essex (aged eighteen).
1683.   Anne, daughter of Henry and Anne Dunch, Little
Wittenham, Berks. (aged ten months).

ANNE, DAUGHTER OF HENRY DUNCH, 1683,
LITTLE WITTENHAM. BERKS.

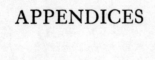

APPENDICES

A.

From *The Antiquities of Warwickshire*, by Sir William Dugdale, 2nd edition, revised by William Thomas, D.D. London, 1730, Vol. I., pp. 445-46.[1]

"On the southside, and adjoining to the Quire of this Church, stands that stately and beautifull Chapell dedicated to the honour of the B. Virgin, the fabrick whereof was begun by the Executors of Richard Beauchamp Earl of Warwick (according to the appointment of his Will) in 21. H. 6. and perfected in 3. E. 4. together with that magnificent Tombe for the said Earl, inferior to none in England, except that of K. H. 7. in Westminster Abby; the charge of all which came to no less than 2481li. 04s. 07d. ob. as by the particular accompts appeareth : but to how vast a sum such a piece of worke would have amounted to in these days, may be easily guest by that great disproportion in the prizes of things now, from what they were then, the value of an Oxe being about that time xiiis. ivd. and of a quarter of bread corne iiis. ivd.

"That the beauty of this goodly Chapell and Monument, through the iniquity of later times, is now much impaired, all that have seen it may easily discern, and thereby guess at the glory wherein it once stood ; to such therefore would there be no great need to say more thereof ; but for the satisfaction of others, I have here thought fit to insert a brief of the Covenants betwixt the said Executors, viz. Thomas Huggeford, Nich. Rodye, and Will. Berkswell, and the severall Artists that were employed in the most exquisite parts of its fabrick and ornaments, as also of the costly Tombe before specified, bearing date xiii. Junii 32. H. 6.

"John Essex Marbler, Will. Austen Founder, and Thomas Stevyns Copper Smyth, do covenant with the said Executors, that they shall make, forge, and worke in most finest wise and of the finest Latten, one large plate to be dressed and to lye on the overmost stone of the Tombe under the Image that shall lye on the same Tombe ; and two narrow plates to go round about the stone. Also they shall make in like wise, and like Latten, an Hearse to be dressed and set upon the said stone, over the Image, to beare a covering to be ordeyned ; the large plate, to be made of the finest and thickest Cullen plate, shall be in length viii. foot, and in bredth iii. foot and one inch. Either of the said long plates for writing shall be in bredth to fill justly the casements provided therefore ; the Hearse to be made in the comliest wise, justly in length, bredth, thickness, and height thereof, and of every part thereof, and in

1 See also *Description of the Beauchamp Chapel adjoining to the Church of St. Mary at Warwick, and the Monuments of the Earls of Warwick in the said Church and elsewhere,* by Richard Gough, Esq. New edition. London, Nichols, 1809, p. 9.

workmanship in all places and pieces such, and after an Hearse of timber which the Executors shall make for a pattern : and in ten panells of this Hearse of Letters the said workmen shall set, in the most finest and fairest wise, ten Scutcheons of Armes, such as the Executors will devise. In the two long plates they shall write in Latine in fine manner all such Scripture of Declaration as the said Executors shall devise, that may be conteined and comprehended in the plates ; all the champes about the Letter to be abated and hatched curiously to set out the Letters. All the aforesaid large plates, and all the said two plates through all the over sides of them, and all the said Hearse of Latten, without and within, they shall repair and gild with the finest gold, as finely, and as well in all places through, as is or shall be any place of the aforesaid Image, which one Bartholmew Goldsmyth then had in gilding ; all the said workmanship, in making, finishing, laying and fastning to be at the charge of the said workmen. And for the same they have in sterling money Cxxvli.

"Will. Austen Citizen and Founder of London xiv. Martii 30. H. 6. covenanteth, &c to cast, work, and perfectly to make, of the finest Latten to be gilded that may be found, xiv. Images embossed, of Lords and Ladyes in divers vestures, called Weepers, to stand in housings made about the Tombe, those Images to be made in bredth, length and thickness, &c to xiv. patterns made of timber. Also he shall make xviii. lesse Images of Angells, to stand in other housings, as shall be appointed by patterns, whereof ix. after one side, and ix. after another. Also he must make an Hearse to stand on the Tombe, above and about the principall Image that shall lye in the Tombe, according to a pattern ; the stuffe and Workmanship to the repairing to be at the charge of the said Will. Austen. And the Executors shall pay for every Image that shall lye on the Tombe, of the weepers so made in Latten, xiiis. ivd. And for every Image of Angells so made vs. And for every pound of Latten that shall be in the Hearse xd. And shall pay and bear the costs of the said Austen for setting the said Images and Herse.

"The said Will. Austen, xi. Feb. 28. H. 6. doth covenant to cast and make an Image of a man armed, of fine Latten, garnished with certain ornaments, viz. with Sword and Dagger ; with a Garter ; with a Helme and Crest under his head, and at his feet a Bear musled, and a Griffon, perfectly made of the finest Latten, according to patterns ; all which to be brought to Warwick, and layd on the Tombe, at the perill of the said Austen ; the said Executors paying for the Image, perfectly made and laid, and all the ornaments, in good order, besides the cost of the said workmen to Warwick and working there to lay the Image, and besides the cost of the carriages, all which are to be born by the said Executors, in total xl li.

"Bartholomew Lambespring Dutchman, and Goldsmyth of London, 23. Maii 27. H. 6. covenanteth to repair, whone, and pullish, and to make perfect to the gilding, an Image of Latten of a man armed that is in making, to lye over the Tombe, and all the apparell that belongeth thereunto, as Helme, Crest, Sword, &c. and Beasts; the said Executors paying therefore xiii li.

"The said Bartholomew and Will. Austen xii. Martii 31. H. 6. do covenant to pullish and repare xxxii. Images of Latten, lately made by the said Will. Austen for the Tombe, viz. xviii. Images of Angells, and xiv. Images of Mourners, ready to the gilding; the said Executors paying therefore xx li.

"The said Bartholomew 6. Julii 30. H. 6. doth covenant to make xiv. Scutcheons of the finest Latten, to be set under xiv. Images of Lords and Ladyes, Weepers, about the Tombe; every Scutcheon to be made meet in length, bredth, and thickness, to the place it shall stand in the Marble according to the patterns. These xiv. Scotcheons, and the Armes in them, the said Bartholomew shall make, repare, grave, gild, enamil, and pullish as well as is possible; and the same Scutcheons shall set up, and pin fast, and shall bear the charge of all the stuff thereof, the said Executors paying for every Scutcheon xv s. sterling, which in all amounteth to x li. x s.

"The said Bartholomew xx. Julii 31. H. 6. doth covenant, &c. to gild, pullish, and burnish xxxii. Images, whereof xiv. Mourners, and xviii. Angells to be set about the Tombe, and to make the visages and hands, and all other bares of all the said Images, in most quick and fair wise, and to save the gold as much as may be from and without spoiling, and to find all things saving gold; the said Executors to find all the gold that shall be occupied thereabout, and to pay him for his other charges and labours, either xl li. or else so much as two honest and skilfull Goldsmyths shall say upon the view of the work, what the same, besides gold and his labour, is worth: and the Executors are to deliver money from time to time, as the work goeth forward, whereof they pay Li li. viii s. iv d.

"The said Bartholomew iiiᵒ Martii 32. H. 6. doth covenant to make clean, to gild, to burnish, and pullish the great Image of Latten, which shall lye upon the Tombe, with the Helme and Crest, the Bear and the Griffon, and all other the ornaments of Latten; and the said Bartholomew shall finde all manner of stuffe for the doing thereof, saving gold, and all workmanship at his charges, the said Executors providing gold, and giving to the said Bartholomew such sum and sums of money for his charges and workmanship, as two honest and skilfull Goldsmyths, viewing the work, shall adjudge, whereof some of the money to be payd for the borde of the workmen, as the work shall go forward, whereof they pay xcv li. ii s. viii d.

"John Bourde of Corff Castle in the County of Dorset Marbler 16. Maii 35. H. 6. doth covenant to make a Tombe of Marble, to be set on the said Earle's grave; the said Tombe to be made well, cleane, and sufficiently, of a good and fine Marble, as well coloured as may be had in England. The uppermost stone of the Tombe and the base thereof to contain in length ix. foot of the standard, in bredth iv. foot, and in thickness vii. inches: the course of the Tombe to be of good and due proportion to answer the length and bredth of the uppermost stone; and a pace to be made round about the Tombe of like good marble, to stand on the ground ; which pace shall contain in thickness vi. inches, and in bredth xviii. inches. The Tombe to bear in height from the pace iv. foot and a half. And in and about the same Tombe to make xiv. principall housings, and under every principall housing a goodly quarter for a Scutcheon of copper and gilt, to be set in ; and to do all the work and workmanship about the said Tombe to the entail, according to a portraicture delivered him ; and the carriages and bringing to Warwick, and there to set the same up where it shall stand : the entailing to be at the charge of the Executors : after which entailing the said Marbler shall pullish and clense the said Tombe in workmanlike sort : and for all the said Marble, carriage and work he shall have in sterling money xlv li.

"The said Marbler covenanteth to provide, of good and well-coloured Marble, so many stones as will pave the Chapell where the Tombe standeth, every stone containing in thickness two inches, and in convenient bredth, and to bring the same to Warwick and lay it : and for the stuff, workmanship, and carriage of every hundred of those stones, he shall have xls. which in the totall comes to iv li. xiii s. iv d."

B.

From *Ancient Funerall Monuments within the United Monarchie of Great Britaine, Ireland, and the Islands adiacent, with the dissolued Monasteries therein contained : their Founders, and what eminent Persons haue beene in the same interred. . . . Whereunto is prefixed a Discourse of Funerall Monuments. Of the Foundation and fall of Religious Houses. Of Religious Orders. Of the Ecclesiasticall Estate of England. . . .* "Composed by the Studie and Trauels of John Weever. . . . London. Printed by Thomas Harper, 1631. And are to be sold by Laurence Sadler at the signe of the Golden Lion in little Britaine."

"*The Author to the Reader—*

"Having seene (judicious Reader) how carefully in other Kingdomes, the Monuments of the dead are preserved, and their Inscriptions or Epitaphs registred in their Church-Bookes ; and having read the Epitaphs of Italy, France, Germany, and other Nations, collected and put in print by the paines of *Schraderus, Chytræus, Swertius,* and other forraine Writers—And also knowing withall how barbarously within these his Majesties Dominions, they are (to the shame of our time) broken downe, and utterly almost all ruinated, their brasen Inscriptions erazed, torne away, and pilfered, by which inhumane, deformidable act, the honourable memory of many vertuous and noble persons deceased, is extinguished, and the true understanding of divers Families in these Realmes (who have descended of these worthy persons aforesaid) is so darkened, as the true course of their inheritance is thereby partly interrupted : grieving at this unsufferable injurie offered as well to the living, as the dead, out of the respect I bore to venerable Antiquity, and the due regard to continue the remembrance of the defunct to future posteritie ; I determined with myselfe to collect such memorials of the deceased, as were remaining as yet undefaced ; as also to revive the memories of eminent worthy persons entombed or interred, either in Parish, or in Abbey Churches ; howsoever some of their Sepulchres are at this day no where to be discerned, neither their bones and ashie remaines in any place to bee gathered. Whereupon with painefull expences (which might have beene well spared perhaps you will say) I travailed over the most parts of all England, and some parts of Scotland," etc. . . .

Chapter X.—

[Page 50.] "*Of the rooting up, taking away, erazing and defacing of Funerall Monuments in the reignes of King* Henry *the eighth, and* Edward *the sixth. Of the care Queene* Elizabeth, *of famous memory, had for the preservation of the same. Her Proclamation in the second of her raigne against defacing of Monuments.*

"Toward the latter end of the raigne of *Henry* the eight, and throughout the whole raigne of *Edward* the sixth, and in the beginning of Queene *Elizabeth*, certaine persons of every County were put in authority to pull downe, and cast out of all Churches, Roodes, graven Images, Shrines with their reliques, to which the ignorant people came flocking in adoration. Or any thing else, which (punctually) tended to idolatrie and superstition. Under colour of this their Commission, and in their too forward zeale, they rooted up, and battered downe, Crosses in Churches, and Church-yards, as also in other publike places, they defaced and brake downe the images of Kings, Princes, and noble estates ; erected, set up, or pourtraied, for the onely memory of them to posterity, and not for any religious honour : they crackt a peeces the glasse-windowes wherein the effigies of our blessed Saviour hanging on the Crosse, or any one of his Saints was depictured ; or otherwise turned up their heeles into the place where their heads used to be fixt ; as I have seene in the windowes of some of our countrey Churches. They despoiled Churches of their copes, vestments, Amices, rich hangings, and all other ornaments whereupon the story, or the pourtraiture, of Christ himselfe, or of any Saint or Martyr, was delineated, wrought, or embroidered ; leaving Religion naked, bare, and unclad ; as *Dionysius* left *Iupiter* without a cloake, and *Aesculapius* without a beard. . . .

[Page 51.] But the foulest and most inhumane action of those times, was the violation of Funerall Monuments. Marbles which covered the dead were digged up, and put to other uses (as I have partly touched before) Tombes hackt and hewne apeeces; Images or representations of the defunct, broken, erazed, cut, or dismembred, Inscriptions or Epitaphs, especially if they began within an *orate pro anima,* or concluded with *cuius animæ propitietur Deus.* For greedinesse of the brasse, or for that they were thought to bee Antichristian, pulled out from the Sepulchres, and purloined; dead carcases, for gaine of their stone or leaden coffins, cast out of their graves, notwithstanding this request, cut or engraven upon them, *propter misericordiam Iesu requiescant in pace.* These Commissioners, these τυμϐώρυχοι, these Tombe-breakers, these gravediggers, made such deepe and diligent search into the bottome of ancient Sepulchres, in hope there to find (belike) some long-hidden treasure; having heard or read that *Hircanus ex Davidis Sepulchro tria millia auri talenta eruit:* That *Hircanus* tooke three thousand talents of gold out of King *Davids* Sepulchre; *Crimen Sacrilegio proximum,* a sinne the nearest unto Sacriledge. Not so much for taking out the money, for *Aurum Sepulchris juste detrahitur, ubi Dominus non habetur,* as for the drawing out, and dispersing abroad the bones, ashes, and other the sacred remaines of the dead. And hereupon the grave-rakers, these gold-finders are called theeves, in old Inscriptions upon Monuments.

Plutoni sacrum munus ne attingite fures.

And in another place: *Abite hinc pessumi fures.*

" But I have gone further then my commission, thus then to returne.

" This barbarous rage against the dead (by the Commissioners, and others animated by their ill example) continued untill the second yeare of the raigne of Queene *Elizabeth,* of famous memory, who, to restraine such a savage cruelty, caused this Proclamation (following) to bee published [page 52] throughout all her dominions; which after the imprinting thereof, shee signed (each one severally) with her owne handwriting, as this was, which I had of my friend, Master *Humphrey Dyson.*

" ELIZABETH.

" *A Proclamation against breaking or defacing of Monuments of Antiquitie, being set up in Churches, or other publike places, for memory, and not for superstition.*

" The Queenes Majestie understanding, that by the meanes of sundrie people, partly ignorant, partly malicious, or covetous; there hath been of late yeares spoiled and broken certaine ancient Monuments, some of metall, some of stone, which were erected up aswell in Churches, as in other publike places within this Realme, onely to shew a memory to the posterity of the persons there buried, or that had beene benefactors to the building or dotations of the same Churches or publique places, and not to nourish any kinde of superstition. By which meanes, not onely the Churches, and places remaine at this present day spoiled, broken, and ruinated, to the offence of all noble and gentle hearts, and the extinguishing of the honourable and good memory of sundry vertuous and noble persons deceased ; but also the true understanding of divers Families in this Realme (who have descended of the bloud of the same persons deceased) is thereby so darkened, as the true course of their inheritance may be hereafter interrupted, contrary to Iustice, besides many other offences that doe hereof ensue to the slander of such as either gave, or had charge in times past onely to deface Monuments of idolatry and false fained images in Churches and Abbeyes. And therefore, although it be very hard to recover things broken and spoiled : yet both to provide that no such barbarous disorder bee hereafter used, and to repaire as much of the said Monuments as conveniently may be : Her Majestie chargeth and commandeth all manner of persons hereafter to forbeare the breaking or defacing of any parcell of any Monument, or Tombe, or Grave, or other Inscription and memory of any person deceased, being in any manner of place, or to breake any image of Kings, Princes, or nobles Estates of this Realme, or of any other that have beene in times past erected and set up, for the onely memory of them to their posterity in common Churches, and not for any religious honour ; or to breake downe and deface any Image in glasse-windowes in any Church, without consent of the Ordinary : upon paine that whosoever shal herein be found to offend, to be committed to the next Goale, and there to remaine without baile or mainprise, unto the next comming of the Iustices, for the delivery of the said Goale ; and then to be further punished by fine or imprisonment (besides the restitution or reedification of the thing broken) as to the said Iustices shall seeme meete ; using therein the advise of the Ordinary, and if neede shall bee, the advise also of her Majesties Councell in her Starre-chamber.

"And for such as bee already spoiled in any Church, or Chappell, now [page 53] standing : Her Majestie chargeth and commandeth, all Archbishops, Bishops, and other Ordinaries, or Ecclesiastical persons, which have authoritie to visit the Churches or Chappels ; to inquire by presentments of the Curates, Churchwardens, and certaine of the Parishoners, what manner of spoiles have been made, sithens the beginning of her Majesties raigne of such Monuments ; and by whom, and if the persons be living, how able they be to repaire and reedifie the same ; and thereupon to convent the same persons, and to enjoyne them under paine of Excommunication, to repaire the same by a convenient day, or otherwise, as the cause shall further require, to notifie the same to her Majesties Councell in the Starre-chamber at Westminster. And if any such shall be found and convicted thereof, not able to repaire the same ; that then they be enjoyned to doe open penance two or three times in the Church, as to the qualitie of the crime and partie belongeth under like paine of Excommunication. And if the partie that offended bee dead, and the executours of the Will left, having sufficient in their hands unadministred, and the offence notorious ; The Ordinary of the place shall also enjoyne them to repaire or reedifie the same, upon like or any other convenient paine, to bee devised by the said Ordinary. And when the offendour cannot be presented, if it be in any Cathedrall or Collegiate Church which hath any revenue belonging to it, that is not particularly allotted to the sustentation of any person certaine, or otherwise, but that it may remaine in discretion of the governour thereof, to bestow the same upon any other charitable deed, as mending of highwayes, or such like; her Majestie enjoyneth and straightly chargeth the governours and companies of every such Church, to employ such parcels of the said sums of money (as any wise may be spared) upon the speedy repaire or reedification of any such Monuments so defaced or spoiled, as agreeable to the originall, as the same conveniently may be.

"And where the covetousnesse of certaine persons is such, that as Patrons of Churches, or owners of the personages impropriated, or by some other colour or pretence, they do perswade with the Parson and Parishioners to take or throw downe the Bels of Churches and Chappels, and the lead of the same, converting the same to their private gaine, and to the spoiles of the said places, and make such like alterations, as thereby they seeke a slanderous desolation of the places of prayer: Her Majestie (to whom in the right of the Crowne by the ordinance of Almighty God, and by the Lawes of this Realme, the defence and protection of the Church of this Realme belongeth) doth expresly forbid any manner of person, to take away any Bels or lead of any Church or Chappel, under paine of imprisonment during her Majesties pleasure, and such further fine for the contempt, as shall be thought meete.

"And her Majestie chargeth all Bishops and Ordinaries to enquire of all such contempts done from the beginning of her Majesties raigne, and to enjoyne the persons offending to repaire the same within a convenient time. And of their doings in this behalfe, to certifie her Majesties privie Councell, or the Councell in the Starre-chamber at Westminster, that order may be taken herein.

[Page 54.] *"Yeven at Windsor the xix of September the second yeare of her Majesties raigne. God save the Queene.* Imprinted at London in Pauls Churchyard by *Richard Iugge* and *John Cawood,* Printers to the Queenes Majestie. *Cum privilegio Regiæ Majestatis.*

"This Proclamation was seconded by another, to the same purpose, in the fourteenth yeare of her Majesties raigne, charging the Iustices of her Assise to provide severe remedie, both for the punishment and reformation thereof.

"But these Proclamations tooke small effect for much what about this time, there sprung up a contagious broode of Scismatickes; who, if they might have had their wills, would not onely have robbed our Churches of all their ornaments and riches, but also have laid them levell with the ground; choosing rather to exercise their devotions, and publish their erronious doctrines, in some emptie barne, in the woods, or common fields, then in these Churches, which they held to be polluted with the abhominations of the whore of Babylon."

C.

Note on vestments showing personal devices, as illustrated
by the exhibition of the Burlington Fine Arts Club,
1905.

In the remarks made on pp. 83-4 concerning the ornamentation of
Mass Vestments as they are shown on brasses, we mention the rare
occurrence of personal devices and of figures of saints on chasubles.[1]
Although the latter are rare on brasses, they are not uncommon on the
orphreys of actual chasubles, which are still in existence, especially in the
form of representations of sacred subjects, such as the Crucifixion or
Assumption.   But personal and heraldic[2] devices are more rarely found.
In the *Exhibition of English Embroidery, executed prior to the middle of the
Sixteenth Century*, held by the Burlington Fine Arts Club, 1905, were
included some good examples of this form of decoration, *e.g.* :—

Chasuble (Case A, No. 3), of early sixteenth century work, with the
   initials " R T " combined with pastoral staff and mitre, for
   Robert Thorneton, Abbot of Jervaulx (1510-1533); lent by
   the Victoria and Albert Museum.

Chasuble (M, 3), early sixteenth century, inscribed *Pray for y^e
   sowlls of Thoms | Sales and Helene hys wyfe;* lent by St. George's
   Cathedral, Southwark.

Chasuble (M, 5), early sixteenth century, decorated with the
   badges of Henry VIII. and Catherine of Aragon ; lent by
   the Right Rev. Bishop Knight.

Chasuble (G, 2), middle sixteenth century, ornamented with the
   letters " P " and " R " and gloves, with inscription on cruciform orphrey, *Orate p[ro] a̅i̅a famli tui P* [a glove] *R,* for Glover ;
   lent by Downside Abbey, Bath.

Chasuble orphrey (B, 2), middle fourteenth century, with arms of
   John Grandisson, Bishop of Exeter, 1327-1369 ; lent by the
   Marquis 'of Bute.

Chasuble (I) of red velvet, embroidered with the lions of England
   in gold, and with the arms of Solms on the orphrey, probably
   made from a horse-trapper of fourteenth-century work ; lent
   by H.H. Prince Solms-Braunfels.

Chasuble (V), fifteenth century ; on cross-shaped orphrey the
   Crucifixion, flanked by two shields with bear and griffin sup-
   porters, each bearing the arms of Henry Beauchamp, Duke of

---

[1] Personal devices are not infrequently found on copes shown on brasses (*see*
pp. 89-90).   Figures of saints on the orphreys of copes are common, and are found on
brasses (*see* p. 93).   Fine examples were shown at the Burlington Fine Arts Club
Exhibition, and splendid copes figure in several pictures in the National Gallery.

[2] Good examples of heraldic chasubles are in the collection at the South Kensington
Museum.

Warwick (*d.* 1445 or 1446):—Quarterly, 1, Beauchamp; 2, Clare; 3, Despenser; 4, Newburgh; impaling those of his wife Cecily Nevill, sister of the King-Maker:—Quarterly, 1 and 4, Montacute quartering Monthermer; 2 and 3, Nevill with a label of three points. Lent by Mr. R. C. Adams Beck.

Chasuble (X, 1), fifteenth century, with the arms of Plantagenet, Stafford, De Bohun, Clare, and FitzWalter; the shields supported by swans; the Stafford knot figuring in the decoration; lent by Colonel J. E. Butler-Bowdon.

Chasuble orphrey (Z, 17), early sixteenth century, showing below the Crucifixion the arms of John de Vere, Earl of Oxford (*d.* 1513), impaling those of his second wife, Elizabeth, daughter of Sir Richard Scrope and widow of William, Viscount Beaumont; lent by Lieutenant-Colonel Croft-Lyons.

A fine heraldic Stole (E, 3) and Maniple (E, 2) of fourteenth-century work, the former decorated with forty-six shields, were lent by Miss Weld, of Leagram, and a Stole (E, 4), of similar date, containing thirty-eight shields, by Lord Willoughby de Broke.

Two other examples of church needlework, showing personal devices, must be mentioned. (i.) An altar cover (M, 8) made from fragments of three vestments, showing a rebus, consisting of the letters "Why" in gold on red velvet and the figure of a church, for William Whychurch, Abbot of Hayles, near Buckland, in 1470; lent by the Rector and Churchwardens of Buckland Broadway. (ii.) A Hanging (BB) made from parts of two vestments (?copes), showing an angel supporting a shield with the arms of Ralph Parsons,[1] *d.* 1478 (Argent on a chevron sable three roses or); a scroll below reading, *Orate p[ro] āīa dn̄i R̄ādi p[ar] s̄os;* lent by the Vicar and Churchwardens of Cirencester.

---

[1] His brass is at Cirencester, showing him in mass vestments and holding a chalice with wafer. See *The Monumental Brasses of Gloucestershire,* by Cecil T. Davis. London. 1899. Pages 75-6.

ADDENDA ET CORRIGENDA

ADDENDA ET CORRIGENDA

P. 29, line 17, *for* Blomfield *read* Blomefield.

P. 34, line 18, *for* Bowers Giffard *read* Bowers Gifford.

P. 40, line 2, *for* Widville *read* Wideville.

„ line 10, *for* fourteeth *read* fourteenth.

P. 43, line 16, *for* Topcliff *read* Topclyff.

P. 44, line 8, *insert* Bishops *before* Burchard ; *for* Iohn *read* Johan.

„ line 22, *side note*, Flemish palimpsests *should be here.*

P. 50, line 8, *for* enamelling *read* colouring.

P. 52, line 20, *read* Bishop Johan de Mul.

„ line 27, *for* Topcliff *read* Topclyff ; also p. 53, line 3.

P. 55, footnote 2, line 6, Grave ; Stone ; line 8, rivited & fastened ; line 9, cleane ; line 10, *add* Proved 8 June 1631.

P. 70, lines 3-4, *for* Gamma (γ) *read* Y.

„ line 10, *for* Horsemonden *read* Horsmonden.

„ line 16, *for* Shottesbrook *read* Shottesbrooke.

P. 71. The dates *c.* 1411, 1472, must not be considered to include the paragraphs following ; but merely the first brass in each paragraph.

P. 76, footnote, line 4, *for* 1630 *read* 1630-1.

P. 80, footnote 3, line 2, *for* William Neele, 1510, *read* William Jombharte, *c.* 1500.

P. 82, line 7, *for* through *read* owing to.

P. 84, footnote 4, line 4, *for* sixteenth *read* fifteenth.

Add A Richard Standon or Stondon, Friar Preacher, was appointed a papal chaplain, 1413, 6 Kal. Feb. *See* p. 175, *Calendar of Entries in the Papal Registers relating to Great Britain and Ireland. Papal Letters,* Vol. VI., A.D. 1404-1415, 1904 ; and the same, p. 381.

P. 86, footnote 2, line 3, *add* 1895, p. 41.

P. 87, line 20, *for* Butler *read* Buttler.

P. 88, line 10, *for* Clothal *read* Clothall.

P. 94, line 4, *for* Penhalluryk *read* Penhallinyk.

P. 95, line 19, *for* c. 1490 *read* c. 1400.

P. 102, line 30, *for* Wimington *read* Wymington.

P. 105, footnote 1, line 1, *for* Crishall *read* Chrishall.

P. 106, line 15, *for* Laycock *read* Lacock.

P. 108, footnote 2, line 6, *for* Redfarn *read* Redfern.

P. 111, footnote 2, line 21, *for* Badelsmere *read* Badlesmere.

P. 112, footnote 1, line 3, *for* Ruthyn *read* Ruthin.

P. 127, footnote 3, line 8, *for* Maltheureux *read* Malheureux.

P. 129, line 12, *for* Yslyngtone *read* Yslyngton.

P. 131, line 7, p. 132, line 6, *for* Sowthe *read* Lowthe.

P. 134, line 33, *for* Jacob *read* James.

P. 140, *add* to footnote :—In the Losely Chapel, St. Nicholas' Church, Guildford, is the sculptured effigy of Canon Arnald Brocas, Rector, 1395, showing him in cassock, surplice, grey almuce, and red cope, with the close-fitting buttoned sleeves of a red undergarment appearing at the wrists. The brass inscription describes him as "baculari' ut'usq[ue] iuris."

P. 141, line 27, *for* 1430 *read* 1434. See *Winchester Scholars*, by Thomas Frederick Kirby, M.A., London, 1888, p. 54. (An illustration of this brass forms the frontispiece.)

P. 150, line 26, *for* Neyland *read* Nayland.

P. 155, line 14, *after* torteaux *add* gules, over all a label of three points.

P. 161, line 14, *for* Iohn *read* John.

P. 169, line 1, *for* Sir John Leventhorpe *read* John Leventhorpe, Esq.

P. 170, line 11, *for* Sir John Throckmorton *read* John Throckmorton, Esq.

P. 175, line 5, *for* Anstey *read* Ansty.

P. 179, line 7, *for* Lyttcot *read* Lytkot.

P. 179, line 11, *for* Redcliff *read* Redcliffe.

P. 181, line 15, *for* Heveningham *read* Hevenyngham.

P. 183, line 4, *for* Ralph *read* Raphe.

P. 185, line 25, *for* Arundell *read* Arundel.

P. 190, line 27, *for* Sir Thomas Peryent *read* John Peryent, Esq.

P. 190, line 31, *for* Arnold *read* Arnald.

P. 191, line 28, *for* Sir Thomas de St. Quintin *read* Thomas de St. Quintin, Esq.

P. 192, line 10, *for* Sergeant *read* Serjeant.

P. 193, line 16, *for* Coates *read* Cotes.

P. 200, line 16, *for* Agnes *read* Agneys.

P. 201, line 28, *for* Frankelein *read* Civilian.   See p. 200.

P. 207, line 33, *for* Lechdale *read* Lechlade.

P. 208, line 16, *for* Smith *read* Smyth.

P. 212, line 33, *for* Hatch *read* Hatche.

P. 214, line 22, *for* Rawmarch *read* Rawmarsh.

P. 216, line 31, *for* William *read* Walter (Septvans).

P. 218, line 4, *for* Brown *read* Browne.

P. 228, line 1, *for* Bingham *read* Byngham.

    „   line 5, *for* Urswyke *read* Urswyk.

P. 232, line 22, *for* Laycock *read* Lacock.

P. 234, line 20, *for* Willesdon *read* Willesden.

P. 244, line 14, *for* Hellesden *read* Hellesdon.

P. 245, line 1, *for* Topcliff *read* Topclyff.

P. 249, line 1, *for* Stapelton *read* Stapleton.

P. 250, line 14, *for* Crishall *read* Chrishall.

P. 251, line 19, *for* Kerdiston *read* Kerdeston.

P. 261, line 18, *for* Mellicent *read* Millicent.

    „   line 27, *for* Quartermain *read* Quartremayn.

P. 263, line 4, *for* Launcelyn *read* Launceleyn.

P. 265, line 16, *read* Furneaux Pelham.

„   line 17, *for* Quartermain *read* Quartremayn.

P. 268, line 10, *for* Sir Thomas Shernborne *read* Thomas Shernborne, Esq.

P. 268, line 22, *omit* ? *after* Catherine.

P. 271, line 18, *for* Ingleton *read* Ingylton.

P. 275, line 16, *for* Herling *read* Harling.

P. 276, line 8, *for* Laycock *read* Lacock.

„   line 23, *for* Ardingly *read* Ardingley.

P. 279, line 1, *for* Dauntesay *read* Dauntsay.

P. 284, line 24, *for* Sir William Coke *read* William Coke, Esq.

P. 296, line 33, *for* c. 1480 *read* c. 1475.

P. 298, line 30, *for* Ruthyn *read* Ruthin.

P. 299, lines 3-4, *for* Braybrook *read* Braybrok.

INDICES

1. OF PERSONS

2. OF PLACES

3. OF COSTUME

4. GENERAL

OF PERSONS[1]

Names of Authors cited in italics.

A

ABBOT, Alice, 115; Archbishop George, 115; Maurice, 115; Bishop Robert, 115
Abell, William, 13, 82, 102
Aberfeld, John, 139
Acklam, George, 15
Adams, Richard, 95, 102
Adrianson, Adrian, 56
Aileward, Thomas, 90, 91, 93
Ailmer, John, 207, 263; Margery, 263
Airay, Provost Henry, 14, 117
Alban, St., 47
Albemarle, Isabel de Fortibus, Countess of, 147 n.; William de Fortibus, Earl of, 147 n.
Albinus, Cardinal, 86
Albyn, Robert, 160
Alcala, Don Parafan de Ribera, Duke of, 25
Aldeburgh, William de, 157, 159, 160
Alderburne, John, 71
Aldrych, Robert, 235
Alfounder, Robert, 216
Alnwyk, John, 136
André, J. Lewis, F.S.A., 98 n., 247 n., 286 n.
Andrewes, Agnes, 281; Thomas, Esq., 281
Anjou, Geoffrey Plantagenet, Count of, 5 : René d', 272 n.
Anne Boleyn, Queen, 283 n.
Ansty, John, Esq., 175, 270, 316
Antiquaries, Society of, 214 n.
Anyell, Dame Juliana, 98

Appleton, Mary, 283; Roger, 283
Arden family, lady of, 280
Arderne, Anna, 297; Bridgett, 297; Dame Catherine, 268, 317; Elizabeth, 297; John, Esq., 217, 297; Dame Matilda, 206 n.; Sir Peter, Chief Baron, 227, 268; Susanna, 297; Sir Thomas, 206 n.
Argentein, John, 128, 133
Argenteine, *see* D'Argenteine
Argentine, Margery, 265
Armstrong, W., 52 n.
Arthur, Robert, 93
Arundel and Surrey, Beatrice Fitz-Alan, Countess of, 258, 262; Thomas Fitz-Alan, Earl of, 258
Arundel, the Lady Ann, 292; Ann, 292; Sir John, 216, 292; John, Esq., 185, 216, 292, 316; Archbishop Thomas, 90 n.
Arundell, family of, 45; Edward, 214; Eleanor, Lady, 189 n.; the Lady Elizabeth, 281; George, Esq., 285; Isabel, 285; Sir John, 182, 281; Sir John, of Trerice, 182, 286; John, 166 n.; Dame Juliana, 286; Dame Katherine, 281; Margery, 257, 261; Dame Mary, 286; Richard, 166 n.; Thomas, Esq., 261
Asger, John, 217
Asheley, Robert, 166 n.
Asheton, Nicholas, 116
Ask, Margaret, 266; Richard, Esq., 172, 266
Asscheton, Mathew de, 91 n.

---

[1] *See also* List of Illustrations.

INDICES

327

Coke, Sir Edward, 222n.
Coke, William, Esq., 229, 284, 317
Cokyn, William, Esq., 179
Colard, John, 234
Cole, Arthur, 92, 135
Cole, Rev. Thomas, 1, 95n.
Coles, Eleanor, 293 ; George, 293 ; Sarah, 293
Colman, John, 211
Colte, Joan, 191, 273 ; Thomas, Esq., 191, 273
Coly, Thomas, 102, 137
Compton family, member of, 178n., 278 ; wife of, 278
Conquest, Elizabeth, 278 ; Richard, Esq., 179, 278
Constable, John, 15 ; Katherine, 15 ; Sir Marmaduke, 23n.
Constantine, Emperor, 76
Cooke, Joan, 294 ; John, 218, 294
Cookesey, Walter, Esq., 190
Cooper, C. H., F.S.A., 247n.
Corbet family, man of, 282 ; wife of, 282
Corbet, Jane, 286 ; John, Esq., 286
Cornelius, St., 56
Corner, G. R., F.S.A., 224n., 226n.
Cornewaylle, Dame Elizabeth de, 245
Cornish, Bishop Thomas, 80n.
Cornwall, John of Eltham, Earl of, 152n.
Corp, Elyenore, 244n., 254 ; John, 201, 254
Cortewille, Ludowic, 9n., 10, 56
Coryton, Jane, 282 ; Peter, Esq., 180, 282
Cosowarthe, John, 183
Cosyngton, John, Esq., 168, 262 ; Sarra, 262
Cotman, J. S., 1, 33, 49n., 53, 64n., 167, 187n., 235, 248n.
Cotrel, James, 24n.
Cottesmore, John, C.J., 227
Couderborch, Asscheric van der, 7
Coulthirst, Robert, 216

Courtenay, Sir Edward, 208 ; Sir Peter, K.G., 186 ; Sir Philip, 279 ; Archbishop William, 79
Courthope, James, 87, 95
Covell, Thomas, Esq., 216
Covert, Elizabeth, 280 ; Henry, Esq., 178 ; Richard, Esq., 280
Covesgrave, John, 202
Cracherood, Agnes, 283 ; John, 283
Cradock, Jane, 292 ; John, 292
Crafford, Arthur, Gent., 215
Crane, Edward, 213 ; Sir Francis, 188n. ; Henry, 140n. ; Joan, 269 ; Margaret, 269 ; William, 269
Cranley, Archbishop Thomas, 78, 79
Cranmer, Archbishop Thomas, 110
Crauden (Crowden), John de, 96
Crawford and Balcarres, Earl of, 48n.
Creeny, Rev. W. F., 1, 3, 7, 17, 25n., 26, 43n., 47, 58-9, 64n., 73, 83, 126n., 129, 153n., 244n.
Creke, Dame Alyne de, 13, 241, 242 ; Sir John de, 152
Cremer, John, 215
Crespin, St., 189n.
Crespinian, St., 189n.
Cressett, Richard, 15
Cressy, Cristina, 262, 265 ; John, 262
Crewaker, John, 71
Creyghton, Bishop, 108n.
Crispe, Elizabeth, 290 ; Henry, 290
Crofton, William, Gent., B.C.L., 234
Croke, John, 218
Cromwell, Ralph, Baron, K.G., 67n., 174, 186, 204 ; Humphrey Bourchier, Lord, 296
Crosse, Ric., 15
Croston, Edmund, 94
Croyland, Abbot Godfrey de, 21n., 96

PERSONS

Dillon, Viscount, 156n., 168n., 177n.

Dirckz, Dirck Alewyn, 289n.

D'Iseni, Sir William, 150

Disney, Rev. Dr., 56n.; Jane, 287; Margaret, 284n.; Nele, 287; Richard, 287; William, Esq., 56; 184n.; 284

Dixon, Nicholas, 231

Dixton, Richard, Esq., 173

Dobrée, H. C. P., 126n., 133n.

Dod, Robert, 224n.

Dodding, Margaret, 290; Myles, Esq., 290

Dodschone, Hen., 70

Donne, Dr., 23

Doreward, Isabella, 261; John, Esq., 261

Douce, Francis, 49

Dowsing, Samuel, 31n.

Dowsing, William, 30, 31

Drake, Mr., 32

Drake, Francis, Esq., 299; John, 299

Drax, Richard, 140

Drayton, Sir John, 190

Dreux, Robert, Count of, 14n.

Drew, Edward, Esq., S.L., 230n.

Drury family, lady of, 283; Dame Margery, 256; Sir Roger, 256

Du Cange, Charles du Fresne Seigneur, 94n.

Dudley, *see* Northumberland

Dugdale, Sir William, 9n., 96, 223n., 225, 303

Duke, Anne, 283; George, Esq., 283; George, Gent., 215

Dunch, Anne, 300; Anne, 300; Henry, 300

Dunkin, E. H. W., 103

Duyse, Mons. van, 7

Dye, William, 116

Dymoke, Dame Elizabeth, 261n.; Sir Thomas, 261n.

Dynne, Henry, Esq., 234

Dyson, Master Humphrey, 308

Dyson Richard Randall, 185-6n.

Dyve, Sir John, 40, 263

Dyxon, Adam, 40; "vycar," 40

E

Echyngham, Elizabeth, 295; Dame Joan, 259; Thomas, 295; Sir William de, 161; Sir William, 169, 259

Edgcomb, Thomas, 137n.

Edvarod, Joane, 287n.; Valontyne, 287n.

Edward I., 19, 145, 243n.

Edward II., 20, 150, 232n.

Edward III., 21, 38, 42, 52, 155, 156, 161, 186, 198n., 243n., 248, 253n., 254, 270

Edward IV., 169, 229, 271, 277, 303

Edward VI., 30, 102n., 107, 193n., 284, 307

Edward the Black Prince, 6, 157n.

Edward the Confessor, 168n.

Edward, John, 226, 232

Elcok, Christopher, 212; Ralph, 94

Eleanor, Queen, 58n.

Eligius, St., 52

Eliot, Barbara, 290; Roger, 290

Elizabeth, Queen, 24, 102n., 107n., 108, 110n., 114, 133, 177, 183, 192, 193n., 213, 230n., 232n., 284, 285, 287, 288, 307, 308-10

Elizabeth Woodville, Queen, 277

Ellacombe, Rev. H.T., M.A., F.S.A., 87n.

Ellenbridge (Elyngbrigge), Thomas, Esq., 64n.

Elliott, Rev. H. L., M.A., 279n.

Elmebrygge, Roger, Esq., 169

Eltham, John of, *see* Cornwall

Elys, William, 231; William, 231

Empoli, Jacopo da, 67n.

Engliss', Beneit, 199

Englissh, Sir Henry, 252; Dame Margaret, 252

Eric Menved, King, 44, 58

H

HACOMBLEYN, Robert, 95

Haines, Rev. Herbert, 1, 2, 3n., 5, 6, 7, 14, 17n., 19, 24, 26, 27, 29-30, 39n., 53, 64n., 96, 108n., 123, 124, 129, 131, 134-41, 161n., 166n., 167, 185, 189n., 201, 202, 205, 207, 214n., 217, 279n., 285n.

Haitfeld, Ada de, 256; Robert de, 203, 256

Hakebech, Sir Adam de, 150

Hakebourne, Richard de, 63, 71, 83

Halle, Elizabeth, 258; Peter, Esq., 167, 168, 258; Thomas, Esq., 179

Hallum, Bishop Robert, 57, 187n.

Halsham, Sir Hugh, 167, 259; John, 259; Dame Joice, 259; the Lady Philippa, 259

Hampden, Sir John, 181; John, Esq., 179

Hampton, Dame Alice, 99; Isabella, 272n., 298; John, 99; Thomas, Esq., 176, 272n., 298

Hamsterley, Ralph, 25

Hanensee, Eghardus de, 72; 126n.

Hansard family, knight of, 168n.

Hansart, Anthony, Esq., 178n., 279; Katherine, 279

Hanson, Robert, 39

Hardy, T. Duffus, 115n.

Hardyng, Robert, 193

Hare, Nicholas, Esq., 232

Harflet or Harflete, see Septvans

Hargreve, Geoffrey, 138

Harlakynden, Thomas, Esq., 181

Harlestone, Alice, 279

Harpedon, Sir John, 169, 264

Harper, Dame Margaret, 287; Sir William, 183, 218, 287

Harris, George, 15

Harsick, Dame Catherine, 248; Sir John, 161, 248

Harsnett, Archbishop Samuel, 30, 55, 75, 76n., 108, 113-14

Hart, Boneface de, 21n.

Harte, Malyn, 284; Thomas, 284

Hartshorne, Albert, F.S.A., 189n.

Hartshorne, Rev. C. H., 8

Harvey, W., 209n.

Harvye, Sir Jarrate, 184

Harwedon, Margery, 265; William, Esq., 265

Hastings, Sir Hugh, 8, 43, 49-50, 51, 53, 154; Ralph, 204n.; see Pembroke

Hatche, Henry, 212, 276, 316; Joan, 276

Hatton, Mary, 290; Richard, 290

Hauley, Alice, 248; Joan, 248; John, Esq., 163, 248

Haultoft, Gilbert, 231; Margaret, 231

Hautryve, William, 125, 130

Hawberk, John, 299; Sir Nicholas, 264, 299

Hawford, Edward, 129

Hawkesworth, William, 127n.

Hawkins, Aphra, 290; Henry, 290; Thomas, Esq., 184

Haydock, Dr. Richard, 14

Hayton, Robert, Esq., 164n.

Hayward, Richard, 126, 130

Heere, Gerard de, 44, 51; John de, 44, 51

Hefner-Alteneck, J. H. von, 124n., 297n.

Heies, Humphrey, 215; Humphrey, junr., 215

Heigham, Dame Anne, 286; Dame Anne, 286; Sir Clement, 229, 286

Hellard, Stephen, 139

Hemenhale, Sir Robert, 264

Henry II., 5n.

Henry IV., 22, 156, 157n., 164, 189n., 202, 206n., 227n.

Henry IV. of France, 289n.

Henry V., 57, 156n., 164, 192, 227

Henry VI., 164, 166n., 169, 186, 224, 231, 303, 304

Y

Z

OF PLACES[1]

A

---

[1] *See also* List of Illustrations.

PLACES Carshalton, Surrey, 64*n.*, 85, 191
Cartmel, 97*n.*
Casterton, Little, Rutland, 162, 190, 253
Castle Ashby, Northants, 72*n.*, 90, 93
Castle Donnington, Leics., 174, 268
Cawood, Yorks., 115*n.*
Cawston, Norfolk, 105*n.*
Chalcedon, 81
Chalfont St. Peter, Bucks., 39, 64*n.*
Chalgrove, Oxon., 173
Chalons-sur-Marne, 7
Channel Islands, 27
Charlton Makerel, 230*n.*
Charlwood, Surrey, 180, 282
Chart, Great, Kent, 178, 182, 185, 210, 269, 293
Chartham, Kent, 93, 94, 137, 145-7
Charwelton, Northants, 281
Cheam, Surrey, 28, 82, 200, 201, 213, 281, 298
Checkendon, Oxon., 230
Cheddar, Somerset, 165, 169
Chedzoy, Somerset, 178*n.*
Chelsea, *see* London
Chelsfield, Kent, 82, 271
Cheltenham, Gloucs., 228
Cheriton, Kent, 36, 104
Chesham Bois, Bucks., 182
Cheshunt, Herts., 11, 12, 231
Chester, See of, 114; Holy Trinity, 187; St. Peter, 232
Chesterford, Great, Essex, 283
Chesterford, Little, Essex, 266
Chevening, Kent, 116
Chichester Cathedral, 14*n.*, 79*n.*, 137*n.*
Chigwell, Essex, 30, 55, 75, 108, 114
Childrey, Berks., 131, 166, 167, 259, 294
Chingford, Essex, 214*n.*
Chinnor, Oxon., 64, 128, 244, 251
Chipping Campden, Gloucs., 201, 207, 208, 210, 253

Chipping Norton, Oxon., 34, 207
Chiselhurst, Kent, 235
Chittlehampton, Devon, 273
Cholsey, Berks., 21
Chrishall, Essex, 105*n.*, 208, 250, 274, 315-16
Christchurch, Hants, 31, 33, 109*n.*, 127*n.*, 163*n.*
Church Oakley, Hants, 106
Churchill, Somerset, 183, 287
Cirencester, Gloucs., 85, 104*n.*, 173, 175, 203, 207, 216, 263, 264, 297, 312
Clapham, Sussex, 181, 279
Clavering, Essex, 104
Claydon, Middle, Bucks., 166*n.*
Clehongre, Herefordshire, 151*n.*, 152*n.*, 175, 272
Clerkenwell, *see* London
Cleves, 59
Cley-next-the-Sea, Norfolk, 102, 106, 129
Clifford Chambers, Gloucs., 183
Clifton, Pro-Cathedral of the Apostles, 123*n.*
Clifton, Beds., 179
Clifton, Notts., 215
Clifton Campville, Staffs., 145*n.*, 247
Clippesby, Norfolk, 184, 289
Clothall, Herts., 88, 116, 139, 140, 315
Clynnog, Carnarvonshire, 299
Clyst St. George, Devon, 294*n.*
Coates, Great, Lincs., *see* Cotes
Cobham, Kent, 20*n.*, 86, 87*n.*, 93, 94, 158, 160, 180, 240, 245, 250, 251, 264, 278, 297, 299
Coburg, 59*n.*
Coggeshall, Great, Essex, 274, 283
Colan, Cornwall, 183
Colchester, 114*n.*
Coleshill, Warwickshire, 13, 82, 102, 116
Collingbourne Ducis, Wilts., 299
Cologne, 9, 56
Constance Cathedral, 57, 187*n.*

L

PLACES 243*n*., 248, 253*n*., 254, 264,
303; Westminster. Courts at,
223*n*., 224*n*., 309, 310; West-
minster Hall, 222, 277*n*.; West-
minster, St. Margaret's, 31
Longforgan, Perthshire, 206*n*.
Louvain, University of, 129
Lowick, Northants, 264, 266
Lowthorp, Yorks., 15
Lübeck, 44, 47, 52
Lucca, 77*n*.
Ludlow, Salop, 258*n*.
Lullingstone, Kent, 179
Luton, Beds., 33, 132, 205, 267
Lydd, Kent, 139, 284
Lytescary, 230*n*.

M

MABLETHORPE, Lincs., 296
Macclesfield, Cheshire, 64*n*., 101
Magdeburg, 79
Maids' Moreton, Bucks., 296
Maidstone, All Saints', 79
Malling, East, Kent, 95, 102, 210, 273
Malling, West, Kent, 102*n*., 281
Malmesbury, Wilts., 58*n*.
Malvern, Great, Worcs., 192*n*.
Manchester Cathedral, 80, 94, 139, 266
March, Cambs., 178*n*., 279
Marden, Herefordshire, 288
Margate, Kent, 45, 173, 185, 205, 207
Markham, East, Notts., 257, 261
Marston Morteyne, Beds., 174, 266
Marsworth, Bucks., 231
Mattishall, Norfolk, 233
Mawgan-in-Pydar, Cornwall, 45, 88, 214, 285
Mayence, 77, 79
Meaux Cathedral, 7
Mecklinburg, 44
Meissen, 59
Melbury Sampford, Dorset, 184
Melford, Long, Suffolk, 184, 272, 273, 297

Melton, Suffolk, 104, 206, 264
Melverley, 97*n*.
Mendlesham, Suffolk, 167*n*.
Meopham, Kent, 33
Mepshall, Beds., 263
Merevale, Warwickshire, 167, 256
Mereworth, Kent, 213
Meriden, Warwickshire, 292
Merstham, Surrey, 299
Merton, Norfolk, 180*n*., 276
Messing, Essex, 281
Methley, Yorks., 109*n*.
Methwold, Norfolk, 150*n*., 161*n*.
Middleburgh in Walcheren, 56
Middleton, Essex, 4
Middleton, Lancs., 70*n*., 82, 102, 186, 293
Middleton, Warwickshire, 228, 267
Milan, 87*n*.
Mildenhall, Suffolk, 189*n*.
Milton, Cambs., 229, 284
Milton Abbas, Dorset, 96*n*., 184, 231
Milton-next-Sittingbourne, Kent, 175, 278
Mimms, North, Herts., 7, 43, 49, 50, 52, 53, 70, 101, 178, 286
Minchinhampton, Gloucs., 99
Minehead, Somerset, 268
Minety, Wilts., 185, 290
Minster, Kent, 56, 150*n*., 152, 242
Minsterley, Salop, 294*n*.
Mirival, Warwickshire, 29
Missenden, Little, Bucks., 39
Monewden, Suffolk, 116
Monkton, Kent, 70*n*.
Morland, Westmorland, 27*n*.
Morley, Derbyshire, 174
Mugginton, Derbyshire, 191, 296
Musgrave, Great, Westmorland, 84

N

NARBONNE CATHEDRAL, 48*n*.
Narburgh, Norfolk, 193, 218, 229, 231, 278, 282, 286
Naudhausen, 68

INDICES

363

Tew, Great, Oxon., 151*n*., 163, 191, 253
Tewkesbury Abbey, 58*n*.
Teynham, Kent, 191
Thame, Oxon., 171, 175, 181, 182, 261, 265, 268
Thannington, Kent, 179
Thaxted, Essex, 136
Theddlethorp, Lincs., 164*n*.
Thetford Priory, Norfolk, 187
Theydon Gernon, Essex, 88
Thirsk, Yorks., 43
Thorn, in Prussian Poland, 44, 49, 52, 244*n*.
Thornbury, Gloucs., 287
Thorncombe, Devon, 204, 206, 259
Thornton, Bucks., 175, 232, 269, 271
Thornton-le-Street, Yorks., 15
Thruxton, Hants, 168
Thurcaston, Leics., 92*n*.
Thurlow, Great, Suffolk, 266, 283
Thurrock, West, Essex, 215
Ticehurst, Sussex, 40
Tideswell, Derbyshire, 81
Tilbrook, Beds., 203, 256
Tillingham, Essex, 215
Tilty, Essex, 96
Tingewick, Bucks., 14, 116
Tintagil, Cornwall, 262
Tintinhull, Somerset, 93
Tisbury, Wilts., 214
Todwick, Yorks., 215
Tolleshunt Darcy, Essex, 45, 81, 138*n*.
Tong, Salop, 94, 100, 102, 136, 171, 172, 175, 264, 266, 271
Topcliffe, Yorks., 43, 45, 48, 50-2, 201, 244, 247
Toppesfield, Essex, 283
Tormarton, Gloucs., 210
Tor Mohun, Devon, 287
Torrington, Devon, 262
Tottenham High Cross, 185*n*.
Totternhoe, Beds., 97*n*.
Tredington, Worcs., 89, 94

Trotterscliffe, Kent, 234
Trotton, Sussex, 13, 57, 168, 186, 187*n*., 190, 206, 239, 257
Trumpington, Cambs., 17, 20, 145-7
Trunch, Norfolk, 13*n*.
Tuxford Hall, Notts., 127*n*.

U

Ufford, Suffolk, 274
Ufton, Warwickshire, 116
Ulverstone, Lancs., 290
Upchurch, Kent, 199, 241, 247
Upminster, Essex, 81, 84, 268, 296
Upsala, 43*n*.
Upton Cressett, Salop, 15
Upton Lovel, Wilts., 71
Upwell, Norfolk, 66, 68, 71

V

Vauluisant Abbey, 242*n*.
Verden, 16, 63
Vernon, Normandy, 175*n*.
Verona, 77*n*.
Vienne, 94*n*.
Villers, Brabant, 7

W

Walcheren, 56
Waldingfield, Little, Suffolk, 211, 283
Wales, 27
Walkern, Herts., 45, 234
Wallop, Nether, Hants, 98
Walsham, North, Norfolk, 100
Walsingham, Little, Norfolk, 100
Waltham Abbey, 95*n*., 96*n*.
Waltham, Lincs., 297
Waltham, Little, Essex, 174
Walthamstow, Essex, 140*n*.
Walton-on-Thames, Surrey, 24, 289
Walton-on-Trent, Derbyshire, 101

COSTUME fringe of, 160, 163, 164, 167, 168; gussets of, 157, 171, 174, 178; see Camail, Chausses, Habergeon, Hawberk
Mail, collar of, 171
Mail skirt, 171, 175, 177, 178, 181-3; period, 177-83, 188, 192
Mammelières, 152n., 153
Μανδύας (cope), 88
Manicæ (episcopal gloves), 73
Maniple, 41, 46, 47, 68-9; shape of, 82; absence of, 82, 134; crosses on, 83n.; heraldic, 312
Manipulus (maniple), 68
Mantle, male, fastened on right shoulder, 49, 141, 198, 200, 203, 205; fastened on left shoulder, 182; absence of, 201-2; dagged, 198n.; civic, 183, 217; Judge's, 223n., 225, 226, 228; absence of, 229; regal, 58; see Garter
Mantle, female, 240, 241, 243, 244, 246-8, 250-5, 257, 258, 260n., 263, 264, 268, 270, 272-5, 277-9, 296; absence of, 242; diapered, 252; how fastened, 241, 244, 246; ermine-lined, 266, 269; hood of, 247; cords of, 246; slide, 244, 246; brooches or studs of (tasseaux, fermailes), 241; heraldic, 181, 187, 188, 252, 254, 259, 269, 273, 275, 276, 278-82, 285; monastic, 98; absence of, 99
Mantling, see Helm
Mappula (maniple), 68
Martel de fer, 192
Mentonière, 172, 176
Mirror hanging from waist, 285
Misericorde, 159-61, 165, 173, 174, 178, 192; absence of, 168, 169, 171, 173-5
Mitra (mitre), 74-5; aurifrigiata, 75; pretiosa, 46, 75, 82; simplex, 75
Mitre (episcopal), 41, 47, 48, 55n.,

67n., 74-5, 81n., 96, 108, 114, 126n., 311; strings of (infulæ, labellæ, vittæ), 75
Mitre head-dress, 258, 269, 270
Mitten sleeves, see Cote-hardie, Kirtle, Subtunica, Undertunic
Monastic habit, male, 95-7; female, 98-9
Monial (ornament of episcopal gloves), 73
Morning star (morgenstern), 193
Morse of almuce, 87; of cope, 88, 91-2
Moton, 170, 171
Mourning, 246n., 247n.
Moustache, see Hair
Muff-warmer, 277

N

NEBULÉ head-dress, 244, 245, 249-51, 253
Necklace, 254, 258, 259, 270, 272, 273, 277, 292; pendant of, 254, 258, 259; see Chain
Network, see Head-dress

O

OCULARIA, see Helm
Ὀθόνη (maniple), 68
Ὠμοφόριον (pall), 78
Ὠράριον (stole), 66
Orarium (stole), 66-7; (Roman costume), 78
Oreillettes, see Helmet
Orle, see Bascinet
Orphreys of vestments, 65n.

P

PÆNULA, 69
Palettes, 165, 167-70
Pall, archiepiscopal, 67, 77n., 78; lineæ of, 78n.; crosses on, 78
Pallium, archiepiscopal, 78; or cloak (Roman costume), 67, 78

GENERAL

See also List of Contents

General

DATE DUE
